ST/CTC/130

Transnational Corporations and Management Division
Department of Economic and Social Development

World Investment Report 1992
Transnational Corporations as Engines of Growth

United Nations New York, 1992

NOTE

The Centre on Transnational Corporations in the Transnational Corporations and Management Division of the United Nations Department of Economic and Social Development serves as the focal point within the United Nations Secretariat for all matters related to transnational corporations and acts as secretariat to the Commission on Transnational Corporations, an intergovernmental subsidiary body of the United Nations Economic and Social Council. The objectives of the work programme are to further the understanding of the nature of transnational corporations and of their political, legal, economic and social effects on home and host countries and in international relations, particularly between developed and developing countries; to secure effective international arrangements aimed at enhancing the contribution of transnational corporations to national development goals and world economic growth while controlling and eliminating their negative effects; and to strengthen the negotiating capacity of host countries, in particular the developing countries, in their dealings with transnational corporations.

The *World Investment Report* is published annually by the Centre on Transnational Corporations with a view to contributing to a better understanding of transnational corporations, their activities and their economic, legal, political and social impact.

The term "country" as used in this paper also refers, as appropriate, to territories or areas; the designations employed and the presentation of the material do not imply the expression of any opinion whatsoever on the part of the Secretariat of the United Nations concerning the legal status of any country, territory, city or area or of its authorities, or concerning the delimitation of its frontiers or boundaries. In addition, the designations of country groups are intended solely for statistical or analytical convenience and do not necessarily express a judgement about the stage of development reached by a particular country or area in the development process.

The following symbols have been used in the tables:

Two dots (..) indicate that data are not available or are not separately reported. Rows in tables have been omitted in those cases where no data are available for any of the elements in the row;

A dash (—) indicates that the item is equal to zero or its value is negligible;

A blank in a table indicates that the item is not applicable;

A slash (/) indicates a financial year, e.g. 1988/89;

Use of a hyphen (-) between dates representing years, for example, 1985-1989, signifies the full period involved, including the beginning and end years.

Reference to "dollars" ($) means United States dollars, unless otherwise indicated.

Annual rates of growth or change, unless otherwise stated, refer to annual compound rates.

Details and percentages in tables do not necessarily add to totals because of rounding.

The material contained in this volume may be freely quoted with appropriate acknowledgement. Comments should be sent to the Centre on Transnational Corporations in the Transnational Corporations and Management Division of the United Nations Department of Economic and Social Development, Office of the Director, United Nations, Room DC2-1220, New York, NY 10017, U.S.A. Telephone: (212) 963-2990; Fax: (212) 963-2146; Telex: 661062 UNCTNC.

ST/CTC/130

UNITED NATIONS PUBLICATION

Sales No. E.92.II.A.19

ISBN 92-1-104396-4

PREFACE

A major challenge facing the world economy today is the revival of economic growth, especially among developing countries, most of which have suffered serious setbacks during the 1980s. Transnational corporations and foreign direct investment can play an important role in meeting this challenge. Since the early 1980s, world investment flows have been expanding rapidly, much faster than other key economic variables such as world trade and world output. A number of major new developments in the global economic situation—the enhanced role of the private sector and a greater reliance on market forces, major technological breakthroughs, the globalization of firms and industries, the ascendancy of the services sector and trends towards a regionalization of markets—has placed foreign direct investment in a central position to influence the pace and the nature of economic growth in most countries. Finally, developing countries themselves have implemented notable and, in many cases, dramatic policy changes, in order to open their economies to greater contributions by transnational corporations.

The question of how, to what extent and under what circumstances transnational corporations can contribute to economic growth of developing countries forms the core of the analysis in the ***World Investment Report 1992,*** the second in this annual series. Growth itself is a complex process, involving familiar elements, such as capital accumulation, the creation and dissemination of new technology, the development of human resources, access to markets and, of course, the environmental sustainability of growth. How these elements are combined varies substantially across regions and countries, with different results in terms of growth. The contribution of transnational corporations can also vary substantially, due, among other factors, to the structural conditions and policy environments in host economies.

The evidence provides ample cause for optimism, as transnational corporations have made important and positive contributions to some of the most successful recent cases of economic revival in developing countries. At the same time, transmitting such success to a greater number of countries is a formidable task. The lessons learned from the analysis in this Report about the contributions being made by transnational corporations to growth in developing countries can hopefully assist in policy formulation and the design of technical assistance in an increasing number of countries, and thereby help make the 1990s a decade of renewed economic development.

Hamdan BenAissa
Director
Transnational Corporations and Management Division

New York, June 1992

The present Report was prepared by a team led by Karl P. Sauvant and comprising Marita Andersson, Victoria Aranda, Persephone Economou, Michelle Gittelman, David Gold, Torben Huss, Azizul Islam, Peter Koudal, Padma Mallampally and Paz Estrella Tolentino. Specific inputs were received from Vincent Casim, Norman Edinberg, Alejandro Grinspun, Hiroshi Kawamura, Charles Lipton, Anita Mathur, Ike Minta, Anna Theofilopoulou and Zbigniew Zimny. Principal research assistance was provided by Jag Alexeyev, Mohamed Chiraz Baly, Ming-Wah Lam, Zane Nobbs and Dorothy Woo. The team received extensive advice from John Dunning, Senior Economic Adviser to the Director of the Transnational Corporations and Management Division, Peter Hansen and Goran Ohlin. The Report was edited by Betty Hamnett and was desktop-published by Valerian Monteiro. Production of the Report was carried out by Marie Antoine, Carmelita Aquilizan, Maria Luisa De Jesus, Juliet Capili, Kanayalal Israni and Armi Manamtam.

Experts from within and outside of the United Nations system provided many substantial inputs that were utilized for the Report. They included Manuel Agosin, Susan Bartholomew, John Cantwell, Edward M. Graham, David Hartridge, John Kline, Samuel Laird, Charles Pearson, Dominick Salvatore and Arvind Subramanian.

In view of the multitude of issues covered by the theme of this Report, a wide range of experts were consulted and commented on various chapters. Extensive comments were received during various stages of preparation from Paul Bailey, Marino Baldi, Ramon De Reyna, Dennis Encarnation, Arghyrios A. Fatouros, Geza Feketekuty, Harris Gleckman, Khalil Hamdani, Nurul Islam, Mario Kakabadse, Georg Kell, Robert Lipsey, Michael Minor, Theodore H. Moran, Michael Mortimore, M. Ishaq Nadiri, Maurice Odle, Sylvia Ostry, Terutomo Ozawa, Thomas Schroeter, William Stibravy and Raymond Vernon.

Contents

Page

Page

Page

Page

List of boxes

Page

(List of boxes, cont'd.)

List of figures

List of tables

Page

(List of tables, cont'd.)

Page

(List of tables, cont'd.)

INTRODUCTION

Transnational corporations have become central organizers of economic activities in an increasingly integrated world economy.

Since the mid-1980s, world-wide flows of foreign direct investment have grown at unprecedented rates, to reach $225 billion of outflows in 1990. Their nominal annual average growth rate of 34 per cent between 1985 and 1990 exceeded by far that of merchandise exports (13 per cent) and nominal GDP (12 per cent). For many developing countries, foreign direct investment has become the principal source of foreign capital: its share in the total long-term capital inflows from private sources of over 90 developing countries increased from 30 per cent during the period 1981-1985 to 74 per cent during the period 1986-1990. Foreign direct investment also accounts for an increasing share of total investment in most countries. Although, on an economy-wide basis, this share rarely exceeds 10 per cent, in selected (typically key) industries, it is frequently much higher; moreover, transnational corporations have come to account for a substantial part of the assets, employment and trade in selected industries of many host countries.

Investment flows are an underestimating measure of the activities of transnational corporations in host countries. Associated with those flows are transfers of technology from parent firms in home countries to their foreign affiliates in host countries through both equity and non-equity arrangements. A good part of international technology flows, as captured by the payment of licensing and other fees, originates from transnational corporations. Most of those payments are made on an intra-firm basis, that is, as flows between firms belonging to the same corporate ownership system. In fact, a large share of the world's research-and-development activities is undertaken by transnational corporations; the combined expenditures for research and development of the 10 largest United States transnational corporations, for example, exceed those of France or the United Kingdom. Foreign direct investment is also an important source of such soft technologies as the know-how, training and organizational skills that are of central importance for the production of modern goods and services. By the end of the 1980s, the volume of goods and services sold by foreign affiliates amounted to an estimated $4.4 trillion, almost double that of world exports (excluding a substantial volume of intra-firm trade). In other words, production by foreign affiliates is of greater importance than exports in delivering goods and services to markets world-wide. Foreign direct investment, and the flows of capital, technology, training and trade that are part of it, have become the primary means by which a growing number of countries are integrated in the international economy.

But, as documented in chapters I and II of Part One of the Report, the growth of foreign direct investment has not been evenly distributed. As shown in the *World Investment Report 1991: The Triad in Foreign Direct Investment*, some three fourths of world investment flows take place among developed countries and, in particular, are concentrated in the Triad (the United States, the European Community and Japan). In addition, some two thirds of all investment flows to developing countries are directed to just 10 countries. Despite the growing role of foreign direct investment in the world economy, therefore, most developing countries currently do not receive as much as they need to help stimulate development. At the same time, the amount of investment that developing countries do receive is, for many of them, of relatively high importance, partly because the qualitative impact of such investment often exceeds its quantitative measure. Furthermore, the improved growth prospects of many developing countries, combined with a more favourable macro-environment, liberalization policies and privatization programmes, may make them more attractive for foreign direct investment during the next years. Increased flows to a number of developing countries in Asia and, most recently, in Latin America, suggest that transnational corporations are already increasing their involvement in some developing countries.

Within this overall picture, an important trend is the emergence of foreign-direct-investment clusters, in which foreign direct investment in developing and Central and Eastern European countries is dominated by a single investing country. Those clusters are centred on individual Triad members which, in turn, can become growth poles for the developing countries associated with them, be it informally or in the context of regional integration efforts. In North America, for instance, the affiliates of United States transnational corporations located in Mexico account for nearly 40 per cent of that country's total trade with the United States, Mexico's largest trading partner. In fact, in some cases, regional integration at the policy and institutional levels may be driven by underlying integration at the production level which takes place as a result of the regional strategies of transnational corporations. Where countries are joined in such regional production networks, pressure is likely to mount for deeper integration at the policy level, implying greater coordination and convergence of policies among regional neighbours.

Reflecting its growing importance, foreign direct investment is receiving greater attention as a policy issue. On the global level, a draft of the first-ever multilateral framework governing international transactions in services is nearing completion in the Uruguay Round of GATT, following five years of negotiations. Such an agreement would provide a framework for, among other things, services-sector foreign direct investment, which accounts for 50 to 55 per cent of total outflows from most major home countries. Draft agreements are also being finalized in the Uruguay Round on trade related investment measures and trade related aspects of intellectual property rights, both of which bear directly on the activities of transnational corporations. On the regional level, the instruments of the Organisation for Economic Co-operation and Development affecting transnational corporations were recently strengthened, especially in the areas of national treatment and the environment. On the bilateral level, the number of treaties for the promotion and protection of foreign direct investment has expanded markedly, with 64 such treaties signed in the first 18 months of the 1990s alone (by comparison, only 199 treaties were signed during the entire decade of the 1980s). Finally, more and more countries have opened up their economies to foreign direct investment, as illustrated by the fact that, of 82 policy changes made in relation to foreign direct investment by 35 countries in 1991, 80 were in the direction of greater liberalization. In addition, privatization programmes in over 70 countries offer new opportunities for foreign direct investment, especially in the services sector; Central and Eastern Europe alone could absorb an estimated $50 billion of foreign direct investment during the course of this decade. These developments, discussed in chapter III of Part One, illustrate that competition among countries for investment is becoming more intense than ever before. At the same time, they show that a more coherent international policy approach towards foreign direct investment is needed and may, indeed, be emerging.

* * * * *

It is against this background that the *World Investment Report 1992* focuses, in Part Two, on the role of transnational corporations in the economic growth of developing countries. That focus derives its importance not only from the role of transnational corporations in the world economy, but also from a number of other developments, some recent, others more long-standing, which point to a rapidly changing context for economic growth, along with a growing role for transnational corporations in that process. Among them, five (outlined in chapter IV) stand out as particularly important: an increasing emphasis on market forces and a growing role for the private sector in nearly all developing countries; rapidly-changing technologies that are transforming the nature of international production and the organization and location of such activity; the globalization of firms and industries, whereby production chains span national and regional boundaries; the rise of services to become the single largest sector in the world economy; and regional economic integration, involving the world's largest economies as well as selected developing countries.

Transnational corporations are at the centre of all of those trends, which are setting new policy agendas for developing countries. For example, the scope for acquiring technology through arm's-length transactions rather than through foreign direct investment is narrowing, as product life cycles become shorter, the costs of research and development become very high and inter-firm technology networks proliferate. Similarly, global industries are re-defining the ways in which countries develop their manufacturing and services-sector capabilities, such that countries (including developing ones) are increasingly becoming part of multi-country production and service networks, organized and managed by transnational corporations primarily from developed countries.

The growth of foreign direct investment in the context of the new world economy poses a critical question: to what extent can transnational corporations, as central organizers of international economic activities, be engines of growth? This question promises to be a critical issue for the 1990s, because that decade is likely to be characterized by increased competition among countries and yet—somewhat paradoxically—a deepening of cross-national economic ties. It is of particular importance for developing countries which, although they receive less than one fifth of world-wide investment flows, depend more heavily than developed countries on transnational corporations for investment, technology, training, market access, environmentally sound technology and other growth stimuli.

While the context for growth is undoubtedly changing, the basic factors that, taken together, drive economic growth remain the same: a country's ability to save and invest in productive activities; to develop, acquire and utilize technology effectively; to raise the productivity of its human capital; to engage in international trade; and to take adequate environmental safeguards to ensure the long-term sustainability of its growth path. Chapters V through IX look separately at the impact of transnational corporations on each of those key determinants of economic growth. Since the linkages to growth of capital formation, technology, human resource development, trade and the environment are already well established, the analysis in the present Report focuses on the ways in which transnational corporations contribute to each of those linkages and, through them, to growth.

As these chapters show, the contribution of transnational corporations to each growth determinant varies considerably. Foreign direct investment contributes to capital formation in host countries, particularly in those industries that are important for growth (for example, technology-intensive manufacturing and services industries). It is also frequently accompanied by the supply of new plant and equipment, which embody advanced technology and can raise the productivity of both the existing and new stock of capital. Higher rates of labour and capital productivity of foreign affiliates can positively impact the effectiveness of domestic investment and trigger greater efficiency on the part of domestic firms through competitive pressures, demonstration and learning effects and backward and forward linkages with local suppliers and consumers. But the contribution of transnational corporations is perhaps strongest in the areas of technology and trade because, in those areas, firms can draw on their firm-specific advantages, especially in relatively high-technology, globalized industries. Indeed, transnational corporations are major actors in the development of technology. Fifty transnational corporations, for example, accounted for more than one-quarter of all United States patents granted to firms during the 1980s. Transnational corporations have also made a significant contribution to technology transfer to developing countries through increased research-and-development expenditures, higher factor productivity and diversification of output and exports in favour of technology-intensive products with high growth potential. In the area of trade, foreign affiliates account for upwards of 50 per cent of manufactured exports from several developing countries, thus permitting levels of production and efficiency that could not be sustained solely by domestic demand. Transnational corporations also facilitate the growth of exports through their far-flung trading networks, and alleviate potentially growth-retarding supply shortages through the import of capital goods. Foreign affiliates can also impact the development of human resources of host countries, especially by providing vocational training for manual and skilled workers, formal and informal training for managerial staff and by raising the level of employment. Finally, by observing environmental standards that can be higher than those enforced by Governments of host countries and by introducing environmentally sounder technologies, transnational corporations can contribute to sustainable long-term growth.

Important as those individual contributions are, it is a distinguishing characteristic of foreign direct investment that it combines, often in a synergistic manner, capital, technology, training, trade and environmentally sounder practices. In other words, as discussed in chapter X, transnational corporations bring an integrated *package* of tangible and intangible assets to host countries, which operates as a growth stimulus. Moreover, to the extent that foreign affiliates are linked to the local economy through forward and backward linkages, demonstration and learning effects as well as various other mechanisms, these growth stimuli can directly enhance the growth potential of firms in host countries. Thus, transnational corporations are not only responsible for a substantial share of international flows of capital, technology, skills and trade, but they also integrate those flows within their equity and non-equity networks of affiliates, make them subject to unifying corporate strategies and link them to local economies. It is, above all, the organizational and managerial capacity to integrate the factors and conditions of production on a world-wide scale that make transnational corporations potentially very efficient productive agents.

In fact, the growth of cross-national production networks of goods and services of some 35,000 transnational corporations and their more than 150,000 foreign affiliates is beginning to give rise to an international production system, organized and managed by transnational corporations. In terms of economic impact, therefore, transnational corporations play a critical role in the allocation of resources world-wide, in improving the competitiveness of both host and home countries in the new world economy and in stimulating processes of economic integration. As central wealth-creating organizers of international economic activities, transnational corporations can be important engines of growth.

The role of transnational corporations as integrating agents for a broad spectrum of economic activities also means that host-country policies in a correspondingly wide range of areas need to be sensitive to the potential contributions of those firms. Indeed, all chapters in Part Two highlight the importance of host-country market and factor conditions, within an enabling national policy framework, as key determinants of the extent to which transnational corporations can contribute to economic growth. In particular, economic policies need to be seen in the light of their impact on the strategic decisions of firms. Typically, policymakers have focused on trade and financial policies to govern their external economic relations; now much greater attention needs to be given to the coordination of all policies that affect the contribution of transnational corporations to host countries within a holistic policy framework that explicitly and prominently pays attention to foreign direct investment. At a minimum, policies relating to foreign direct investment need to be re-defined and broadened, to take into account the expanding role of transnational corporations as integrating and growth-promoting agents in the world economy.

* * * * *

Beyond the immediate implications for national policies, however, the emergence of an international production system for goods and services raises a much broader question, namely, from which perspective should international economic transactions be viewed? And, ultimately, what international governance framework is most appropriate for the new world economy?

Traditionally, trade has been considered to be the driving force of international transactions, and an international framework that reflects that perspective was established. But in a world in which the sales of foreign affiliates are more important than exports in serving international markets, and in which technology and other flows are associated with foreign direct investment, international economic transactions need to be seen from the perspective of international production by transnational corporations. *Foreign direct investment, as managed by transnational corporations, is increasingly the driving force of international economic transactions*. Trade and technology transfers are being more and more structured by foreign direct investment. A fundamental *change of perspective* is needed to understand the new world economy fully and to devise policies that are appropriate for it. In Part Three of the present Report a few important policy issues are explored from that vantage point, in a first attempt to view the world economy from the perspective of foreign direct investment, transnational corporations and international production.

For example, as discussed in chapter XI, international policy discussions have typically focused on how investment policies might influence trade flows in a distortive manner, as reflected in the fact that trade related investment measures (TRIMs) are an important subject of the Uruguay Round. By the same token, trade policies can have a significant impact on the locational decision-making of transnational corporations and, hence, on the global patterns of investment flows. From that perspective, investment related trade measures (IRTMs) are as important, if not more so, as TRIMs for the international allocation of resources; yet, IRTMs have not even received conceptual recognition, let alone become a subject of international discussions or negotiations. Similarly, strategic trade policies have been the subject of extensive academic analysis, and have also found their way into policy discussions. But very little, if any, attention has been given to strategic foreign-direct-investment policies, be it on the basis of a narrow rent-snatching or a broader developmental approach. Such is the importance of the perspective from which international economic transactions are viewed.

Quite naturally, if one takes an international production perspective, the institution central to it, the transnational corporation, comes into focus. And so do the problems that arise if and when a transnational corporation fails. Given the great number of transnational corporations, such incidents are likely to happen from time to time, as the recent examples of BCCI and Maxwell Communications Corporation illustrate. Yet, the international community is utterly unprepared to deal with such occurrences in a cooperative, equitable and efficient manner.

A changed perspective would also have important institutional implications. Trade-supporting measures, aimed at encouraging exports, for instance, are quite common and, at the international level, have found their expression in the creation of UNCTAD nearly 30 years ago. In the investment area, however, little is being done to promote outward investment beyond insurance and protection guarantees. Perhaps what is needed are foreign-direct-investment facilities at the national and international levels, aimed at accelerating the flow of investment to developing countries and enhancing its growth-promoting role. In that regard, it may also be useful to increase the transparency of national foreign-direct-investment regimes and to introduce multilateral reviews of foreign-direct-investment policies. This would allow Governments to disseminate information about their own policies and to learn from each others' experiences, and it would make it easier for foreign investors to obtain information important for decision-making—in brief, it would facilitate a better functioning of the international market mechanisms.

In the longer run, as suggested in chapter XII, however, a more comprehensive governance system may be needed. Given the growing role of international production, a stable, predictable and transparent international framework that defines, in a balanced manner, the rights and responsibilities of Governments and investors, would greatly assist the smooth functioning of the new world economy. Equally important, a multilateral institutional focal point may be needed, especially to safeguard competition in a world of globalizing firms and industries and interwoven international economic transactions. Such an institution would finally realize the vision that stood at the beginning of today's international institutional arrangements.

In summary, the international public policy framework needs to keep pace with the rapid globalization of firms and industries that is now under way, and with the emergence of a highly competitive world foreign-direct-investment market. Bold steps are needed to ensure that the emerging international production system functions smoothly, with a view to creating the best possible framework within which transnational corporations can act as engines of growth, especially for developing countries. Some possibilities in this regard, along the lines indicated above, are sketched in Part Three of the present Report, in order to stimulate thinking and discussion about how the international community can best meet the challenges it now faces.

PART ONE

RECENT TRENDS

Chapter I

TRENDS IN FOREIGN DIRECT INVESTMENT

A. Global trends

Foreign direct investment (FDI) continued to grow in 1990, although at a rate below that of the late 1980s. World-wide FDI *outflows* reached $225 billion (for an *outward stock* of $1.7 trillion). In 1990, the total number of transnational corporations (TNCs) exceeded 35,000, with more than 150,000 foreign affiliates (box I.1). The growth of FDI outflows represented an increase of 7 per cent over 1989 and a decline from the average annual growth rate of 14 per cent for the 1980s (table I.1). At the same time, there was a decline in world-wide FDI *inflows* in 1990, to $184 billion (box I.2). The rate of growth of outflows in 1990 was higher than what might have been expected, given the slow-down in economic growth in a number of large countries and the difficulties experienced by many financial institutions. Preliminary data for 1991 for the five largest outward investors show, however, a sharp decline of outflows (table I.2).

The slow-down in the growth of outflows in 1990 and the expected decline in 1991 can largely be attributed to a slow-down in the growth of outflows from Japan, a possible plateauing of outflows from the United States and a decline in outflows from the United Kingdom (table I.2). Outflows of FDI from developed countries, except for Japan, the United Kingdom and the United States, grew by 27 per cent in 1990, a rate of growth equivalent to the global average for 1983-1990. Outflows from developing countries had grown substantially in the late 1980s, driven by the growth in outflows from the Asian newly industrializing economies, but declined in 1990 when compared with 1989.

Box I.1. How many transnational corporations and foreign affiliates are there?

According to estimates of the Transnational Corporations and Management Division, based largely on official sources, the number of parent TNCs in the world is about 35,000, with some 150,000 foreign affiliates (table 1). The reported number of TNCs and affiliates, however, should be used with great caution, given the

Table 1. The geographical distribution of parent transnational corporations and foreign affiliates
(Number)

Region/economy	*Parent corporations*	*Foreign affiliates* [a]	*Year*
Developed countries	30,900	73,400	1989
of which:			
Austria	880	2,492	1988
Denmark	800	647 [b]	1992
Finland	1,350	1,524 [b]	1991
France	2,000	3,671 [c]	1984
Germany	6,984	10,978 [d]	1990
Japan	3,331	2,884	1990
Norway	1,115	2,799	1989
Sweden	2,750	..	1986
Switzerland	3,000	..	1992
United Kingdom	1,533	3,411 [e]	1981
United States	3,712	13,582	1989
Developing economies	3,800	62,900	1989
of which:			
Brazil	576	7,110	1986
China	553	15,966	1988
Hong Kong	500	2,464 [d]	1982
India	176	926	1988
Malaysia	153	578 [e]	1981
Pakistan	57	560 [f]	1988
Republic of Korea	668	2,821	1988
Taiwan Province of China	405	4,764	1988
Yugoslavia	112	3,949	1991
Central and Eastern Europe	300	10,900	1991
Bulgaria	26	117	1991
Commonwealth of Independent States	68	2,296	1991
Czechoslovakia	26	592	1991
Hungary	66	2,140	1991
Poland	58	2,168	1991
Romania	20	3,527	1991
World total [g]	35,000	147,200	1990

Source: United Nations, Department of Economic and Social Development, Transnational Corporations and Management Division, based on *World Investment Directory* (New York, United Nations, 1992) and national official and secondary sources.

a Represents the number of foreign affiliates as reported by host countries.
b For 1986.
c For 1971.
d For 1989.
e For 1988.
f For 1987.
g Includes data for countries not shown in the table.

/.....

The changes observed for 1990 can largely be explained by conditions within the United States. Inflows into the United States fell from $71 billion in 1989 to $37 billion in 1990 as the onset of a recession made investments less profitable. The slow-down of outflows from Japan and the United Kingdom, noted above, is to a significant extent a result of changing economic conditions in the United States, where Japan and the United Kingdom are the largest investing countries, and that trend seems to have continued in 1991 (table I.2).[1] A recession in the United Kingdom and larger domestic investments

(Box I.1, cont'd.)

limitations and discrepancies in the data: several countries do not report the number of TNCs or foreign affiliates, while others report only those affiliates with sales or assets above a minimum size, or exclude affiliates in certain industries.[1] The number of TNCs and foreign affiliates should therefore be considered as an underestimate. The inclusion of non-equity forms of investment (not included in table 1) would further increase the number of foreign affiliates, especially in developing countries.

Most TNCs are small or medium-size companies. A small number of TNCs, however, accounts for the majority of outward FDI in individual countries. For example, the fifty largest TNCs from the Federal Republic of Germany, less than 1 per cent of the total number, account for nearly 60 per cent of the total outward stock.[2] In France, 350 TNCs accounted for 80 per cent of all outward flows during the period 1981-1984.[3] Similarly, eighty TNCs from Finland account for 90 per cent of the total outward stock.[4] For a number of countries, FDI is highly concentrated in a small number of TNCs.

While the great majority of parent TNCs originates in developed countries (about 90 per cent), half of the foreign affiliates are located in developing countries. The concentration of parent TNCs in developed countries mirrors the fact that these countries are the main sources of outward FDI. France, Germany, Japan, the United Kingdom and the United States alone account together for about 70 per cent of world-wide investment outflows and for about half of the total number of TNCs. At the same time, with the rapid growth of FDI from the newly industrializing economies, the number of TNCs from developing countries has risen and can be expected to increase further in the future. The fact, however, that half of the foreign affiliates are located in developing countries is in sharp contrast with the relatively small share of FDI received by these countries. Given that developing countries have been receiving on average less than 20 per cent of world-wide FDI during the 1980s, the foreign affiliates located there are likely to be small or medium-size affiliates.

---

1 For example, the Deutsche Bundesbank includes only affiliates whose assets are at least DM 500,000; the United States Department of Commerce estimates for 1989 exclude banks, as well as affiliates whose assets, sales and net income are below $3 million (although an estimate of such affiliates, based on 1982 data, has been included in table 1); the Ministry of Finance of Japan excludes financial, insurance and real estate companies; and the United Kingdom only includes companies with at least £20 million directly invested overseas.

2 Deutsche Bundesbank, unpublished data.

3 Bank of France, *Bulletin Trimestriel*, No. 60 (1986), p. 51.

4 Suomen Pankki-Finlands Bank, unpublished data.

Table I.1. Inflows and outflows of foreign direct investment, 1986-1990

Country group	*1986*	*1987*	*1988*	*1989*	*1990*	*1980-1985*	*1986-1990*	*1980-1985*	*1986-1990*
	(Billions of dollars)					*Share in total (Percentage)*		*Growth rate (Percentage)*	
Developed countries									
Inflows	64	108	129	165	152	75	83	-3	24
Outflows	86	135	161	201	217	98	97	-2	26
Developing countries									
Inflows	14	25	30	30	32	25	17	4	22
Outflows	2	2	6	10	8	2	3	1	47
All countries									
Inflows	78	133	158	195	184	100	100	-1	24
Outflows	88	137	167	211	225	100	100	-2	26

Sources: International Monetary Fund, balance-of-payments tape, retrieved in December 1991; OECD estimates; and Transnational Corporations and Management Division, *World Investment Directory* (New York, United Nations, 1992).

by Japanese corporations also contributed to a reduced growth in outflows from those countries. [2] In addition, a decline in world-wide merger-and-acquisition activity (a result of slower growth, rising equity market valuations and uncertainties in financial markets) exerted a dampening influence on FDI outflows.

Among the reasons given for the lower level of FDI in the United States in 1990 was the weakness of its economy owing to the onset of recession. [3] That raises the question of the impact of cyclical fluctuations on the investment outlays of TNCs, as well as the attractiveness of host countries facing a recession. In the past, the volatility of investment flows has been closely related to cyclical fluctuations (figure I.1). [4] In 1990, a year of recession or low growth for many developed countries, FDI continued to grow, although at a considerably lower rate compared to 1989 (table I.2). Since FDI outflows for the five largest home countries declined in 1991 compared to 1990, this would suggest that cyclical fluctuations have contributed to the decrease in the rate of growth of investment outflows. Among the five largest home countries, outflows from Germany increased by about 60 per cent in 1990 from their 1989 level and did not decline in 1991; however, that country grew at a relatively high rate in comparison to the others. Outflows from France jumped 80 per cent in 1990, as changes in government policies stimulated a substantial growth in cross-border mergers and acquisitions by French TNCs, but declined considerably in 1991. [5]

The fact, however, that the combined investment outflows from the five major home countries grew at a modest rate in 1990, [6] a year of slow growth, and that the level of FDI in that year and even in 1991 was above the average level of those outflows during 1987-1989 (a period of high growth) in all of these countries except the United Kingdom, suggests that TNCs may become less influenced by cyclical fluctuations (or influenced with a time lag). Transnational corporations may be more tuned to long-term global strategic objectives, such as penetrating markets or increasing market share, with one factor explaining that behaviour being the growing realization that global expansion is necessary to increase competitive advantages.[7] By pursuing long-term goals, TNCs are, therefore, less likely to be influenced by cyclical fluctuations. For example, the expansion of TNC activity in Central and Eastern Europe, despite severe weaknesses in many of the economies in that region, attests to the importance of long-term goals in corporate planning. Such considerations would suggest that the recent divergence between the growth rates of FDI and GDP would continue in the 1990s, even if the explosive growth of investment observed in the late 1980s were not repeated. At the same time, it is possible that a slow-down in growth could affect FDI with a lag, with investment continuing to grow slowly or even to decline in 1991 and 1992. In fact, the decline in outflows of FDI from the largest home countries in 1991 (table I.2) indicates that, indeed, recessionary forces continue to exert an impact on investment decisions of TNCs. The fact, however, that the fall in FDI in 1991 is mainly concentrated in Japan and France, which could be attributed to circumstances specific to those countries, might reflect the decreasing importance of cyclical fluctuations on TNC investments. If the recession should spread and deepen, however, slow growth in the short term might influence the long-term plans of TNCs and lead to a temporary decline of investment flows.

Box I.2. The discrepancy between inflows and outflows

Inflows and outflows of FDI should balance, in principle; however, in practice, similar to other balance-of-payments items, they do not. Although this is not a recent phenomenon, the size of the discrepancy between world investment inflows and outflows has been increasing and has become a cause for concern. In 1990, the discrepancy reached $41 billion, a sizeable amount and one that potentially distorts the picture for 1990. The size of the discrepancy is actually higher given the fact that reinvested earnings are not included in outflows reported by Japan. Since Japanese outflows grew rapidly during the late 1980s, reinvested earnings are likely to be sizeable. Several reasons have been cited as the cause of the discrepancy, including differences in the threshold definition between inward and outward investment (which, however, has not been found to be a significant source of discrepancy); differences in the treatment of unremitted branch profits between inward and outward investment; treatment of unrealized and realized capital gains and losses; the recording of transactions of "offshore" enterprises; differences in the recording of reinvested earnings between inward and outward investments; differences in the method of collection and reporting of FDI between countries; and differences in the treatment of real estate and construction investment.[1] The use of outflows for analysing FDI trends is based on the premise that most of those flows originate from a small number of developed countries which have collection systems that are more suited to take the above factors into account than many of the recipient countries and, as such, provide a more reliable picture of the trends.

---

1 For a discussion of the causes of the discrepancy between investment inflows and outflows, see Neil Patterson, "The world statistical discrepancy on foreign direct investment capital flows: provisional comparisons and adjustments", a paper prepared for the third meeting of the Working Party on the Measurement of International Capital Flows, Washington D.C., 13-15 September 1990.

Table I.2. Outflows of foreign direct investment from five major home countries, 1986-1990

Country	1986	1987	1988	1989	1990	1991[a]	1980-1985	1986-1990	1980-1985	1986-1990
	Outflows (Billions of dollars)						*Share in total (Percentage)*		*Growth rate (Percentage)*	
France	5	9	15	19	35	21	6	10	-6	59
Germany, Federal Republic of	10	9	11	14	23	23	8	8	4	22
Japan[b]	15	20	34	44	48	31	10	20	22	35
United Kingdom	18	31	37	36	21	18	20	17	-1	6
United States[c]	14	28	14	29	29	29	26	14	-16	20
Total	61	97	112	142	156	122	69	72	-5	26

Sources: International Monetary Fund, balance-of-payments tape, retrieved in December 1991; Deutsche Bundesbank, *Statistische Beihefte*, No. 3 (March 1992); Bank of Japan, *Balance of Payments Monthly*, No. 306 (January 1992); Central Statistical Office, unpublished data provided by the British Trade Office in New York; United States, Department of Commerce, unpublished data; Ministère d'Economie, des Finances et du Budget, "La balance de paiements en 1991", communiqué of 19 March 1992.

a Preliminary estimates.

b Data for Japan do not include reinvested earnings.

c Excluding outflows to the finance (except banking), insurance and real estate sectors of the Netherlands Antilles. Also excludes currency translation adjustments.

Inflows of FDI to developing countries grew by 7 per cent in 1990. Developing countries received 17 per cent of all inflows in 1990, equal to their share for the last half of the 1980s. Continued strong growth of flows to East, South and South-East Asia and an increase of flows to Latin America and the Caribbean were partially offset by a drop in flows to Africa. The growth in the share of FDI going to developing countries in 1990 was a result of an increase in the size of such flows, as well as a slackening in world-wide flows. Among developing countries, the 10 largest host countries continued to receive approximately two thirds of all inflows. Flows of investment to the least developed countries grew slightly in 1990, to $250 million—equivalent to the inflows to Pakistan. Foreign direct investment to Central and Eastern Europe increased sharply, but remained at low levels.

The sectoral composition of the outward stock of FDI by major home countries at the end of the 1980s is shown in table I.3.[8] The rapid increase in investment flows in the 1980s was accompanied by a shift in the sectoral composition of both flows and stocks towards services. For all but Canada and the

United Kingdom, the services sector continued to be the single largest sector, and reached, for outward investment, over two thirds of the stock of Japan and over 40 per cent of the stock in most of the other countries. In terms of outflows from these countries, the services sector accounted for 50 to 55 per cent of the total during the late 1980s. Despite fluctuations in annual sectoral flows, including a decrease (albeit, from often considerably high levels) in the share of services in outflows from all of the countries in table I.3 (except the Netherlands and France) in the most recent year for which data are available, the shift towards services, reflecting long-term structural changes, seems likely to continue.

B. Regional trends

1. Developed countries

The slow-down in the growth of investment flows to and from the developed countries in 1990 is largely owing to a slowing down of economic activity, especially in the United States, which entered a recession in the middle of the year, and to some extent in Western Europe. [9] The slow-down in growth,

Figure I.1. Foreign direct investment, gross domestic product and domestic investment, 1970-1990

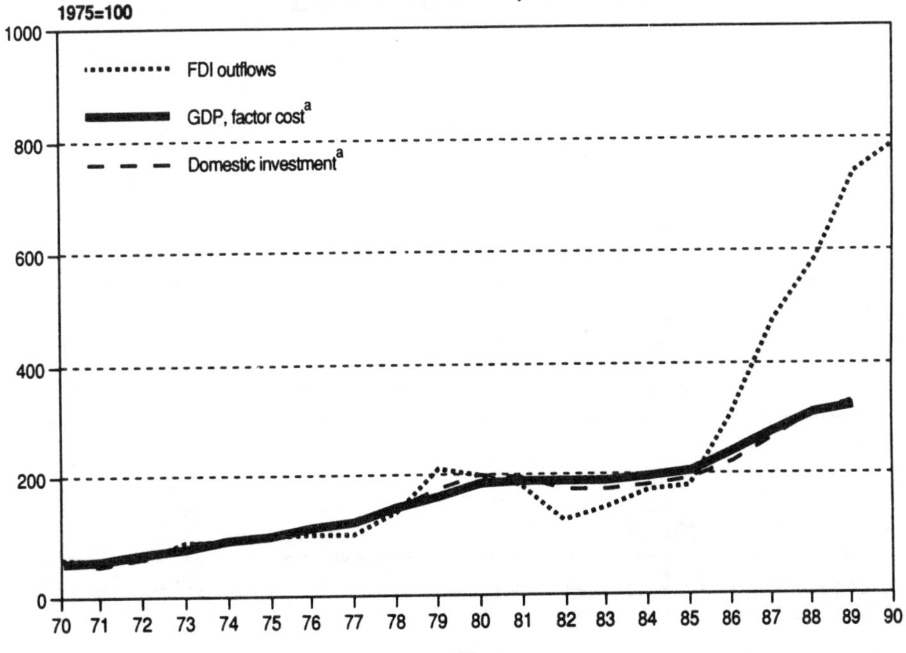

Source: International Monetary Fund, balance-of-payments tape, retrieved in December 1991; World Bank, world tables database.

a Data for 1989 are preliminary.

Table I.3. Sectoral composition of the stock of outward foreign direct investment of major home countries

(Percentage share and annual growth rate of stock)

Country	Period	Sectors			Total
		Primary	*Secondary*	*Tertiary*	
Canada					
Composition	1975	9	62	29	100
	1990	6	51	43	100
Growth rate	1975-90	13	14	18	15
France [a]					
Composition	1975	22	38	40	100
	1990	13	38	49	100
Growth rate	1975-90	23	27	29	27
Germany, Federal Republic of					
Composition	1976	5	48	47	100
	1990	2	49	59	100
Growth rate	1976-90	6	10	14	12
Japan					
Composition	1976	28	32	40	100
	1990	6	27	67	100
Growth rate	1976-90	10	21	28	23
Netherlands					
Composition	1975	47	39	15	100
	1989	35	24	41	100
Growth rate	1975-89	6	5	17	12
United Kingdom					
Composition	1984	33	32	35	100
	1988	25	38	37	100
Growth rate	1981-88	2	14	11	9
United States [b]					
Composition	1975	26	45	29	100
	1990	8	44	47	100
Growth rate	1975-90	-	8	12	12

Source: Estimates of Transnational Corporations and Management Division, based on Transnational Corporations and Management Division, *World Investment Directory* (New York, United Nations, 1992).

a Based on cumulative flows of direct investment from 1972.

b The vertically-integrated petroleum industry is included in the primary sector in 1975. In 1990, only the extractive portion of the industry is included in the primary sector, with processing included in the secondary sector and marketing and distribution in the tertiary sector.

combined with rising private-sector debt burdens and emerging structural weaknesses within the financial systems in a number of countries, was behind a slowing down in global merger-and-acquisition activity, the most important mode of cross-border investment for firms from developed countries. The major exception was France, whose TNCs increased their cross-border mergers and acquisitions in 1990. [10]

There are also indications that 1990 represented a year in which TNCs began to consolidate their positions within North America and Western Europe, as firms approached their desired investment positions after a period of rapid growth. Japanese TNCs expanded investments in domestic production facilities in response to an increased government demand stimulus, as the growth of outward FDI slowed down. [11] The slow-down in Japanese outflows may also be attributed to the substantial direct investments abroad accumulated by major Japanese TNCs during the 1980s in automobile and electronics production, and lesser amounts of finance available for outward FDI as Japanese banks—the key financiers for overseas investments—incurred substantial losses during the crumbling of the stock and real estate markets at the start of 1990, while having to increase their reserves to meet reserve requirements of the Bank for International Settlements.

Flows of FDI to Japan increased in 1990 from negative flows in 1988 and 1989, when a number of foreign investors, including such firms as Chrysler, General Motors and Honeywell, disinvested, apparently, at least in part, to realize capital gains accumulated during the boom in Japan's stock and real estate markets. The stock of FDI from Japan remains high in comparison with that of other large developed countries, when expressed in relation to the stock of inward investment and when the latter is expressed in relation to the level of GDP in the host economy (table I.4). Government restrictions on inward FDI in existence from 1950 through 1980 explain, in part, the low level of the stock of inward investment. But at least some TNCs do not appear to have adopted their most effective competitive stance in approaching the Japanese market. For example, only a few TNCs in the automobile industry, such as BMW, have established their own distribution networks in Japan. At the same time, the competitive advantages of Japanese corporations within their home market continue to raise difficulties for foreign TNCs seeking to operate within Japan. While there are signs indicating that a significant increase in FDI inflows is possible, such an increase has yet to materialize. [12]

The growth of inflows and outflows to and from the non-EC Western European countries (44 and 27 per cent, respectively, during 1985-1990; for values of these flows see annex table 1), combined with the already large amounts of EC inward and outward FDI, is an indication of the emergence of the European Economic Area (EEA) as a powerful economic region. In the case of the Nordic countries, the surge of inward investment after 1984 reflects the determination of Governments to pursue policies more favourable to TNCs prior to the onset of wider European economic integration. [13] Companies from Sweden, as well as other EFTA countries, have launched aggressive merger-and-acquisition offensives inside the European Community to gain a stronger foothold in the Single Market, while firms from within the Community have also invested in EFTA countries. During the period from 1985 to 1989, approximately 51 per cent of total inflows and outflows of investment in and from the EFTA member countries were accounted for by both EC and EFTA members.

Table I.4. Inward and outward foreign direct investment in the largest developed market economies, 1989
(Billions of dollars; percentage share; ratios)

Item	*European Community* [a]	*Japan* [b]	*United States*	*France*	*Germany, Federal Republic of*	*United Kingdom*
Inward stock of FDI	249	28	374	51	74	135
Percentage of world total	22	2	27	4	5	10
Outward stock of FDI	370	156	376	75	122	213
Percentage of world total	32	11	27	5	9	16
Ratio of outward stock to inward stock	1.5	5.6	1.0	1.5	1.6	1.6
Ratio of inward stock to GDP	0.05	0.01	0.07	0.05	0.06	0.17

Source: Calculations by Transnational Corporations and Management Division, based on Transnational Corporations and Management Division, *World Investment Directory* (New York, United Nations, 1992).

a Excludes intra-EC FDI.

b The stock of FDI in Japan is estimated using data on outward investment from Australia, Canada, the European Community, Norway, Switzerland and the United States.

Despite the decline in FDI inflows into the developed countries, those countries continued to account for more than four fifths of world-wide inflows in 1990. The Triad, consisting of the EC, Japan and the United States, accounted for approximately 70 per cent of world-wide inflows, a proportion unchanged from the average for the decade of the 1980s, and 83 per cent of outflows, a small decline from the average for the 1980s. In the 1990s, the emerging Triad may be more aptly described as including Japan, North America (Canada and the United States) and the European Economic Area (EC and EFTA). Cross-holdings of stocks of FDI within this emerging Triad amounted to $572 billion in 1989 (figure I.2).

The continuing concentration of transnational corporate activity in the Triad has made FDI an increasingly important instrument of global economic integration in these countries. The growth and concentration of FDI in the Triad at the beginning of the 1990s are associated with several structural and cyclical factors. Among the former are sustained technological competition and cross-border, intra-industry production; significant economic developments in those countries, such as the regionalisation of markets with the EC and its extension to EFTA countries; the United States-Canada Free Trade Agreement and the likely inclusion of Mexico in a wider North American Free Trade Agreement;

privatization and deregulation in services industries and their opening to FDI; and fears of rising protectionism as regional markets grapple with their relations with the rest of the world. High growth rates relative to most other regions of the world are among the cyclical factors. The economic slow-down of the early 1990s may have reduced the impact of some of these trends, but it is not likely to alter them in any substantial way.

Figure I.2. Intra-Triad foreign direct investment, 1989

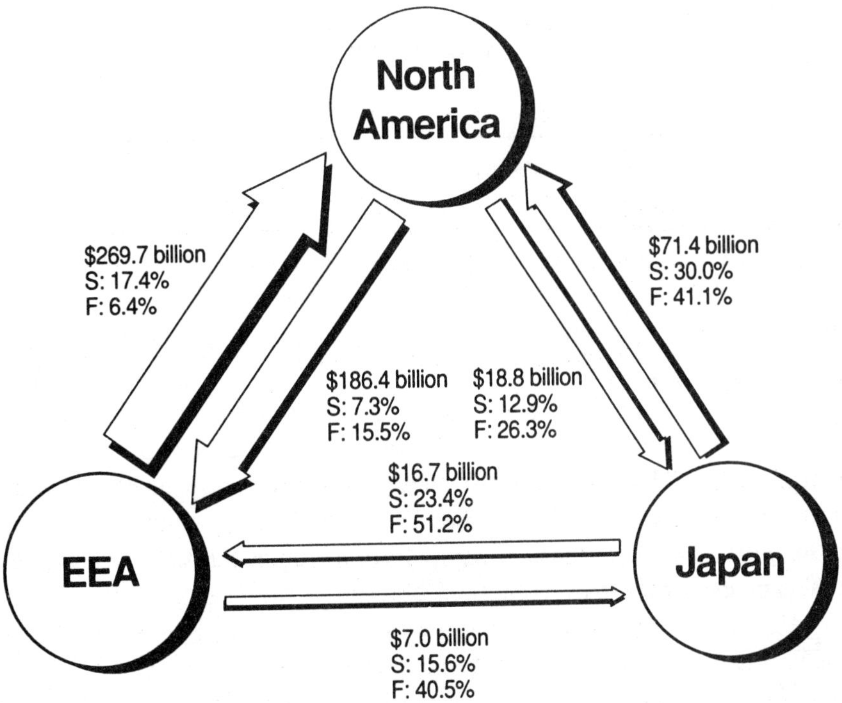

S = Stocks; F = Flows

Source: Transnational Corporations and Management Division, *World Investment Directory* (New York, United Nations, 1992).

Note: Dollar figures show estimated value of stock of foreign direct investment based on data on inward and outward investment from North America and the European Economic Area (EEA), excluding Iceland and Liechtenstein. Intra-North American investment and intra-EEA investment has been netted out. Percentages show average annual growth rates for stocks (1980-1989) and flows (1985-1990). North America includes Canada and the United States. The European Economic Area includes the European Community (EC) and the European Free Trade Association (EFTA), excluding Iceland and Liechtenstein.

2. Developing countries

Foreign direct investment to developing countries grew in 1990, reaching a total of $32 billion, thus continuing the substantial growth in inflows to developing countries that began in the mid-1980s (table I.5 and annex table 1). The Asian region attracted the majority (61 per cent) of inflows to developing countries. Flows to Latin America and the Caribbean grew in 1990 (to reach a share of 32 per cent), as a number of countries in that region were showing signs of a significant economic revival. Flows to Africa (7 per cent) and to the least developed countries (0.7 per cent) have remained at low levels, and show no signs of significant growth.

While the quantity of flows to developing counties as a whole, and Asia and the Pacific and Latin America and the Caribbean in particular, continued to increase, the share of FDI going to developing countries declined over time, reflecting strategies of TNCs that increasingly favour the locational advantages of developed countries. (The share of inflows to developing countries increased in 1990, largely owing to the sharp drop in inflows to the United States, the size of which is not likely to be repeated in succeeding years.) Among developing countries, a large proportion of inflows of investment was directed to a small number of countries (annex table 2). Thus, while FDI flows to developing countries as a whole increased, those flows were not evenly distributed.

(a) Asia and the Pacific

In 1990, the position of East, South and South-East Asia and the Pacific as the leading recipients of FDI flows among developing countries was further consolidated, with Asia and the Pacific accounting for almost 60 per cent of total flows to all developing countries in that year. [14] At the same time, that group of countries accounted for an overwhelming share of investment outflows from developing countries (about 86 per cent in 1990), with the Asian newly industrializing economies being the leading source. Moreover, the Republic of Korea and Taiwan Province of China have become net exporters of investment and, along with the other Asian newly industrializing economies, are responsible for an increasing share of all investment flows to Asia.

East, South and South-East Asia and the Pacific, having overtaken Latin America and the Caribbean as the largest recipients of investment among developing regions in 1986 (on average, during 1989-1990, investment *inflows* have been almost twice as large in Asia and the Pacific as in Latin America), continued to surpass all other developing regions in terms of the size of inflows. Flows of investment to Asia and the Pacific continued to grow in 1990, reaching approximately $18 billion, an 18 per cent increase over the previous year. Attracted by high rates of domestic growth, relatively low production costs and increasingly lucrative domestic markets due to rising consumer purchasing power, investment flows to those countries have grown at the highest rate among all developing regions: by 20 per cent throughout the 1980s and by 29 per cent during the period 1986-1990. Flows of FDI to East, South and South-East Asia are likely to continue on an upward path, given that China has reconfirmed its open policy and

Table I.5. Average inflows of foreign direct investment to developing regions, by region, 1970-1979, 1980-1985 and 1986-1990

Host region and economy	*1970-1979*	*1980-1985*	*1986-1990*	*1970-1979*	*1980-1985*	*1986-1990*	*1970-1979*	*1980-1985*	*1986-1990*
	(Billions of dollars)			*(Share of all inflows) (Percentage)*			*(Annual growth rate) (Percentage)*		
All countries	22	50	150	100	100	100	16	-1	24
Developing countries	5	13	26	24	25	17	21	4	22
Latin America and the Caribbean	3	6	9	13	12	6	20	-5	17
West Asia	0.3	0.4	0.5	1	1	0.4	..	53	37
East, South and South-East Asia	1	5	14	6	9	9	16	7	28
Oceania	0.02	0.1	0.1	0.1	0.3	0.1	28	-1	-5
Africa	1	1	3	3	3	2	22	52	6
Other [a]	0.03	0.04	0.05	0.1	0.1	0.03	15	-8	..
Least developed countries	0.1	0.2	0.2	0.5	0.4	0.1	27	-16	116
Ten largest host countries [b]	1970-1979: 4	1980-1990: 13		1970-1979: 16	1980-1990: 13		1970-1979: 23	1980-1990: 11	

Sources: Estimates of Transnational Corporations and Management Division, based on International Monetary Fund, balance-of-payments tape, retrieved in December 1991; OECD estimates; and Transnational Corporations and Management Division, *World Investment Directory* (New York, United Nations, 1992).

a Malta and Yugoslavia.

b For a list of these countries, see annex table 2.

continues to attract substantial investments and given the substantial liberalization of India's FDI regime and other changes in the economy of that country. (See also the box on India in chapter III.)[15]

The share of Western Asia in total FDI inflows to developing countries continued to decline during the second half of the 1980s compared to the first half, although, in absolute terms, inflows increased. Oil exporting countries have been the major recipients of FDI, accounting for roughly two thirds of those investments to Western Asia. In 1990, Cyprus experienced its highest inflow of investment capital over the past two decades and accounted for over half of all flows to non oil-producing countries of that region.

Investment *outflows* from East, South and South-East Asia, valued at almost $8 billion in 1990, fell slightly from the previous year's record high of over $8 billion. On average, investment outflows from Asia grew by 47 per cent during the 1980s and 75 per cent during 1986-1990. In the cases of both the Republic of Korea and Taiwan Province of China, outflows have exceeded inflows, a pattern usually reserved for developed countries (figure I.3). China has also emerged as a major investor from that region during the past decade, with investment outflows reaching $830 million in 1990 (an annual average growth rate of 17 per cent since 1986), reflecting the efforts on the part of Chinese TNCs to penetrate new markets and to acquire technology and management skills.[16]

Figure I.3. Foreign-direct-investment inflows and outflows, Republic of Korea and Taiwan Province of China

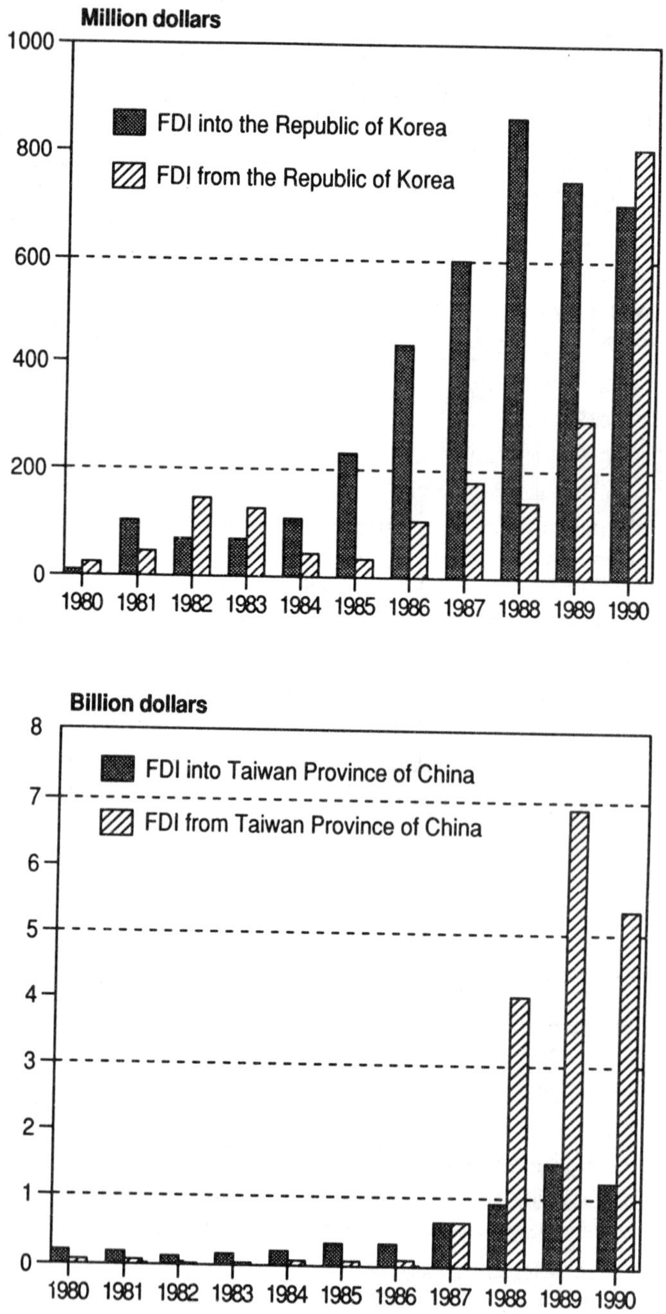

This unprecedented growth of FDI from the East, South and South-East Asian region, overwhelmingly from the newly industrializing economies in which a growing number of domestic firms have become global competitors, can be attributed to the "push" factors of the appreciation of national currencies and labour shortages exerting upward pressure on domestic production costs, the large current account surpluses experienced by some of these countries and the removal of restrictions on outward capital flows. In addition, the loss of generalized system of preference status for those economies is likely to have contributed to the increase of outward investment and influenced its pattern, particularly regarding the location of investments by TNCs in the industries most affected by the removal of that status, such as electrical equipment and food processing. The main "pull" factors have been protectionist threats by developed countries, which have encouraged firms from those economies to invest in North America and Europe in order to secure market access and maintain a presence in their main export markets. Another important factor was access to technology, which enables firms to upgrade their production processes and move up the value-added chain to retain export market shares and increase the capital intensity of output in the face of domestic labour shortages.

Most of the total FDI stock from the newly industrializing economies in developed countries (64 per cent of total outward stock for Taiwan Province of China in 1990) is concentrated in the North American and European markets. In those regions, FDI is concentrated in the manufacturing sector, although the services sector has also attracted a significant share of investment from those economies.[17] At the same time, TNCs from the newly industrializing economies are increasingly focusing on Asia as a low cost production base for supplying the region and the rest of the world[18] and as a means of diversifying export markets in the face of growing protectionism in developed countries.[19] As a result, intraregional flows of investment in East, South and South-East Asia and the Pacific expanded rapidly during the second half of the 1980s (mostly in manufacturing) and account for a growing share of the inward investments of the recipient countries (table I.6). In particular, the newly industrializing economies accounted for an increasing share of total annual average investment

Table I.6. Investment flows to South and South-East Asia, China and the Asian newly industrializing economies from the Asian newly industrializing economies, 1983-1986 and 1987-1990 [a]

(Percentage share of total average annual inflows)

Host economy	*1983-1986*	*1987-1990*
South and South-East Asia		
India	1	3 [b]
Indonesia	11	19
Malaysia	19	41
Philippines	6	18 [c]
Thailand	13	31
Newly industrializing economies		
Republic of Korea	3	5 [b]
Taiwan Province of China	10	14
China	55	66 [b]

Source: UNCTC, *World Investment Directory 1992, Vol. I, Asia and the Pacific* (United Nations publication, Sales No. E.92.II.A.11).

a As reported by the host economy.
b 1987-1988.
c 1987-1989.

flows to countries in South and South-East Asia and to other newly industrializing economies. While outward investment from those economies is driven primarily by supply factors (low production costs and the need to retain export competitiveness), investments in the latter are motivated by the growth in domestic demand.

(b) Latin America and the Caribbean

The resurgence of economic growth in a number of countries in Latin America and the Caribbean, policy changes that have allowed foreign investors greater access to the region's resources and markets, and stronger efforts to achieve regional economic integration are leading to a revival of FDI in the region. The proposed North American free trade agreement, if concluded, will enhance the locational advantages of Mexico as a host country for FDI, a process that has already begun and which is further discussed in section D. At the same time, outflows of investment from the region declined substantially. Transnational corporations from Latin America and the Caribbean, with a few exceptions, have not developed into international competitors. The role of import-substituting trade and industrialization strategies in the region may have contributed to the slow expansion of TNCs from Latin America and the Caribbean.[20]

Successes in managing external debt burdens, combined with concessions to debtor countries through the Brady debt initiative, allowed indebted countries to adopt more stimulative economic policies, increased the confidence of both foreign and domestic investors and helped to stimulate FDI inflows to a number of countries in the region. Debt-for-equity swaps have been important in facilitating FDI flows, especially in Chile, Brazil and Venezuela (table I.7).[21] Economic policy changes, especially in Argentina, Chile and Mexico involving a greater liberalization of policies towards TNCs and more of an outward orientation of economic policies have been manifested in the

Table I.7. Total foreign direct investment and foreign direct investment financed through debt-equity swaps, 1985-1989

(Millions of dollars)

	Total investment flows		*Foreign direct investment through debt-equity swaps* [a]	*Foreign direct investment through debt-equity swaps as percentage of total foreign direct investment*
Country	*1980-1984*	*1985-1989*	*1985-1989*	*1985-1989*
Argentina	2 195	3 646	731	20
Brazil [b]	10 499	7 687	4 529	59
Chile [c]	1 210	3 947	3 160	80
Mexico	7 497	10 098	3 053	30

Source: Transnational Corporations and Management Division, *Debt-Equity Swaps and Development* (New York, United Nations, forthcoming).

a Includes only that portion of swaps which corresponds to foreign direct investment.

b Excludes informal conversions.

c Excludes chapter XVIII transactions.

privatization of State-owned enterprises, including in such services industries as telecommunications, banking and public utilities, the lowering of trade barriers and greater efforts to control fiscal deficits (box I.3). A number of countries in the region have stepped up efforts at fostering regional integration, in part with the objective of enlarging markets and attracting larger amounts of FDI.

Box I.3. Foreign direct investment in Argentina

Inflows of FDI to Argentina began to increase in the late 1980s, particularly in gas and petroleum, food processing, tourism, motor vehicles, petrochemicals and the financial industry. The recent increase in FDI inflows can be largely attributed to the efforts of the Government of Argentina to boost foreign equity participation in the country's economy.

Investment in the petroleum sector increased significantly, following the broad deregulation of the sector initiated by the so-called Houston Plan of 1985. Foreign oil companies were invited to participate, through concession contracts, in the exploitation of several of Argentina's marginal oil fields (*areas secundarias*). Since 1990, foreign oil companies have also been awarded concession rights in some of the country's richest oil fields (*areas centrales*).

Investment in the food-processing and automotive industries was greatly encouraged by the signing of a Complementarity Agreement between Argentina and Brazil in 1986. This trade agreement led to a major restructuring of the automotive sector, including the merger of two of the largest TNCs, Ford and Volkswagen, into a joint venture, Autolatina. Autolatina, whose goal is to rationalize and integrate its Argentine and Brazilian operations, has since set up a wholly-owned subsidiary, Transax, to produce gear boxes for export to Brazil. The Complementarity Agreement has also boosted investment in the agro-industrial sector, including significant commitments by the Swiss firm Nestlé.

In addition, Argentina operated a formal debt capitalization scheme during the period 1987-1989 with a view to promoting new investments through the direct conversion of bank debt. Investment projects approved under the debt-conversion scheme were heavily concentrated in agri-business, tourism, automobiles and pharmaceuticals. Since 1988, there has also been growing foreign participation in the country's telecommunications market, particularly in cellular telephone and data-transmission services.

Since 1989, the policy of stimulating FDI has gathered increasing momentum. The new administration amended the already liberal investment law of 1980, gave new impetus to the full-scale privatization of State-owned companies and implemented several policy reforms aimed at easing trade and exchange restrictions and restoring macroeconomic equilibrium. The new FDI law of 1989 made approval of foreign investments virtually automatic. Registration is now required only for statistical purposes. Limits on profit and dividend remittances were lifted, and so were restrictions on foreign ownership of local companies. The new law also reduced the tax burden on foreign investors and increased their access to domestic financing. The only areas in which FDI is not permitted are defence-related industries and the mass media. In addition, changes were introduced in the mining code, allowing national and provincial Governments to call for international bids for the exploration and exploitation of mineral reserves held by the State.

The new administration has also embarked upon a massive privatization programme. It involves the sale of some of the largest State-owned companies through the ample use of debt-equity swaps. For that purpose, a law passed in 1989 gave the executive branch of the Government extraordinary powers to take all appropriate

/.....

The proposed free trade agreement being negotiated by Mexico with the United States and Canada (and discussed further in section D below) has already increased the attractiveness of Mexico as a low-cost production location for the entire North American market. Majority-owned foreign affiliates of United States companies planned to increase capital spending by 20 per cent in 1991 in Mexico, as of July 1991, as compared to a planned 9 per cent increase for the region as a whole, and up from a 6 per cent planned increase in December 1990, in response to the prospect of the free trade agreement and an improving investment climate.[22] Although investment inflows into Mexico declined by $405 million in 1990, a number of indications point to the rapid expansion of FDI in the next years. For example, actual inflows of FDI were about $5 billion in 1991.[23]

The implementation of the North American free trade agreement is likely to have long-term impacts on countries in Central America and the Caribbean. Some of the export-oriented labour-intensive investments presently being undertaken in Central American and Caribbean countries and geared towards the North American market may be diverted to Mexico. Countries in the region appear to have benefited from policies of the Government of the United States designed to stimulate trade with the United States market. The creation of twin plants for production-sharing between Puerto Rico and its Caribbean neighbours, such that labour intensive operations are carried out in a Caribbean or Central American country and final processing is performed in Puerto Rico, have allowed United States and other foreign producers to tap into the region's low-cost, abundant labour force, with low turnover rates and rapid turnaround potential.[24] Transnational corporations from the Asian newly industrializing economies,

(Box I.3, cont'd)

steps to privatize public sector companies fully or partially, without the need to obtain congressional approval. A salient feature of the Argentine privatization programme is that, from its very inception, foreign investors were targeted as a priority. The law allows majority foreign ownership and control in most sectors, reserving only the media and defence-related industries for local companies.

Several privatizations took place during the first two years of the programme, including those of ENTEL (telecommunications), Aerolineas Argentinas (the country's flag carrier airline) and several petrochemical firms. The sale of ENTEL involved a debt-equity swap of over $5 billion, the largest so far in Latin America. In most cases, the participants are foreign consortia involving a transnational bank, a foreign company and several local groups which plan an important role during the bidding process. Additional privatizations are scheduled in 1992-1993. They include most public utilities (electricity, water and gas), the national road and railway networks, ports and shipping and petrochemical companies. Also included are the giant state concerns SOMISA and Altos Hornos Zapla (steel), as well as YPF (oil), the largest Argentine company. Foreign participation in future privatization deals is being actively encouraged.

During March 1991, the Presidents of Argentina, Brazil, Paraguay and Uruguay signed the Treaty of Asunción creating the Southern Cone Common Market (Mercosur), the goal of which is the establishment of a single external tariff and the elimination of non-tariff barriers by 1995. Furthermore, Argentina is concluding negotiations with IMF for an extended fund facility. The expected inclusion of Argentina in the Brady Plan in 1992 could lead to a significant reduction in the country's foreign debt. Together, those factors may well create additional incentives for FDI in Argentina.

especially the Republic of Korea and Taiwan Province of China, have located some of their labour-intensive manufacturing in Caribbean countries, partly because of the latter's free trade status with the United States.[25] While the proposed free trade agreement will increase the attractiveness of Mexico as a location for such export-oriented industrial FDI, those investments will not enjoy the locational advantages of the Central American and Caribbean countries that emerge from their preferential access to the EC through the Lomé Convention. In addition, those countries would continue to be an important host area for investment in agro-business by TNCs.

Outflows of FDI from Latin America and the Caribbean were $1.1 billion in 1990, a 59 per cent increase from the previous year. The largest sources of FDI from that region are Brazil and Venezuela. Investment outflows from Latin America and the Caribbean grew by 14 per cent during the period 1986-1990 in comparison to 75 per cent for South and South-East Asia. The slower growth of outflows from Latin America and the Caribbean in comparison to East, South and South-East Asia may be explained by the earlier trade and industrialization strategies adopted by the two regions. The emphasis placed on greater outward orientation and economic growth through export expansion in a number of Asian countries, particularly the newly industrializing economies, may have contributed to the greater competitiveness of their firms in trade and international production. That has resulted in larger amounts of exports and, later, export-oriented outward investment from Asia. By contrast, the emphasis on greater inward orientation and economic growth through domestic demand in a number of Latin American countries may have contributed to the relatively slower growth of Latin American firms that are internationally competitive in either trade or international production. In addition, the slower pace of growth in Latin America owing to macroeconomic difficulties, including debt-servicing problems, helps to explain why the growth of TNCs from Latin America and the Caribbean has been surpassed by the more rapid development of Asian TNCs in recent years.[26]

(c) Africa

Flows of FDI to Africa fell to $2.2 billion in 1990—slightly more than what Portugal received in that year—a decrease of 50 per cent from 1989. Although investment inflows were significantly lower in 1990, their level was similar to that reached during most years in the late 1980s, implying that the 1989 level was exceptionally high. The fall in investment inflows was experienced primarily by the oil exporting countries in Africa, particularly Nigeria and Egypt, whose share of the total fell from 80 to 66 per cent between 1989 and 1990. For the latter, the impact of political tensions in the Persian Gulf on the investment climate is the main explanatory factor. Non-oil exporting countries in Africa, most of which are classified as least developed countries, received on average less than $0.5 billion per year during the second half of the 1980s—roughly what Papua New Guinea alone attracted during the same period.[27]

The low levels of FDI flowing to Africa underline the increasing marginalization of the region. Continuing uncertainty regarding prospects for economic development have deterred investments by TNCs from the major home countries, as those companies favour countries with high growth rates or large domestic markets.[28] The low level of new investments in Africa by TNCs from the major home countries, indicated by the small proportion of equity capital in total FDI outflows to that region reported by those countries (less than 10 per cent during the late 1980s), further illustrates that most investment is undertaken by affiliates that already have investments in Africa. There are also examples of large TNCs acquiring existing foreign-owned companies without contributing to the overall amount of FDI.[29]

In recent years, a number of countries in Africa have sought to attract greater amounts of FDI, primarily by reducing or removing legal and regulatory restrictions on the activities of foreign companies. Despite those extensive efforts at liberalization, the quantity of FDI flowing to the region has remained small, largely because, as indicated above, the economic advantages of the countries in the region appear not to be sufficient to attract larger flows of new investment. Thus, a greater involvement by national and international agencies may be needed to help attain the necessary economic conditions and infrastructural requirements to attract significant amounts of FDI.

3. Central and Eastern Europe

The number of joint ventures and wholly-owned affiliates registered in Central and Eastern Europe more than doubled between the beginning of 1991 and January 1992, to reach a total of over 34,000. Foreign equity participation committed to those enterprises as of October 1991 amounted to over $9 billion (table I.8).[30] The amounts actually invested, however, remain small by international standards. Divergence in the economic performance of Central and Eastern European countries and political uncertainty regarding the future of the members of the Commonwealth of Independent States led to changes in the pattern of investment in the region. By the beginning of 1992, Hungary and Romania had become the largest host countries in terms of the number of registered joint ventures and wholly-owned foreign affiliates.

Table I.8. Foreign investment registrations in Central and Eastern Europe, by number and value of foreign equity participation, beginning of 1992

Country	*Number*	*Foreign equity*[a] *(Millions of dollars)*
Bulgaria	900	300
Commonwealth of Independent States	5 400	5 650
Czechslovakia	4 000	480
Hungary	11 000	2 089
Poland	5 100	670
Romania	8 022	231
Total	34 422	9 420

Source: Transnational Corporations and Management Division and ECE, *World Investment Directory 1992, Central and Eastern Europe* (New York, United Nations, 1992).

[a] As of 1 October 1991.

While most companies that invest in Central and Eastern Europe are attracted by the size of the

the domestic market, companies from particular industries, such as automobiles and electrical goods, consider that region (primarily Czechoslovakia, Hungary and Poland) as an extension of Western Europe and are establishing production facilities there with a view to supply the entire European market (box I.4). In the automobile industry, a number of Japanese, United States and Western European manufacturers have established plants in Central and Eastern Europe to supply both domestic and foreign markets. [31] Similar examples can also be found in electrical machinery and consumer goods, with TNCs setting up plants in Eastern Europe to serve all of the European market. [32] Viewing Central and Eastern Europe in the context of a regional core network strategy on the part of TNCs is likely to increase further the locational advantages of that area, such as proximity to Western Europe, the availability of a skilled labour force and relatively low labour costs. With improvements in the overall economic situation of these countries, this is likely to lead to sizeable increases in FDI. Although benefits to existing investments may not materialize in the short run, possible "first-mover" advantages and long-term prospects have already induced many companies to invest there.

Economic and political developments in the members of the Commonwealth of Independent States place those countries increasingly apart from the other countries in the region. Transnational corporations are less likely to include these countries in their regional core network strategies, not only owing to continuing political and economic uncertainties, but also to the distance of a number of those countries from Western Europe, combined with a lack of infrastructural facilities and distribution channels and the regulatory and administrative infrastructure required for the functioning of a market economy. It would be unlikely, therefore, that TNCs would invest in a major way in the Asian part of the former Soviet Union to supply the European market. It is only in natural resources (where distance plays a less

Box I.4. Foreign investments in automobiles in Central and Eastern Europe: an example of regional core network strategies

Several automobile manufacturers, including Fiat (Italy), General Motors (United States), Volkswagen (Germany) and Suzuki (Japan), have already invested, or are in the process of investing, in the manufacture of automobiles or automobile components in Central and Eastern Europe. Those investments are examples of regional core network strategies on the part of those automobile manufacturers. Transnational corporations, encouraged by the desire of Central and Eastern European countries to integrate themselves with Western Europe, view their investments in that region as part of a wider regional strategy of supplying both the potentially sizeable domestic markets of those countries as well as the markets of other European countries. For example, General Motors' recently established plant in the eastern part of Germany incorporating the latest production technology, and its new engine plant and a small automobile assembly operation in Hungary may be considered as part of the regional core network strategy of that company aiming at supplying components or finished products to the whole European market. Some companies, notably Fiat, have had a long-term involvement in automobile manufacturing activities in the region through licensing and production agreements and have benefited considerably from the experience gained in negotiating with those countries and in solving particular difficulties. Nevertheless, even late-comers have moved rapidly to establish a strong presence in the region by acquiring existing companies, committing funds for the modernization of existing plants and providing technical and managerial assistance, and by capitalizing on their existing marketing networks.

significant role) that some TNCs have shown a strong interest.[33] On the other hand, those natural resources, as well as skilled labour and large potential markets, make these countries attractive locations for FDI in the future. Their proximity to TNCs from developing countries in Asia and from Japan has encouraged some of those companies to invest in the Asian part of the former Soviet Union (including the Nakhodka Free Trade Zone), as a means of penetrating the potential markets of the members of the Commonwealth of Independent States, as well as using them as a base for exporting to the rest of the region.[34]

Although the present levels of FDI in Central and Eastern Europe are small by international standards—about the same level as the FDI flows to Belgium and Luxembourg in 1990—investments in that region could expand significantly. To a large extent, this will depend on the success of Governments to implement market reforms and remove remaining legislative obstacles, and on the degree of commitment on the part of Western countries to provide financial and technical assistance to the region as a whole. By one estimate, cumulative FDI in Central and Eastern Europe could rise to $75 billion-$100 billion by the late 1990s; other estimates arrive at similar figures.[35] Using, for comparative purposes, FDI flows in the 1980s to Brazil, Mexico and Portugal—countries with levels of per capita GDP similar to those of many of the countries in the region—cumulative investment flows could surpass $50 billion by the end of the 1990s.

C. Foreign-direct-investment clusters of the Triad members and newly industrializing economies

The clustering of Central and Eastern European and host developing countries around one or more Triad members, as determined by FDI stocks and flows, was discussed for the first time in the *World Investment Report, 1991*, which found that, from the perspective of a large number of host countries, most FDI originates from one or more Triad members. It was also found that, between the early and late 1980s, the clustering of FDI had become more pronounced, with host countries tending to be clustered around a single Triad member located in the same geographical region. That pattern was consistent with the emerging strategies of TNCs to build regional core networks of affiliates centred on their home country.

Updating FDI stock and flow data to 1989 shows that the pattern is not significantly different from that which was described in the *World Investment Report, 1991* (figure I.4 and annex table 3). The distribution of host countries around Triad members shows that the United States continues to be the dominant investor in most Latin American countries and in a few Asian countries. In terms of FDI flows, which better than stocks reflect recent shifts, the position of Japan as a source of FDI for Asia was further strengthened as Singapore and Taiwan Province of China were added to its cluster. The European Community continues to be the dominant investor in Central and Eastern Europe, Africa and a few Asian countries, where its member countries have strong historical ties. The newly industrializing economies continue to be dominant in China and in a few other Asian countries; the number of countries in that

Figure I.4. Foreign-direct-investment clusters of Triad members, 1986-1989
(Economies in which one Triad member dominates
average annual investment inflows)

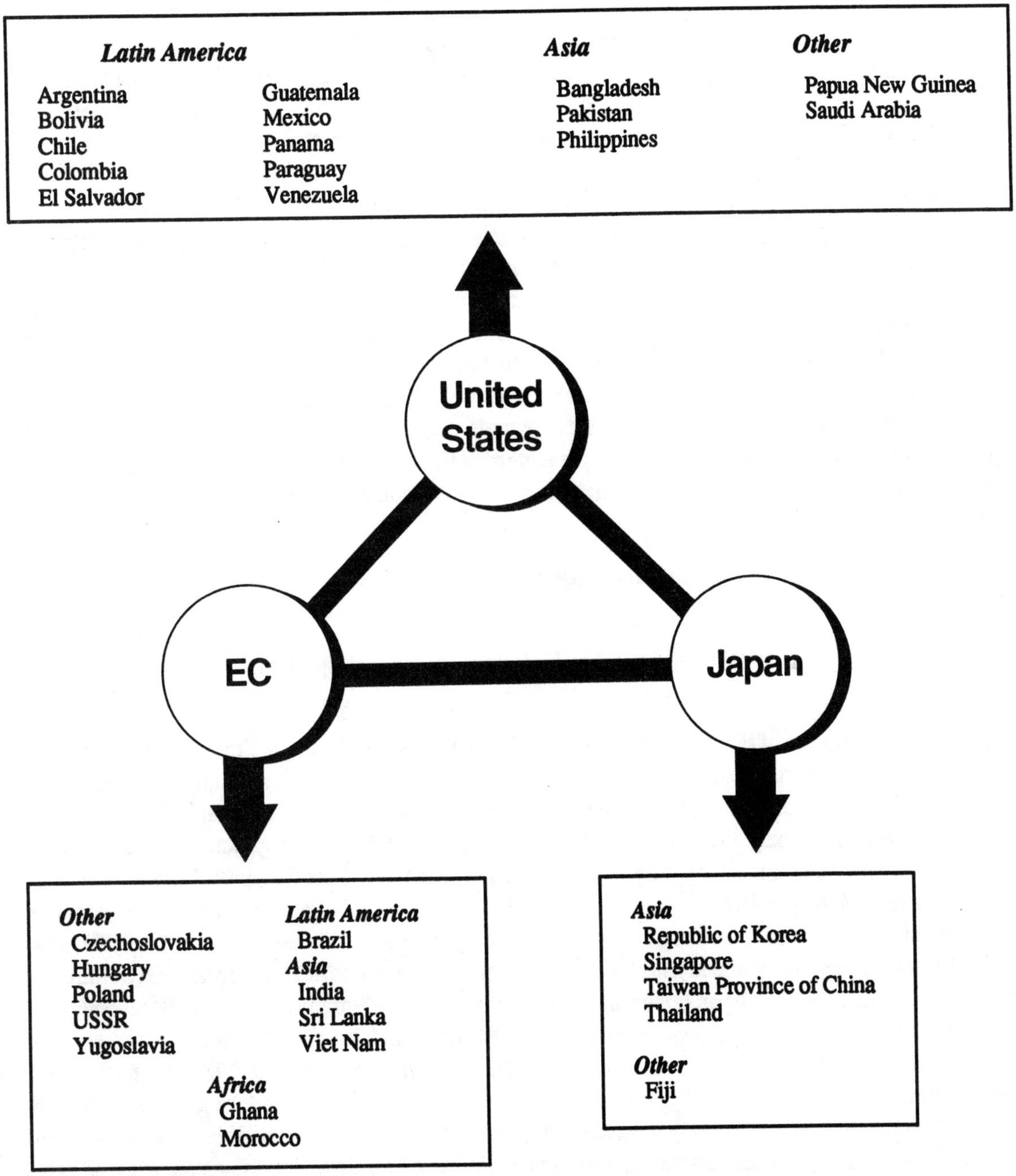

Source: Annex table 3, based on Transnational Corporations and Management Division, *World Investment Directory* (New York, United Nations, 1992).

cluster might be expected to increase in view of the fact that Taiwan Province of China was the largest source of FDI in Indonesia and Viet Nam in 1991.[36]

The stability of the pattern described above is not surprising. Adding two years to FDI flows and stocks is not likely to alter significantly the relationship between host countries and Triad members. The most notable observation is the continuing consolidation of Japanese TNCs in Asia. The observed pattern reflects the regional core network strategies of Japanese TNCs, a phenomenon that is likely to become more visible for TNCs from the United States and the European Community, respectively, in South America and Central and Eastern Europe. Moreover, there is evidence that TNCs from each Triad member are expanding their FDI in the host countries clustered around the other Triad members, in order to remain competitive throughout the Triad. To a certain extent, this is a response to growing regional links and to the impending formation of trade and investment blocs in Latin America (NAFTA) and Europe (EEA). Transnational corporations from the newly industrializing economies are pursuing similar strategies, as evidenced by their investments in Latin and Central America (especially in Mexico) and in Central and Eastern Europe, in order to ensure access to the markets of the United States and the European Community. The trend of TNCs from one Triad member investing in countries clustered around another Triad member is likely to continue as efforts towards regional integration become stronger. One implication of that might be the weakening of the pattern of FDI clusters of host countries around a single Triad member and an increase in the incidence of shared dominance by two Triad members.

D. Regionalization: issues and analysis

1. Policy-led versus investment-led integration

The regionalization of FDI in developing countries centred around a single Triad member described above underlies, to a certain extent, the acceleration of regional economic integration, particularly in North America, Europe and Asia. An analysis of trading patterns in the 1980s reveals that trade within regions has outpaced world trade to a large extent; intraregional trade in goods now accounts for 61 per cent, 41 per cent, and 35 per cent of the total trade in goods of the European Community, Asia and North America, respectively.[37] It is likely that there is a close relationship between the growth of intraregional FDI and rising intraregional trade. More specifically, the strategies of TNCs to build regionally-integrated, independently sustainable networks of overseas affiliates around each of the three poles of the Triad is likely to be an important factor in the growth of intraregional trade. In recent years, for example, intra-EC FDI has grown faster than intra-EC trade and, by 1988, EC countries themselves accounted for one third of the EC's total outward FDI, up from one-quarter in 1980.[38] In the Asian region, intraregional trade (including Japan) has grown by 23 per cent a year during the period 1986-1989.[39] Much of this growth is likely to have been driven by rapidly rising intra-Asian FDI, which grew even faster, at about 25 per cent a year in terms of stock in the 1980s. In many Asian countries, as noted earlier, FDI from other Asian countries (including Japan) now accounts of upwards of 50 per cent of total inward FDI. In North America, the United States accounts for about two-thirds of total Canadian outward FDI stock and, reflecting the relative size of their economies, Canada accounts for one-fifth of total United States outward FDI.[40] Clearly, the investments that flow within a region are a key element in understanding the nature and extent of economic integration in that region. While current moves towards regional integration are occurring more or less simultaneously, they differ in several respects, among which is the relationship between integration at the policy level and integration at the production level. Differences in respect to that relationship may be critical in determining the ultimate success of an integration effort. Hence, it is useful to examine integration efforts from that perspective, in order to understand current trends in the area of regionalization, the role of TNCs in those trends and the potential for success of integration agreements.[41]

Most integration programmes aim at improving the economic performance of their member States by providing them, at the very least, with increased opportunities for trade and stimulating greater economic competition. In addition, regional integration is often meant to encourage firms to expand their operations in the region so as to attain economies of scale which may have been constrained by the small size of domestic markets. As firms expand across national borders, intraregional FDI flows increase, as do the trade flows associated with it. The result is integration at the production level.

The development of a regional production system based on intraregional FDI requires a far greater degree of policy co-ordination between States than does increased intraregional trade. Regional trade integration involves mostly the liberalization of barriers to cross-border flows of goods and services; it remains, therefore, relatively "shallow". Regional production integration goes beyond trade integration and extends to the liberalization of barriers to cross-border flows of capital, technology, skills and, to some extent, people; it is, therefore, relatively "deep". More specifically, the policies that allow for such movements go much further in integrating national economies and regulatory systems than policies designed to support intraregional trade, since adjusting to a regional production system implies harmonizing (or, at least, recognizing and coordinating) a wide range of national practices and policies, rather than only liberalizing trade. Indeed, policies to promote a regional production system may extend to the harmonization of fiscal, monetary and industrial policies among member countries and the adoption of common standards in a variety of fields, such as labour, health and safety. It appears that successful regional integration involves a combination of integration at the levels of both policies and production. However, many regional integration programmes fail to reach this stage of deep integration, that is, a regionalized production system governed by a regional policy framework, and, therefore, often do not last.

Policy-led integration programmes are those in which initiatives at the policy level initiate the economic integration of participating States. Typically, the policy measures focus on reducing barriers to trade among member States, usually by liberalizing trade between member countries, to create a free trade area and, if a customs union is formed, by adopting common external trade policies *vis-à-vis* third countries. Integration policies may go even further towards harmonization, if a given level of cross-border trade has already been reached. The essential characteristic of such integration efforts is that the institutional framework for integration precedes actual integration at the production level.

In contrast, FDI-led integration (or TNC-led integration) occurs when the activities of firms, not policies, serve as the principle drivers of regional integration, that is, TNCs perceive advantages to integrating their operations across countries in the region. Such advantages may include country and process specialization, and the economies of common governance over a set of geographically-dispersed activities. While liberal trade policies may encourage firms to implement regional strategies (which often entail intra-firm, intraregional trade), such integration may also occur in the absence of specific regional integration policies. In other words, the integration of States in a region may be thought of as originating from one of two possible starting points: from the regional integration policies of States or from the regional integration strategies of TNCs—assuming, of course, an overall enabling framework.

In practice, the line between policy-led and FDI-led integration is not so sharp. As noted above, policy-led integration is often geared towards promoting intraregional trade in the initial phases of an integration process, by reducing trade barriers. Once a given level of intraregional trade has been reached, firms within the region may adjust to the larger market by making cross-border investments, thus beginning to form a regional production system. Indeed, a minimum level of cross-border trade within a region is likely to be necessary before intraregional FDI flows begin to grow. At some stage, however, the efforts of firms to create efficient operations on a regional scale may be hampered by the lack of an appropriate regional policy framework. For example, non-tariff barriers (such as different national technical standards) may block attempts to integrate production at a regional level. Furthermore, disputes may arise between member States regarding the treatment of firms that have established regional operations. Thus, the degree of production integration already achieved may create pressures to deepen the integration programme at the policy level to bring about an environment that would allow for further integration at the production level. Regional policies at this stage may cover such areas as harmonized standards *vis-à-vis* firms and their output, a common company law and even closer integration of fiscal and monetary policies. In this manner, policy-led integration triggers a process of FDI integration, which in turn leads to further integration measures at the policy level. Thus, while it is difficult to classify regional integration efforts as being purely policy-led or FDI-led (most tend to fall between the two extremes) the ways in which integration programmes evolve have different implications for the subsequent degree and nature of regional integration.

An examination of various regional integration policies sheds light on the relationship between policy-led and TNC-led integration. The 1989 United States-Canada Free Trade Agreement provides an example in which early integration measures (such as the Automotive Pact) and years of intraregional tariff-lowering led to a large degree of integration at both the trade and the production levels. Indeed, trade in automobiles was low before the 1965 Automotive Pact removed tariffs on automobiles between the two countries; thereafter, automotive trade, most of it intra-firm, grew rapidly, as did flows of FDI in the industry. Furthermore, tariffs between the two countries had been substantially lowered even before the 1989 Agreement, and there was already a great deal of FDI between Canada and the United States. However, it was argued that firms were unable to reap the full benefits of cross-border integration because of the lack of a policy framework which would assure an open trading environment and closer policy coordination between the two countries. The 1989 Agreement thus promoted further TNC integration by including many FDI-related issues, such as national treatment, performance requirements, screening procedures and FDI and trade in services. The signing of a bilateral agreement in and of itself signalled to firms that their integration across national borders would be assured in the long term. Similarly, in the case of the current integration efforts between the United States and Mexico, there has also been a significant degree of pre-existing integration at both the trade and production levels (see the section 2(a) below on NAFTA). Any agreement which emerges, therefore, is likely to focus explicitly on ratifying current integration at the production level, and promoting increased FDI in the future. It is thus likely that the current activities of TNCs will play a significant role in determining the outcome and eventual success of the agreement.

The European Community presents an interesting case of the relationship between policy-led and FDI-led integration. In that case, early policy efforts (beginning in 1957 and continuing until about 1985) focused mainly on removing intraregional barriers to trade, although the right of establishment and national treatment were early principles governing Community relations (largely excluding, however, services industries). Indeed, intraregional trade did grow rapidly following the formation of the Common Market. At the same time, integration at the production level also occurred, but the primary actors in that process were, for a variety of reasons, United States manufacturing TNCs; many TNCs from the Community remained relatively national in orientation. A major aim of the 1992 Single Market programme was to address this imbalance, by promoting region-wide integration at the production level by Community TNCs in both the industrial and the services sectors. In particular, the 1992 Single Market programme included, for the first time ever, an extensive opening up of services markets to FDI, thus permitting regional strategies by transnational services corporations. Not surprisingly, therefore, major Community TNCs were among the key proponents of the 1992 programme during its inception period, precisely because they perceived their international competitiveness to be hampered by the lack of a unified regulatory regime in their home region. Some of the policy measures taken encouraged a regional production system directly (that is, by adopting a system to develop EC-wide industrial standards and adopting an EC-wide competition policy), while others encouraged regionalization of production indirectly (by, for example, harmonizing certain fiscal policies and placing limits on government subsidies to firms and industries). Through those and other measures, the 1992 Single Market programme—the best example of far-reaching integration at the policy level—facilitated intraregional FDI flows and encouraged the further regionalization of production, as witnessed by the rapid growth since 1985 of intra-EC (mostly services) FDI. The case of EC, therefore, represents a situation in which early moves in the policy arena triggered economic integration in the area of trade and FDI, which in turn promoted further policy measures to facilitate integration of member States at the production level. As a result of this process, which has been evolving for over three decades, the Community represents a case of deep integration, in which regional (rather than national) economic policies and a regional (rather than national) production system are beginning to dominate.

The admission of the EFTA countries into the framework of the European Community through the creation of the European Economic Area (EEA) is another case of deep integration (box I.5). In the area of trade, the Community is the largest trading partner of EFTA, accounting for 58 per cent of the latter's exports and 61 per cent of its imports in 1990.[42] Similarly, EFTA is the largest trading partner of the Community, accounting for about one quarter of the latter's imports and exports (excluding intra-EC trade). Regarding FDI, EFTA countries are rapidly integrating their economies with the EC, although the reverse may not be the case. Average annual FDI outflows from EFTA to the EC during the period 1985-1987 were 38 per cent of the former's world-wide outflows; that share rose to 56 per cent in 1988 and to 69 per cent in 1990 (the latter figure represents Sweden and Switzerland only). On the other hand, average annual FDI outflows from EC to EFTA between the periods 1985-1987 and 1988-1989 rose from 5 to 6 per cent of world-wide outflows from the former (most FDI from the EC goes to the United States and to the EC itself).[43] From a host country perspective, however, the EC is the dominant foreign investor in EFTA countries, accounting from 38 per cent of total inflows to EFTA in the period 1985-1988. The 1992 programme has prompted a great deal of FDI, both offensive and defensive, from

Box I.5. The European Economic Area

In late 1991, the countries of the European Free Trade Association (EFTA) and the EC concluded negotiations to create a "European Economic Area" (EEA), with an agreement scheduled to enter into force on 1 January 1993.[1] Even before the new agreement, free trade in goods had been established between the two groupings following the creation of a free trade area in 1972. The EEA agreement creates, among other things, a single space for intra-European FDI flows, and it is likely to encourage further integration between EFTA and the EC at the production level.

Under the framework of the EEA, EFTA countries will join the EC internal market by removing a variety of mostly non-tariff barriers to the intraregional flow of goods, services, capital and people, to create a common economic space of approximately 380 million people in 19 countries. In addition, the EFTA countries will participate in a number of EC regional programmes and projects, such as those in the areas of research and development, the environment and education. The EFTA countries will also be able to participate on an expert level in the formulation of new legislation in relevant areas ("decision shaping" as opposed to the formal "decision making").

Despite their participation in the single market, EFTA countries will not take part in several key policy areas. Specifically, EFTA will not adopt EC's external policies *vis-à-vis* third parties (including the common trade policy and development cooperation), nor will it entail economic, fiscal and foreign policy coordination. EFTA will also be excluded from the common agricultural and fishery policies of EC.

The EEA agreement contains a number of provisions that will have a direct bearing on FDI. It establishes provisions for the free movement of capital, by removing all remaining restrictions and regulations relating to payments, investments, capital-market flows and other types of capital movements, although the EFTA countries have been allowed a safeguard clause to limit capital movements temporarily in the event of serious imbalances. In that area, the EEA framework goes further than the OECD Codes on the Liberalisation of Capital Movements because it provides for complete elimination of restrictions by all signatories, whereas the OECD Codes basically provide for a standstill and contain only a political commitment to further liberalisation (rollback).

Closely linked to capital movements are the rights of establishment and national treatment. The EEA agreement will require EFTA countries to adopt a number of EC Directives to replace regulations and controls

/.....

EFTA members (particularly Sweden). Under the framework of the EEA, further production integration between the two groupings will be encouraged, as FDI flows between them are being liberalized.

An example of TNC-led integration is currently under way in the Asian region, even though initiatives at the level of regional policy have been relatively weak. Intraregional FDI and trade are significant, and regional core networks of TNCs centred on Japan have emerged. The openness of Asian trade regimes and the complementarity of their economies explain in part the dynamism of intra-Asian FDI. A certain degree of regional production integration appears to be beginning in the absence of a regional policy framework. At some stage, however, further production-level integration in Asia may be hampered by the lack of a regional policy framework that would ratify the integration that has been taking

(Box I.5, cont'd)

that had earlier constituted barriers to the right of establishment. EEA companies will be free to establish subsidiaries, branches and agencies in all other EEA countries, whether through new investment or acquisition, and will be granted the same treatment as accorded the host country's citizens. In this context, the agreement allows EEA business persons and companies to buy real estate for the purposes of their activities, including forests and other natural resources.

In the area of services, the agreement provides for national treatment for service companies throughout the EEA. This is likely to increase the flow of cross-border FDI in the services sector. In the area of financial services, a certain minimum EEA-wide harmonization of legislation has been established. Apart from that, affiliates of EEA based transnational banks, insurance companies and securities firms in the EEA will be subject to the rules and regulations of their home, rather than their host country, in areas such as disclosure of information and required equity ratios.

Cross-border flows of FDI in services, many of which rely on specialized personnel, will be assisted by the mutual recognition of diplomas and certificates, along with the free movement of persons. Under these measures, a person from any EEA country has the right to move between, to work and to live in, all other EEA countries. The labour market will be governed by common elements regarding the social security system.

Finally, the EEA will indirectly affect FDI by extending the competition policy of EC to the whole EEA territory. For that purpose, a new regional institution, the EFTA Surveillance Authority, will be created. Under this framework, the two surveillance authorities have, among other things, the right to examine and eventually block a merger that they deem to affect competition in the EEA if the total turnover of a combined business entity exceeds a certain amount (at present, 5 billion ECUs).

In sum, the EEA provides for a liberal FDI regime that eliminates a number of barriers to the movement of factors of production, including capital and labour. Such liberalization is likely to contribute to a further expansion of FDI flows within the EEA and to result in an even deeper integration at the production level across Western Europe.

---

1 EFTA members are Austria, Finland, Iceland, Liechtenstein, Norway, Sweden, Switzerland. The agreement was signed on 2 May 1992. Before entering into force in 1993 the agreement will have to be ratified by Parliaments in all signatory States as well as the European Parliament.

place and that would allow for further intraregional activity; indeed, signs of such efforts have become visible in recent years. The resulting framework would bring into balance TNC-led integration efforts with the policy framework and advance deep integration among member countries, going beyond harmonization of trade policies to extend to a broad range of national regulatory areas.

In contrast to the above examples, many integration efforts among developing countries, both past and ongoing, are primarily policy-led. At best, they occur in the context of weak intraregional trade flows; and typically they involve very little FDI. It is unlikely that, in the absence of underlying integration at the production level, integration policies will lead to a unified regional economy. Such regional groupings would have to consider national policies to promote increased cross-border investment as a precondition for lasting deep regional economic integration.

2. Foreign direct investment and regional integration in North America: the possible impact of a North American Free Trade Agreement

(a) Foreign direct investment-led integration in North America

A rapid process of regional economic integration is taking place in North America, with TNCs at the forefront. In January 1989, the United States and Canada entered a Free Trade Agreement, which removes the remaining barriers to the free movement of goods and services between the two countries. The United States, Canada and Mexico are presently negotiating a North American Free Trade Agreement (NAFTA) under "fast-track procedures".[44] The NAFTA negotiations may be a first step in the eventual creation of a Western Hemisphere free trade zone extending from Alaska to Tierra del Fuego, envisioned in the "Enterprise for the Americas Initiative" proposed by the United States. To that end, the Government of the United States has already signed bilateral trade and investment framework agreements with twelve Latin American States.[45] Even though these agreements do not contain substantive trade and investment provisions, they represent a starting point for future substantive bilateral arrangements which, together, could lead to a regional framework centred on the United States. They may become particularly important if the Uruguay Round will not be concluded successfully.

When assessing the likely impact of a NAFTA agreement on economic integration between Mexico and the United States, one has to bear in mind that substantial economic integration already exists between the two countries, similar to what existed between the United States and Canada before their 1989 Agreement. Regional integration in North America can, therefore, be characterized as being primarily FDI-led rather than policy-led. Indeed, a great deal of TNC-led integration occurred between the United States and Mexico during the 1980s, whereas policy integration has only become an issue in the past two or three years. On the level of trade, Mexican exports to the United States increased by 70 per cent from 1982 to 1990, excluding exports from the *maquiladora* industries. By 1990, 71 per cent of Mexico's exports were destined for the United States (against 53 per cent in 1982). Exports from the United States to Mexico increased by 105 per cent in the same period, from 6 to 7 per cent of total United States exports.[46]

The growing trade integration between the two countries is largely prompted by FDI.[47] From 1982 to 1989, United States affiliates operating in Mexico increased their share of Mexican exports to the United States nearly fourfold, to over one-quarter of total (table I.9). At the same time, the proportion of United States affiliates in Mexico's imports from the United States increased to over 40 per cent. Nearly all of that trade is on an intra-firm basis. Much of that increase was due to a more liberal trading environment, but policies in this regard were of a global nature rather than couched specifically in the context of a regional integration programme. As early as the 1970s, United States TNCs in the automobile industry increased their intra-firm exports from Mexico to the United States. However, it was not until trade was liberalized between the two countries in 1984 that such exports expanded rapidly, to be followed by further trade policy liberalization in 1989.

Thus, the trade of United States affiliates operating in Mexico with the United States is almost entirely intra-firm, that is, between affiliates and their parent companies, indicating that many United States-based TNCs have integrated their operations across the United States-Mexican border during the 1980s. Indeed, the fact that United States affiliates account for a growing share of Mexico's exports to the United States is a result of both new export-oriented greenfield investments in Mexico by United States

Table I.9. Mexico-United States trade, by United States affiliates in Mexico, 1982 and 1989[a]

(Millions of dollars and percentage)

Item	*1982*	*1989*
Mexican exports to the United States	11 315	15 776
of which: Exports by United States affiliates (Percentage of total Mexican exports to the United States)	774 (7)	4 268 (27)
of which: Intra-firm exports to the United States parent (Percentage of total affiliate exports to the United States)	727 (94)	4 198 (98)
Mexican imports from the United States	8 959	15 755
of which: Imports by United States affiliates in Mexico (Percentage of total imports from the United States)	2 328 (26)	6 640 (42)
of which: Intra-firm imports from the United States parent (Percentage of total affiliates' United States imports)	2 095 (90)	5 996 (90)

Sources: Comercio Exterior, vol. 6, No. 11 (February 1984) and vol. 41, No. 4 (April 1991); United States, Department of Commerce, *U.S. Direct Investment Abroad: 1982 Benchmark Survey Data* (Washington, D.C., 1985), tables III.E.1., III.E.4., III.G.3. and III.G.5.; and *U.S. Direct Investment Abroad: 1989 Benchmark Survey, Preliminary Results* (Washington, D.C., 1991), tables 40, 42, 68 and 69.

a Excludes trade relating to *maquiladora*.

TNCs, as well as the restructuring of existing United States affiliates in Mexico towards a greater emphasis on exports. This is reflected in the fact that the export propensity of United States affiliates operating in Mexico has increased from 7 per cent in 1982 to 26 per cent of sales in 1989.[48]

A number of non-United States TNCs are also increasingly utilizing their Mexican affiliates to supply the United States market.[49] In the automobile industry, for example, Volkswagen decided that, from 1990, the successor to the Golf and Jetta models would be exported exclusively to the United States from its Mexican plant. Nissan has announced that, from the summer of 1992, the company will ship 200,000 engines a year to the United States from its Mexican subsidiary.

The booming *maquiladora* industry along the Mexican—United States border is another indication of FDI-based economic integration between the two countries. (The *maquiladora* programme allows foreign investors to set up in-bond assembly plants in Mexico; United States tariffs are only paid on the value-added generated in Mexico, if the products assembled originate from the United States.) From 1986 to 1988, *maquiladora* exports nearly doubled, from $5.6 billion to $10.1 billion, and their value-added increased from $1.3 billion to $2.3 billion. If NAFTA reaches an accord on duty free access of goods between Mexico and the United States, and Mexico further eases restrictions on FDI; there would be no need for a continuation of the *maquiladora* programme in its present form.

The above discussion underlines that, by the time moves on the policy level were taken for a NAFTA, TNCs had already engaged in a substantial amount of cross-border regional production integration an example of TNC-led integration. As such, the policy framework that is emerging is likely to ratify and advance the integration that is already taking place at the level of production. The following section examines how this process is currently occurring, and analyses the possible impact of a NAFTA on economic integration in the region.

(b) The possible impact of a North American Free Trade Agreement

A NAFTA would, above all, establish a firm and stable framework within which trade and FDI could prosper. At the same time, it would further strengthen the pre-existing process of regional economic integration through FDI. The NAFTA negotiations are taking place under six headings: market access, trade rules, services, investment, intellectual property and dispute settlement.[50] In the area of trade, the incentive for the United States to enter a NAFTA agreement with Mexico is to achieve rapid export growth in areas in which Mexico still has trade protection or high tariffs. While the United States is relatively open to Mexican exports, the average Mexican tariff is 12.5 per cent, with maximum rates of 20 per cent, and other products under quota (such as electronic equipment, automotive products, steel, textiles and services).[51] Given the low level of Mexican tariffs, the principal aim of NAFTA is to facilitate the rationalization of production by TNCs by providing a stable regulatory framework and access to the North American market. To that end, a NAFTA will create new investment opportunities in Mexico that will allow North America-based TNCs to further gear their production in Mexico towards serving the North American market. Mexico offers low-cost and high-quality labour, which could improve the international competitiveness of United States and Canadian TNCs. By further liberalizing trade in a regional policy framework, NAFTA would allow North American TNCs that have not yet already done so to incorporate their Mexican affiliates into a regional network strategy, which entails a significant amount of cross-border trade. Such a free trade arrangement could raise the locational advantages of Mexico as a host country for a number of activities, and could result in a shift of some investment in Asia aimed at sourcing of labour-intensive products and components to North America. In one recent example, the Zenith Electronics Corporation, a TNC from the United States producing television sets, announced that it will close down its manufacturing facilities in Taiwan Province of China, and move the production to Mexico. The move may be explained by lower labour costs in Mexico and the prospects of NAFTA.[52]

NAFTA could attract FDI not only from the United States and Canada, but also from Europe and Asia. The agreement, depending on how it is structured, could provide non-United States TNCs with an important incentive to build an export capacity in Mexico, as it would assure long-term, duty-free access to the United States market. In that respect, one of the key issues in the negotiations related to FDI concerns rules of origin and local content, which set the minimum amount of North American value-added to qualify for duty-free status. On this issue, pre-existing regional economic integration at the production level is affecting the shape of integration at the policy level, and thus is an illustration of TNC-led regional integration influencing subsequent integration policies. In the automotive industry, the three United States car manufacturers, all of which already operate in Mexico (General Motors, Ford and Chrysler), are promoting local-content requirements of 60 to 70 per cent for goods in this industry to qualify for duty-free access to the NAFTA countries. That would place most European and Asian car manufacturers in a disadvantaged position because they would not be able to rely on sourcing from their home countries in order to qualify for duty-free status in NAFTA. However, in more globalised industries, such as the electronics and business-equipment industries, United States TNCs are *not* in favour of high local-content requirements, because they source many of their parts and components outside of North America.[53] While high local-content requirements could discourage foreign investors in some industries from establishing themselves in North America, such requirements might benefit Mexico if they served to attract additional FDI; they might also ensure that foreign investors do not only locate assembly ("screwdriver") activities in Mexico.

Apart from high local-content requirements, United States car manufacturers are also urging that separate rules should apply to firms already established in Mexico versus rules applying to newcomers.[54] They have suggested that, for the five companies with Mexican plants, cross-border tariffs should be eliminated immediately and the local-content requirements reduced. Newcomers to Mexico, however, should comply with the existing tariffs and local-content requirements for the next five years, with the existing barriers to be lowered gradually over a 10-year period.

To date, moves towards NAFTA appear to have already increased the locational advantages of Mexico. However, the expansion of FDI in 1990 is largely owing to increases in portfolio investment following the liberalization of the foreign investment regulation in May 1989, which eased restrictions on foreign participation in the Mexican stock market. Despite the fall in FDI inflows in 1990, the upward revised plans of United States affiliates to increase capital spending in Mexico point to the growing attractiveness that country has for FDI. German TNCs have also pledged large investment projects in

Mexico: Hoechst has announced that it will invest $800 million in a Mexican petrochemical plant; Mercedes-Benz is considering building an assembly line for luxury cars in Mexico; and other German companies plan to invest $600 million in the tourism industry. [55] Volkswagen, which (as mentioned above) had already planned to make Mexico its production location for the Golf and Jetta models, recently announced that it would increase its Mexican production capacity by 60 per cent, to 390,000 cars a year by 1994. [56] Nissan plans to invest $1 billion in its plant, which supplies both the Mexican and United States markets, while other Japanese automakers which do not already have Mexican operations, are waiting for the outcome of the NAFTA negotiations before considering investments in that country. [57]

Closer economic integration in the region is also likely to increase Mexican investment in the United States in industries in which Mexican firms enjoy comparative advantages. Some of the large Mexican conglomerates, like Vitro (glass) and Cemex (cement), are building production plants in the United States in order to expand into that market. With sales reaching $2.5 billion in 1990, Vitro is one of the world's leading glass container manufacturers. In 1990, Vitro consolidated its position in the United States market by acquiring Anchor Glass Container and Latchford and, in 1991, the company entered an agreement with Corning, the United States glass group, to form an $800 million joint venture for consumer housewares. [58] Such investment in the United States by Mexican firms is likely to increase if NAFTA opens up the Mexican market to increasing competition, which may induce Mexican firms to invest directly in the United States.

3. Regional integration in the 1990s: building blocs or stumbling blocs?

The accelerating trend towards regionalization has raised concerns that new regional groupings might pose a threat to the GATT principles of an open, multilateral trading system and replace it with a small number of large, relatively closed regional blocs. Policies such as rules of origin, managed trade arrangements and harmonization of standards may be constructed in such a way as to discriminate against countries not included in an integrating region. Regional blocs may thus deviate from principles contained in the GATT framework, which seek to promote liberalization on a multilateral basis, thus allowing countries to benefit equally from reductions in trade barriers. Hence, regional integration programmes in EC and North America are sometimes viewed as "stumbling blocs" for the multilateral system.

In the area of FDI, however, no multilateral framework exists to provide a benchmark from which to deviate and against which to judge policy changes in the context of regional integration. In the context of FDI, therefore, regional integration programmes may be seen as building blocs towards a multilateral system, since they combine the regulatory FDI regimes of individual countries; in fact, deep integration, as described above, entails a certain amount of harmonization of policies and practices regarding TNCs. At a minimum, national treatment—a principle often contained in free trade arrangements—ensures that firms from one member country will be granted the same treatment as domestic firms, while national regulatory environments may still remain quite different in other respects. Deep integration will often go further and entail the harmonization policy regimes of member countries. Such policy convergence among groups of countries may be achieving at a regional level what has not yet been achieved at an international level, namely, an agreed set of principles and norms that govern the international activities of firms. Achieving cooperation among a small number of regional groupings is likely to be more feasible than among a large number of countries with very different regulatory regimes.

Regional integration may also exert pressures on non-member countries to bring their policies in line with those adopted by regional members. This is particularly true of countries which may ultimately wish to join an integrated grouping, such as EFTA and Central and Eastern European countries *vis-à-vis* EC, and Central and South American countries in regard to NAFTA. Other countries, too, may find it necessary to move towards the policy standards adopted by regional groupings with which they have significant economic relations, in order to maintain and deepen economic ties with the integrating region. It may well be that regional integration presents a challenge to the multilateral system in the area of trade; but in the context of FDI, regionalisation may serve as a first step towards creating such a system.

Finally, the increasingly global activities of TNCs may also exercise certain pressures to harmonize FDI policies on the global level, stemming from the fact that TNCs are engaged in extensive FDI across regions in addition to increasing FDI within them. For example, TNCs from the European Community have invested more in the United States than they have in other EC countries, while Japanese TNCs invest more in the United States and Europe than they do in Asia. Such activity is leading to increasing economic integration on a global level, such that production systems are in some cases extended not only within regional boundaries but also across regional blocs. Just as FDI-led regional integration creates pressures for the emergence of regional policy frameworks, FDI-led global integration may increase pressures to harmonize policies across regional blocs. In particular, competition policy is likely to need to converge to some extent in order to reflect the impact of competitive conditions in one region on those of another. In other words, TNC-led integration is not confined to a regional context only, but may, increasingly, extend to the multilateral level. Regarding developing countries, globalisation may increasingly place pressure on many of them to bring their policy frameworks in line with those of developed countries, in order to increase their participation in the international economy. The strong trend towards the liberalization of many developing countries' policy frameworks, documented in chapter III, may in part be a result of that process. In the future, developing countries may have to go beyond liberalization and increasingly align their policy frameworks and national standards with those of developed countries in order to keep pace with the increasing globalisation of economic activity. The growing international interdependence brought about by globalization may thus provide the basis for increasing convergence and harmonization of policies on a multilateral level.

E. Conclusions

The continued growth of world-wide FDI flows in 1990, while at a rate below that of the late 1980s, occurred in a context of reduced economic growth in a number of large economies. The willingness of TNCs to expand investment despite a slow-down in profits and adverse economic conditions attests to the increasing global nature of business operations, which, at least to a certain extent, are becoming somewhat less dependent on the performance of specific markets. It is not clear, however, how robust this willingness is, since FDI flows have declined in 1991. Nevertheless, the rapid growth of FDI during the second half of the 1980s has made TNCs central actors in the world economy.

While FDI continues to be concentrated in the developed market economies, and especially within the Triad members, the continuous growth of FDI in developing countries in Asia and, more recently, the increase of FDI in Latin America and the Caribbean, is an important development. In addition, a number of developing countries in Asia are themselves becoming important home countries to TNCs. Foreign direct investment in the countries of Central and Eastern Europe continues to grow, but FDI to Africa and to the least developed countries continues to stagnate. The pattern of distribution of host countries, whereby host developing, Central and Eastern European countries are clustered around a single Triad member located in the same geographical region, remains stable. That pattern underlies the FDI-led integration of international production in North America and Asia, which strengthens initiatives for the formation of regional blocs in those regions. In this context, NAFTA as an example of the emerging policy framework strengthening the pre-existing integration at the production level led by TNCs. NAFTA is likely to increase investment in Mexico from United States TNCs seeking to rationalize production further and from European and Asian TNCs seeking access to the North American market.

Notes

[1]Jim Carlton, "Outlook for Japanese spending on U.S. real estate is bleak", *The Asian Wall Street Journal Weekly*, 6 January 1992; "Japanese investment in Midwest increased in slower pace in '91", *The Wall Street Journal*, 7 February 1992.

[2]A reduction in inter-company loans between United Kingdom TNCs and their foreign affiliates accounts for much of the decline in FDI outflows from the United Kingdom. Some of those changes may reflect United Kingdom firms disinvesting from foreign affiliates in response to home country financial difficulties. See Bank of England, *Quarterly Bulletin*, vol. 31 No. 4 (November 1991), p. 529.

[3]Eduardo Lachica, "European firms slow investment activity in U.S.", *The Wall Street Journal*, 24 September 1991. In this context, a period of recession is defined as two consecutive quarters of decline in real GNP.

[4]See DeAnne Julius, *Global Companies and Public Policy* (London, Pinter Publishers, 1990), and "Foreign direct investment: the neglected twin of trade", Group of Thirty, Occasional Paper No. 33 (Washington, D.C., Group of Thirty, 1991). Julius found a positive correlation between real growth of FDI and real growth of GNP over the period 1963-1988 for France, the Federal Republic of Germany, Japan, the United Kingdom and the United States, taken together. She also found that the volatility of FDI was three to four times higher than that of GNP. Actual FDI growth during the period 1983-1989 was six to eight times higher than that of GNP, suggesting that factors besides the economic recovery in those countries after the recession of the early 1980s played a role.

[5]William Dawkins, "Groups pause for reflection", *Financial Times*, 22 October 1990.

[6]Investment outflows grew substantially in certain industries. For example, outflows from the United States into communications and public utilities and in business services increased considerably between 1989 and 1990, reflecting long-term factors influencing the decisions of TNCs to invest abroad.

[7]Committee for the Study of the Causes and Consequences of the Internationalization of United States Manufacturing, *The Internationalization of U.S. Manufacturing: Causes and Consequences* (Washington, D.C., National Academy Press, 1990). As an illustration, United States outflows in 1990 (a year of recession) at $29 billion were the same as in 1989.

[8]For a discussion of the role of TNCs in natural resources and services see, respectively, Bruce McKern, ed., *Transnational Corporations and Natural Resources. United Nations Library on Transnational Corporations* (London, Routledge, forthcoming), and Karl P. Sauvant and Padma Mallampally, eds., *Transnational Corporations and Services. United Nations Library on Transnational Corporations* (London, Routledge, forthcoming).

[9]For a detailed overview of FDI trends in developed market economies, see Transnational Corporations and Management Division, *World Investment Directory 1992: Developed Countries* (New York, United Nations, 1992).

[10]Randall Smith, "French firms pass British, Japanese as leading acquirors of U. S. concerns", *The Wall Street Journal*, 24 April 1991.

[11]Dennis M. Engbarth, "Japanese investment drops, hitting US the hardest", *Business International*, 22 July 1991; Edward Balls, "Expansion abroad curtailed", *Financial Times*, 15 July 1991; "Japan foreign investment falls", *The Wall Street Journal*, 3 June 1991; and Stefan Wagstyl, "Japanese overseas investment in first fall since 1983", *Financial Times*, 4 June 1991.

[12]Dennis J. Encarnation and Mark Mason, "Neither MITI nor America: the political economy of capital liberalization in Japan", *International Organization*, vol. 44, No. 1 (Winter 1990), pp. 25-54.

[13]Robert Taylor, "Sweden eases foreign ownership restrictions", *Financial Times*, 29 October 1991; John Burton, "Sweden to lift curbs on foreign ownership", *Financial Times*, 13 February 1991; Enrique Tessieri, "Finns to clear path for foreigners", *Financial Times*, 14 February 1991; Charles Leadbeater, "Politicians follow where business has been forced to tread", *Financial Times*, 23 October 1991.

[14]For a detailed overview of FDI trends for Asia and the Pacific, see UNCTC, *World Investment Directory 1992, Vol. I, Asia and the Pacific 1992* (United Nations publication, Sales No. E.92.II.A.11).

[15]According to *The Wall Street Journal*, FDI approved in the past two and a half years in China exceeded the total reached in the previous ten years ("China attracts investment", 10 March 1992). By the end of 1991, cumulative FDI in operation in China was about $23 billion, including joint ventures for oil exploration; Suman Dubey, "GE is raising level of business in India", *The Wall Street Journal*, 6 March 1992.

[16]For a discussion of the motives of Chinese TNCs to invest abroad, see Ye Gang "Chinese transnational corporations from Shanghai", *Transnational Corporations*, vol. 1, No. 2 (forthcoming).

[17]By 1990, cumulative investments in the manufacturing sector of Western Europe and North America by the Republic of Korea and Taiwan Province of China, were 47 per cent and 55 per cent of their respective total outward investments; the corresponding shares for the services sector were 39 per cent and 45 per cent, respectively. UNCTC, *World Investment Directory 1992, Vol. I, Asia and the Pacific* , op. cit.

[18]UNCTC, *World Investment Report, 1991: The Triad in Foreign Direct Investment* (United Nations publication, Sales No.E.91.II.A.12).

[19]Kim Soo Mi, "Auto makers in South Korea set plant plans", *The Wall Street Journal*, 11 November 1991.

[20]For a detailed overview of FDI trends for Latin America and the Caribbean, see, Transnational Corporations and Management Division, *World Investment Directory 1992: Latin America and the Caribbean* (New York, United Nations, 1992).

[21]Damian Fraser, "Venezuelan debt swap for project investment," *Financial Times*, 5 July 1991.

[22]Mahnaz Fahim-Nader, "Capital expenditures by majority-owned foreign affiliates of U.S. companies, revised estimates for 1991", *Survey of Current Business*, vol. 71, No. 9 (September 1991), pp. 32-38; Raymond J. Mataloni, "Capital expenditures by majority owned affiliates of United States companies, latest plans for 1991", *Survey of Current Business*, vol. 71, No. 3 (March 1991), pp. 26-33.

[23]Banco de Mexico, unpublished data.

[24]Santiago Fittipaldi, "CB II holds promise for Caribbean Basin, serves as model for Andean initiative", *Business Latin America*, 3 December 1990.

[25]Shelly Emling, "Asian tigers leap into Central America", *Business Latin America*, 16 December 1991; and Che-Hung Chen, "Taiwan's foreign direct investment", *Journal of World Trade Law*, vol. 20, No. 6 (November-December 1986), pp. 639-664.

[26]Some of the other factors that foster international production in the case of the Asian newly industrializing economies are the need to take advantage of greater geographical proximity or preferential trading status of host countries to important export markets (as in the case of host countries in the Caribbean) and, in the case of Hong Kong, the need to overcome uncertainty surrounding the return of the territory to China. See Paz Estrella E. Tolentino, *Technological Innovation and Third World Multinationals* (London, Routledge, 1992).

[27]For a detailed overview of FDI trends for Africa, see, Transnational Corporations and Management Division, *World Investment Directory 1992: Africa and Western Asia* (New York, United Nations, 1992).

[28]For example, a recent survey of overseas investment plans of Japanese firms showed that, for the period 1991-1993, the European Community, ASEAN and the Asian newly industrializing economies will be the most popular destinations of these firms (The World Bank, Debt and International Finance Division, "Financial flows to developing countries: current developments", *Quarterly Review*, March 1991, p. 8). At the same time, Japanese companies seem to have selected South Africa as the place to invest in the region (*Africa Analysis*, No. 129 (23 August 1991), p. 5.)

[29]Laurence Cockcroft and Roger C. Riddell, *Foreign Direct Investment in Sub-Saharan Africa*, Policy, Research, and External Affairs Working Papers (Washington, D.C., The World Bank, 1991), p. 27.

[30]See Transnational Corporations and Management Division and ECE, *World Investment Directory 1992, Central and Eastern Europe* (New York, United Nations, 1992), for an analysis of FDI trends in that region.

[31]Nicholas Denton, "GM puts further DM100m into its Hungary venture", *Financial Times*, 6 November 1991; and "Hungary: UT Automotive's new European plant site", *Business Eastern Europe*, 22 April 1991, p. 123.

[32]*Business Eastern Europe*, 22 April 1991, p. 126.

[33]Ariane Genillard, "Japanese, Slovaks to link up for Russian oil search", *Financial Times*, 12 November 1991; John Lloyd, "Western companies await decision by Soviets on oil", *Financial Times*, 15 May 1991; and Leyla Boulton, "The lure of oil's final frontier", *Financial Times*, 6 March 1992. Foreign investment in the oil sector in the former Soviet Union was put at $200 million. In the Russian Republic, which accounted for 80 per cent of the former Soviet Union's crude oil output, only 16 joint ventures operate in the oil sector.

[34]Preston Torbert, "First Soviet free zone will give firms access to Pacific Basin markets", *East Asian Executive Reports*, 13 (March 1991), pp. 9, 16-17; James Rupert, "Central Asia's ties that bind", *International Herald Tribune*, 2 December 1991. On free economic zones in Russia in general, see, UNCTC, *The Challenge of Free Economic Zones in Central and Eastern Europe: International Perspectives* (United Nations publication, Sales No. E.90.II.A.27).

[35]John Dunning, "International direct investment patterns in the 1990s". A paper prepared for the UNCTC Symposium on Globalization and Developing Countries, The Hague, 30 March 1992 (forthcoming); *The Economist* ("Business in Eastern Europe", 21 September 1991) estimated investments of $7 billion per year into the region until 1995. This would give a total of $28 billion between 1992 and 1995 and, assuming the same annual increase, about $63 by the end of the 1990s.

[36]"Foreign investment in Indonesia", *The Wall Street Journal*, 13 February 1992; and Urban C. Lehner, "Japanese prepare for Vietnam gold rush", *The Wall Street Journal*, 21 February 1992.

[37]The corresponding figures for 1980 were 56 per cent, 37 per cent, and 27 per cent, respectively. Asia includes Japan; North America consists of the United States and Canada only. United Nations, Department of International Economic and Social Affairs, *Monthly Bulletin of Statistics*, vol. XLV, No. 6 (June 1991).

[38]UNCTC, *World Investment Report, 1991: The Triad in Foreign Direct Investment*, op. cit.

[39]Asian Development Bank, *Asian Development Outlook 1991* (Manila, Asian Development Bank, 1991), p. 43.

[40]Transnational Corporations and Management Division, *World Investment Directory* (New York, United Nations, 1992).

[41]For a review of research on this subject, see Peter Robson, ed., *Transnational Corporations and Economic Integration. United Nations Library on Transnational Corporations* (London, Routledge, forthcoming). More generally, see Miroslav N. Jovanovic, *International Economic Integration* (London, Routledge, 1992).

[42]Estimates of the European Free Trade Association Secretariat, Economic Affairs Department.

[43]Transnational Corporations and Management Division, *World Investment Directory* (New York, United Nations, 1992). FDI data for EFTA represent Finland, Norway, Sweden and Switzerland. FDI data for EC represent Denmark, France, Germany, the Netherlands and Spain.

[44]Under "fast-track procedures", the United States Congress can only vote "yes" or "no" on the final agreement, that is, cannot amend it.

[45]See chapter III.B below.

[46]See *Comercio Exterior*, March 1984 and April 1991. See also International Monetary Fund, *Direction of Trade Statistics Yearbook, 1983* and *1991*.

[47]For details, see UNCTC, *Foreign Direct Investment and Industrial Restructuring in Mexico* (United Nations publication, Sales No. E.92.II.A.9).

[48]The export-to-sales ratio is calculated from United States, Department of Commerce, *U.S. Direct Investment Abroad: 1982 Benchmark Survey Data* (Washington, D.C., 1985), tables II.D.3, II.E.4, and *U.S. Direct Investment Abroad: 1989 Benchmark Survey* (Washington, D.C., 1991), tables 32 and 42.

[49]See UNCTC, *Foreign Direct Investment and Industrial Restructuring in Mexico*, op. cit.

[50]See "Mexican minister expects US free trade deal soon", *Financial Times*, 12 July 1991. Even though the negotiations currently are well under way, a 1992 signature of the treaty is uncertain, because of the recession and the November 1992 presidential elections in the United States. See "Mexico guards its precious oil business", *The Wall Street Journal*, 20 January 1992.

[51]See Rudiger Dornbusch, "North American free trade: what it means", *Columbia Journal of World Business*, vol. 26, No. 2 (Summer 1991), pp. 73-76.

[52]See *The Wall Street Journal*, 12 November 1991.

[53]Bernard Simon, "Vehicle dispute drives a wedge through NAFTA talks", *Financial Times*, 25 October 1991, p. 6.

[54]See UNCTC, *Foreign Direct Investment and Industrial Restructuring in Mexico*, op. cit.

[55]*Financial Times*, 4 July 1991.

[56]Kevin Done, "VW steps up Mexico output by 60 per cent", *Financial Times*, 6 March 1992.

[57]"Detroit South", *Business Week*, 16 March 1991.

[58]*Financial Times*, 7 August 1991.

Chapter II

THE RELATIVE IMPORTANCE OF THE ACTIVITIES OF TRANSNATIONAL CORPORATIONS

A. In the world economy

1. Foreign direct investment, domestic investment and output

During the 1980s, world-wide FDI flows grew faster than world-wide domestic investment and domestic output and, to the extent that greenfield investments followed the same trend, output by foreign firms has contributed an increasing share to that output. Foreign direct investment, domestic output and domestic investment grew at similar rates throughout the 1970s. During the early 1980s, the rate of growth of FDI began to diverge from that of domestic output and domestic investment and since 1985 the rate of growth of FDI has accelerated, outpacing that of the other two (chapter I, figure I.1). During the period 1985-1990, global FDI grew almost four times as fast as domestic output and more than twice as fast as domestic investment (annex table 4). In spite of the fact that FDI flows grew faster in developed than in developing countries, flows to developing countries increased more than twice as fast as domestic investment and domestic output between 1985 and 1990 (annex table 5). To a large extent, the rapid growth of FDI represents the growth of international mergers-and-acquisitions, especially among developed countries. However, mergers-and-acquisitions activity would not be reflected in domestic investment (gross domestic capital formation) in so far as the change in ownership does not lead to an addition in the existing stock of capital. The fact that only greenfield investments or additions to the capital stock attributed to international mergers and acquisitions are included in domestic capital formation could explain the divergence between the growth of FDI and the growth of domestic investment during that period. Given that international mergers-and-acquisitions activity grew rapidly during the second half of the 1980s—a phenomenon which was reflected more in the growth of FDI than in the growth of domestic investment—it could be possible that this activity did not usually lead to an increase in the stock of capital.

Figure II.1. The importance of foreign direct investment and domestic investment in domestic output for the six largest host countries,[a] 1980-1990

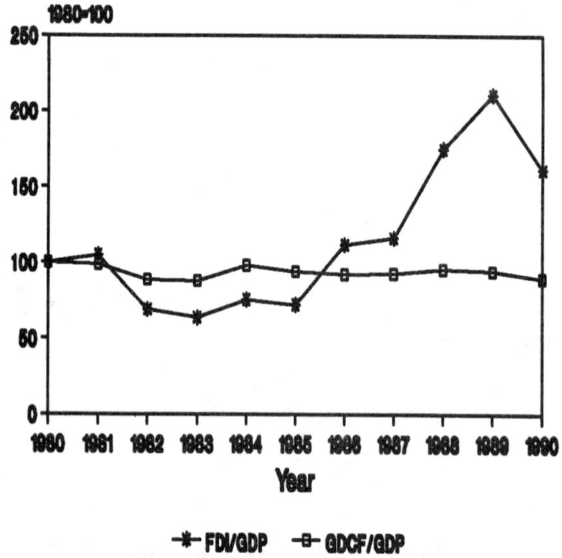

Sources: International Monetary Fund, balance-of-payments tape, retrieved in December 1991; and United Nations, Department of Economic and Social Development, data base on major economic indicators showing historical development trends.

a Australia, France, the Netherlands, Spain, the United Kingdom and the United States.

The ratio of combined FDI inflows to domestic output (gross domestic product) for the six largest host economies of the 1980s (which together accounted for 65 per cent of global inflows during that period) grew faster than the corresponding ratio of domestic investment to domestic output for the second half of the 1980s, except 1990 (figure II.1). The share of that output contributed by FDI (to the extent that it represents additions to the existing stock of capital) increased, while the share contributed by domestic investment decreased during that period, underlining the rising importance of FDI in the growth of domestic output. Although the ratio of FDI to domestic output is low in comparison to the ratio of domestic investment to domestic output, its value is increasing owing to the faster growth of FDI in these countries, which seems to have outpaced the growth of domestic investment during the late 1980s.

2. Foreign direct investment, trade, technology and sales

During the second half of the 1980s, FDI flows grew faster than other key international flows, namely, trade and technology (annex tables 4 and 5). The link between FDI, trade and technology flows implies that the growth of FDI is increasingly related to the growth of the other two types of flows. [1] For example, it is estimated that intra-firm transactions in royalties and licence fees (which include mostly receipts for the use of trademarks, processes, techniques, copyrights and patents) between firms related by ownership account for over 80 per cent of the total value of these transactions (chapter VI, table VI.10). Intra-firm trade between TNCs is also substantial, accounting for an estimated 25 per cent of world-wide trade, although it is substantially higher for individual countries (see chapter VIII, section B). To a certain extent, therefore, the growth of royalties and licence fees and trade is associated with the growth of FDI.

Figure II.2. Investment outflows, exports and royalty and fees receipts, 1970-1990

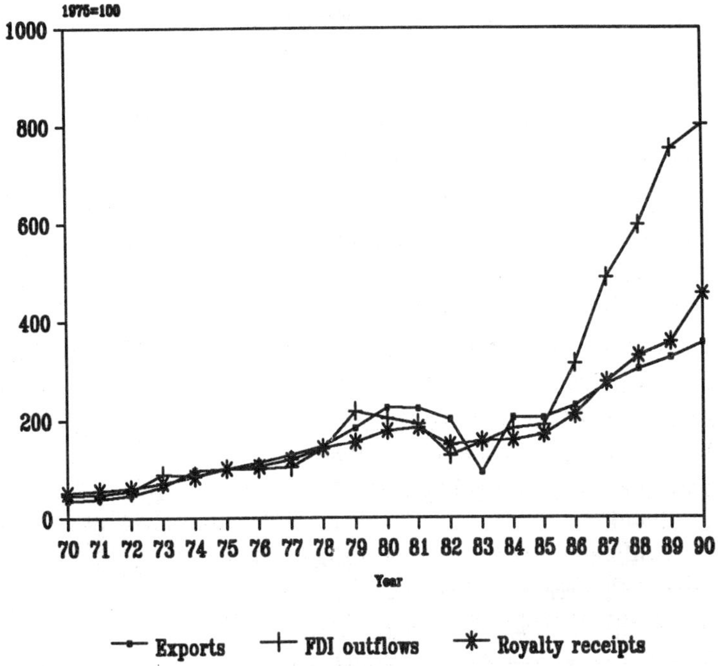

Sources: International Monetary Fund, *Direction of Trade Statistics Yearbook*, various issues; International Monetary Fund, balance-of-payments tape, retrieved in December 1991 and January 1992; OECD estimates; and Transnational Corporations and Management Division, *World Investment Directory* (New York, United Nations, 1992).

While global FDI outflows, receipts of royalties and fees and exports grew at similar rates throughout the early and mid-1970s, those rates of growth began to diverge during the 1980s (figure II.2). Since 1985, FDI outflows grew about one-and-a-half times faster than receipts of royalties and fees and about two-and-a-half times faster than exports. To a certain extent, the growth of receipts of royalties and fees reflected the rapid growth of FDI flows. The divergence between the rates of growth of FDI and exports, in spite of the link between FDI and trade, suggests the possible existence of time lags or the influence of exchange rates on exports.

For developing countries overall, technology flows may also be approximated by payments of royalties and licence fees (paid mostly to developed countries), by imports of capital goods and by technical cooperation grants from developed countries (annex table 5). For those countries, the growth of FDI inflows was also nearly two times higher than that of the above indicators of technology flows and almost one-and-a-half times higher than that of all imports. In other words, FDI is growing faster than either trade or technology flows for developing countries, although not at the same pace as for developed countries.

Since FDI data measure investment and not the value of output, they tend to underestimate the extent of the activities of TNCs (see box II.1). Using FDI as a proxy for international production and comparing it with other measures of serving international markets, such as trade, could therefore lead to misleading conclusions. Global sales of foreign affiliates in host countries are an alternative indicator of the activities of TNCs, and are better suited for comparisons with trade flows. Estimates of world-wide sales have been obtained by extrapolation, using sales of foreign affiliates abroad of TNCs based in the Federal Republic of Germany, Japan and the United States (three of the largest outward investors) and the share of those countries in world-wide outward FDI stock.[2] According to this method of estimation, world-wide sales of foreign affiliates in 1989 were $4.4 trillion, compared to world exports of $2.5 trillion, including world exports of commercial services and excluding intra-firm trade (table II.1). Global sales of affiliates are considerably more important than exports in delivering goods and services to markets world-wide, which underlines the importance of TNCs in structuring international economic relations. Actual data for three of the five largest home countries for which time-series data are available confirm the overall pattern, namely, that sales by foreign affiliates are considerably more important than total exports, by a factor of about 2 to 5 (table II.2). Global sales of affiliates of TNCs from the United States are higher than those of the Federal Republic of Germany and Japan because of the longer history of that country as an outward investor, reflected by the size of its FDI stock abroad. Beyond that, however, the pat-

Box II.1. Imperfections of foreign-direct-investment data

Foreign direct investment is the most commonly used measure of the activities of TNCs. It is, however, an imperfect measure since:

- It does not capture non-equity linkages of TNCs, such as contractual arrangements and turnkey agreements, which account for a substantial part of the activities of these corporations in certain industries (for example, the hotel industry). Non-equity forms of involvement of TNCs, though not easily quantifiable, may be more widespread as a form of conducting business in developing than in developed countries.
- It underestimates the amount of FDI since reinvested earnings are unavailable for several home countries—some of which are significant outward investors—and, hence, are not included in total flows. As such, investment flows underestimate the extent of foreign involvement by TNCs in host countries.
- It underestimates the total amount of investment by foreign affiliates in so far as it does not include capital that is raised in the host country (locally-raised capital is frequently used to finance international mergers-and-acquisition, as well as greenfield investments). The exclusion of domestically-raised capital has more serious repercussions in the estimation of FDI in developed than in developing countries because mergers-and-acquistions activity is concentrated in the former and financial markets in the latter are not highly developed. The implication of this is that the share of developing countries in world investment flows may be overestimated.

Since comparable FDI data that include estimates of locally-raised capital and non-equity forms are not available, FDI flows and stocks are commonly used as the main indicators of the importance of the activities of TNCs. Foreign-direct-investment flows, however, greatly underestimate the full extent of TNC activity, not coutning such other activities of TNCs as transfer of technology, trade and human resource development (see Part Two).

tern diverges, with the ratio falling in the United States and increasing in the Federal Republic of Germany and Japan during the late 1980s. The rise in that ratio for the latter countries reflects, in part, the appreciation of their currencies *vis-à-vis* the dollar since 1985.

Global sales of affiliates have grown at an annual average rate of 15 per cent since the mid-1980s, significantly above their growth during the first half of the 1980s. The rapid growth of sales in recent years concurs with the growth of FDI. Nevertheless, the ratio of global sales to exports has remained fairly constant, since exports grew at similar rates. This reflects in part the declining ratio of sales to exports for the United States during the 1980s, which is largely the result of a resurgence of exports from that country during the second half of the 1980s, owing to, in particular, a depreciation of the dollar exchange rate, higher economic growth abroad (especially in Western Europe) and stronger demand for United States capital goods, which account for a considerable share of its exports.[3]

Table II.1. Estimated worldwide sales of foreign affiliates and total exports, 1982-1989, and average annual growth rates 1982-1984 and 1985-1989

Year	*Sales* [a]	*Exports* [b]	*Ratio of sales to exports*
	(Trillions of dollars)		
1982	2.4	1.5	1.6
1983	2.3	1.3	1.7
1984	2.5	1.4	1.7
1985	2.5	1.4	1.8
1986	2.9	1.7	1.7
1987	3.5	2.0	1.7
1988	4.2	2.4	1.8
1989 [c]	4.4	2.5	1.8
	1982-1984	*1985-1989*	
Average annual growth rates			
Sales	3	15	
Exports	-2	15	

Sources: International Monetary Fund, *Direction of Trade Statistics Yearbook, 1988* and General Agreement on Tariffs and Trade, *International Trade 1990/91*, vol. II; Jeffrey H. Lowe and Raymond J. Mataloni, Jr., "U.S. direct investment abroad: 1989 benchmark survey results", *Survey of Current Business*, vol. 71, No. 10 (October 1991), p. 29; Ministry of International Trade and Industry, *Wagakuni Kigyo no Kaigai Jigyo Katsudo* and *Kaigai Jigyo Katsudo Kihon Chosa: Kaigai Toshi Tokei Soran*, various issues; Deutsche Bundesbank, *Statistische Beihefte der Monatsberichte*, various issues; and United States, Department of Commerce, Bureau of Economic Analysis, *U.S. Direct Investment Abroad: Operations of U.S. Parent Companies and their Foreign Affiliates*, various issues.

a World-wide estimates of sales by foreign affiliates of home-based TNCs were calculated by extrapolating the sales of foreign affiliates of TNCs from the Federal Republic of Germany, Japan and the United States on the basis of the relative importance of these countries in world-wide FDI outward stock.

b World-wide exports have been adjusted to exclude intra-firm trade, estimated by applying the share of intra-firm trade by TNC affiliates in total exports from the United States to world-wide exports.

c Preliminary estimates extrapolating the sales of foreign affiliates of TNCs from the Federal Republic of Germany and the United States on the same basis as that described in (a).

3. Foreign direct investment and capital flows

By the end of the decade, FDI had become the principal source of private foreign capital for the major-

Table II.2. Sales of foreign affiliates and total exports for selected home countries, 1982-1989, and average annual growth rates, 1982-1984 and 1985-1989

Country and year	Sales (Billions of dollars)	Ratio of sales to exports	Exports [a]
United States			
1982	936	5.5	169
1983	886	6.0	147
1984	899	5.3	168
1985	895	5.6	159
1986	929	5.1	182
1987	1 053	4.8	218
1988	1 195	4.3	278
1989	1 266 [b]	4.1	307
Japan [c]			
1982	192	1.8	105
1983	195	1.9	100
1984	290	2.5	118
1985	214	1.8	117
1986	263	1.8	148
1987	379 [d]	2.2	172
1988	534 [d]	2.6	203
Germany, Federal Republic of			
1982	173	1.3	136
1983	171	1.4	118
1984	184	1.5	123
1985	192	1.5	124
1986	237	1.3	176
1987	290	1.3	220
1988	349	1.4	246
1989	372	1.5	251

Average annual growth rates	*United States*		*Japan*		*Germany, Federal Republic of*	
	Sales	*Exports*	*Sales*	*Exports*	*Sales*	*Exports*
1982-1984	-2	-0.3	23	6	3	-5
1985-1989	9	18	36 [e]	20 [e]	18	19

Sources: Jeffrey H. Lowe and Raymond J. Mataloni, Jr., "U.S. direct investment abroad: 1989 benchmark survey results", *Survey of Current Business*, vol. 71, No. 10 (October 1991), p. 29; Ministry of International Trade and Industry, *Wagakuni Kigyo no Kaigai Jigyo Katsudo* and *Kaigai Jigyo Katsudo Kihon Chosa: Kaigai Toshi Tokei Soran*, various issues; International Monetary Fund, *Direction of Trade Statistics Yearbook, 1988* and *1991*, General Agreement on Tariffs and Trade, International Trade 1990/91, vol. II; Deutsche Bundesbank, *Statistische Beihefte der Monatsberichte*, various issues; and United States, Department of Commerce, Bureau of Economic Analysis, *U.S. Direct Investment Abroad: Operations of U.S. Parent Companies and their Foreign Affiliates*, various issues.

a Adjusted to exclude intra-firm trade, estimated by applying the share of intra-firm trade by TNC affiliates in total exports from the United States to all exports reported here.

b Not strictly comparable with the previous estimates because of a break in the series resulting from improved coverage of the survey universe in 1989.

c Fiscal years. Sales for Japan represent only sales by those affiliates that replied to the corresponding question in the survey questionnaire.

d Including sales by subsidiaries owned by foreign affiliates.

e 1985-1988.

ity of developing countries. The non-debt-creating nature of FDI and the fact that outflows from host countries related to the activities of foreign affiliates, such as the repatriation of profits, are linked to their performance, make these investments desirable in relation to other flows from private sources. Foreign direct investment accounts for an increasing proportion of all capital flows to developing countries owing primarily to the decline in net lending by private sources. More specifically, FDI inflows accounted for three fourths of *total long-term capital flows from private sources* (excluding non-guaranteed credit and including FDI) to 93 capital-importing developing countries during the period 1986-1990, compared with 30 per cent during the period 1980-1985. In the mid-1980s, FDI flows exceeded flows of net disbursements of debt from private sources, with the gap between the two widening further more recently (figure II.3). Thus, FDI has become the primary source of foreign savings for capital importing developing countries. To the extent that foreign savings help alleviate the savings-investment gap facing many of these countries, FDI can contribute to the realization of their growth potential.

Foreign direct investment in relation to long-term capital flows from private sources became particularly significant for the heavily indebted developing countries during the second half of the 1980s. Those countries (which, on average, accounted for 54 per cent of debt from private sources of the capital-importing developing countries and nearly half of FDI flows to developing countries during the 1980s) have experienced a reversal in the relative importance of investment flows. A substantial drop in loans from private sources, combined with a recovery in investment flows in the second half of the decade, have been the main factors for this reversal. For the least developed countries, capital flows from private sources have been insignificant; even then, however, FDI was the largest single source of flows from private sources, although, in terms of magnitude, it is small.

Although FDI has increased as a proportion of long-term flows from private sources, its importance has not changed significantly in relation to *official flows*. Disbursements of official development assistance to developing countries from members of the Development Assistance Committee of OECD, multilateral organizations and members of OPEC grew during the 1980s at rates similar to those of FDI (in nominal terms), primarily owing to the growth of bilateral official development assistance (ODA) flows. In terms of their order of magnitude, ODA flows are substantially higher than investment flows, which emphasizes the continuing importance of that form of capital to developing countries (figure II.3). Nevertheless, significant disparities exist in the importance of FDI in relation to ODA among developing countries. For the heavily indebted countries, investment flows have exceeded flows of ODA. In contrast, for the least developed countries, ODA is the primary source of foreign capital and greatly exceeds all other flows, including FDI.

Among private capital flows, world-wide portfolio investment flows [4] grew rapidly between 1980 and 1990, at an annual rate of 9 per cent. Portfolio investments are confined primarily to developed countries, with only a small number of developing countries having limited participation in these investments owing to the lack or small size of their securities markets. [5] In developed countries, portfolio investment flows increased rapidly, primarily because of the expansion of investments in those countries by institutional investors (such as pension funds, insurance companies and investment trusts). Nevertheless, FDI flows to those countries grew more rapidly than total portfolio investments, as well as the

Figure II.3. Investment flows, debt from private sources[a], official development assistance[b] and portfolio investment for 93 capital importing developing countries, heavily indebted developing countries[c] and least developed countries, 1970-1990

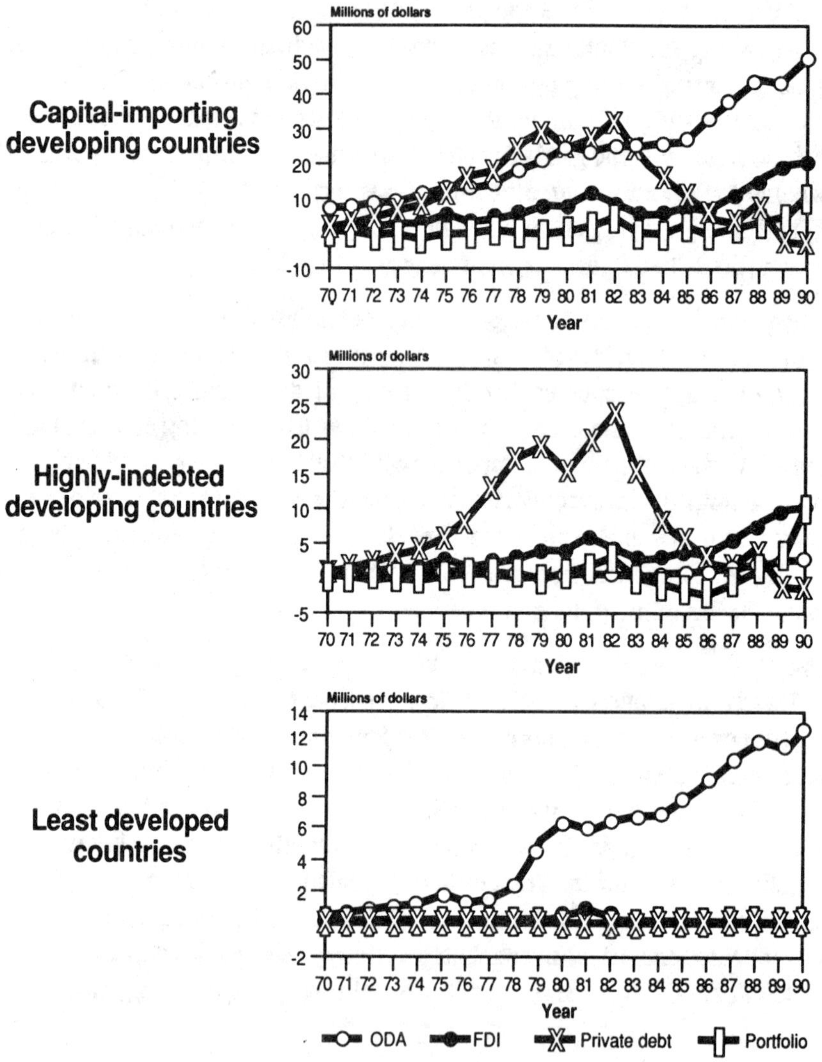

Sources: World Bank, world-debt-tables-data tape, retrieved in January 1992; International Monetary Fund, balance-of-payments tape, retrieved in December 1991 and January 1992; OECD estimates; Transnational Corporations and Management Division, *World Investment Directory* (New York, United Nations, 1992), and OECD, *Development Co-operation Report*, various years.

a Net disbursements of public and publicly guaranteed debt, excluding debt owed to official creditors.

b Official development assistance to all developing countries, excluding countries in the Middle East.

c Argentina, Bolivia, Brazil, Chile, Colombia, Côte d'Ivoire, Ecuador, Mexico, Morocco, Nigeria, Peru, Philippines, Uruguay, Venezuela, Yugoslavia.

corporate equity component of those investments. The stock market crash of October 1987 had a temporary adverse effect on the growth of portfolio flows, while FDI flows, responding more to long-term motives, have been less affected.

Although securities markets in developing countries have traditionally played a small role in attracting foreign capital, the inclusion of portfolio investment in capital flows from private sources reduces the relative importance of FDI in total private capital flows, especially during the second half of the 1980s. The rapid growth of portfolio investment to developing countries during that period (though fluctuating more than that of FDI flows) occurred particularly in East, South and South-East Asia, aided by the growth of bond issues in some Latin American countries. The rise of portfolio investment can be attributed to the removal of many restrictions on foreign participation in securities markets and the easing of exchange controls on the part of many developing countries. Eventually, the opening of securities markets to foreign investors can also lead to higher FDI flows, as investors accumulate more sizeable shares of investment in domestic firms.

For developing countries, the share of FDI in total financial flows during the 1990s will depend on a number of factors, foremost among which is, of course, the growth of FDI inflows themselves. But flows of private credit to those countries will also be important (as they recover from the effects of the debt crisis), as will be the continuing liberalization of financial markets and exchange control regulations (which is likely to encourage further the flow of portfolio, as well as direct investment). Competition for ODA is likely to increase as Central and Eastern European countries attempt to reintegrate themselves into the world economy, thus increasing the importance of FDI for developing countries as a source of capital.

B. In host countries

Reflecting the growing importance of FDI in the world economy, the activities of TNCs are becoming increasingly important to the economies of individual host countries. Specifically, the share of total exports, sales and assets accounted for by foreign affiliates in a number of host countries is not only sizeable, but, at least for a sample of countries, has been increasing over time. The ratio of FDI flows to domestic investment (GDCF), an indicator of the significance of FDI in domestic capital formation, has risen for most developed and developing countries (figure II.4 and table II.3). Moreover, the ratio of FDI stock to domestic output (GDP), an indicator of the importance of those investments in relation to the size of the economy of host countries has also been rising over time. In this section, the importance of TNCs in individual host countries will be examined, with particular attention being paid to regional differences and to differences arising in these indicators according to the level of development of host countries.

Since the mid-1970s, FDI has been more significant in the domestic investment of developing rather than that of developed countries, as indicated by the higher ratio of FDI flows to gross domestic capital formation [6] in the former (figure II.4 and annex table 6). During the second half of the 1980s, however, the rapid growth of FDI to developed countries brought about an increase in its importance relative to domestic investment above the corresponding increase for developing countries. In other words, while the ratio of foreign to domestic investment rose for both developed and developing countries during the 1980s, that increase has been higher for the former. This has led to a narrowing of the gap in that ratio between developed and developing countries, and the return to a situation similar to that prevailing during the early 1970s, but at a higher level (4.1 and 4.2 for developed and developing countries, respectively). This ratio, however, is a more meaningful indicator of the relative importance of FDI for developing than developed countries, where FDI flows are likely to represent greenfield investments. Among developing countries, FDI in relation to domestic investment has increased in importance in all regions except West Asia, but the increase has been most dramatic in Asia and the Pacific and, since the mid-1970s, in Africa (figure II.4). With respect to Asia and the Pacific, this reflects the rapid growth of investment flows to that region during the late 1980s (exceeding the growth of FDI to any other region); in the case of Singapore, a major recipient of FDI, the ratio of FDI to gross domestic capital formation reached over 30 per cent during the period 1986-1989. With respect to Africa, the high ratio does not reflect a substantial increase in investment flows, but rather a substantial drop in domestic investment, which resulted in a higher ratio of the two for that region.

Figure II.4. The ratio of investment inflows to gross domestic capital formation, by region, annual average, 1971-1975, 1976-1980, 1981-1985, 1986-1989 [a]

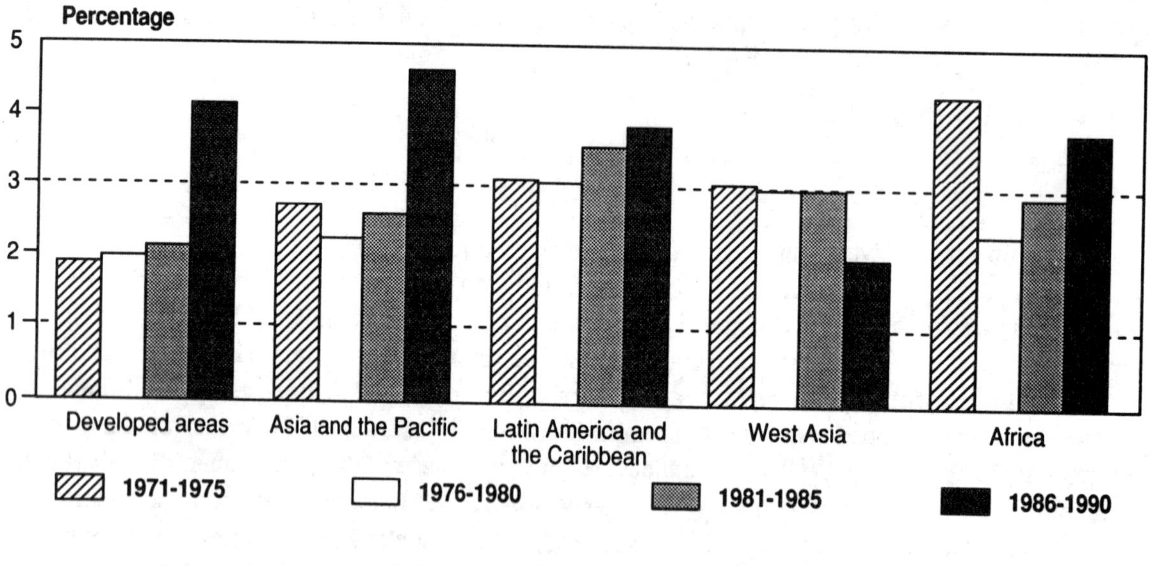

Sources: International Monetary Fund, balance-of-payments tape, retrieved in December 1991; OECD estimates; Transnational Corporations and Management Division, *World Investment Directory* (New York, United Nations, 1992); and United Nations, Department of Economic and Social Development, database on major economic indicators showing historical development trends.

a For some countries, data for individual years might be missing; in those cases, ratios have been estimated only on the basis of those years for which data are available.

Table II.3. The relative importance of investment inflows in gross domestic capital formation, 1986-1989

Percentage	*Economy*
Less than 5 per cent	Algeria, Austria, Bangladesh, Barbados, Bolivia, Brazil, Canada, Chile, Denmark, Ecuador, El Salvador, Fiji, Finland, France, Gabon, Federal Republic of Germany, Ghana, India, Indonesia, Ireland, Israel, Italy, Jamaica, Jordan, Kenya, Kuwait, Madagascar, Morocco, Nepal, Norway, Pakistan, Paraguay, Peru, Republic of Korea, Sri Lanka, Sudan, Sweden, Switzerland, Taiwan Province of China, Thailand, Togo, Trinidad and Tobago, Tunisia, Uganda, Venezuela, Yemen
5.1 to 10 per cent	Argentina, Australia, Colombia, Congo, Costa Rica, Côte d'Ivoire, Cyprus, Dominican Republic, Egypt, Greece, Honduras, Liberia, Malaysia, Malta, Mauritius, Mexico, New Zealand, Oman, Philippines, Portugal, Rwanda, Spain, Uruguay, United States
10.1 to 15 per cent	Belgium, Netherlands, Nigeria, United Kingdom
15.1 to 20 per cent	Guatemala, Hong Kong, Papua New Guinea
Over 20 per cent	Botswana, Seychelles, Singapore, Swaziland

Sources: International Monetary Fund, balance-of-payments tape, retrieved in December 1991; OECD estimates; Transnational Corporations and Management Division, *World Investment Directory* (New York, United Nations, 1992); and United Nations, Department of Economic and Social Development, database on major economic indicators showing historical development trends.

While the average ratio of foreign to domestic investment between developed and developing countries is moving towards convergence, the same cannot be said for developing regions; West Asia, in particular, has experienced a slower growth of inflows, contributing to the divergence of those ratios among developing regions. That divergence in the ratio of FDI to gross domestic capital formation among developing regions has increased during the late 1980s compared to the late 1970s and early 1970s, reflecting to some extent the regional differences in the growth rates of the former.

If countries are classified by income group the ratio of foreign to domestic investment has increased on average, for all income groups, especially for the lower middle-income countries, where that ratio has doubled between the second half of the 1970s and the second half of the 1980s (figure II.5). In this regard, most noteworthy are the high-income developing economies (oil producing countries in West Asia, Hong Kong and Singapore). For them, this ratio—over 20 per cent—is significantly above that of the average for the other income groups and has more than doubled, reflecting, however, almost exclusively the high and growing importance of FDI for Singapore. Although domestic investment increased rapidly in several middle-income countries during the 1980s, foreign investment growth has been even greater, resulting in high ratios overall.

Figure II.5. The ratio of investment inflows to gross domestic capital formation for developing countries by income group, annual average, 1971-1975, 1976-1980, 1981-1985, 1986-1989 [a]

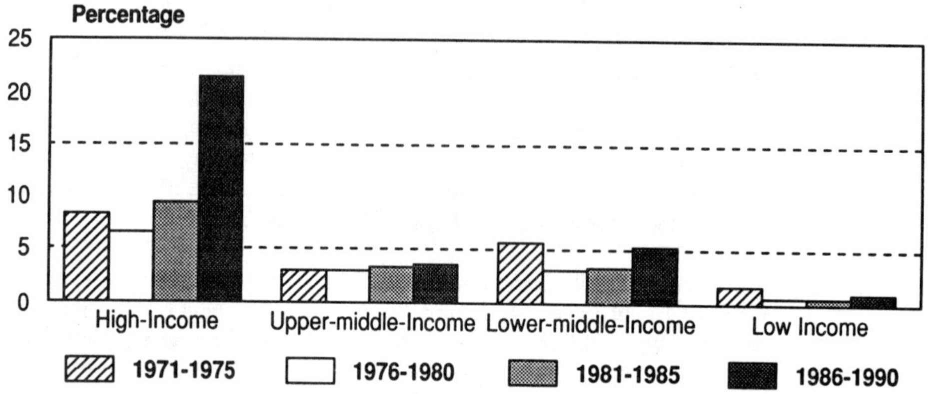

Sources: International Monetary Fund, balance-of-payments tape, retrieved in December 1991; OECD estimates; Transnational Corporations and Management Division, *World Investment Directory* (New York, United Nations, 1992); United Nations, Department of Economic and Social Development, database on major economic indicators showing historical development trends; and World Bank, *World Development Report, 1991* (New York, Oxford University Press, 1991).

a For some countries, data for individual years might be missing; in those cases, ratios have been estimated only on the basis of those years for which data are available.
b Over $10,000 1989 GNP per capita.
c $1,500-$9,999 1989 GNP per capita.
d $500-$1,499 1989 GNP per capita.
e Less than $499 1989 GNP per capita.

The importance of FDI in relation to domestic capital formation becomes more pronounced when compared to the component of that formation attributed to the private sector. This is not surprising, given that, in a number of countries, public investment accounts for a substantial share of total domestic investment. On the other hand, FDI is usually, though not exclusively, concentrated in the private sector. Excluding residential investment from total domestic investment of host countries further boosts the importance of FDI in their economy.

The ratio of FDI stock to domestic output (gross domestic product), another indicator of the importance of these investments in host countries, shows significant increases for many developed and developing countries (annex table 7; see also table II.4). This ratio rose significantly during the 1980s for most developed countries, more than doubling in some cases (for example, Portugal and the United States) but, in some cases, starting from lower values compared to corresponding ratios for developing countries. For the latter, that ratio also increased substantially, particularly for countries in East, South and South-East Asia (for example, Singapore and Indonesia). Considering that domestic output grew rapidly in that region during the 1980s, the increasing significance of FDI there suggests a link between the two.

On the sectoral level, the relative importance of FDI for countries represented in annex table 7 has been consistently greater in manufacturing than in the services sector and, with few exceptions, in the extractive sector. Thus, despite the large FDI inflows in services during the 1980s, FDI in this sector still lags behind that in manufacturing in terms of relative importance for host countries. This discrepancy may, however, narrow or even disappear during the 1990s, if services remain the largest sector in FDI outflows of major home countries and new capital-intensive services industries, such as telecommunication, transportation and public utilities, as well as banking in a number of developing countries are privatized and being opened to FDI.

Other indicators of the significance of the activities of TNCs include sales, assets and exports of foreign affiliates located in host countries. From the perspective of host countries, activities of foreign affiliates are important, but perhaps more so in developing than in developed countries (annex table 8). Foreign affiliates in host developing countries play an important role in manufacturing, particularly in electrical and transportation equipment.[7] Limited as data on sales, assets and exports are, they, too, suggest that, over time, foreign affiliates are assuming a relatively more important role in host economies, developed and developing alike (annex table 9). On the sectoral level, there are some notable differences, with foreign affiliates in the primary sector accounting for a smaller share of total assets and exports, as developing countries assumed control of previously foreign-owned assets in resource-based industries. In contrast, that share for manufacturing—having declined during the 1970s and first half of the 1980s—is again increasing.

* * * * *

Table II.4. The relative importance of foreign-direct-investment stock in the domestic economy, 1988

Percentage	*Economy*
Less than 5 per cent	Bangladesh, China, Finland, France, India, Japan, Nepal, Norway, Pakistan, Philippines, Republic of Korea
5.1 to 10 per cent	Austria, Federal Republic of Germany, Indonesia, Italy, Morocco, New Zealand, Nigeria, Portugal, Spain, Sri Lanka, Thailand, United States
10.1 to 15 per cent	South Africa
15.1 to 20 per cent	United Kingdom
Over 20 per cent	Australia, Canada, Fiji, Hong Kong, Malaysia, Netherlands, Papua New Guinea, Singapore

Sources: Transnational Corporations and Management Division, *World Investment Directory* (New York, United Nations, 1992); United Nations, Department of Economic and Social Development, database on major economic indicators showing historical development trends.

The assessment of the relative importance of FDI to host countries depends, to some extent, on the indicators of the activities of TNCs that are available. Although for some developed and developing countries the extent of foreign involvement in the domestic economy has not changed substantially over the past two decades, for most countries, foreign affiliates appear to have become more significant in their economic activities. Some developing countries with a large foreign presence in their economies in the 1970s experienced a drop in that presence by the mid-to late 1970s resulting, to some extent, from policies aimed at reducing foreign ownership of productive assets. During the late 1980s, however, the values of most of these measures began to increase and, by the end of the 1980s, foreign involvement in the economies of several host countries had risen significantly. In general, differences in the extent of involvement of the TNCs in developed and developing countries are becoming less pronounced as foreign involvement in developed countries is increasing more rapidly than in developing countries. Foreign direct investment is, therefore, becoming more important in relation to world-wide investment, output, trade, technology and capital flows, and TNCs are playing a more important role in the economies of individual countries.

Notes

[1]For a discussion of this, see UNCTC, *World Investment Report, 1991: The Triad in Foreign Direct Investment* (United Nations publication, Sales No. E.91.II.A.12), chapter 3.

[2]Since both exports and sales of foreign affiliates abroad include intra-firm transactions, some double-counting is involved. For example, a product shipped by a parent company to its foreign affiliate and then sold would be included in both exports and sales. This is discussed in DeAnne Julius, *Global Companies and Public Policy* (London, Pinter Publishers, 1990), p. 78. A partial solution is to subtract from exports the share of intra-firm trade by affiliates of TNCs. That share is available for the United States and has been applied to world-wide exports.

[3]Stephen Cooney, *Can the U.S. Export Drive Continue?* (Washington, D.C., National Association of Manufacturers International Economic Department, December 1991).

[4]Foreign direct investment differs from portfolio investment in that the former involve a lasting interest in firms; for the purpose of data collection, this distinction usually involves an ownership threshold below which all foreign investments are considered as portfolio.

[5]The total market capitalization of equity markets in developing countries is only 6 per cent of that in developed countries, according to one estimate, see Philip Turner, "Capital flows in the 1980s: a survey of major trends", Bank for International Settlements Economic Papers, No. 30 (April 1991), p. 51.

[6]Gross domestic capital formation represents changes in the existing stock of capital and, therefore, it is not, strictly speaking, comparable to foreign direct investment, which may include acquisitions of existing assets.

[7]UNCTC, *World Investment Report 1991: The Triad in Foreign Direct Investment* op. cit. pp. 99-100; and annex tables 8 and 9.

Chapter III

RECENT POLICY DEVELOPMENTS

During 1991, a number of important policy developments of relevance to TNCs took place at the multilateral, regional, bilateral and national levels. At the multilateral level, the most significant developments on FDI took place in the context of the Uruguay Round. After almost five years of negotiations, the Uruguay Round of Multilateral Trade Negotiations entered its final phase when, on 20 December 1991, Director-General of GATT submitted a draft final act embodying the results of the negotiations, including texts on the so-called new issues, namely, services, trade related investment measures (TRIMs) and trade related aspects of intellectual property rights (TRIPs). [1] Section A of the present chapter reviews the results achieved so far in those areas, as they are of particular importance for the emerging multilateral regime for FDI.

At the regional level (section B.1), besides new developments towards regional integration already discussed in chapter I, the Council of Ministers of OECD reviewed in June 1991 the OECD instruments on TNCs and agreed on a number of changes to strengthen them. At the bilateral level (section B.2), the network of bilateral treaties for the promotion and protection of foreign direct investment continued to expand, and an antitrust cooperation agreement between the United States and the European Community was concluded.

At the national level (section C), the liberalization of inward FDI regimes continued unabated, with some 30 countries introducing or continuing policy changes, the overwhelming number of which were in a liberalizing direction. At the same time, many countries introduced or continued privatization programmes, in many of which foreign investors are encouraged to participate. Special attention is, therefore, being given to that issue.

Finally, section D provides a brief discussion of self-regulation, an approach that has received special attention in the context of promoting environmentally sustainable growth.

A. The Uruguay Round

1. Services

The more than five years of negotiations in the framework of the Uruguay Round of Multilateral Trade Negotiations resulted in a draft of the first-ever multilateral framework to govern international transactions in services, the General Agreement on Trade in Services (GATS).[2] Although still a draft as submitted by the Director-General of GATT, most of the proposed provisions command broad consensus. The framework, which aims at expanding trade in services under conditions of transparency and progressive liberalization, consists of two principal components: general obligations (Part II) and specific commitments (Part III). Countries will be obliged to implement the former when the agreement is adopted. In distinction to general obligations, specific commitments, however, will not apply automatically. They are subject to negotiations among countries, which are still ongoing. To be actually implemented, specific commitments have to be included in the country schedules attached to the agreement, specifying industries and kinds of transactions with regard to which a country undertakes the commitments.

The scope of GATS is broad in terms of both service industries and kinds of transactions covered. All services are included, except those supplied in the exercise of governmental functions. Given the peculiarities and importance, however, of services such as telecommunications, financial services and air-transportation, special rules and provisions supplementing or interpreting the rules set out in the main text were added in the form of sectoral annexes. The agreement also covers all possible modes of delivery of services, including cross-border trade, the movement of factors of production and the movement of consumers. In other words, for the purpose of the agreement, FDI is fully covered. The main general obligation is the most-favoured-nation (MFN) principle, which is defined as "non-discrimination across foreign sources of supply", meaning that all parties to the agreement must receive the most favourable transaction terms available to any other party. Another important general obligation is the provision on transparency, which requires that any rules and regulations affecting transactions in services be published. The specific commitments cover, among other things, market access and national treatment. Naturally, the implementation of the agreement raises a number of practical questions because, so far, most countries (and especially developing countries) have had little experience with the issues related to the liberalization of FDI and trade in services (box III.1).

Since economic development, especially that of developing and least developed countries, has been recognized as a central element of the proposed framework, the Preamble and a number of Articles deal explicitly with concerns of developing countries. Contrary to past practice, therefore, this issue is not being dealt with by way of special treatment for developing countries in the form of derogations from

Box III.1. Issues in the liberalization of foreign direct investment and trade in services

The Uruguay Round has undoubtedly contributed to placing services on the agenda of policy-makers around the world. If and when GATS is adopted, policy makers in all signatory states will have to review their domestic regulatory framework in light of the provisions contained in that agreement. Other factors will nudge countries in the same direction, especially the recognition that international competitiveness is increasingly associated with access to modern producer services, and the expectation that FDI in services will play a major role in shaping investment flows in the 1990s.

Issues that arise in this context are both conceptual and practical. Conceptual issues relate to the hierarchy of national objectives and competing objectives. What do "liberalization" and "efficiency" mean in the context of various market situations in various service industries and in countries at different levels of development? What do those concepts mean in the context of services with differing degrees of tradability? What are the implications of the changing tradability of services, owing to technical progress in telematics? For example, do service providers throughout the world, including in developing countries, have sufficient access to networks—the electronic highways of world services trade—and under conditions that are not biased? What are the costs and benefits of liberalizing FDI, trade and, to a certain extent, labour movement in services? Is there an appropriate sequence in liberalizing services industries, or should an across-the-board approach be favoured? If an industry-by-industry approach is selected, what are the industry-selection criteria? To what extent do measures known and tested in the area of FDI and trade in goods apply to international transactions in services? What are their costs and benefits, and what experiences have countries gained with them so far? Can liberalization proceed at one pace in the area of trade and at another in the area of FDI and labour movement? What are the costs and benefits of different speeds of liberalization with respect to the various modes of delivery?

One of the legacies of the neglect of the services sector is that few answers are known to those questions. In the case of trade (and, to a certain extent, FDI) in goods, economists have debated the questions for years, and policy makers could gain experience during the 40 years over which liberalization was implemented in the framework of GATT. But in the area of liberalizing international services transactions, little research and experience exist to guide actions. At the same time, the likely adoption of the GATS and the factors mentioned above require immediate and broad-based action.

That calls for urgent research that is policy- and technical-assistance oriented, to put decision-makers—especially in developing countries—in a better position to cope with the new challenge. As a first step in that direction, the Division of Transnational Corporations and Management of the United Nations Department of Economic and Social Development and the World Bank, supported by UNDP, have embarked on a joint project designed to address some of the questions mentioned above. Its first output will be a *Handbook on Issues Related to the Liberalization of Foreign Direct Investment and Trade in Services*. It will be followed by technical assistance in a number of requesting developing countries to provide practical help in the area of national policy-making.

general rules and principles. In addition, GATS recognizes the right of parties to regulate in the area of services (and particularly the need of developing countries to exercise that right), when deemed necessary to meet national policy objectives. Furthermore, the agreement stipulates that the increasing participation of developing countries in international trade in services should be facilitated through negotiated commitments, to allow firms from those countries access to technologies, information networks, distribution channels and markets in industries of export which are of interest to them. Other rules provided for by GATS cover issues such as payments and transfers, exceptions and safeguards (for example, for balance-of-payments reasons), economic integration, monopolies and restrictive business practices, rules for negotiation, dispute settlement and institutional procedures.

The emerging GATS will have important implications for how FDI policies in the services sector are formulated and implemented in the future. [3] It covers modes of delivery that require FDI, including the movement of production factors such as capital and labour, and commercial presence through the establishment of offices in the importing country. Commercial presence may take the form of "any type of business or professional establishment, including through (i) the constitution, acquisition or maintenance of a juridical person" (a corporation, partnership, joint venture, sole proprietorship or association) or "(ii) the creation or maintenance of a branch or a representation office" (Article XXXIV). One mode of delivery, as well as one of the annexes to GATS, provides for the temporary movement of natural persons—in other words, service providers themselves as well as employees of service providers—provided that requirements with regard to qualifications, standards, visa and work permits are met. Thus, TNCs providing services may place key personnel in the importing country. In sum, all forms of FDI in the services sector are covered by the agreement.

A number of other provisions of GATS may affect FDI policies to various degrees. Its MFN obligation means that any preferential treatment given by parties (for example, in the context of bilateral or regional investment arrangements) has to be granted to all other parties on an MFN basis, unless such arrangements are notified and exempted from the MFN obligation in schedules of commitments of the parties. (A party may invoke such exemptions under the Annex on Article II exemptions.) Those exemptions, however, are time limited (no longer than 10 years), and subject to periodic review and negotiation in subsequent trade-liberalization rounds. Agreements concluded under Article V of GATS dealing with economic integration, which further liberalize FDI policies affecting trade in services between the parties concerned, will also be exempted from the MFN principle; such agreements would have to be notified to all other parties. According to the provision on transparency, all FDI-related rules and regulations affecting trade in services will have to be published. Parties are also requested to inform each other, at least annually, of the introduction of any new changes to such rules and regulations. The framework does not deal explicitly with the right of establishment, but it provides a procedure under which such commitments can be negotiated as part of a national schedule. The rules also allow the transfer of payments, including those related to FDI (transfer of earnings). The safeguard clause of GATS, however, may be applied for balance-of-payment reasons.

The extent to which FDI (and the movement of natural persons) as modes of delivery will be concretely governed by the agreement will be determined by the ongoing negotiations of liberalization commitments. In other words, countries are identifying service activities for which they will undertake specific commitments regarding market access (access by services *and* service-providers to a foreign market) and national treatment (treatment no less favourable than that accorded to like domestic services *and* service-providers). If a party wishes to limit access to its market or national treatment, it is required to specify such limitations in its schedule of commitments. The schedule could include measures that restrict access by service-providers that require specific types of legal entities or joint ventures through which they may provide a service and that limit the participation of foreign capital in terms of maximum percentages of foreign shareholding, or of the total value of individual or aggregate FDI. In the ongoing negotiations of the initial liberalization commitments, offers indicate that countries wish to maintain certain restrictions relating to commercial presence, such as requirements that FDI take place only through incorporation, with a specified foreign-equity ceiling, or only via a joint-venture arrangement. There are also offers indicating restrictions with regard to the participation of foreign capital in many services industries. Negotiations are under way to reduce or eliminate those and other kinds of investment restrictions to trade in services, through inclusion of specific commitments in national schedules.

If and when GATS is adopted, its immediate impact on the liberalization of FDI may vary from negligible to substantial, depending on the results of the ongoing negotiations of liberalization commitments to be included in the national schedules. At the beginning of 1992, the initial offers of developed countries concerning FDI-related transactions were more comprehensive than those of developing countries. In general, countries seemed to proceed with caution. Offers indicated a tendency among countries to bind their regulations, in most cases, below the existing levels of liberalization, rather than to make substantial progress in the opening of markets. A few countries with more open markets in telecommunication and financial services have even suggested that those services be exempted from MFN treatment until other countries reach the same levels of liberalization. But even if the cautionary approach prevails at that stage, there may be progress in liberalization, because, as a result of the MFN obligation, a number of existing bilateral or regional investment and related arrangements (for example, the Convention on a Code of Conduct for Liner Conferences) may be "multilateralized", requiring the extension of their provisions to non-member countries. In addition, the immediate effect of GATS—if adopted—would be to reduce uncertainty for providers of services by increasing the transparency of regulatory regimes and reducing the scope of discrimination across the sources of supply.

In the long run, the process initiated by the Uruguay Round, and GATS specifically, will not only increasingly determine the formulation and implementation of FDI policies in the services sector, but also may accelerate the liberalization of FDI policies in other sectors. The reason is that GATS, if adopted, includes, for the first time ever, multilateral binding rules on FDI. Although they would apply only to one part of FDI, they may eventually be extended to other sectors as well.

2. Trade related investment measures

The Uruguay Round negotiations on trade related investment measures (TRIMs) have attempted to establish multilateral standards to govern the use of TRIMs by host countries. TRIMs were a controversial issue during the negotiations in that member countries had diverging views concerning the interpretation of the Punta del Este negotiation mandate, which stipulated that further provisions under GATT that might be necessary in order to avoid trade-restrictive and distortive effects of investment measures on trade were to be elaborated, as appropriate. A broad range of TRIMs relating mainly to performance requirements were discussed during the negotiations (table III.1).[4] It was also suggested that investment incentives, home-country measures (for example, export limitations on foreign affiliates, preferential taxes for income on investments) and corporate measures (restrictive business practices) be considered TRIMs, to the extent that they influence patterns of trade and investment.[5] Those measures, however, did not receive nearly the same attention as performance requirements.

A good part of the discussion concerned the extent to which TRIMs are trade distorting and would need to be addressed by new GATT rules. Some developed countries were seeking to prohibit TRIMs and related investment measures *per se*, whereas other developed and developing countries considered that the Punta del Este mandate was solely to address the trade-restrictive and trade-distortive effects of investment measures, particularly those that were not already covered by GATT.[6] Developing countries also argued that TRIMs, applied by a country for the purposes of achieving socio-economic development objectives, should fall outside the negotiating mandate.[7]

The draft Decision on TRIMs, included in the Draft Final Act[8] released in December 1991, covered TRIMs related to trade in goods only. It requires each Party to notify the GATT Secretariat of the publications in which TRIMs may be found, and to be prepared to consider in a positive way requests of other parties for information and/or consultations on TRIMs. A Committee on TRIMs would be established to monitor the operation and implementation of the Decision. With regard to consultation and the settlement of disputes, the GATT mechanism (Articles XXII and XXIII and related instruments) would apply. Parties would review the operation of the Decision within five years, and at that time would consider whether its scope should be broadened to include provisions on investment and competition.

An illustrative list attached to the draft Decision (box III.2) identifies the TRIMs that are seen as inconsistent with the provisions of GATT on national treatment (Article III) and the general elimination of quantitative restrictions (Article XI). Those measures concern performance requirements, such as requirements for import substitution, domestic sales, trade balancing and local content. The last three measures are already covered by existing GATT rules. The list also covers foreign-exchange restrictions, but only those to be used for trade-balancing. The list is non-exhaustive in nature, which reflects a recognition that there might be other TRIMs that are inconsistent with Articles III and XI of GATT. It should be noted that the list does not include export-performance requirements, which are among the most frequently used TRIMs in developing countries, and which were the subject of intense negotiations. Negotiators, however, have so far not been able to agree upon a discipline for that type of TRIM. TRIMs that are inconsistent with the Decision should be notified and eliminated within two years by developed

Table III.1. Trade related investment measures and their possible impact on trade and investment

Measures	*Possible economic impact*
Investment incentives [a]	**Influence location of investments**
Tax concessions	
Tariff concessions	
Subsidies	
Investment grants	
Performance requirements	
Local-equity requirements [a]	Require ownership of investments
Licensing requirements [a]	Require technology transfer
Remittance restrictions [a]	Restrict external financial transfers
Foreign-exchange restrictions [b]	Restrict external financial transfers
Manufacturing limitations [b]	Restrict production
Transfer-of-technology requirements [c]	Require technology transfer
Domestic sales requirements [d]	Displace imports
Manufacturing requirements [e]	Displace imports
Product-mandating requirements [e]	Displace other exports
Trade-balancing requirements [e]	Displace other exports
Local-content requirements [f]	Displace imports
Export requirements [f]	Displace other exports
Import-substitution requirements	Displace exports
Corporate measures (resrictive business practices) [g]	
Market allocation	Restrict exports
Collusive tendering	Excessive pricing for imports
Refusal to deal	Restrict exports/imports
Exclusive dealing	Export prohibition
Tied sales	Displace other imports/exports
Resale price maintenance	Excessive pricing for imports
Price fixing	Excessive pricing
Differential pricing	Excessive pricing
Transfer pricing	Excessive pricing for imports; Low pricing for exports
Home-country measures	
Export limitation on foreign affiliates	Restricts trade
Preferential taxes for income on investments	Subsidize investments

Source: UNCTC, *New Issues in the Uruguay Round of Multilateral Trade Negotiations*, UNCTC Current Studies, Series A, No. 19 (United Nations publication, Sales No. E.90.II.A.15).

Note: The countries identifying particular measures in the Uruguay Round are indicated as follows:

a United States.
b European Community and the United States.
c Japan and the United States.
d European Community, Japan and the United States.
e European Community, Japan, Switzerland and the United States.
f European Community, Japan, Switzerland, the Nordic countries and the United States.
g India.

countries, within five years by developing countries and within seven years by least developed countries. The need for special treatment of developing countries is stipulated in the Preamble and in a number of the Articles, of which one (that is, longer transition periods) has already been mentioned.

Developing countries would also be free to deviate temporarily from the provisions of the Decision, that is, they would be allowed to apply, temporarily, TRIMs that are prohibited, but that may be needed to promote government policy objectives regarding socio-economic growth and development. In short, the draft Decision (Article IV) essentially reaffirms that relevant Articles of GATT, giving developing countries the right to use trade restrictions for balance-of-payment measures and allowing them to protect infant industries, would continue to apply; no additional rights are conferred on developing countries by Article IV. At the same time, all exceptions under GATT would apply.

With regard to transitional arrangements, member countries that have notified a TRIM inconsistent with the Decision may, during the transition period and under certain conditions, apply the same TRIM to a new investment in order not to disadvantage established enterprises subject to the notified TRIM. They must be terminated, however, at the same time.

Box III.2. Illustrative list of "unacceptable" trade related investment measures

1. TRIMs that are inconsistent with the obligation of national treatment provided for in Article III:4 of the General Agreement include those which are mandatory or enforceable under domestic law or under administrative rulings or compliance with which is necessary to obtain an advantage, and which require:

- the purchase or use by an enterprise of products of domestic origin or from any domestic source, whether specified in terms of particular products, in terms of volume or value of products, or in terms of a proportion of volume or value of its local production;
- that purchases of an enterprise or use of imported products be limited to an amount related to the volume or value of local products that it exports.

2. TRIMs that are inconsistent with the obligation of the general elimination of quantitative restrictions provided for in Article XI:1 of the General Agreement include those which are mandatory or enforceable under domestic law or under administrative rulings or compliance with which is necessary to obtain an advantage, and which restrict:

- the importation by an enterprise of products used in or related to its local production, generally, or to an amount related to the volume or value of local production that it exports;
- the importation by an enterprise of products used in or related to its local production by restricting its access to foreign exchange to an amount related to the foreign exchange inflows attributable to the enterprise;
- the exportation or sale for export by an enterprise of products whether specified in terms of particular products, in terms of volume or value of products, or in terms of a proportion of volume or value of its local production.

Source: Quoted from the annex to the Draft Decision on trade related investment measures, Section N of the Draft Final Act Embodying the Results of the Uruguay Round of Multilateral Trade Negotiations (MTN.TNC/W/FA, 1991).

The potential implications of the draft Decision on TRIMs are difficult to foresee, because there is no commonly accepted method of drawing a line between so-called "legitimate" and "illegitimate" measures (in home or host countries) that may affect the location of production and the associated flows of goods, services, technology and capital among markets. The TRIMs included in the illustrative list of the draft Decision are mainly various performance requirements whose major economic impact may be the displacement of exports or imports. There is, however, no common agreement on how, precisely, such measures actually affect firm behaviour, or what their impact is on trade and development. Furthermore, in the competition for FDI, developed countries frequently use market access, tariff escalation and investment incentives to attract foreign investors in the same way that developing countries use TRIMs. [9]

Given the fact that GATT already allows developing countries greater flexibility in the use of trade-restrictive measures for a variety of reasons, including balance-of-payments problems and infant industry and development considerations, [10] the Decision, if adopted, will not affect significantly the use of TRIMs by those countries. In any event, most developing countries have substantially liberalized their FDI regimes (see below) with a view to increasing inward FDI flows. Such liberalization may tend to reduce the possibility of violations of the Decision on TRIMs, if it is adopted.

While the Uruguay Round negotiations have focused on efforts to control, reduce and prohibit TRIMs, the distortionary effects of TRIMs, as compared with other types of locational policies (for example, cash grants or tax breaks), are still being debated. In particular, prohibiting one type of policy instrument potentially affecting locational decisions of TNCs, while leaving others intact, might in itself be distortionary. Therefore, a more balanced multilateral approach may be needed, incorporating all locational policies affecting FDI, especially performance requirements and investment incentives. Those matters are likely to be discussed in a newly established Committee on TRIMs, in which contracting parties may consult on matters relating to the operation and implementation of the Decision. The provisions on transparency will further contribute to a more effective decision- and policy-making process by allowing Governments, companies, investors and others increased access to information on TRIMs applied by national authorities.

Considering the major divergences in views on TRIMs by member countries at the time of the launching of the Uruguay Round, the present draft text is certainly an achievement. At the same time, the outcome of the TRIMs negotiations so far represents mostly a reaffirmation of existing GATT rules. Since the final provisions of the Decision provide, however, that investment and competition policies will be considered for potential inclusion into the scope of the Decision within five years, it may well be that the seeds have been planted for a broader multilateral framework for FDI and related policy issues. [11]

3. Trade related aspects of intellectual property rights

The draft agreement negotiated in the Uruguay Round on trade-related aspects of intellectual property rights (TRIPs), including trade in counterfeit goods, contains three major elements of potential importance for TNCs:

- First, it sets minimum standards of protection for seven categories of intellectual property rights: copyright and related rights, trademarks, geographical indications, industrial designs, patents, layout-designs of integrated circuits and undisclosed information (trade secrets);
- Second, it sets out the obligations of member Governments on the civil, judicial and administrative procedures to be available under national law, both internally and at the border, for the enforcement of those rights;
- Third, it sets up a multilateral procedure for the settlement of any disputes that might arise between member Governments.

The standards of protection provided, especially in the technology-related areas of patents, integrated circuits and undisclosed information, would be generally higher than those prevailing hitherto, notably in a number of developing countries. It is intended that the agreement will form part of the overall results of the Uruguay Round and will be adopted by over 100 countries.

In considering the economic impact of higher standards of intellectual-property protection, two considerations need to be borne in mind. First, the impact is likely to be greater in industries in which cheap or costless imitation is relatively easy, such as pharmaceuticals, chemicals and computer software, than in high technology areas in which the co-operation of the inventor is more essential for technology diffusion. It is in the former category that intellectual- property regimes have hitherto varied most sharply; those differences would be eliminated or significantly narrowed by a TRIPs agreement. It is in the areas in which copying is easier that the role of intellectual-property protection has been most significant in preventing the appropriation of R&D activity. In other areas, inventors can more easily use other means, such as secrecy, advertising and increasing returns to scale, to secure the benefits of their research and create barriers to entry, so that intellectual-property protection as such is relatively less important. Second, the economic effects of higher intellectual-property protection, including those on market structure, prices, output and profits, are influenced by a host of other measures relating to, especially, competition policy, price controls, advertising and taxation, which a TRIPs agreement would not regulate. For example, the increase in prices that better patent protection could bring about could, to a certain extent, be offset by price controls.

In the long term, better intellectual-property-right protection may be expected to induce more R&D generation by TNCs, though it is difficult to predict the size and nature of such effects. Given that the change in intellectual-property regimes will be more pronounced in developing countries and, therefore, that much of the improvement in corporate performance, such as may occur, would be derived from markets in those countries, it may be that the incentive to innovate in product areas of special interest to developing countries, such as tropical medicine and inputs for tropical agriculture, would also be enhanced. If that happened, it would be an important departure from past trends whereby intellectual-property rights in developing countries were used predominantly for trade purposes rather than for investment and local production. In general, if the induced effects on R&D were strong, the dynamic benefits of increased intellectual-property protection, in the form of lower production costs, lower prices and greater product variety, could be considerable.

It is also likely that stronger protection of intellectual property will facilitate technology transfer, since there is some evidence that companies have been unwilling to export the latest technology in the absence of security against appropriation. In the short run, however, as imitation-based technology is substituted by protected technology whose costs may be higher, technology diffusion in some sectors may be slowed down. In the long term, higher protection should encourage the invention of cheaper and better technology, which would increase global welfare.[12]

In sum, the impact of the agreement, if adopted, on foreign direct investment should in general be favourable, partly through the reduction of disincentives to technology transfer (mentioned above) and partly through the creation of a policy climate more favourable and receptive to FDI. In industries that have hitherto been supplied largely by imitation-based production, such production could in principle be replaced by imports, by FDI or by local production under licence. The effect of a TRIPs agreement in the patent area is to put those three means of supplying the market on an equal footing, so that decisions on investment and industrial location are more likely to be based on commercial considerations and less likely to be affected by government policy on patents.

B. Regional and bilateral developments

1. The 1991 review of OECD instruments

On the interregional level, the most important development was the review of the OECD Declaration on International Investment and Multinational Enterprises, adopted in 1976.[13] The latest review of that instrument was endorsed by the OECD Council of Ministers in 1991. Among the main changes approved were the following:

- The Decision on National Treatment was revised by strengthening the obligation of notification of measures that are contrary to the principle of national treatment. Also reinforced were the existing examination procedures with a view to accelerating liberalization;
- The existing provisions on the environment in the Guidelines for Multinational Enterprises were strengthened and expanded into a full new chapter dedicated to that topic;

- It was agreed to incorporate in the Declaration an earlier agreement on general considerations and practical approaches to take into account in adopting legislation that may lead to conflicting requirements being imposed on TNCs.

The 1991 review clarified that the obligations of the revised national-treatment instrument apply to all member countries and at all levels of Government (federal, state and local Governments). Moreover, under the strengthened procedures, all exceptions to national treatment will be notified and listed in an annex to the Decision. Other measures having a bearing on national treatment will also be subject to notification for transparency purposes. Instead of the periodic examination of compliance conducted on the basis of categories of measures, as was done until now, in the future there will be country-by-country comprehensive reviews. Follow-up procedures to determine the effect given to the recommendations after a country has been examined are specified. It was also agreed that exceptions to national treatment will be examined in conjunction with the Committee on Capital Movements and Invisible Transactions. A significant new development was the adherence for the first time of the European Community to the section of the Declaration dealing with national treatment in those aspects which are within its competence. Moreover, according to its Article 7, the Revised Decision on National Treatment is now open for accession by the European Community.

With respect to environmental protection, a new chapter was introduced in the Guidelines for Multilateral Enterprises, thus stressing the importance attached to that topic by OECD and emphasizing the linkages between economic objectives and environmental concerns. The new chapter on environment strengthens cooperation between Governments and industry by suggesting practical ways of solving major international environmental issues. Under the new guidelines, TNCs will be expected to undertake several preventive measures, such as assessment of environmental and health risks in decision-making, and disclosure of relevant information to competent authorities regarding the potential impact of their operations. Under the new provisions, both transnational and domestic enterprises are subject to the same expectations, with respect to the duty to protect the environment and avoid creating environmental problems. The specific measures recommended to prevent and minimize risks include those related to the use of safe technology and processes; environmental protection at the enterprise level, including, where appropriate, environmental auditing; provision of adequate equipment and information to local enterprises; education and training programmes; and support for public-information programmes.

The overall strategy of OECD member States with respect to FDI is also reflected in a new initiative taken by that Organisation to study the advantages and feasibility of a comprehensive investment instrument that would apply to all levels of Government and cover entry and establishment of FDI, as well as treatment of already established foreign affiliates. The instrument might draw upon the OECD Liberalisation Codes, the National Treatment Instrument, as well as other international instruments, which it would consolidate, in order to strengthen and enlarge the OECD framework on FDI.

2. Bilateral arrangements

During 1991, the network of bilateral treaties for the promotion and protection of FDI continued to expand, to reach a total number of 440 by mid-1991 (table III.2 and annex table 10). As of mid-year, 19 new treaties had been concluded, mainly by Western countries with States in Central and Eastern Europe, as well as Latin America. The network confirms a trend that began a few years ago when, for the first time, some countries in Latin America and Central and Eastern Europe joined in the practice of concluding bilateral investment treaties, as one of the policy measures adopted by those countries with a view to creating a favourable climate for foreign investors. By mid-1991, Poland had concluded 16 treaties; the USSR signed 14; Czechoslovakia 13; and Hungary had signed 18 bilateral treaties. As to Latin America, 10 new treaties were signed between 1990 and mid-1991, and others were under negotiation. The conclusion of bilateral investment treaties by countries such as Argentina, Bolivia, Chile, Peru and Venezuela marked a significant policy change in the approach of those countries towards foreign investors. Until recently, the countries of that region had rejected bilateral investment treaties as being incompatible with their adherence to the Calvo Doctrine.[14]

Table III.2. Distribution of bilateral investment treaties between OECD countries and developing regions and Central and Eastern Europe, by ten-year period

Region	*1950s*	*1960s*	*1970s*	*1980s*	*1990-1991*[a]	*Total*
Africa	-	56	38	33	13	140
Asia	1	1	28	46	3	79
Latin America and the Caribbean	1	6	3	32	12	54
Middle East	-	1	12	9	1	23
Central and Eastern Europe	-	-	11	42	25	78
Memorandum						
Among OECD countries	-	5	2	9	2	18
Among developing countries	-	3	5	15	6	29
Between developing countries and Central and Eastern Europe	-	-	4	13	2	19
Among Central and Eastern European countries	-	-	-	-	-	-
Total	2	72	103	199	64	440

Source: UNCTC and ICC, *Bilateral Investment Treaties 1959-1991* (United Nations publication, Sales No. E.92.II.A.16).

a First six months of 1991 only.

Overall, the format of bilateral investment treaties has not changed very much over the years. Bilateral investment treaties continue to provide a number of general standards of treatment (that is, fair and equitable, national and most-favoured-nation treatment), as well as specific standards for the most sensitive issues in investment relations, namely, expropriation, transfer of payments, subrogation and settlement of disputes between investors and the Governments, of their host countries. Although the question of entry and establishment has traditionally been left out of the treaties (to be determined by the laws of the host country), there is, nevertheless, a clear emphasis in the treaties on the facilitation of entry and establishment of foreign investments from the other contracting party. Recent treaties, notably those concluded by the United States, prescribe that the entry and establishment of investors from the other contracting party should be granted on the basis of national and most-favoured-nation treatment. Specific issues related to operational conditions are usually left to be determined by the laws of the contracting States. Provisions relating to performance requirements are not a common feature of bilateral investment treaties, but the United States treaties include a clause specifically prohibiting performance requirements between the contracting States. [15]

A significant new development since mid 1990 has been the conclusion, by the United States, of 15 trade and investment framework agreements involving a total of 31 Latin American and Caribbean countries (only Cuba, Haiti and Suriname are not parties to any such agreement). Thirteen such agreements were concluded with individual countries (Bolivia, Chile, Colombia, Costa Rica, Dominican Republic, Ecuador, El Salvador, Guatemala, Honduras, Nicaragua, Panama, Peru, and Venezuela). The other two agreements were signed with the Southern Cone Common Market (Mercosur) [16] and with the Caribbean Community (CARICOM). [17] The arrangements are meant to be policy-building blocs that could eventually lead to full free trade and investment agreements. While they do not prescribe binding commitments on trade and investment liberalization, they seek to monitor relations in these two areas. They establish working groups to put in motion a series of policy goals aimed at increasing access to markets and diminishing trade restrictions. They also seek to strengthen the protection of intellectual-property rights, and set up mechanisms for dispute settlement. [18]

Another significant bilateral undertaking is the antitrust cooperation agreement concluded between the United States and the Commission of the European Communities on 23 September 1991. [19] The agreement permits the United States to request the European authorities to take action against anti-competitive conduct occurring in Europe and vice versa. To that effect, the agreement contains, among other things, the following:

- a commitment to notify the other party of antitrust enforcement activities that may affect important interests;
- an undertaking to take into account the important interests of the other parties at all stages of their antitrust implementation activities;
- coordination of enforcement activities, if it is mutually advantageous;
- ad hoc consultations to resolve issues as they arise;
- regular meetings to exchange information and views on antitrust policy.

Because of the extraterritorial nature of some of the existing antitrust laws, and the different approaches adopted by various national regulations in that area, there have been many instances of conflicting requirements and conflicts of jurisdiction in the application of antitrust legislation. Those problems have interfered with the establishment of trans-border mergers within the EC and the United States. The adoption of the agreement would, therefore, help minimize those difficulties and intensify intergovernmental cooperation in the area of competition law, thus paving the way for further harmonization and integration efforts still to come.

C. National developments

1. Regulatory changes

The trend towards liberalization of government policies on FDI that started in the 1980s continued—even accelerated—during 1991 (table III.3 and annex table 11).[20] During that year, especially countries in Central and Eastern Europe liberalized their FDI regimes (for example, Albania, Bulgaria), as part of their efforts to attract and facilitate FDI flows. In other countries, the pattern of liberalization that was initiated in the past few years has continued and even intensified, for example, in India (see box III.3), Viet Nam and Saudi Arabia. On the other hand, a few Western countries traditionally associated with liberal attitudes towards foreign investors (for example, the United States), introduced some controls on business operations affecting foreign investment, although, overall, the framework for FDI in all developed countries is now liberalized to a very large extent.[21] Moreover, as some regional integration institutions assume stronger functions, some aspects of investment regulation are now being dealt with at the regional level, for instance, by the EC, CARICOM, PTA and MERCOSUR.

In the developing world, many countries had already introduced new laws on FDI, or modified existing ones during the 1980s. Still, in 1991, some countries that had not undertaken a comprehensive review of their FDI regimes introduced new policies aimed at liberalizing some of the existing restrictions. But the pace of changes varies considerably from country to country. The new liberalizing measures adopted by developing countries typically included the lifting of local ownership requirements and sectoral restrictions (for example, in service industries such as banking, tourism and telecommunications), the simplification of approval procedures and the introduction of more liberal rules for the repatriation of capital and payments. In addition, developing countries continued to offer a wide variety of incentives to attract foreign investors (mainly tax exemptions, tax holidays and custom exemptions). In many countries, incentives were granted on the condition that certain performance requirements were met by the investor, related either to the size and importance of the project or to requirements such as local content or levels of exports. In general, most incentives differentiated between local and foreign enterprises and between different industries. But there appeared to be some efforts aimed at harmonizing incentives granted to foreign investors within particular regions.

The most dramatic changes in FDI regimes during 1991 continued to take place in Central and Eastern Europe. The fundamental economic and political changes initiated in 1989 have required the introduction of new laws reflecting market principles in virtually all aspects of economic activity. Foreign

Table III.3. Main changes in investment regimes in 1991

	Effected by		Type of measure									
			Foreign ownership/ sectoral restrictions		Approval procedures		Incentives		Guarantees		Controls	
Region	New law	Revision of law	More liberal	Less liberal	More liberal	Less liberal	More liberal	Less liberal	More liberal	Less liberal	More liberal	Less liberal
Asia	China						x					
	India		x		x							
	Mongolia						x					
	Philippines		x									
	Republic of Korea				x							
		Taiwan Province of China	x				x					
		Viet Nam	x									
Africa	Egypt		x									
	Uganda				x		x					
	Zambia				x		x					
Middle East		Bahrain	x									
	Saudi Arabia				x							
	Syrian Arab Republic						x		x			
	Yemen						x		x			
Latin America and the Caribbean	Bolivia		x		x				x			
	Colombia		x		x				x		x	
	Ecuador		x		x				x		x	
	Jamaica										x	

/.....

(Table III.3, cont'd.)

	Effected by		Type of measure									
			Foreign ownership/ sectoral restrictions		Approval procedures		Incentives		Guarantees		Controls	
Region	New law	Revision of law	More liberal	Less liberal	More liberal	Less liberal	More liberal	Less liberal	More liberal	Less liberal	More liberal	Less liberal
Latin America and the Caribbean (cont'd.)	Nicaragua		x		x				x		x	
	Peru		x		x				x		x	
Central and Eastern Europe	Albania		x				x		x		x	
	Belarus		x				x				x	
	Bulgaria		x				x		x		x	
		Czechoslovakia							x			
	Estonia		x						x			
	Poland				x		x		x		x	
	Romania		x		x		x		x		x	
	Russian Republic		x		x		x		x		x	
	Ukraine		x		x				x			
	Uzbekistan		x		x				x		x	
OECD	Japan		x		x				x			
	Sweden		x				x					
	Switzerland											x
		United States										x

Source: United Nations, Department of Economic and Social Development, Transnational Corporations and Management Division, based on annex table 11.

Box III.3. India: a new pragmatism

Despite the advantages of a rapidly-expanding market, a well-developed infrastructure and industrial base, a large pool of scientific and engineering personnel and a tradition of medium-scale entrepreneurship, India has received far less in FDI compared with other developing countries (table 1). The main reason has been negative investor perception, whether well founded or not, of national commitment to foreign capital.

Inheriting a distrust of TNCs as a legacy of colonial domination, the Government evolved a complex legal and institutional labyrinth to ensure a marginal and highly circumscribed role for FDI in the economy. As a corollary, the normal ceiling on foreign-equity participation was limited to 40 per cent, and FDI was largely restricted to priority industries requiring sophisticated technology, undertakings with high export-earnings capacity, industries lacking in indigenous technology or industries in which a critical production gap existed. While earlier reservations towards FDI had given place to a more realistic appraisal of the need for technology and investment liberalization measures, particularly in the period 1985-1990, the basic structure of controls and regulations on TNCs did not change significantly to encourage FDI and technology imports.

In a series of bold moves, the industrial policy unveiled on 24 July 1991 moved the Indian economy from a very restrictive industrial regime towards a market-friendly, outward-looking one. More liberal and sweeping than at any time in the past, the across-the-board reforms set out a clear objective of resuscitating the faltering economy, improving the investment climate and integrating India into the world economy. The reforms liberalized many of the industrial-licensing, foreign-exchange and anti-monopoly regulations; partially freed the financial system from controls on interest rates; allowed partial convertibility of the rupee; proposed a more limited role for the public sector; revamped trade policy to make exports more profitable; and simplified the taxation structure. Overall, the reforms signalled a fundamental shift in attitude towards FDI.

Table 1. Investment inflows, 1990
(Billions of dollars)

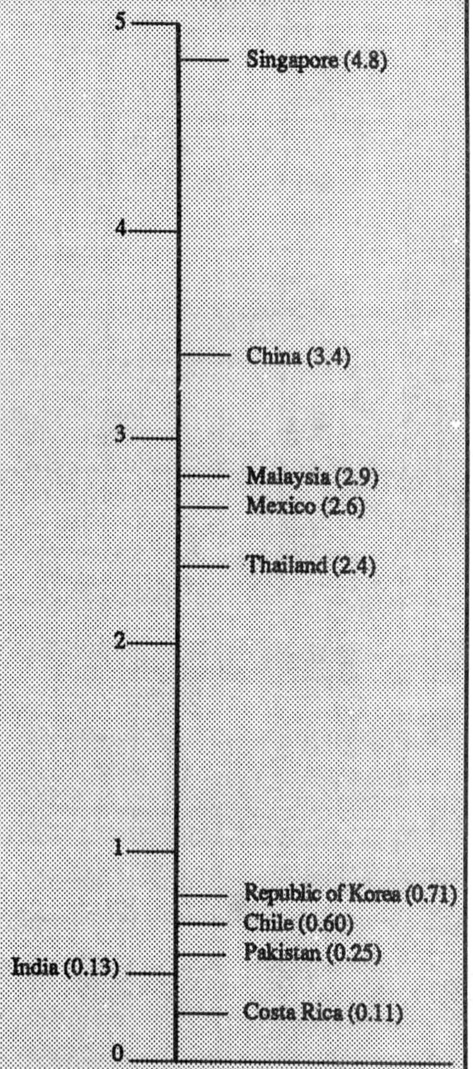

Source: International Monetary Fund, balance-of-payments tape, retrieved in December 1991.

The role of the public sector will be restricted to eight core industries (including arms, atomic energy, mineral oils, rail transport and mining), opening new investment opportunities for foreign and domestic capital

/.....

(Box III.3, cont'd)

in other industries. In a sharp break from the past, the new policy abolished the requirement of licensing for all but 18 industries and swept away the limitations under the Monopolies and Restrictive Trade Practices (MRTP) Act. The MRTP companies, foreign and domestic, with assets of $30 million or more, will no longer require licences for starting new industries, expanding existing ones and merging with or taking-over other companies.

The cornerstones of the new policy are, however, the measures designed to attract FDI and increase the national technology base and international competitiveness. Automatic approval will be given to joint ventures with up to 51 per cent (up from 40 per cent) foreign-equity participation in 34 high-priority industries, provided foreign equity covers the foreign-exchange requirement for imported capital goods. Changes have also been made in the very restrictive Foreign Exchange Regulation Act (FERA), which effectively required foreign companies to limit equity participation to 40 per cent or face stringent controls. A few TNCs (like IBM and Coca-Cola) preferred to divest in 1977 rather than dilute their equity holdings. IBM is now returning to India, in a 50-50 joint venture with the Tata group, to produce personal computers and software packages for export, as well as for sale to the local market. Foreign partners in several existing ventures in India are increasing their equity participation to take advantage of the relaxed ownership restrictions. For instance, Suzuki has been allowed to raise its equity in Maruti Udyog to 50 per cent from 40 per cent. Lesaffre (France) will also increase its equity to 51 per cent from 40 per cent in its local yeast plant, Safyeast Ltd.

In a further policy relaxation, FERA companies (companies with more than 51 per cent foreign interest) have been allowed to set up trading offices and branches, borrow money and accept deposits, deal in immovable property and use foreign trademarks. Formerly, for example, Pepsico could market its drinks only with a local prefix to its international brand name, Lehar Pepsi. In essence, under the new policy initiatives, FERA companies have been placed on a par with Indian companies for all operational purposes.

To further streamline the FDI applications process, the Government has pledged to take no more than 36 days to reach a decision. Furthermore, a high-powered Foreign Investment Promotion Board has been constituted to invite, negotiate and facilitate investment proposals from large foreign companies that may fall outside the usual parameters and procedures. In a clear and positive signal to prospective foreign investors, for example, the Government has expeditiously granted approval to proposals from a number of major TNCs (table 2).

In another policy reversal, the Government has lifted its ban on foreign participation in the oil and gas industry, including the exploration and development of existing fields, production, refin-

Table 2. Foreign-collaboration approvals, August 1991-February 1992
(Millions of dollars)

Joint venture	*Industry*	*Investment*[a]
IBM-Tata	Computer systems, software	9.8
BMW-Escorts	Motorcycles	3.8
Ford/Sumitomo-Maruti	Aluminium radiators	3.1
Fujitsu-PSEDPS	Digital electronic-switching systems	12.8
Kellogg's	Food processing	16.6
Coca-Cola-Pillai	Snack food and beverages	20.0
General Motors-Hindustan Motors	Automobiles and parts	30.0
General Electric-Godrej	Kitchen appliances	20.0

Sources: Indian Investment Centre; *India Today*, 15 December 1991.

[a]Estimates.

/.....

(Box III.3, cont'd)

ing and marketing. The reversal will favour the proposals submitted by Shell, Caltex, Chevron and Total. British Gas and Gaz de France have also submitted a proposal with the Gas Authority of India for joint distribution of gas in Bombay. Similarly, in telecommunications, the Government has reversed its previous policy of indigenous development and is now inviting FDI; for example, it is discussing joint ventures with Motorola, AT&T, Siemens, Ericsson, NEC and Fujitsu. The drive of the Government to attract more FDI in all sectors of the economy may well lead to greater protection of intellectual-property rights.

To harness both domestic and international savings in its industrialization process, the new policy allows foreign pension funds and the like to invest in the Indian stock market. The investment will not only boost share prices and bring in foreign equity, but will also mark the first steps towards an integration of the Indian stock markets with the international ones. In addition, a plan approved on 7 February 1992 allows Indian companies to issue equity to foreign investors through convertible instruments. Further, if approved, the foreign collaboration between Unit Trust of India and Alliance Capital Management LP will be the first to provide investment-management services to Indian investors.

The new policy also spells out more incentives to attract FDI from non-resident Indians (NRIs). On a non-repatriable basis, areas like housing, real estate and infrastructure have been opened to NRIs. Interestingly, in a calculated move to take advantage of the special privileges extended to NRIs, including entry into restricted areas, easier approvals and 100 per cent equity, Coca-Cola teamed with a Singapore-based NRI to secure its recent investment decision under liberal conditions.

Competing for scarce international capital, the Government has found it necessary to market India aggressively in high-powered business and official forums at home and abroad. In order to strengthen the diplomatic missions abroad in that respect, the Government is considering a proposal to induct personnel from the corporate sector in the commercial wing of the missions. A further indication of the changing attitude towards TNCs is the growing competition between state Governments to attract foreign investors.

The reforms have generated considerable interest in several foreign companies that are seeking to take advantage of the more liberal environment as the ability of the Government to back its policy assertions with actions becomes apparent. The most recent estimates indicate that the amount of FDI approved between August and December 1991 was more than nine times that approved in the corresponding period in 1990: $165 million against $18 million. Several other TNCs have announced plans for new projects in India. In light of the recent changes, some firms like Fujitsu and Alcatel are submitting revised proposals rejected in the past. At the same time, firms already operating in India are seeking more liberal conditions.

Still, while as many as 760 foreign proposals have been approved since the announcement of the new policy (August-December 1991), the foreign equity involved has fallen far short of what the Government had hoped for. And, in nearly all cases, the ventures had been formulated before the new policy announcements.

The shortfall might well simply reflect the normal lags in the reaction of investors to policy change, or it could mean that, given the fierce global competition for capital, liberalization measures in India may have to go further to attract a substantially increased stream of FDI. For, despite the substantial progress made in several areas, what matters to investors is not what dramatic departures from past practices have been introduced by the new policy, but how the new climate compares with investment opportunities elsewhere.

Sources: Government of India, *India's New Economic Policies* (New Delhi, Ministry of External Affairs, 1991); UNCTC, *Foreign Direct Investment and Technology Transfer in India* (United Nations publication, Sales No. E.92.II.A.3); *Far Eastern Economic Review*, various issues; *Financial Times*, various issues; *India Abroad*, various issues; *Times of India*, various issues; *Financial Express*, various issues; *The Wall Street Journal*, various issues; *Business Asia*, various issues; *The New York Times*, various issues.

direct investment was among the priority areas targeted for new legislation. By the end of 1991, most countries in the region had adopted legislation providing liberal conditions for FDI, including (in most cases) 100 per cent foreign ownership, free transfer of profits and the repatriation of capital (although restrictions on currency exchange and convertibility continue), guarantees for expropriation, and incentives, mainly tax holidays (table III.3).[22] Moreover, after only a few years of being in force, some of the new-generation FDI laws passed in that region are being clarified and amended, building now upon experience gained with their application. Given the fact that, until recently, all industries were in the hands of the public sector, major privatization programmes have also been set in motion. The new privatization rules being implemented are also important elements of the FDI regimes, since main major industrial enterprises are expected to attract foreign investors, at least until the indigenous industrial and financial base of those countries is modernized. In many respects, the new regimes reflect state-of-the-art provisions in areas such as environmental protection, competition and intellectual-and-industrial property protection. Yet, gaps in basic economic legislation (contractual and company law, financial markets, banking legislation) render the application of the new laws difficult.

Within the OECD area, several countries have adopted new legislation affecting FDI, including the liberalization of rules on take-overs and mergers. Thus, for example, Japan lifted existing restrictions including the requirement of prior notification for effecting inward investments. In addition, the recently completed agreement between the EC and EFTA countries (described in chapter I) will have many and immediate consequences for the legal frameworks of the latter countries. Many of those countries are now compelled to align their legislation with EC regulations in a number of significant areas, such as company law, consumer protection, the environment and restrictive business practices, as well as those applying to specific industries. In the past few years, liberalization efforts among Western countries have gained momentum, mainly in response to closer integration ties being developed among groups of countries within that region. Within the OECD area, those efforts have concentrated mainly on the liberalization of cross-border flows of capital and services and on the lifting of existing government measures that discriminate between foreign and national enterprises.

Despite the overall pronounced liberal attitude towards FDI, some policies and practices have emerged in the OECD area that may suggest a more regulatory approach towards TNCs. In the United States, most importantly, the Exon-Florio amendment to the Defence Production Act has become, since 1991, a permanent fixture of the United States legislation, and grants the President authority to screen out specific foreign-investment projects on the grounds of national security. In fact, it has been argued that the Exon-Florio amendment could be implemented in such a way that competition from foreign investors could be limited, and incentives for domestic firms to develop technologies equal or superior to those held by foreigners would be removed. Such implementations could in the long run have the effect that the competitiveness and productivity of United States firms would be hampered.[23]

2. Privatization

Privatization of former state-owned enterprises has become an increasingly attractive option in developed and developing countries alike, alongside the liberalization of investment policies, and as part of an increasing application of free-market economic policies.[24] With active privatization efforts in more than 70 countries, the annual number of privatizations world-wide more than quintupled between 1985 and 1990, to around 130.[25] By the end of the 1980s, the value of state enterprises sold was reported to have reached over $185 billion, with no sign of a slow-down.[26] Although only limited statistical evidence is available, the role of TNCs in privatization efforts (table III.4) seems to be important in developing countries, especially in Latin America (in Asia, privatization has been of less significance, despite ambitious plans of many Governments in the region).[27] In Central and Eastern Europe, TNC participation in privatization programmes has become crucial in the transition from centrally-planned to market economies.

The increasing utilization of privatization programmes in a large number of countries arises from a number of factors. Most important among them are the disappointing performance of many public-sector enterprises, exemplified by the recent collapse of the centrally planned economies, as well as economic stagnation (and correspondingly large budgetary deficits) in many developing countries with large public sectors. While there may be ideological underpinnings in some privatization efforts, the main rationale seems to be a pragmatic one, namely, the need to improve the provision of goods and services to meet demand, to reduce public-sector deficits and to develop the requisite entrepreneurial capacity for sustained economic growth. It follows that Governments often adopt a selective approach towards privatization, maintaining certain activities in the public domain in order, for example, to keep down the costs to the public of certain services (for example, domestic transportation), or to ensure their availability to all sections of the population (for example, health care). Other enterprises that Governments retain in the public sector tend to be natural monopolies (for example, postal services), or of a strategic nature (for example, oil), or those that involve defence-oriented activities (for example, armaments firms).

The role of FDI in any privatization programme depends on at least two factors. One is the willingness of foreign investors to invest in enterprises that are being privatized. Another concerns the political willingness to admit foreign capital which, in turn, is also a function of the extent to which domestic capital and entrepreneurial resources are able to absorb and operate the available public-sector enterprises. There is, quite often, a considerable resource-gap in the latter respect in many developing countries, as well as the countries of Central and Eastern Europe, thereby making FDI a crucial element in the success of privatization programmes. Some estimates indicate that domestic private capital resources available in some countries, such as Hungary and Poland, would cover less than 25 per cent of the public-sector assets likely to be put on the market.[28] Consequently, an infusion of foreign capital, through loans or FDI, is in many cases required if privatization is to occur, unless Governments decide to transfer ownership of enterprises to the public through a mass distribution of shares (for example, as initiated in Czechoslovakia and proposed in Poland and Romania).

Table III.4. Examples of recent privatizations with the participation of transnational corporations

Host country	*Privatized enterprise*	*Year*	*Industry*	*Foreign TNC*	*Home country*	*Value of the equity sold off (Millions of dollars)*	*TNC share of the equity sold off (Percentage)*	*TNC share of total equity in the enterprise (Percentage)* [a]
Argentina	Aerolineas Argentinas	1990	Air transportation	Iberia	Spain	531[b]	24	20 (with option to buy additional 10)
	ENTEL	1990	Telecommunications	Telefónica de España Citibank Societa Finanziaria Telefónica France Telecom	Spain United States Italy France	964[c]	100	60
Czechoslovakia	Rakona	1991	Detergents	Procter & Gamble	United States	20	100	100
	Skoda	1991	Automobiles	Volkswagen	Germany	409[d]	100	31 (increasing to 70 by 1995)
Hungary	Tungsram	1989	Light bulbs	General Electric	United States	150	100	51
Mexico	Teléfonos de Mexico (Telmex)	1990	Telecommunications	Southwestern Bell France Telecom	United States France	1 760	48	10 (with option to buy additional 5)
Poland	Alima	1991	Fruit juice and baby foods	Gerber Products Co.	United States	11	100	60
	Pollena Bydgoszcz	1991	Detergents	Unilever	Netherlands	20	80	80
	Wedel	1991	Chocolates	Pepsico Inc.	United States	25	100	40
Venezuela	CANTV	1991	Telecommunications	GTE AT&T Telefónica de España	United States United States Spain	1 885	72	29
	Viasa	1991	Air transportation	Iberia	Spain	146	75	45

Source: United Nations, Department of Economic and Social Development, Transnational Corporations and Management Division, based on various sources.

a Since state enterprises are not always sold in their entirety (that is, the Government keeps a certain share of the equity) or since a part of them is sold to domestic investors, the percentages in this column can differ substantially from those in the preceding column.

b Estimated cash price on the basis of the cash value of $130 million in cash, $130 million in cash over five years and $2 billion in debt paper.

c Estimated cash price on the basis of the cash value of $214 million in cash and $5 billion in Argentinean debt paper.

d The amount is equal to DM620 million, at an exchange rate of DM1.516=$1. Volkswagen also pledged to invest $6.4 billion in Skoda over the following ten years.

The willingness of TNCs to invest in host countries is also an important determinant of their participation in the privatization programmes of those countries. That willingness depends on factors such as the overall investment climate in a host country and the industry in which TNCs operate. In several countries, little FDI has been forthcoming, despite liberalized investment legislation and incentives. This is particularly true of several African and certain Central and Eastern European countries. Privatization programmes may, in and of themselves, improve the overall investment climate; however, other factors, such as adequate physical and communication infrastructure, attractive markets, and a stable legal framework, are likely to be more important in this regard. Regarding the industry-specific aspects of privatization, TNCs often tend to operate in relatively globalized manufacturing industries characterized by a high degree of technological, capital and marketing intensity; in vertically integrated resource-based industries; as well as in such services industries as telecommunications, airlines, banking and business services. The creation of private enterprises, therefore, often involves the need to establish equity linkages with foreign firms to obtain the technology, capital and market connections required to become internationally competitive. The linkages are particularly important in economies which, parallel to privatization programmes, also liberalize the framework for external transactions. It may also be necessary for host country financial institutions to establish closer linkages with international financing bodies, in order to obtain financial participation and support for privatized enterprises. On the other hand, in the case of firms in industries that are primarily oriented towards the domestic market and in which international competition may be more limited (for example, utilities), the incidence of TNC participation tends to be lower, except for countries with large and growing markets, such as Brazil, China and India.

Active TNC participation, to the extent that it is available, can have considerable impact on in host-country privatization programmes. The participation of foreign investors in the bidding process increases the number of potential buyers and may increase the sales revenues for the Government. Participation by TNCs may also improve the balance-of-payments position of the host economy. In many instances, TNC participation in host-country privatizations may also lead to the transfer of knowledge by the foreign investor to the privatized enterprise, for example, in the form of production, marketing and management skills; such transfers may be greater than those from a host-country buyer. That may be particularly the case in those countries that are short of the skills and technology required to compete internationally, such as in Central and Eastern European countries, which have little recent prior experience with the management of private enterprises in a market economy.[29] In this regard also, the export performance of a privatized business might be increased through the use of the global networks of TNCs and their knowledge of product needs in other countries. The recognition of those potential benefits by the host-country Government, together with the need to reduce external debt, has led to an increase in the use of debt-equity swaps in privatization programmes particularly in Latin America in the late 1980s.[30] Additionally, when debt-equity swaps are undertaken in the context of a privatization programme, the potentially inflationary impact of such swaps can be greatly reduced, since this investment does not necessarily involve the creation of new money.

The negative aspects of allowing TNCs to participate in privatization programmes concern, in particular, the programmes associated with a de-nationalization of enterprises, especially when the enterprises are in economically or strategically important sectors and occupy the commanding heights of the economy. Furthermore, foreign investors may, sometimes, buy a privatized enterprise primarily to acquire its market share. In those cases, production (or part of it) would be phased out, plants would be closed and the market would be served from production facilities abroad. This may occur occasionally where established facilities are quite outdated (and hence require substantial modernization efforts), and are located in countries not far from existing, modern production facilities of the foreign investor, Thus, it may be necessary for Governments to agree with foreign investors on certain targets regarding future investment and employment in the privatized enterprise to ensure its future development. Additionally, the risk that a former state monopoly might become a foreign-owned monopoly could also be a source of concern. As a condition for privatization, however, Governments may have to allow TNCs some form of (temporary) monopoly to make it attractive for those firms to invest. The allowance was exemplified by the 1990 privatization of Teléfonos de Mexico (Telmex), in which equity stakes were sold off to Southwestern Bell of the United States, France Telecom and a local partner. The Government of Mexico had to guarantee Telmex a monopoly through 1996, as a compensation to the new owners for making substantial net investments in the telephone system by installing 4.5 million new lines, improving rural services by 100 per cent, introducing optical fibre communication, increasing digitalization by at least 65 per cent and upgrading 480,000 obsolete lines, in addition to maintaining prices in real terms until 1996, with a 3 per cent annual decrease thereafter.[31] Thus, certain agreements with the new owners may sometimes be necessary to secure public-policy goals in the industry.

* * * * *

A few conclusions emerge from the discussion of the role of TNCs in the privatization process. Since TNCs facilitate the transfer of capital, technology and skills, the industries in which TNC participation appears to be relatively more important are those in which host-country investors lack those resources. Moreover, when the competitiveness of a firm is best sustained through a global presence, TNC involvement may be particularly important.

British Telecom's recent investment in the Belize telecommunication system illustrates the important combination of technology transfer and capital infusion. The Belize telecommunication system lacked experience in the modern and highly technology-intensive telecommunications industry that is critical for competitiveness in that industry. Furthermore, it was also unable to develop much-needed customer service, a decisive element in attracting investors to the country. British Telecom, itself a state-owned enterprise until 1984, took an ownership stake in the Belize telephone system, thereby securing technological and managerial know-how for the enterprise.[32]

In many cases, particularly in former centrally planned economies, privatization entails a degree of transformation of the economic culture of the country and the introduction of new concepts, ideas and systems of economic management, with which the cadre of personnel in that country is relatively unfamiliar. In such cases, there is a need to introduce training programmes in certain areas, such as in business administration and accounting, which involves, essentially, a re-tooling of manpower resources, in addition to the re-shaping of the macroeconomic and legal environment. By the same token, the relatively low development of an entrepreneurial class possessing the necessary capital and skills to manage a major enterprise effectively, which characterizes many economies in transition and developing economies, also indicates the need for programmes oriented towards management and entrepreneurial development, in which TNCs may play an important role.

Where such programmes have to be carried out in the midst of an economic crisis, FDI becomes a critical element in the economic recovery effort. But, since many TNCs may shy away from investing in a turbulent and risky economy, privatization must often go hand-in-hand with the overall promotion of FDI, in addition to the promotion of domestic private investment. It is thus crucial for those countries to establish attractive policy and regulatory regimes for FDI, in order to carry forward their privatization programmes successfully.

D. Self-regulation

National laws and regulations, together with international agreements, are the main instruments through which the rights and responsibilities of Governments and firms are defined. In market economies, furthermore, there is also a certain degree of self-regulation that sometimes even has quasi-official status (in the area of professional activities, including, for example, in accounting). In the area of FDI, the International Chamber of Commerce (ICC), the principal international organization of the business community, addressed the question of treatment of foreign investors by the Governments of their host country as early as in the 1940s, when it issued its "International Code of Fair Treatment for Foreign Investments". In 1972, the same issue became the subject of the highly publicized ICC "Guidelines for International Investment", which was followed by a number of voluntary sector-specific codes and guidelines. In addition, many corporations adopted their own corporate behaviour codes. [33]

There are many reasons why industry engages in self-regulation. Self-regulation may be used to shape or avoid future legislation. Voluntary guidelines adopted by the business sector may be more stringent than national legislation and therefore make such legislation unnecessary. In some cases, self-regulation may be more effective than national regulations themselves, especially in those countries in which enforcement mechanisms are weak. For regulators, self-regulation by business fulfills a useful function in that the resulting self-imposed standards can provide practical internal guidance while responding to public-interest questions. Thus, self-imposed standards can be instruments against which the position of firms on public policy issues can be measured.

In those and other respects, a distinction should be made between self-regulation by business associations and self-regulation through specific codes or guidelines of firms. There are similarities in the motivations and functions of the two kinds of instruments, but there are also important differences.

Self-regulation by associations involves the imposition of certain common standards on *all* firms in the industry. The sanctions for non-compliance involve the good name of the firm, its acceptance by other firms in the specific context of the industry represented by the association and any other sanctions the association may impose. In other words, the other members of the association are charged with ensuring compliance with the association's standards. That type of self-regulation is similar to the kind of self-regulation that has long been the hallmark of the liberal professions, and which often has had a quasi-official status.

Corporate codes or guidelines do not function in that manner. Their role is to impose certain disciplines within the firm, without necessarily involving other firms or others to ensure compliance. Adherence to certain strict corporate standards that go beyond existing legislation can become a competitive tool, for example, by saving money in the use of resources, energy use and waste disposal; on the other hand, voluntary self-regulation by a firm can result in costs that may place it at a competitive disadvantage *vis-à-vis* non-self regulating firms. Furthermore, enterprise self-regulation is often seen as an issue of corporate responsibility *vis-à-vis* shareholders, customers and the public at large. Self-policing by firms can also be an effective public-relations technique, especially at a time when consumers increasingly scrutinize industry performance before making purchasing decisions. For business generally, self-regulation of that kind is a preferable alternative to codes of conduct developed by international organizations, or to those prepared by non-governmental organizations.[34]

* * * * *

In the past few years, self-regulation received a particular impetus in the area of environment, especially in preparation for the United Nations Conference on Environment and Development. (In fact, international business was invited by the Secretary-General of the Conference to develop proposals for its participation in the Conference and for follow-up action.) Efforts in that area reach back to 1974, however, two years after the United Nations Conference on the Human Environment, held in Stockholm, when the first attempts by industry to self-regulate its environmental performance were made. The ICC issued "Environmental Guidelines for World Industry",[35] which attempted to balance corporate environmental responsibility with financial realities; but the document provided only general guidance. In April 1991, the ICC launched the "Business Charter for Sustainable Development",[36] which is a set of 16 principles aimed at providing common guidance on environmental management to all types of business and enterprises around the world, and aiding them in the development of their own environmental policies and programmes. The stated intent of the Charter is to lay the foundations of policies that will lead corporations towards overall sustainability of their operations in the context of working towards sustainable development in general. Although the Charter contains no specific references to the application of the principles to a corporation's transnational operations, one would presume that they are also covered as well.

Apart from the ICC, a number of industrial and national associations have generated voluntary codes and guidelines.[37] The environmental guidelines developed by the Chemical Manufacturer's Association and the Conseil Européen des Federations de l'Industrie Chimique address a number of important issues, such as product stewardship and the provision of information to the public for contingency procedures. As with the ICC Business Charter, environmental responsibilities *vis-à-vis* the foreign affiliates of corporations are not discussed, although again, presumably, they are also covered. The subject, however, is addressed explicitly by Keidanren, the Japanese industry association, in its environmental guidelines.[38] In fact, Keidanren expects its members to go beyond compliance with national laws in developing countries, where environmental standards are less stringent than those in Japan; furthermore, the transfer of most advanced technology and know-how related to environmental management measures is advocated.

The transnational nature of the environmental performance of a corporation is increasingly addressed by individual corporations that have developed formal corporate-wide policy statements on their commitment to the protection of the environment. The benchmark survey of international corporate environmental policies conducted by UNCTC in 1991 found that, among the 169 responding firms, 43 per cent stated that they have developed formal international environmental policies (although, of course, their focus and specificity vary). In addition, the survey found that 75 per cent of the responding

Box III.4. Environmental policy of Chevron

The following is an excerpt from the environmental policy statement of Chevron. In addition to socially responsible behaviour, the corporation pledges integration of environmental concerns in all business decisions, participation in the formulation of pertinent legislation, openness in its operations as they affect safety and the environment and efficiency in the use of natural resources.

It is the policy of Chevron Corporation to conduct its business in a socially responsible and ethical manner that protects safety, health and the environment. ...To that end, the Company will:

- Integrate safety, fire, health and environmental protection into every aspect of its business activities;
- Comply with all safety, fire, health and environmental laws or regulations without regard to the degree of enforcement;
- Seek opportunities to participate in the formulation of safety, fire, health and environmental legislation, regulation or policy issues that may significantly impact our business. Work actively with the appropriate governmental agencies to ensure timely, reasonable and cost-effective solutions for issues wherever possible;
- Encourage employees to initiate and maintain an open dialogue within the Company and with the public or its agents regarding safety, fire, health and environmental matters. This includes recognizing and responding as appropriate to Company and community concerns about such matters...;
- Exhibit socially conscious leadership and demonstrate exemplary safety, fire, health and environment performance;
- Conserve Company and natural resources by careful management of emissions and discharges and by eliminating unnecessary waste generation. This also includes wise use of energy in our operations. Discretionary environmental, health and safety expenditures should be managed prudently to enhance Chevron's long-term competitive position.

Source: Excerpts from Chevron Corporation, "Strategic management in the environmental era", in brochure containing Chevron's Corporate Policy No. 530 for Safety, Fire, Health and the Environment, p. 5.

firms had between 1 and 23 specific environmental policies on issues such as air, water, health and safety, or waste reduction that go beyond the requirements of national legislation (boxes III.4 and III.5).

Some corporations have taken steps to improve their environmental performance, even if doing so means sacrificing a line of business. [39] Other companies pledge to improve product and resource efficiency within target dates. [40] At times, environmental responsibility is extended to outside of the boundaries of a corporation, to include its business associates. [41] Self-regulation is sometimes the result of corporations seeking to address pro-actively major areas of concern, [42] while other corporations seek to increase energy and resource-use efficiency by reducing pollution at its source and by pledging to discontinue certain environmentally harmful processes. [43]

Box III.5. Self-regulation and environmental protection

Below are illustrations of self-regulatory responses of a few firms to inadequate local environmental regulations. The corporations make a commitment in their environmental policy statements to apply their own standards where adequate protection to health, safety and the environment is not provided for by the law.

Company	*Statement*
Eli Lilly and Company	***Environmental Policy:*** "The company will comply with or exceed all applicable laws and regulations. Where existing laws and regulations are not adequate, the company will adopt its own environmental quality standards".
Allied Signal	***Health, Safety and Environmental Policy:*** "Adopt its own standards where laws or regulations may not be adequately protective, and adopt, where necessary, its own standards where laws do not exist".
Pennzoil Company	***Corporate Policy Manual:*** "...it shall be the company's policy to comply with all applicable federal, state and local regulations. Should the company believe that existing laws and regulations are not adequately protective, risks are unacceptable, or if proper regulations are nonexistent, Pennzoil may develop more demanding company environmental, safety, and health standards".
Apple Computer, Inc.	***Environmental Health and Safety Policy:*** "Adopt our own corporate standards for protection of human health and the environment in those areas where Apple believes that current laws and regulations either don't exist or are inadequate"
Boise Cascade Corporation	***Environmental Policy:*** "Adopt our own environmentally sound operating practices in areas where laws and regulations are inadequate or nonexistent".
Bayer AG	***Policy Guidelines for Environmental Protection:*** "Not only does Bayer comply with the legal and official requirements relating to environmental protection, but it also takes additional measures on its own initiative and out of its own sense of responsibility".

Source: UNCTC "Benchmark corporate environmental survey 1990-91" (New York, UNCTC, 1991), mimeo.

* * * * *

Self-regulation offers a number of benefits to industry and the regulatory authorities. As some of the examples show, corporations can pursue more stringent standards than those legislated by the State. At the same time, self-regulatory instruments can often be phrased in relatively general terms, can be self-serving, and compliance with them by all firms can typically not be enforced. Thus, voluntary initiatives cannot be expected to replace regulation, nor can they function effectively in a regulatory vacuum. Indeed, 63 per cent of the respondents to the UNCTC benchmark survey indicated that changes in home-country legislation were the main reason for developing their own company-wide environmental policy. Still, self-regulation can be one means through which the sometimes adversarial position between industry and the authorities can become one of cooperation and mutual consultation.

Notes

[1]For a discussion of these issues as far as they relate to transnational corporations, see UNCTC, *New Issues in the Uruguay Round of Multilateral Trade Negotiations,* UNCTC Current Studies, Series A, No. 19 (United Nations publication, Sales No. E.90.II.A.15).

[2]On 20 December 1991, the Draft Final Act embodying the results of the Uruguay Round of Multilateral Trade Negotiations was released by the Director-General of GATT. The draft GATS (which is part of the Draft Final Act) consists of three parts: the articles of the agreement; a set of annexes that cover, among other things, sectoral specificities for financial-, telecommunication- and air-transportation services, the movement of natural persons providing services under the agreement, and exemptions; and a number of decisions and understandings concerning institutional arrangements, certain dispute settlement procedures, environmental concerns in relation to services trade, commitments in the area of financial services and substantive guidelines for the negotiation of initial commitments during the Uruguay Round. They all form an integral part of the draft GATS.

[3]On TNCs and FDI in services, see Karl P. Sauvant and Padma Mallampally, eds., *Transnational Corporations and Services. United Nations Library on Transnational Corporations* (London, Routledge, forthcoming).

[4]See UNCTC and UNCTAD, *The Impact of Trade-related Investment Measures on Trade and Development* (United Nations publication, Sales No. E.91.II.A.19), annex.

[5]The last two types of measures were suggested by developing countries.

[6]UNCTAD, *Trade and Development Report, 1991* (United Nations publication, Sales No. UNCTAD/TDR/11), p. 143.

[7]UNCTC, op. cit., p. 86.

[8]When the Draft Final Act embodying the results of the Uruguay Round of Multilateral Trade Negotiations was released in December 1991, it was done with the understanding that no single element of the Draft Final Act would be considered agreed until the total package was agreed.

[9]UNCTC and UNCTAD, op. cit.

[10]The FIRA-panel case; see UNCTC, op. cit., p. 13.

[11]For a review of the international regulatory framework on FDI, see A. A. Fatouros, ed., *The International Legal Framework for Transnational Corporations. United Nations Library on Transnational Corporations* (London, Routledge, forthcoming).

[12]See also UNCTC, op. cit.

[13]The Declaration contains four instruments: the "Guidelines for Multinational Enterprises" and the Decisions on "National Treatment", "Incentives and Disincentives" and "Conflicting Requirements". Together with the Codes of Liberalisation of Capital Movements and Current Invisible Transactions, they constitute the OECD framework for foreign direct investment. The Codes and Decisions are binding upon States. The Guidelines are a set of recommendations addressed to TNCs.

[14]The Calvo doctrine (which takes its name after the Argentinean jurist who formulated it) has traditionally determined the practice of the Latin American States. It affirms that, under international law, States are required to accord to aliens the same treatment as that accorded to their nationals under their national laws; that disputes by aliens against the host State must be decided exclusively by the courts of that State; and that a foreign affiliate does not have the right to diplomatic protection by its home State.

[15]For a more in-depth analysis of recent bilateral treaties, see UNCTC, "Other international, regional and bilateral arrangements and agreements relating to transnational corporations: report of the Secretary-General" (E/C.10/1991/9, of 25 February 1991). For the most recent list of bilateral investment treaties, see UNCTC and ICC, *Bilateral Investment Treaties 1959-1991* (United Nations publication, Sales No. E.92.II.A.16).

[16]Members of Mercosur are Argentina, Brazil, Paraguay and Uruguay.

[17]*International Trade Newsletter*, vol. 6, No. 3 (September 1991), pp. 1-2.

[18]See *International Trade Newsletter*, op. cit., pp. 1-20.

[19]United States, Department of Justice, *Press Release*, 23 September 1991, annex.

[20]For a review of domestic regulatory issues relating to TNCs, see S. Rubin and D. Wallace, eds., *Transnational Corporations and National Law. United Nations Library on Transnational Corporations* (London, Routledge, forthcoming).

[21]See OECD, *Foreign Direct Investment: Policies and Trends in the OECD Area* (Paris, OECD, 1992).

[22]The relevant laws are contained in Transnational Corporations and Management Division and ECE, *World Investment Directory: Central and Eastern Europe* (New York, United Nations, 1992).

[23]Edward M. Graham and Michael E. Ebert, "Foreign direct investment and US national security: fixing Exon-Florio", *The World Economy*, vol. 14, No. 3 (September 1991), p. 267.

[24]For a review of the issues involved, see B. Balassa, "Public enterprises in developing countries: issues of privatization" (Washington, D.C., The World Bank, 1989), mimeo; and N. Van de Walle, "Privatization in developing countries: a review of the issues", *World Development*, vol. 17, No. 5 (1989), pp. 601-615.

[25]The figures exclude the ongoing extensive privatizations in the former German Democratic Republic. Caution should be exercised regarding those figures, as they are preliminary data from an ongoing research project at the Division. In particular, the definition of privatization influences estimates on the number of privatizations. However, the increase in the number of privatizations from 1985 to 1990 is clear. The definition used here is that any case of equity sold off from a majority-owned state enterprise represents a case of privatization. According to the German Treuhandanstalt, in charge of the privatization programme in the former German Democratic Republic, more than 5,500 firms (of a target of more than 10,000 firms), valued at about $70 billion, have been sold to private investors, as of 31 January 1992. Of those privatizations, FDI accounts for around 12 per cent. See *Deutschland Nachrichten*, 6 March 1992, p. 4.

[26]Caution should be exercised in interpreting this figure, since no information on source, definition of a privatization or period studied was disclosed. See John B. Goodman and Gary W. Loveman, "Does privatization serve the public interest?", *Harvard Business Review*, vol. 69, No. 6 (November-December 1991), p. 26.

[27]Matthew Montagu-Pollack, "Privatization: what went wrong", *Asian Business*, vol. 26, No. 8 (August 1990) pp. 32-39. For an extensive review of the role of FDI in the privatization process, see Maurice Odle, "Privatization in developing countries: the foreign direct investment dimension." Paper submitted to the Conference on Management of Privatization Process, Islamabad, Pakistan, 2-6 March 1992, mimeo.

[28]David Fairlamb, "The privatizing of Eastern Europe", *Institutional Investor*, vol. 24, No. 4 (April 1990), p. 173.

[29]See, for example, Jan Vañous, "Privatization in Eastern Europe: possibilities, problems, and the role of Western capital", *PlanEcon Report*, vol. V, No. 38-39 (1989), pp. 1-32.

[30]Transnational Corporations and Management Division, *Debt-Equity Swaps and Development* (ST/CTC/126, forthcoming). For a discussion of the role of debt-equity swaps in the privatization process, see also Antoine Basile "The role of debt-equity conversions in privatization and deregulation processes", in Dennis J. Gayle and Jonathan N. Goodrich, eds., *Privatization and Deregulation in Global Perspective* (Westport, Connecticut, Quorum Books, 1990), pp. 139-155.

[31]Matt Moffett, "Rewiring a nation: Teléfonos de Mexico makes promising start on a daunting task", *The Wall Street Journal*, 19 February 1992; Odle, op. cit., p. 36.

[32]Richard Molz, "Privatization in developing countries", *Columbia Journal of World Business*, vol. 25, No. 1-2 (Spring/Summer 1990), p. 18.

[33]For a discussion of the history of voluntary guidelines by industry see John M. Kline, *International Codes and Multinational Business* (Westport, Connecticut, Quorum Books, 1985).

[34]For a discussion, see ibid., pp. 89-97; Charles S. Pearson, *Down to Business*, World Resources Institute, Study 2 (January 1985), pp. 69-71; "The greening of corporate America", *Business Week* (23 April 1990), pp. 96-103.

[35]International Chamber of Commerce, *Environmental Guidelines for World Industry* (Paris, ICC, 1974), revised in 1981, 1986 and 1990.

[36]International Chamber of Commerce, *The Business Charter for Sustainable Development* (Paris, ICC, 1991).

[37]For a discussion of sectoral and national industry environmental guidelines (such as those of the Chemical Manufacturers Association and the Conseil Européen des Federations de l'Industrie Chimique), see Business and Industry Advisory Committee to the OECD, "Voluntary agreements and initiatives in environmental policy", first draft, 9 October 1991, mimeo.

[38]Keidanren, *Keidanren Global Environmental Charter* (Tokyo, 1991).

[39]For example, E.I. Du Pont de Nemours and Company, which accounts for 25 per cent of the world production of chlorofluorocarbons (CFCs), announced after the adoption of the Montréal Protocol that it would support a complete phase-out of CFCs before either the United States or the European Community announced a similar intention.

[40]Kubota Corporation, for example, has a policy to reduce the usage of electricity and oil by 20 per cent by March 1994. Toyota has plans to reduce by 10 per cent the electricity use by 1995 and to stabilize the level of carbon dioxide through afforestation. Texas Instruments Japan has as a corporate goal the abolition of the use of CFCs by the end of 1993. See UNCTC, "Benchmark corporate environmental survey" (New York, UNCTC, 1991), mimeo.

[41]For example, the Bank of America pledged to "...make a special effort to identify businesses and organizations that are attempting to find solutions to environmental problems and provide appropriate support"; see Bank of America, "Environmental principles", *Bank American* (San Francisco, California, January 1991), p. 1.

[42]Apple Computer, Inc., for example, intended to "...strive to anticipate future environmental, health, and safety risks and regulatory requirements, and have a proactive approach to dealing with them whenever appropriate..."; see Apple Computer, Inc., *Policy on Environmental Health and Safety* (Cupertino, California, 14 March 1990); Gechem/Recticel stated that: "It is our decision that safety and environment concern should become a second nature for all of us... The Recticel Management ensures that all plants shall ... use no raw materials upon which a reasonable doubt lies as to their toxicity or environmental implication... use as little as possible of the natural resources... exhibit a pro-active policy towards new environmental issues"; see Gechem/Recticel, *Management Declaration on Environment and Safety* (Brussels, 1990).

[43]Polaroid, after having been named a major polluter of the Boston harbour by an environmental group in 1987 (even though the company was well within existing dumping regulations), announced plans to slash the amount of toxic chemicals the company used, as well as the amount of overall waste generated by 50 per cent within five years; see Sana Siwolop and Amy Barrett, "Business and the environment", *Financial World*, 23 January 1990, p. 42; in 1975, when legislation in the United States, such as the Clean Air Act, was first being drafted, 3M launched a formal, in-house pollution reduction programme, the first of its type for United States industry at that time. Since 1975, 3M's "Pollution prevention pays" programme has come to embrace 900 projects and has cut air pollution emissions by 120,000 tons. This programme has earned the company top ranking from a social investment fund and has saved the company $450 million. See Arthur Zich, "Keeping tabs on risky business", *Tomorrow*, vol. 1, No. 2 (1991), p. 26; in addition, 3M plans to spend $150 million over three years to control air pollution at some of its United States and overseas plants. More recently, it has started unveiling products that it considers environmentally helpful, including a foam landfill cover that takes up far less dump space than dirt. See Jackey Gold, "The pioneers", *Financial World*, vol. 159, No. 2 (23 January 1990), p. 57.

PART TWO

TRANSNATIONAL CORPORATIONS AND GROWTH IN DEVELOPING COUNTRIES

Chapter IV

TRANSNATIONAL CORPORATIONS AND ECONOMIC GROWTH: A FRAMEWORK FOR ANALYSIS

A. The increasing importance of transnational corporations

By most measures, transnational corporations (TNCs) play a larger role in the world economy today than they have in the past. As examined in chapters I and II, flows and stocks of FDI are larger in absolute terms and in relation to key economic indicators, such as GDP, exports and domestic capital formation, than they have been in the past for the world economy as a whole and for most host countries, both developed and developing. In addition, world-wide foreign sales of TNCs are larger than exports as a means of delivering goods and services to markets.

Those quantitative measures of TNC activities are indicators of both the growing economic importance of TNCs and their potential for shaping world development. There is also a qualitative dimension to the expansion of TNCs, which integrate within themselves the principal modes of international economic activity, namely, investment, trade in goods and services, technology transfer and financial flows. Thus, their activities can be a force for increasing the efficiency of resource allocation on a wide scale and a channel for transmitting a variety of economic impulses, such as production technology and labour skills. At the same time, the channels that transmit growth-inducing factors can also transmit growth-inhibiting factors. For example, TNCs can act monopolistically within host economies, and production techniques introduced by TNCs can have negative environmental impacts.

In both regards, the importance of TNCs extends beyond the presence of FDI in a host economy and involves a variety of means by which TNCs undertake international production, including through both equity and non-equity arrangements. [1]

The increasing importance of TNCs in the world economy is not only an outcome of the recent growth of FDI. In addition, changing perceptions concerning TNCs—particularly among developing countries, but also among many developed ones—ensure that their impact is more significant, regardless of cyclical swings in the amounts of FDI. Because of those changing perceptions, a fundamental shift in policy-making has occurred in that area. The principal aim is no longer to control and contain the activities of TNCs, but rather to encourage FDI (including its entry into industries previously closed to private, let alone foreign, ownership) in order to reap its benefits.

Several concurrent factors that operate in an interrelated manner on the international, regional and national levels, are behind the shift in attitudes *vis-à-vis* TNCs. On the international level, new and changing technologies, the global expansion of key industries and the ascendancy of the services sector are changing the nature of production and the ways in which developing countries participate in the international division of labour. On the regional level, emerging trends point to a concentration of world economic activity in three main regions, Asia, North America and Western Europe, with growth and integration in those regions driven by the Triad members, Japan, the United States and the European Community, respectively. [2] On the national level, recent years have witnessed the opening up of most of the world to private enterprise and some form of a market system, such that there are now few countries and industries into which international capital may not go. Those factors, which are examined in the following section, are defining the shape of the new world economy in the 1990s and establish a context for development that differs markedly from that of previous decades. Transnational corporations are playing a central role in those changes. An understanding of their contribution to economic growth and development, therefore, needs to take into account not only the quantitative impact of TNCs, but also their importance in shaping the emerging international economic system.

B. The new world economy

1. The increasing importance of market forces

The emergence of a new world economy means that the context in which developing countries grow is changing rapidly. One of the most salient features of the changing context is an expanded role for the private sector, including its role in many service industries which, traditionally, have been reserved in most countries for public ownership (for example, telecommunications, utilities and transportation). One illustration of this trend is that, over the period 1986-1988, private investment has increased its share of gross domestic product in a number of developing countries from 10 per cent to 12 per cent, while the share of public-sector investment declined slightly from 8 to 7.5 per cent. [3] In conjunction with the trend towards an expanded private sector, countries that had formerly adopted inward-looking development strategies are, for a variety of reasons, adopting policies to shift to an outward orientation, by liberalizing trade, FDI and exchange control regimes, and by placing greater emphasis, generally, on a more intensive participation in the global economic system. For example, 63 developing countries have liberalized their trade-policy regimes since the beginning of the Uruguay Round, and some 30 developing and Central and Eastern European countries liberalized their FDI regimes in 1991 alone. [4] In part, that shift has been encouraged by the example of high growth rates in several Asian developing countries, which have become models of successful outward-oriented development in which market forces and the extensive participation in the international economy play a crucial role (even while, in many cases, state policies remain interventionist). Another factor is the debt crisis of the 1980s, which substantially narrowed the margin for state-led development strategies and led to structural adjustment programmes in many countries which, in turn, encouraged a greater role for the private sector and the adoption of outward-oriented non debt-creating policies.

The shift towards greater reliance on market forces has been most dramatic in Central and Eastern Europe, where the centrally planned economic system literally collapsed. But it has also been quite marked in Latin America, more recently in Africa and, to a certain extent, in China as well. Transnational corporations are increasingly important in implementing those changes, a role which is reinforced by a continuing low in commercial bank lending. In Latin America, for instance, there have been widespread efforts to privatize large segments of the economy that were previously state-owned, and TNCs are playing an important role in this process. Overall, some 50 developing countries and all Central and Eastern European countries have active privatization efforts.

Liberalization, privatization and fiscal reform are all expressions of the fundamental shift in policy orientations in many parts of the world. Increased competition between firms and between regions (and heightened concerns about unfair competition), focused especially on the Triad, has been one of the consequences. That development has put TNCs, as the leading international market actors, into the centre of economic development, in a world in which now virtually all countries are seeking to integrate themselves into the world economy.

2. Technology and the shrinking of economic space

While those changes are redefining the ideological and regulatory context of development, changes in the nature and uses of technology are redefining the ways in which countries develop. Since the 1970s, economic growth has been increasingly associated with new technologies rather than with the use of natural resources, such as energy and minerals. The change reflects the fact that production itself has become less materials-intensive and more skill-, knowledge- and technology-intensive. Furthermore, new communication technologies are rapidly shrinking the economic distance between countries, and may be viewed as "the electronic highways of the informational age, equivalent to the role played by railway systems in the process of industrialization". [5] New communication technologies are allowing for a far greater degree of economic internationalization than was previously possible. In that regard, it is interesting to note that the volume of international communications mirrors broadly international economic relations and, indeed, current trends in FDI: the highest volume of international telephone calls is between the United States and Canada, the United States and the United Kingdom and the United States and Mexico, while the greatest growth in international telephone traffic is in the Pacific Rim, fuelled by 23 per cent annual growth in outward calls from Japan, versus 18 per cent from the United States. [6] With the current installed capacity of fibre-optic and satellite-communications networks, international calling volumes are doubling every three to five years, while prices of such calls are falling by about 10 per cent a year. [7]

In recent years, the technological capacity to process and send information has proceeded far more rapidly than the ability to adapt organizationally to the new possibilities that such technology presents. For example, the processing power of an integrated circuit has doubled every 18 months, and the transmission capacity of lightwave systems (based on fibre optics) has increased even more rapidly, doubling every year. [8] By the late 1990s, it may be possible to combine the computing of data with photonics, such that computers will be powered by light waves, leading to a new generation of computers that would be far more powerful than that of today. [9]

Although the economic effects of such changes are only beginning to be felt, there are signs that new technologies, particularly information technologies, are leading to a fundamental change in the way in which goods are being produced and services are delivered (and, in fact, *what* goods and services are being produced and delivered), and the organization of production, both within and between countries. [10] In fact, as discussed in chapter X, elements of a new global production system are emerging. Again, TNCs are at the centre of the developments, as far as the generation, application and transfer of the new technologies are concerned.

The relationship between TNCs and technological change is a dual one: TNCs are key actors in the development of technology, yet, at the same time, they are greatly influenced by it. In fact, technological developments are a major factor behind the growing importance of TNCs and their increasingly global strategies, which are often motivated by the need to gain control over the development and use of new technologies. Such strategies imply that a rising share of technology flows world-wide are being generated by TNCs, and that the firms are increasingly important vehicles for the transfer of technology to host countries. That trend, combined with the ever-increasing pace of technological developments along with the rising costs associated with such developments, implies that the scope for countries—both developing and developed—to create a purely indigenous technological base may narrow. Instead, countries may need to rely more on inward and outward FDI in order to gain access to technologies that are critical to their competitiveness. The need is underscored by the fact that licensing may no longer be as effective as in the past for acquiring many technologies, not only because obsolescence occurs more quickly than in the past, but also because effective use requires more training, both initial and ongoing, of human resources. To the extent that TNCs do not transfer technology to indigenous firms, the trend may increase the vulnerability of countries to the loss of technological competence, if such competence is gained only through the presence of large firms over which countries have limited control and which may shift their activities elsewhere. Thus, while technological developments are offering new opportunities for developing countries with adequate infrastructure and human resources to absorb them, the mechanisms through which such technologies are transmitted are converging on TNCs.

The question of access to technology via TNCs is further complicated by the new organizational structures that are emerging in the international economy, built by firms seeking to access and obtain the maximum benefit from new technological developments. Increasingly, inter-firm networks are employed by competing firms in an industry, whereby firms in a network share the information as well as the costs associated with innovation. Strategic alliances, joint ventures and research consortia are all expressions of such inter-firm networks. During the 1980s, strategic partnering accelerated greatly in such high-technology industries as bio-technology, information technology and new materials.[11] A number of changes in the nature of competition in high-technology industries—such as the shortening of product life cycles and the increasing complexity and intersectoral nature of new technologies—are behind the acceleration of inter-firm networks in the 1980s, as advances in information and communication technologies (that are shrinking economic distance) make such networks more feasible. From the perspective of firms, key motivations for joining alliances include the need to reduce uncertainty regarding which technology will emerge as the future industry standard, the desire to share complementary strengths in R&D and pool the costs associated with such activity and the aim to diversify into new lines of business and/or enter new markets. Such multi-firm networks lower the costs of accessing and utilizing new technology for member firms, while the costs for non-members may be raised considerably.

In addition to technology-sharing networks, powerful transnational computer-communication networks owned by single firms or groups of firms are becoming more important, with some TNCs setting up central data-processing centres for an entire continent, with high-speed links connecting them to national offices.[12] In some industries (for example, banking, insurance, hotels, airlines), such electronic networks are becoming the basis for international transactions, and access to them is, therefore, a crucial matter.

While it is difficult to measure the extent of those phenomena, all evidence indicates that both technology-pooling organizational networks and electronic-data networks are located almost exclusively in the Triad. Indeed, over the decade of the 1980s some 95 per cent of all strategic technology alliances were between firms from developed countries. Furthermore, those alliances that did include developing-country partners (most of which were from newly industrializing economies) did not focus as strongly on "core technologies" (including information technologies) as did alliances between firms from developed countries. Overall, 50 per cent of strategic technology alliances among developed-country firms had a strong R&D orientation, versus only 13 per cent of alliances involving firms from developing countries.[13] Given the importance of technology in growth, access to both inter- and intra-firm networks, and the benefits resulting from them, is an issue likely to receive more attention in the years ahead.

3. The globalization of industries and firms

Partly because of greater competition associated with the expanded role for the private sector, and partly because of the impact of new technologies, many firms, markets and entire industries have become global in nature in that value-adding activities occur in numerous countries, both developed and developing, and both within and across regions. In many cases, deregulation and macro-economic shifts have facilitated the trend towards globalization. While finance is an example of a globalized market, the automobile and consumer-electronics industries are examples of globalized industries, in which TNCs integrate, coordinate and control cross-border value-adding activities. One of the possible implications of globalization is that the nation-state is diminishing in importance as the key arena for economic activity.

The globalization of industry means that, to a large extent, the way in which countries grow and develop comparative advantage is changing considerably. As a result of globalization, countries may become specialized locations for one segment of an industry (engines in automobiles, semiconductors in electronics, data entry in insurance, for example) and may become significant players in that industry in the process. In some cases, countries in a given region develop a comparative advantage in an industry concurrently, with growing intraregional, intra-industry trade as a result. Sources of comparative advantage—capital, know-how, experience and technology, for example—are thus transferred across borders in greater quantities, as more and more countries participate jointly in various stages of the value-adding process of an industry. In other words, globalization means that the boundaries that define an industry are increasingly being drawn across countries rather than within them. The implication of the trend is that, in many instances, strategies to develop independent indigenous industries may no longer be appropriate for developing a dynamic comparative advantage, and that the participation in global industries may be a necessary ingredient for the development of a competitive economy.

The intra-industry, cross-border flows of goods, services and technology that characterize a global industry are, to a large extent, channelled by TNCs. Indeed, they are the driving force behind the globalization of industries, although there is a distinction between global industries and global firms. Such firms control a growing share not only of world investment and output, but also of world trade and technology flows. Among other things, the existence of global firms means that competition in certain industries is occurring less between countries than between firms that compete simultaneously in a number of countries. It may now be possible to describe some corporations as stateless, in the sense that their management, organizational structure and value-adding activities are no longer governed by any single country.

Given those developments, the globalization strategies of TNCs are likely to change the ways in which FDI affects the growth of host developing countries. Until recently, most FDI in developing countries could be characterized as being either resource-seeking, market-seeking (particularly if policies favoured protected local industry) or export-oriented, mainly to take advantage of cheap abundant labour. In each of those cases, the contribution of FDI to economic growth was limited by the comparative advantage of the host country in that particular activity; if wages rose, for instance, investments with low fixed costs might be shifted to lower-cost export platforms. Globalization strategies, however, are blurring the boundaries among those types of investment, particularly the last two: investments in developing countries by TNCs are increasingly both market-seeking and export-oriented. Furthermore, cheap labour is frequently not the primary consideration of global corporations that operate in high-technology industries; consequently, rising wages may alter, but do not necessarily lessen, the locational advantages of host countries. A number of developing countries that began with the primary advantage of cheap labour have succeeded in upgrading the technological competence of their work force, with the result that they continue to attract TNCs even after their relative wage advantage has deteriorated. In other words, the globalization of manufacturing firms, in which value-adding activities are dispersed geographically and integrated within a single firm, is leading to a situation in which FDI may become a driver of dynamic comparative advantage, as TNCs upgrade their overseas affiliates from simple assembly-type operations to high-quality, high value-added manufacturing sites that are integrated into a network of overseas affiliates. Foreign direct investment in manufacturing, then, may become an integral part of the growth process for countries included in the globalization strategies of TNCs.

Those strategies and their impacts may not apply to the same extent to TNCs operating in services industries. As most services cannot be traded, TNCs cannot rationalize their operations across countries to the same extent as in manufacturing. In most cases, TNCs in services have to establish affiliates that largely reproduce in host economies the factor proportions used at home. Intra-firm trade in services is typically lower than in manufacturing, while a given amount of FDI in services will represent a greater transfer of soft technology and skills than in manufacturing. However, as tradability in services increases, TNC activities in that sector are likely to become increasingly similar to TNC activities in manufacturing. The developments observed in goods markets, described above, are beginning to emerge in services.

4. The emerging services world economy

The new world economy is increasingly a services economy, and it is beginning to be recognized as such. Services have come to be, in terms of shares of GDP and employment, the largest sector in most economies and the dominant sector in all developed economies. A substantial part of the output (about half in developing countries) of the services sector consists of intermediate or producer services used as inputs in the production of goods and other services. The services intensity of goods is high and growing, as the rising component of value-added in the production of goods and, especially, high-technology goods comes from services activities, regardless of whether they are purchased from outsiders or undertaken in-house. For example, almost 80 per cent of the cost of a computer is attributable to services activities.

The growing importance of services in production has been mirrored in FDI and in the activities of TNCs. Some 50 per cent of the world stock of FDI and 50 to 55 per cent of annual flows are in services. Only 10 per cent of services production is traded internationally, a reflection of the fact that many services are not tradable or their tradability is limited. Technological changes in computers and telecommunications are increasing the tradability of services, although the major beneficiaries to date have been TNCs that use services internally to organize, expand and manage their global operations. As services become more tradable, their role in shaping the new world economy is likely to grow in importance.

5. The regionalization of the world economy and the emergence of the Triad

The regionalization of the world economy is, somewhat paradoxically, a corollary to increasing globalization; it is also re-shaping the context in which developing countries grow. [14] Globalization has not produced a world in which nations interact with others equally, regardless of their location; rather, economic activity, even as it becomes more dispersed, is increasingly being concentrated in three major regions centred on the the Triad members Japan, the United States and the European Community; they represent the core economies in each regions, and act as principal sources of technology, capital and trade for surrounding countries. As shown in chapter I, a noticable trend in recent years has been the clustering of developing countries around each pole of the Triad, in which countries in a region are dominated by investment from a Triad member in that region.

Transnational corporations are playing a much greater role in that phase of regionalization than they have in past periods (as, for example, in early integration efforts in the European Community). Industrial TNCs are implementing regional core-network strategies centred in a Triad member, in the framework of which they establish affiliates in a cluster of countries (both developed and developing) in a region, and integrate their activities through intra-firm merchandise trade. [15] The networks are often supplemented by increased FDI in services from the same home country, as services TNCs follow their industrial clients abroad. Such networks are an outcome of, as well as a factor behind, the increasing regionalization of the world economy and the clustering effect described above. Current trends in national policies, technology and international competition are likely to facilitate the continued growth of regional core networks.

One feature of the new world economy is thus a certain degree of convergence of policy regimes within regions; a key issue in this regard is how regional policy regimes will be constructed to reflect the interests of both home and host countries. Furthermore, the creation of regional policies that may discriminate against outsiders could, in the future, contradict the trend towards the globalization of those economic activities in which FDI flows are increasing *between* regions. Another issue in this regard is whether regional groupings improve FDI flows to countries that do not belong to them, or serve to divert FDI internally towards the regional group. Developing countries have a particular stake in this question. Regionalization implies that, in the 1990s, selected developing countries are likely to forge their primary economic linkages with the Triad member in their region. Regionalization also implies that developing countries that are not linked to a Triad member through FDI may become increasingly marginalized, and their growth prospects may become correspondingly constrained.

C. Economic growth and its elements

The potential that TNCs possess for contributing to growth and development is being increasingly recognized. Among analysts, FDI is being integrated into theories of economic growth and international expansion, and there is a "gains-from-FDI" approach being developed that parallels in many respects the long-standing "gains-from-trade" paradigm. [16] In policy circles, there has been a clear shift towards greater openness of national economies to inward FDI and the activities of TNCs. The shift has been particularly true in many developing countries, where a marked liberalisation of laws and regulations towards TNCs has been under way for the past decade, with a growing number of countries seeking to attract FDI. [17] The experiences of the newly industrializing economies of South and South-East Asia, which have achieved high rates of growth with substantial involvement of TNCs, have raised awareness of the link between TNCs and economic growth.

That link has assumed increasing importance given the experiences of the 1970s and 1980s. Many developing countries borrowed heavily in international markets in the 1970s, in part in an attempt to stimulate economic growth without having to rely upon foreign-controlled investment. But high debt burdens in the 1980s contributed to retrenchment and slow growth, and many countries suffered severe setbacks to their long-term economic development prospects. Given the growing importance of TNCs in the new world economy, it becomes necessary to evaluate the contribution that TNCs can make to reviving and accelerating economic growth in developing countries.

Economic growth is usually taken to be a sustained increase in the national output of goods and services. Economic growth can be measured using different indices. One widely-used measure is increases in per capita GNP or GDP. Increases in potential production is another measure, which may be greater than actual output to the extent that resources remain underutilized. Measures of sustainable growth are being developed to capture effects of economic activities on the natural environment. Throughout the present Report, the concept of economic growth is used in a general sense, and is best described as increases in a nation's aggregate output over an extended period of time.

Economic growth is a complex process, which is an outcome of the interrelationship between a number of factors, many economic, others political and social. The classical political-economy tradition of the nineteenth century emphasized the importance of expanding the quantity of the basic factors of production: capital, land (including natural resources) and labour. Classical political economy also emphasized the role of expanding markets in improving efficiency and productivity within an economy. The Keynesian revolution of the twentieth century brought to the fore the role of demand and the multiplier effects from increases in investment, government purchases and exports.

More recently, research on aggregate production functions by economists such as Robert Solow and Edward Denison has shown the important contribution of technical change to economic growth, over and above the contribution from expanding quantities of productive factors, and the role that can be played by elements such as improvements in the organization of production and exchange. [18] The growth accounting framework introduced by Solow and Denison, whereby the various elements contributing to growth in an economy are identified and measured, has informed a generation of research on that issue, including the work presented in the present volume.

Even more recently, economists have emphasized the role of qualitative improvements in the labour force of an economy, improvements that come about from better health, more education and greater access to training. Investment in human resource development has become an important component of growth and development strategies for both developed and developing economies. Furthermore, consensus is now emerging that environmental protection is also a necessary component of sustainable economic growth. The relationship between the natural environment and the magnitude and quality of growth is only beginning to be understood; despite the newness, any attempt to describe and analyse economic growth needs to take into account its impact on the environment and its implications for the sustainability of a national growth path. An understanding of what drives the growth process is thus a necessary first step in promoting sustainable economic development.

Economic growth can occur in a variety of ways and be driven by different features of an economy. Growth may be stimulated by investment that augments and improves the productivity of national physical resources. Growth can be driven by innovation and technological change, which not only improve the productivity of existing activities, but also create competitive advantages in new ones. The development of labour skills, or investment in human resources, has grown in importance as a source of economic growth. International trade can promote growth by allowing countries to exploit their existing comparative advantages and develop new ones, encouraging a faster and more efficient utilization of domestic resources and enabling the country to reap the benefits of economies of specialization and participation in the international division of labour.

At different points in the history of a country, one of those elements may be the principal engine of national growth; for example, a growth spurt may initially be primarily factor-based and driven by trade, while later, technology and innovation may become the principal means of economic expansion. In most cases, however, the process is not linear, and countries often exhibit characteristics of several stages within a single economy. Furthermore, the elements underlying growth are interdependent, and advances in one can fuel advances in another. Technological progress, for example, can boost both the productivity of a country as well as its trade performance. Similarly, poor performance in one area may have negative spillover effects on another; for example, inadequate investment in human resources may harm the future ability of a country to grow through innovation and technological progress.

D. A framework for the analysis of transnational corporations and growth

Transnational corporations are often thought of as responding to economic growth as, for a variety of reasons, they are induced to invest in economies with large, growing markets and with a sufficiently high base of technology and labour skills. Foreign direct investment by TNCs, however, may also be thought of as a determinant of growth. The new world economy that is emerging in the 1990s constitutes an environment in which the potential for TNCs to affect economic growth has increased considerably, in light of the expanding role of the TNC as an integrating agent. A new look is needed at how the global activities of TNCs are likely to affect growth and development in the coming years.

The present Report analyses how TNCs affect economic growth in host developing countries. The analysis looks separately at the most important elements that contribute to growth: physical capital formation, technology and human resource development, which are the traditional elements that affect growth through a production framework; trade, which affects growth by expanding markets for both outputs and inputs; and the environment, which has become part of a broader analysis of economic growth. In each case, the Report investigates how TNCs affect growth through that element.

Chapter V analyses at the contribution of TNCs to physical capital formation in host developing countries. Investment is one of the principal engines of economic growth, and FDI may have similar growth effects, to the extent that FDI adds to the quantity of the existing capital stock. Thus, viewed as one type of investment, FDI may directly affect host-country growth. In addition, the activities of TNCs in host economies can affect the pace of domestic investment and can affect, either positively or negatively, the efficiency of domestically-owned capital.

The presence of TNCs in host economies may be more critical than the direct impact of FDI, since these firms create channels through which economic impulses can be transmitted. One of the impulses is technology, which is assuming an increasing role in the new world economy. The contribution of TNCs to economic growth through technology is analysed in chapter VI, where the role of TNCs as generators of technology and their activities as international disseminators of technology are evaluated in terms of their contribution to the technological development of host developing countries.

Chapter VII considers the contribution of TNCs to growth in host developing countries through their effect on the quality of human resources, the development of which covers a variety of specific areas, including health and nutrition, general education and worker training. The importance of TNCs in each of these areas in host developing countries may vary widely, but human resource development as a channel for stimulating growth is growing in importance. Chapter VII assesses the contribution that TNCs make to the process of economic growth via human resource development.

International trade makes a contribution to economic growth that differs from that of capital, technology and human resource development. Trade does not directly add to growth. Instead, wider markets can stimulate demand and improve resource allocation within an economy. International trade has long been thought of as a major integrating element in the world economy, but as the world economy takes on new characteristics, the many contributions of TNCs to global integration, including through trade, assume greater importance. Chapter VIII examines at how TNCs affect growth in developing countries through their effect on international trade.

Broadening the analysis of growth to include sustainable growth raises new issues with respect to the role of TNCs in stimulating economic growth. Chapter IX discusses how TNCs can affect sustainable economic growth in developing countries and how that contribution might be improved over time.

Transnational corporations are likely to have a stronger impact upon growth through some of those elements—and their components—than through others; in some instances the role of TNCs will be small. All are included in the analysis because all are potentially important contributors to growth in developing countries. In addition, the analysis identifies both potentially negative, as well as positive, effects of TNCs on economic growth in host developing countries. Chapter X concludes the analysis by providing an integrated assessment of the overall contribution made by TNCs to economic growth in host developing countries in the context of the new world economy.

Notes

[1]John H. Dunning, "Non-equity forms of foreign economic involvement and the theory of international production", in John H. Dunning, *Explaining International Production* (London, Unwin Hyman, 1988), pp. 169-197.

[2]UNCTC, *World Investment Report 1991: The Triad in Foreign Direct Investment* (United Nations publication, Sales No.E.91.II.A.12).

[3]The figures are from a study of 27 developing countries by the International Finance Corporation, reported in "Developing nations increase reliance on private sector", *Financial Times*, 11 September 1990.

[4]See, respectively, GATT, *Press Release*, 12 March 1992, and chapter III. There are even signs that a more open environment for the movement of skilled labour is emerging. As far as unskilled labour is concerned, however, and in spite of—or because of—mounting migration pressures between developing countries, between North and South and between East and West, the trend appears to be towards tighter restrictions, leading to a noticeable asymmetry in the treatment of international factor flows.

[5]Manuel Castells and Jeffrey Henderson, "Techno-economic restructuring, socio-political processes and spatial transformation: a global perspective", in Jeffrey Henderson and Manuel Castells, eds., *Global Restructuring and Territorial Development* (Beverly Hills, California, Sage Publishers, 1987), pp. 1-17.

[6]International Institute of Communications, "Global telecommunications traffic report, 1991", cited in *Network World*, vol. 8, No. 39 (30 September 1991), pp. 21-22.

[7]*Network World*, op. cit.

[8]Eric E. Sumner, "Telecommunications technology in the 1990s", *Telecommunications*, vol. 25, No. 1 (January 1989), pp. 37-38.

[9]For a discussion of technological developments in computing, see H.L. Capron, *Computers, Tools for an Information Age* (Reading, Massachusetts, Addison Wesley, 1990).

[10]For an elaboration, see Karl P. Sauvant, *International Transactions in Services: The Politics of Transborder Data Flows* (Boulder, Colorado, Westview Press, 1986).

[11]Luc Soete, "National support policies for strategic industries: the international implications", in OECD, *Strategic Industries in a Global Economy: Policy Issues for the 1990s* (Paris, OECD, 1991), pp. 51-80.

[12]Monica Horton, "Private networks: backbone of the worldwide corporate structure", *Financial Times*, 7 October 1991.

[13]For a discussion of the regionalization of the world economy, see Allen J. Morrison and Kendall Roth, "The regional solution: an alternative to globalization", *Transnational Corporations*, vol. 1, No. 2 (forthcoming).

[14]"Core technologies" were found to be involved in 74 per cent of the alliances among firms from developed countries versus only 54 per cent among involving firms from the newly industrialized economies and 23 per cent involving other developing-country firms. See Christopher Freeman and John Hagedoorn, "Globalization of technology" (Maastricht, University of Limburg, MERIT, 1992), mimeo.

[15]See UNCTC, *World Investment Report 1991*, op. cit., pp. 41-53, for an elaboration of regional core networks.

[16]Edward M. Graham and Paul Krugman, *Foreign Direct Investment in the United States* (Washington, D. C., Institute for International Economics, 1991), second edition.

[17]UNCTC, *Government Policies and Foreign Direct Investment*, UNCTC Current Studies Series A, No. 17 (United Nations publication, Sales No. E.91.II.A.20).

[18]Robert M. Solow, "Technical change and the aggregate production function," *Review of Economics and Statistics*, vol. 39, No. 3 (August 1957), pp. 313-320; and Edward F. Denison, *Trends in American Economic Growth, 1929-1982* (Washington, D. C., The Brookings Institution, 1985).

Chapter V

TRANSNATIONAL CORPORATIONS, CAPITAL FORMATION AND ECONOMIC GROWTH

A. Capital formation and economic growth

One of the most widely accepted principles in the analysis of economic growth is that countries should devote substantial efforts to increasing the quantity and improving the quality of their stock of physical capital. An emphasis on the contribution of capital to growth is, of course, not new. It was central to nineteenth century classical political economy. The Harrod-Domar growth model of the 1940s, which provided intellectual stimulation for several generations of thinking on the subject of economic growth, gave central importance to increasing the share of output a country devoted to savings and transformed into physical capital. [1] Empirical work on economic growth has built upon the growth accounting framework introduced by Robert Solow and extended by Edward Denison and others. [2] This empirical literature has increasingly emphasized the importance of technology and human capital, while the stock of physical capital continues to play a large role as a component of growth for both developed and developing countries.

More recently, theories of growth have focused on the interrelationships among the various determinants of growth. For example, technological advance has been linked to capital accumulation, either because advances in technology can make capital more productive and provide an incentive for new investment, or because technology is frequently embodied in new plant and equipment and therefore enters an economy in the form of new capital. [3] The accumulation of capital also represents a force for growth, in part because it can be a conduit for various additional factors that determine growth. Control of capital signifies control over decision-making regarding production. Thus, the various channels that determine growth may be linked to capital accumulation, at least in part because they are all influenced by the decision-making processes of firms.

Research on economic growth in developing countries has also emphasized that, while capital is an important determinant of growth, its importance will vary across countries and over time, according to both economic factors, such as the presence of other determinants of growth, and non-economic factors, such as the political and cultural framework within which the economic elements operate. [4] Thus, both general principles and specific historical and institutional analyses are needed to assess the growth experience and prospects in individual economies.

Transnational corporations are important contributors to world-wide savings and investment. They generate savings through retained earnings and, since TNCs are among the largest firms in their home economies, that contribution is likely to be substantial. In addition, they are themselves investors, utilizing both their internally-generated savings and the savings of others, which they obtain through borrowing and the issue of equity.

The focus in the present chapter is on how TNCs might influence the quantity and quality of physical capital formation in host developing countries, thereby affecting the ability of domestic investment to contribute to economic growth. Capital formation is a complex process involving many interrelationships. The primary concern here is how TNCs influence the savings available to, and the quantity and quality of investment in, host developing economies.

B. Sources of savings for host developing countries

Most savings are generated domestically. Research on savings behaviour in developing countries has tended to focus on the household sector, but savings can also be generated by business firms and from foreign sources, and can be affected by government policies. The primary determinants of household savings patterns are demographic variables, such institutional factors as the effectiveness of the financial system, macroeconomic conditions and policies. [5]

Given the importance of economy-wide variables in determining savings behaviour, there are few ways in which TNCs would have a direct impact upon household savings. To the extent TNCs add to domestic employment, there would probably also be an increase in savings. In addition, the wages and salaries paid by TNCs and the income earned by local suppliers of TNCs undoubtedly alter the distribution of income in favour of savers, although such effects are likely to be limited. As employers, TNCs can encourage savings by, for instance, establishing pension plans, instituting direct deposit into savings accounts and offering payroll deductions for purchasing insurance.

Corporations, both those that are domestically owned and those that are affiliates of foreign firms, can also contribute to savings in host countries through retained earnings. Information from balance-of-payments accounts for Brazil and Mexico, which are among the few developing countries for which data on reinvested earnings of TNCs are available, shows substantial annual fluctuations in the share of FDI inflows accounted for by reinvested earnings. Over a 23-year period (1967-1989), reinvested earnings by TNCs accounted for between 15 and 90 per cent of annual inflows of FDI for those two large developing countries. [6] For the United States, approximately a third, and in 1990 almost a half, of flows of FDI to developing countries took the form of reinvested earnings during the period 1982-1990. [7] Over a longer time period (1967-1989) and looking at all FDI outflows, not only those going to developing countries, reinvested earnings accounted for 43 per cent of outflows for the United Kingdom and 17 per cent for the Federal Republic of Germany. [8]

Developing countries have long sought foreign savings as an important contributor to capital formation; since the onset of the debt crisis, they have placed renewed emphasis on attracting FDI to augment domestic savings, among other reasons, to avoid debt-creating sources of finance. National savings rates in both developed and developing countries have been lower since the middle of the 1970s than they had been in previous years. [9] The importance of TNCs in generating savings and as sources of investment spending in host developing countries appears to have been growing, especially in the second half of the 1980s (see chapter II). Thus, for a number of host developing countries, FDI may be filling an important gap (box V.1).

An analysis of FDI as a source of foreign savings also must deal with repatriated earnings. It has been argued that repatriation represents a deduction from host country savings. [10] That may be possible where TNCs have a high degree of monopoly power within the host economy, and are able to appropriate rents that would otherwise contribute to domestic income and savings. Generally, if TNCs have any positive impacts upon growth, exports or the profits of domestic enterprises, their presence will generate additional income and savings. Repatriated profits, then, will be a deduction from a higher level of savings, which they are partly responsible for generating in the first place. Moreover, some repatriation of earnings may be necessary as an inducement for TNCs to enter, or remain in, a host developing economy.

Governments of host countries affect savings through budgetary policies and via tax and regulatory policies. [11] One reason why national savings rates have generally declined since the 1970s is that, as Governments have incurred larger budget deficits, government savings rates have declined. Transnational corporations can contribute to government revenues directly via tax payments, contractual fees, etc., and indirectly through taxes paid by their employees and suppliers. Direct tax payments by the foreign affiliates of United States-based TNCs to foreign Governments amounted to approximately $100 billion in 1989, or about 10 per cent of their foreign sales. [12] The contribution of TNCs to host-country tax revenues will tend to vary across countries, depending upon host country tax rates, enforcement policies and the proportion of international production that is subject to taxation. In addition, TNCs can practise various forms of tax avoidance, as well as require government subsidies or government outlays. [13] For the foreign affiliates of United States-based TNCs, tax payments contributed more than 5 per cent to revenues of Governments of a number of host countries in 1989, although the proportion is smaller for most countries (table V.1). If data for TNCs from other home countries were available, the contribution to revenues of Governments of host countries would be considerably higher.

Box V.1. The contribution of foreign savings to domestic savings

Recent research has suggested that foreign savings may not have been an important source of savings for both developed and developing countries over the past few decades, and that domestic capital formation is largely limited by domestic sources of savings. That conclusion is based upon the finding of high correlations between domestic investment and domestic savings, expressed as shares of gross domestic product, for a large cross-section of countries. In the original research, only OECD countries were studied, but follow-up work has included developing countries with similar results. The conclusion from this work is that countries attract relatively little foreign capital to augment domestic savings, and that international capital mobility is not high. Since those conclusions challenge much conventional wisdom regarding capital mobility, international financial integration and the importance of foreign capital for developing countries in particular, they have been subject to extensive debate.

High correlations between domestic savings and investment, however, do not mean that developing countries are limited to themselves with respect to raising capital. The studies show that the correlations between domestic savings and domestic investment have declined over time, from the 1960s through the mid-1980s, suggesting that foreign savings are growing in importance. Moreover, several studies found lower correlations for developing countries than for developed countries, suggesting that foreign savings may be more important for financing investment in the former than in the latter. In addition, the importance of foreign savings in financing domestic investment also appears to be larger under flexible exchange rate regimes, and to be sensitive to government policies with respect to current account imbalances.

Net foreign savings is the sum of long-term capital inflows into host countries (including FDI) less corresponding outflows. Net foreign savings can be small even when the size of inflows is large relative to domestic savings. There are examples of developing countries that rely heavily on foreign sources of savings, while simultaneously exporting capital. Foreign savings, including FDI, have made significant contributions to domestic savings in a number of instances, such as in the United States in the late nineteenth century. Rather than focusing attention on net inflows, it may be more important to look at how various components of inflows can be affected by changes in incentives. The contribution of FDI to domestic savings will vary across countries, and will not necessarily be identical with the contribution of capital flows as a whole. For example, since greenfield FDI can add to domestic savings and investment simultaneously, its impact can be more direct and larger than alternative forms of external savings.

Sources: Martin Feldstein and Charles Horioka, "Domestic savings and international capital flows", *Economic Journal*, vol. 90 (June 1980), pp. 314-329; Martin Feldstein and Phillipe Bacchetta, "National savings and international investment", National Bureau of Economic Research Working Paper No. 3164 (Cambridge, Massachusetts, National Bureau of Economic Research, November 1989); Norman S. Fieleke, "National savings and international investment", in *Savings and Government Policy*, Conference Series No. 25 (Boston, Massachusetts, Federal Reserve Bank of Boston, 1982), pp. 138-157; Stanley W. Black, "Discussion", op. cit., pp. 158-161; Michael Dooley, Jeffrey Frankel and Donald Mathieson, "International capital mobility: what do savings-investment correlations tell us?" *International Monetary Fund Staff Papers*, vol. 34, No. 3 (September 1987), pp. 503-530; Tamin Bayoumi, "Why are saving and investment rates correlated across countries?", *Finance and Development*, vol. 27, No. 2 (June 1990), pp. 18-19; Linda Tesar, "Saving, investment and international capital flows", *Journal of International Economics*, vol. 31, Nos. 1/2 (August 1991), pp. 55-78; Mira Wilkins, *The History of Foreign Investment in the United States to 1914* (Cambridge, Massachusetts, Harvard University Press, 1989).

Increased tax revenues from TNCs can help Governments raise funds, reduce borrowing requirements and make more savings available for both private and public investment. However, taxes can also be a disincentive to international production within a host country to the extent that their size and incidence cause potential foreign investors to locate elsewhere. Taxes can create incentives for investors to shift resources among sectors and industries, which can be beneficial to the extent activities with high social costs are made more costly for private decision makers, but can also lead to inefficiencies in resource allocation to the extent investors "chase" tax benefits. Thus, while there might be scope for expanding the revenue raised from TNCs for the financing of public investment, there are also limits to how far that can go. Moreover, the evaluation of the impact of government policies on savings may also depend upon how the government revenue is used. For example, tax revenue that is used for infrastructure might be classified as savings, while the same revenue used to pay administrative costs might be considered as consumption.

Even where foreign savings represent a sizeable share of domestic savings, there is the possibility that this could occur at the expense of domestic savings. A number of studies have indicated that increases in foreign savings are accompanied by declines in domestic savings in developing countries. Recent econometric work, using multivariate, multiple-equation models, has found that the regression coefficient of foreign savings on domestic savings is negative, but between zero and one. This implies that foreign savings represent a net addition to national savings in host developing countries.[14]

Not all of the components of foreign savings, including FDI, need behave in the same manner as foreign savings as a

Table V.1. Tax payments by foreign affiliates of United States transnational corporations, as a percentage of total government revenue of the host country, 1989

(Millions of dollars)

Country	*Tax payment*	*Government revenues*	*Percentage*	*United States FDI as share of total inward stock of FDI*
Chile	192	8 500	2.3	49[a]
China	16	62 428	-	16[b]
Ecuador	18	1 288	1.4	54[b]
Egypt	6	20 547	-	
Guatemala	78	504	15.5	22[c]
India	98	39 671	0.2	21
Indonesia	866	16 190	5.3	6[a]
Korea, Republic of	138	38 202	0.4	28[a]
Malaysia	619	9 141	6.8	6[b]
Mexico	1 266	27 448	4.6	64
Peru	174	1 425	12.2	29
Philippines	362	6 716	5.4	56
Thailand	910	12 321	7.4	24[b]
Trinidad and Tobago	151	1 168	12.9	
Total	4 894	245 549	2.0	

Sources: United States, Department of Commerce, *U.S. Direct Investment Abroad: 1989 Benchmark Survey* (Washington, D.C., United States Government Printing Office, 1991); International Monetary Fund, *International Financial Statistics Yearbook, 1991* (Washington, D.C., International Monetary Fund, 1992).

a 1988.
b 1987.
c 1985.

whole. One econometric study that separated FDI from foreign savings in general yielded contradictory results, with the stock of FDI having a negative relation to economic growth in developing countries, while the flow of FDI had a positive relation. [15] Other studies have looked at all private capital inflows, FDI plus debt, and found generally positive impacts upon growth. [16]

C. Transnational corporations and financial intermediation

The contribution of financial intermediation to capital formation and economic growth in developing countries has been the subject of an extensive theoretical and empirical literature. [17] Transnational corporations are themselves intermediaries in that they mobilize savings from their home countries or international markets (for example, retained earnings, new equity, bank loans, bond flotations), which are then invested in host countries. To the extent that TNCs are simultaneously savers and investors within host economies, they reduce the potential for crowding out.

Not all FDI leads to increases in the host country capital stock. Some foreign capital enters a host country in search of a financial advantage, such as favourable tax treatment. While the phenomenon of tax-haven investment is well known, adjusting for it in data on FDI is difficult. Some foreign affiliates utilize capital from their parent corporations to reinvest in a third country, as when foreign affiliates in Hong Kong invest in China. In addition, there is a need to distinguish between greenfield investment, which increases both savings and investment in a host country; mergers and acquisitions by TNCs, which do not directly increase investment; investment by TNCs financed within the host economy, which may increase investment, but competes for domestic savings; and FDI financed within the home economy or on world markets, which can increase both savings and investment for the host economy. Several of those issues will be discussed below in section D; all are plagued by severe measurement problems.

Since transnational banks (TNBs) are themselves TNCs, the role of those firms as intermediaries is broadened. In general, financial intermediation (or "financial deepening") in a host economy can contribute to development, and specifically to greater efficiency in mobilizing savings, so long as it does not lead to excessive speculation or become an instrument of rapid inflation. The issue here is whether TNBs contribute to the intermediation function by, for example, extending banking services, establishing or strengthening markets for securities or foreign exchange, or widening the menu and/or reducing the risks of financial assets.

Studies of financial services in host developing countries have found that, because TNBs have frequently faced restrictions on their activities, their presence in developing countries has been rather small. In a sample of 21 developing countries, the median share of banking assets accounted for by TNBs was 6 per cent. [18] Transnational banks operating in host developing countries have tended to specialize in serving other TNCs and large domestic clients, in part because the international expansion of banks was initially fuelled by the international expansion of FDI. Even when restrictions on their activities have been reduced, TNBs have tended not to compete with domestic financial institutions. [19] Thus, while TNBs may play a substantial role in mobilizing savings internationally, they typically appear to have assumed little or no role in the domestic intermediation process. It is certainly possible, however, that a further removal of restrictions on their activities within host economies may increase the incentives for TNBs to extend their role.

Financial intermediation also occurs through financial markets. Recent examples of financial liberalizations in developing countries appear to have enhanced capital inflows. A number of developing countries have established domestic markets for equity and debt instruments, or have opened previously existing markets to foreign participation. In larger developing economies with broadly-based private sector firms, such as Mexico and the Republic of Korea, those markets have attracted significant amounts of foreign capital as they provide a mechanism for trading shares and a means for valuing company assets. In many countries—the United States is a prime example among developed economies—markets for capital are also markets for corporate control, as effective control over firm decision-making can be acquired through market purchases of equity. In other countries, such as Japan, the legal and institutional structure places control in the cross-holdings of equities among firms and in financial institutions, not equity markets. To the extent that the establishment of, and the granting of access by foreign investors to, markets in corporate securities in developing countries also establishes a market for corporate control, those markets can become a means for converting portfolio capital inflow into direct investment, as potential foreign investors accumulate equity.[20]

The activities of TNCs, both in terms of FDI and non-equity arrangements, can stimulate additional flows of financial resources. Transnational banks frequently lend more easily to projects with some involvement of transnational corporations,[21] and donor-country policies towards bilateral official development assistance has, in some instances, favoured host countries with a significant presence of TNCs from the donor country.[22]

D. The contribution of foreign direct investment to host country investment

1. Aggregate data

Foreign direct investment, as a measure of the inflow of foreign-owned physical capital, can represent a contribution to host country investment and to host country capital stock. Available evidence, summarized in chapter II, indicates that FDI represents a modest addition to domestic capital in most host developing countries. For the 89 countries for which data are available for the period 1986-1989, only in 35 (39 per cent) did FDI account for more than 5 per cent of gross domestic capital formation (annex table 6). For the 16 developing countries for which data on capital stock are available for 1988 (or latest available year), the foreign share was greater than 5 per cent in 63 per cent of the cases, or 10 countries (annex table 7). For most developing countries for which data are available, the share of FDI in gross domestic capital formation grew in the late 1980s as compared with the early part of the decade.

In some instances, that growth reflected a continuing stagnation in domestic investment; but for most developing countries, a substantial growth in FDI inflows accounted for the rise in the share.

Data on FDI do not, however, accurately reflect real investment by foreigners. Foreign direct investment includes acquisitions of existing assets by foreign firms within host economies. To the extent that mergers and acquisitions are an important means of entry into host developing countries, the data on FDI inflows would overstate the contribution of foreign firms to host country capital formation, although the data would still be a measure of the extent of foreign ownership within the host economy. Mergers and acquisitions represent the bulk of FDI inflows for host developed economies. For developing countries, the establishment and opening of securities markets to foreigners (discussed in section C above), as well as efforts by Governments to include foreign investors in privatization plans (see chapter III), suggests that mergers and acquisitions may become a more important mode of entry in the future. Until now, however, mergers and acquisitions do not appear to be nearly as important for developing countries as they are for developed countries.

On the other hand, data on FDI inflows usually do not include reinvested profits, which, on the basis of reporting by a few large host developing countries and a few large home developed countries, appear to be an important source of funds for foreign firms in developing countries (see section B above). Reinvested earnings can be expected to be highest in host economies in which there have been substantial foreign investment for some time, as mature foreign affiliates tend to generate a larger stream of profits, and tend to have established patterns of reinvestment, as compared to newer affiliates.

Thus, while hard evidence on the quantitative importance of those two sources of bias in FDI data is not available, and while cross-national differences in the size of mergers and acquisitions and the reporting of reinvested earnings can be important, it does appear that the understatement of new investment is more important than the overstatement.

The contribution of FDI to domestic capital formation may be more important in terms of impacts on growth than the aggregate data suggest. In many host developing countries, FDI is concentrated in a relatively few industries, and those may be among the most important in terms of their contribution to economic growth. As a result, FDI tends to represent a larger share of host economy investment for private fixed investment than for investment as a whole and for investment in the manufacturing and services sectors as compared with economy-wide investment (table V.2). In part, that reflects the importance of government investment and housing investment in total capital formation for many countries.

Those observed differences also may reflect the attraction of rapidly-growing and high value-added sectors for foreign capital, as well as the potential importance of foreign capital in stimulating growth in those sectors. In the Republic of Korea, a high-growth developing economy where FDI represents a low share of domestic investment (1.6 per cent in the period 1986-1988), FDI has been particularly important in electrical machinery and transportation equipment, two of the leading industries in that country's export-led growth performance. By one estimate, foreign firms contributed almost half the new capital in those industries in the period 1984-1986. [23] A separate study of the role of FDI in the Republic of

Korea concluded that the direct contribution to economic growth by TNCs was significantly higher than the share of those firms in domestic investment would have suggested. During the mid-1970s (1975-1978), the share of the growth of value-added accounted for by foreign production ranged from 5 to 14 per cent, while the foreign share of the growth of value-added in manufacturing was 16 to 45 per cent.[24] Adding the indirect contribution, through spillovers and linkages, would raise the foreign contribution above those figures.

In India, a study of 28 manufacturing industries in 1977-1978 found that, in nine industries, including motor vehicles, electrical machinery, metal products, plastics, chemicals and pharmaceuticals, the foreign ownership share was greater than 20 per cent.[25] A second study of TNCs in India found that foreign-owned firms accounted for more than 30 per cent of sales in manufacturing in 1975-1976 and 1980-1981.[26] Foreign direct investment as a share of gross domestic investment has been very small in India, at 0.1 per cent in the period 1976-1980 and only slightly higher—0.2 per cent—in the late 1980s.

In addition to FDI in host developing countries being more important than suggested by aggregate data, TNCs have been engaging in other forms of involvement as they expand their international activities. Foreign direct investment implies control over production through either majority or a substantial minority ownership. Production can also be controlled through non-equity arrangements, such as franchising, licensing, long-term subcontracting and non-equity joint ventures in which TNCs may contribute technology or management in their relationships with host country firms. It is difficult to obtain

Table V.2. The contribution of foreign direct investment to domestic capital formation, selected countries

	Foreign-owned share in					
Economy	*GDCF* [a]	*Private fixed investment*	*Assets* [b]	*Manufacturing investment*	*Assets* [b]	*Services assets* [b]
Hong Kong	19		18	..	..	..
Korea, Republic of	2	..	..	19-31 [c]	..	..
Malaysia	10	5-10 [c]	19 [d]	..	..	..
Mexico	9	..	..	..	76	34
Philippines	9	..	19 [e]	..	32 [e]	21 [e]
Taiwan Province of China	4	4 [f]	..	6 [f]	..	..
Thailand	5	4-10 [g]	16	..	83	43

Sources: Annex tables 6 and 8; Transnational Corporations and Management Division, *World Investment Directory* (New York, United Nations, 1992); Chung H. Lee and Eric Ramstetter, "Direct investment and structural change in Korean manufacturing", and Chi Schive and Jenn-Hwa Tu, "Foreign firms and structural change in Taiwan", both in Eric Ramstetter, ed., *Direct Foreign Investment in Asia's Developing Economies and Structural Change in the Asia-Pacific Region* (Boulder, Colorado, Westview Press, 1991), pp. 112 and 150.

a 1986-1989. b 1986. c 1984-1986. d 1988
e 1987. f 1987-1988. g 1986-1988.

data on non-equity arrangements that are comparable with FDI, but studies indicate that such arrangements have been growing. Their growth does constitute further evidence for the position that FDI data understate the importance of TNCs within host economies.

It is possible that the presence of FDI can have a deleterious affect upon domestic capital formation, to the extent that foreign firms effectively crowd out domestic producers. That could occur if foreign firms take over markets previously occupied by domestic producers, or if foreign firms use their competitive advantages to obtain key resources, such as minerals or relatively scarce skilled labour. A recent series of case studies of Asian developing economies, including Malaysia, Singapore, Taiwan Province of China and Thailand, found little evidence of crowding out. [27] In addition, a simultaneous equation model of Taiwan Province of China, which explicitly tested for a quantitative link between FDI and domestic investment, found a statistically significant positive relationship, suggesting, at a minimum, that FDI and domestic investment respond to similar conditions within the host economy but also implying that the two are complements and not substitutes. [28]

2. Linkage effects

The presence of foreign-controlled production facilities in a host developing country has the potential to provide a variety of additional benefits. Transnational corporations establish linkages with the host economy, for instance, as they purchase goods and services from local producers or hire local firms as subcontractors. They can also generate forward linkages to the extent that they widen access to markets, both domestic and foreign, or provide resources that can be used in further production within the host economy. Linkages established by TNCs are important for technology transfer, development of human resource and foreign trade.

Linkages are created because TNCs provide something to a host economy—demand for an input, supply of an output, a particular skill or resource—that did not exist before. [29] Empirical studies of TNCs in host countries have found that local sourcing by TNCs tends to increase over time, as affiliates become more aware of, and involved with, local producers. [30] For example, in 1988, Japanese affiliates procured more than 40 per cent of their inputs locally in Asia and 30 per cent in Latin America (table V.3). Procurement levels were high for such medium and high R&D-intensive industries as chemicals, general machinery, electric machinery and transport equipment. Comparing the local procurement levels for those industries, it is apparent that they generally are higher for the newly industrializing economies than for other Asian countries, particularly in more technology-intensive industries. This indicates that existing local technological capabilities influence the extent of procurement.

Some case studies show that affiliates of TNCs have made extensive use of supplier linkages in host countries and impart considerable training and technical and financial assistance to their local suppliers. For example, a recent survey of 63 large foreign affiliates operating in Mexico's manufacturing sector found an extensive use of local subcontracting: almost two thirds of the foreign affiliates subcontracted locally. Of those firms, nearly one third subcontracted more than 25 per cent of their total production value. That outcome was the result of a combination of performance requirements, the existence of a capable supplier network and industry-specific corporate strategies. The survey also found that the local subcontracting of inputs in Mexico by affiliates of TNCs to a large extent was motivated by efficiency considerations, which assumed a greater role in the calculus of TNCs as the country shifted from an import-substitution regime to an export-oriented regime of liberalized trade policy. [31]

In Asian developing economies, studies have found that the extent and effectiveness of TNC linkages depended upon local conditions. A case study of FDI in Singapore concluded that foreign firms had successfully stimulated local suppliers to become effective exporters, and had generated a substantial number of spin-offs as employees of TNCs became successful entrepreneurs, and often became suppliers to their former employer. [32] In both the Republic of Korea and Taiwan Province of China, foreign firms have increased the share of their procurement which is met through local purchases, supporting the general proposition that local procurement rises as firms become more established in a foreign location. [33] In addition, while foreign firms in Taiwan Province of China increased their local purchases over time, recent foreign investors tended to start with higher levels of local sourcing than did earlier investors, suggesting that the economy's ability to support local sourcing had improved. [34] In both Singapore and Taiwan Province of China, a synergistic relationship has been observed as the growth of foreign

Table V.3. Local procurement of Japanese affiliates, by region and industry, 1981 and 1988
(Percentage of total procurement)

	Latin America		*Asia*		*Asian newly industrializing economies* [a]
Industry	*1981*	*1988*	*1981*	*1988*	*1988*
All industries	28	30	27	44	43
Manufacturing	48	51	52	47	50
Food	93	100	93	87	78
Textiles	88	94	61	49	55
Wood and pulp	100	99	61	82	35
Chemicals	69	94	57	60	69
Iron and steel	66	67	29	29	29
Non-ferrous metals	31	100	73	69	83
General machinery	20	63	47	44	46
Electric machinery	27	50	45	44	46
Transport equipment	45	33	54	48	61

Source: Japan, Ministry of International Trade and Industry, *Wagakuni Kigyo no Kaigai Jigyo Katsudo,* No. 12-13 (Tokyo, Toyo Hoki Shuppan, September 1984), p. 96, and No. 18-19 (Tokyo, Okura-sho Insatsu-Kyoku, March 1990), pp. 86-87 and 94-95.

a Hong Kong, Republic of Korea, Singapore and Taiwan Province of China.

production stimulates local entrepreneurship, while "the growing availability of local suppliers attracts more foreign investment". [35]

In Indonesia, however, it seems that affiliates of TNCs used local inputs primarily because of government pressure. [36] In response, most foreign affiliates have preferred to manufacture in-house and subcontract only a few insignificant and non-essential items. Consequently, the technical, managerial and financial linkages between TNCs and their subcontractors have generally been weak. To a significant extent, that is owing to the absence of competitive domestic supplier industries. Similarly, in Malaysia, relatively few local linkages have been observed, a situation attributable to the absence of a strong entrepreneurial class and the concentration on export-oriented FDI within free trade zones. In such situations, TNCs must cross a border in order to source locally, and they may prefer to source in neighbouring countries. [37]

Linkages between TNCs and host country firms can also be important in other areas of business activity. It recent years, the realization that the international success of many Japanese TNCs is based largely upon their ability to organize production more efficiently than their competitors both within their home country and in regional and global networks, has led to an increased emphasis on the organizational features of firms. [38] Since many aspects of "lean" production methods involve less use of labour inputs and a greater concentration of both final and ancillary production facilities within the larger markets, it has been feared that the spread of the new methods will place many developing countries at a competitive disadvantage in world markets. Initial indications are that the new methods, at least in industries such as automobiles, have begun to spread to developing country producers. Further research is needed, however, to evaluate the mechanisms promoting or retarding such a spread.

E. The contribution of transnational corporations to the effectiveness of host country investment

The presence of TNCs as producers within host economies is likely to have impacts upon firms and upon the efficiency of investment within the host economy. Those qualitative impacts, which could aid or impinge upon the competitiveness of host country firms, may be of even greater importance than the quantitative impacts in evaluating the role of TNCs in host country growth. [39]

The entry of TNCs into host developing countries as producers of goods and services is often thought to have substantial impacts on the efficiency of domestic firms, and therefore on the effectiveness of domestic investment. A substantial amount of research has analysed the relative performance of foreign and domestic firms in host developing countries. In general, that research has concluded that the presence of foreign firms tends to be associated with greater industrial concentration, that foreign firms are more technology- and capital-intensive, and make extensive use of marketing, financial and managerial assets, and that foreign firms have higher rates of labour and total factor productivity than domestic firms in the same industry. [40]

In addition, some studies have found that foreign firms are more profitable than their domestic counterparts. However, the differences are not always large or statistically significant and in a few studies, the domestic firms have higher rates of profit. Moreover, profits of foreign firms may not be measured accurately, given the possibility that TNCs can use transfer pricing to shift reported profits out of host economies.[41]

Two recent statistical studies of Brazil and Mexico found positive correlations between the foreign share of an industry, measured as foreign production in relation to total production, and indices of concentration.[42] Those results reinforce earlier research on Brazil, Chile, Malaysia, Mexico and Peru.[43] It would not necessarily be correct, however, to conclude that the presence of TNCs results in an increase in monopolization and a decline in the efficiency of domestic investment. Research has not been able to distinguish between a situation in which TNCs dominate an industry and reduce its competitiveness, versus a situation in which those firms are attracted to an industry because existing entry barriers or economies of scale allow firms to earn above average returns.

It would also not necessarily be correct to conclude that even when TNCs are linked to greater concentration, the result is a decline in productive efficiency. Transnational corporations can bring new products, technology and methods of organization, which can change an industry's cost structure and lead to fewer producers, yet also be associated with substantial positive spillovers and linkages with domestic producers. That may be particularly the case where TNCs bring a new product and create demand for local inputs and labour services that did not exist previously. In addition, TNCs can widen the market and be potential competitors for the products of a host country industry by linking the host economy more closely with world markets, leading to greater competition even as there might be greater local concentration.

The inability to isolate cause and effect in evaluating the relation between FDI and industrial structure is made more difficult by the motivations behind investment by TNCs. In general, firms engage in production outside of their home country in order to exploit the profit opportunities from a firm-specific asset and/or the economies available from internalizing cross-border transactions. It should not be surprising, therefore, that foreign firms may be able to earn higher returns or achieve higher levels of productivity than domestic competitors, since, if foreign firms did not perceive that they held some significant advantage over host country firms, they would not have engaged in foreign investment in the first place. The foreign affiliates of TNCs can bring non-competitive forms of behaviour, including predatory pricing, restrictive business practices and transfer pricing. Their access to the financial, technological and managerial resources of their parent companies gives them greater scope to engage in non-competitive activities than their host country competitors. At the same time, it should be noted that TNCs tend to operate within oligopolistic structures in their home economies and that studies have noted a similarity in structures when industries in home and host countries are compared.[44] This implies that cost and demand conditions, and not just the presence of foreign firms, play a large role in determining market structure in both home and host countries. Thus, both sides of this issue have received empirical support.

Most of the empirical studies examine industrial performance and structure at a point in time, while the key issue is what impact foreign firms have on domestic efficiency over time. Case studies of individual country experience provide some information on impacts over time. For example, a study of TNCs in Kenya found that the entrance of foreign firms tended to weaken the competitive position of previously existing domestic firms, as the foreign firms employed their advantages in product and process technology and in marketing. [45] The weakening and even disappearance of host country firms, however, is not necessarily evidence that TNCs have an adverse effect on host country efficiency. To the extent the freed resources are employed more effectively elsewhere, a situation that apparently did not occur in Kenya, the host economy can benefit.

F. Assessment

The present chapter has presented evidence on the role that TNCs play in affecting the quantity and quality of physical capital formation in host developing countries. Since capital formation is an important determinant of economic growth, and to the extent that TNCs have a positive influence on the formation of capital in host developing countries, they can also have a positive influence on economic growth in those countries.

Capital formation involves savings, financial intermediation and additions to the stock of plant and equipment. Transnational corporations do not have a large impact upon domestic savings in developing countries, although inflows of FDI have been important, especially in periods when other sources of foreign savings inflows are limited. The contribution of TNBs to the intermediation process in host developing countries has been limited both by government restrictions and competitive conditions.

The evidence indicates that FDI inflows make a positive contribution to the quantity of new physical capital in developing countries, and that this quantitative contribution appears more significant in industries that are crucial to growth and development, such as manufacturing. Local purchasing by TNCs has, in many host developing countries, provided a stimulant to local investment. Evidence on the qualitative contribution of TNCs to host country investment is less clear-cut. It is not clear how the presence of TNCs affects industrial structure and the allocative efficiency of host country investment. And TNC management practices provide a model for efficient organization of production that can be learned by host country producers.

The evidence on TNCs and host countries suggests that the benefits from the presence of TNCs may depend as much upon host country conditions as upon the assets brought by foreign firms. For example, TNCs can more effectively expand their local purchasing to the extent that the domestic economy is conducive to local entrepreneurship. When TNCs produce largely in export processing zones, their ability to stimulate domestic investment is reduced.

The general conclusion is that TNCs have had a positive influence on domestic capital formation in host developing countries. It needs to be recognized, however, that the evidence for such a conclusion is drawn from a small number of developing countries, most of which are large and have had some success in stimulating economic growth. Where FDI does play a positive role—as, for example, in Taiwan Province of China—that role appears to be substantial. Thus, the experiences of countries that have had a degree of success both in generating growth and utilizing the contribution of TNCs can provide a window on the possibilities that exist for a larger group of countries.

It also should be recognized that the international expansion of TNCs may make FDI central to growth not just because of the growth-inducing benefits from capital formation, but also as the primary linkage to the remaining channels by which growth is enhanced. Transnational corporations organize production across borders and can improve overall efficiency to the extent that such organization can be carried out more effectively within a TNC instead of among separate national firms linked through arms-length market-based trade. The economies of common governance practiced by TNCs are a source of both efficiency and profitability, and are themselves derived from the ability of TNCs to undertake production across borders.

Since the international activities of TNCs involve the application of firm-specific assets in host country locations, the benefits TNCs impart to host economies are strongly related to the presence of foreign production. Thus, FDI, along with non-equity arrangements, represents a conduit for technology spillovers, training of host country nationals and access to international markets, issues that are discussed in more detail below (chapters VI, VII and VIII).

G. Some policy implications

In many instances, the contribution of TNCs to domestic capital formation is enhanced by the capabilities of host country institutions. Policies adopted by host countries can reinforce those capabilities and increase the likelihood that the host country will benefit from the presence of TNCs.

The evidence indicates that TNCs can stimulate local investment through their purchasing from local enterprises. In many cases, policies can support this linkage, especially policies that support and encourage local entrepreneurship. These could include a reduction of administrative restrictions on new business formation, establishment of programmes to provide training in business skills to potential new-business entrants and employees in small and medium-size enterprises and greater scope for TNCs operating in special enterprise zones to purchase locally.

The general area of industrial policy also provides scope for host countries to enhance the benefits they receive from TNCs with respect to capital formation. In formulating such policies, the issue of whether TNCs can make a significant contribution to the host economy has become more relevant. As such, it may be important to include such firms in any overall industrial strategy. A related area is anti-monopoly policy. With the growing importance of international markets, the global competitiveness of an industry is becoming more important than its competitiveness within a single economy. It cannot be ruled out that TNCs bring with them a degree of monopolistic behaviour when they produce within host developing countries. But if TNCs bring additional benefits, such as a high exporting propensity and access to new markets, or a significant transfer of production technology, any decline in local competitiveness may be minor. On the other hand, if TNCs bring few additional benefits, or even impose costs, such as a decline in environmental quality, the competitiveness issue becomes more important.

Although the evidence does not assign to TNCs a major role in savings or in financial intermediation, and it is not likely that such a role will emerge, policies can improve the ability of TNCs to contribute in this area. Countries that have opened their financial markets to foreign participation have seen an increased inflow of foreign capital. And lifting some of the restrictions on TNBs could lead to a greater use of such enterprises as domestic intermediaries. However, the most important actions a host country can take to attract foreign capital is to maintain a strong domestic economy through monetary and fiscal policy and through policies to support domestic capital formation, both physical and human, in a manner that does not create barriers against FDI.

Notes

[1]Nobel laureate W. Arthur Lewis "saw the problem of raising the rate of growth as that of raising [the rate of savings]", in Nicholas Stern, "The determinants of growth", *The Economic Journal*, vol. 101 (January 1991), p. 124.

[2]Robert M. Solow, "Technical change and the aggregate production function", *Review of Economics and Statistics*, vol. 39, No. 3 (August 1957), pp. 313-320; Edward F. Denison, *Trends in American Economic Growth, 1929-1982* (Washington D. C., The Brookings Institution, 1985).

[3]Maurice Scott, *A New View of Economic Growth* (Oxford, Oxford University Press, 1989); Paul M. Romer, "Increasing returns and long-run growth", *Journal of Political Economy*, vol. 94, No. 5 (1986), pp. 1002-1037; "Economic growth: explaining the mystery", *The Economist*, 4 January 1992.

[4]See, for example, W. Arthur Lewis, "The state of development theory", *American Economic Review*, vol. 74, No. 1 (March 1984), pp. 1-10, and Nicholas Stern, "The economics of development: a survey", *The Economic Journal*, vol. 99 (September 1989), pp. 597-685.

[5]Two recent surveys are Mark Gersovitz, "Saving and development", in H. Chenery and T. N. Srinivasan, eds., *Handbook of Development Economics*, volume I (Amsterdam, North Holland, 1988), pp. 381-424, and Angus Deaton, "Saving in developing countries: theory and review", in *Proceedings of the World Bank Annual Conference on Development Economics*, 1989, pp. 61-96.

[6]Data from International Monetary Fund balance-of-payments tape, retrieved in January 1992.

[7]"U. S. direct investment abroad: detail for historical-cost position and balance of payments flows, 1990", *Survey of Current Business*, vol. 71, No. 8 (August 1991), table 4, and earlier annual articles.

[8]Calculations of the Transnational Corporations and Management Division, based upon cumulative outflows of FDI and reinvested earnings, from IMF balance-of-payments tape, retrieved in February 1992. The higher share of retained earnings in outflows for the United Kingdom relative to the Federal Republic of Germany may reflect the fact that foreign affiliates from the former country would tend to have been established in their host economies for a longer period and are likely to have established higher levels of cash inflow. In addition, domestic profitability in the Federal Republic of Germany has been higher than in the United Kingdom, giving parent companies in the Federal Republic of Germany more resources to invest abroad.

[9]Bijan B. Aghelvi and James M. Boughton, "National savings and the world economy", *Finance and Development*, vol. 27, No. 2 (June 1990), pp. 2-5. The decline in savings rates in developing countries since the mid-1970s has been far from uniform; those countries with the highest growth rates and lowest inflation rates have tended to maintain higher savings rates.

[10]For example, Chinyere Emmanuel Egbe, *The Impact of Foreign Private Investment on the Growth of GNP and Investment in Nigeria*, unpublished PhD dissertation, Washington State University, 1984.

[11]Vittorio Corbo and Klaus Schmidt-Hebbel, "Public policies and saving in developing countries", *Journal of Development Economics*, vol. 36 (July 1991), pp. 89-115, based on a cross country study for 1980-1987, concluded that higher government savings are offset only partially by a decline in private savings, leading to a net increase in national savings.

[12]United States, Department of Commerce, *U. S. Direct Investment Abroad: 1989 Benchmark Survey, Preliminary Results* (Washington, D. C., United States Government Printing Office, October 1991), table 31. The 1989 benchmark survey reported data on taxes paid by affiliates of United States TNCs out of income, as well as tax payments that were considered as business expenses, such as import duties, property taxes etc.

[13]The ability of TNCs to shift a portion of their tax burden to low tax jurisdictions or, in some instances, to avoid taxes altogether, has long been the subject of debate and analysis, including, most recently, in the United States. Walter Darnall Vinyard Jr., "Higher taxes, stricter audits lie in wait", *Financial Times*, 22 August 1990, and Patrick Harverson, "US to tighten tax avoidance rules for foreign companies", *Financial Times*, 17 June 1991.

[14]Pradumna B. Rana and J. Malcolm Dowling, Jr., "The impact of foreign capital on growth: evidence from Asian developing countries", *The Developing Economies*, vol. XXVI, No. 1 (March 1988), pp. 3-11, reviewed the literature and presented a two-equation model in which foreign savings are a net addition to domestic capital formation. Similarly, Kanhaya L. Gupta and M. Anisul Islam, *Foreign Capital, Savings and Growth: An International Cross-Section Study* (Dordrecht, the Netherlands, D. Reidel Publishing Company, 1983) concluded that, while foreign savings has a negative effect on domestic savings, this effect is substantially smaller than shown by earlier studies.

[15]Colin Stoneman, "Foreign capital and economic growth", *World Development*, vol. 3, No. 1 (January 1975), pp. 11-26. For a critique of these results, see Gupta and Islam, op. cit., ch. III.

[16]Gupta and Islam, op. cit., chap. IV.

[17]See, for instance, Maxwell J. Fry, "Financial development: theories and recent experience", *Oxford Review of Economic Policy*, vol. 5, No. 4 (Winter 1989), pp. 13-28; Ronald I. McKinnon, *Money and Capital in Economic Development* (Washington, The Brookings Institution, 1973); and Edward S. Shaw, *Financial Deepening in Economic Development* (New York, Oxford University Press, 1973).

[18]Alan H. Gelb and Silvia B. Sagari, "Banking", in The World Bank and UNCTC, *The Uruguay Round: Services in the World Economy* (Washington, D.C. and New York, The World Bank and UNCTC, 1990), pp. 49-59.

[19]"Role of transnational corporations in services, including transnational banks: role of transnational corporations in other services", (E/C.10/1991/6, 20 February 1991), paras. 14 and 15.

[20]The threshold level when portfolio equity holdings by a single foreign investor become direct investment holdings varies across countries.

[21]There is also the issue of whether FDI and other forms of foreign savings are substitutes or complements. For a discussion, see Constantine Michalopoulos, "Private direct investment, finance and development", *Asian Development Review*, vol. 3, No. 2 (1985), pp. 59-71. At least one empirical study suggested that FDI and private financial flows were complements. See UNCTAD, "Transfer and development of technology in a changing world environment: the challenges of the 1990s" (PHD/B/C.6/153, 25 January 1991), p. 5.

[22]UNCTC, *World Investment Report, 1991: The Triad in Foreign Direct Investment* (United Nations publication, Sales No. E.91.II.A.12), pp. 78-80.

[23]Chung H. Lee and Eric Ramstetter, "Direct investment and structural change in Korean manufacturing", in Eric Ramstetter, ed., *Direct Foreign Investment in Asia's Developing Economies and Structural Change in the Asia-Pacific Region* (Boulder, Colorado, Westview Press, 1991), pp. 107-112. The impact of foreign ownership in the electronics and automobile industries in Malaysia, Singapore, Taiwan Province of China and Thailand was analysed in Linda Y. C. Lim and Pang Eng Fong, *Foreign Direct Investment and Industrialization in Malaysia, Singapore, Taiwan and Thailand* (Paris, OECD, 1991), chaps. 4 and 5.

[24]Bohn Young Koo, "The role of foreign direct investment in Korea's recent economic growth", in Walter Galenson, ed., *Foreign Trade and Investment: Economic Growth in the Newly Industrializing Asian Countries* (Madison, Wisconsin, The University of Wisconsin Press, 1985), pp. 176-216.

[25]Sanjaya Lall and Sharif Mohammad, "Multinationals in Indian big business", *Journal of Development Economics*, vol. 13 (1988), table A.1. Foreign presence was measured as the ratio of dividends paid abroad to all dividends paid by firms in the respective industries. Lall and Mohammad recognized that, to the extent foreign firms earn greater profits on their invested capital than domestic firms, this ratio would be biased upward. It would also be biased to the extent foreign and domestic firms differ in the proportion of profits that are reinvested, although the degree and direction of bias is uncertain. However, even if this estimate were biased upward, the "true" figure would undoubtedly be substantially higher than the share of FDI in aggregate capital formation in India.

[26]Nagesh Kumar, *Multinational Enterprises in India* (London and New York, Routledge, 1990), p. 29.

[27]Lim and Fong, op. cit., pp. 95-6.

[28]Chi Schive and Jenn-Hwa Tu, "Foreign firms and structural change in Taiwan", in Ramstetter, *op. cit.*, pp. 142-171.

[29]Richard E. Caves described such linkages as "many cells of an input-output table of a developing country are empty" and that the presence of TNCs can fill in these cells, thereby improving the ability of the remaining cells to add to output. See *Multinational Enterprise and Economic Analysis* (Cambridge, Cambridge University Press, 1982), p. 271.

[30]Caves, op. cit., pp. 270-272.

[31]UNCTC, *Foreign Direct Investment and Industrial Restructuring in Mexico*, UNCTC Current Studies, Series A, No. 18 (United Nations publication, Sales No. E.92.II.A.9).

[32]Lim and Fong, op. cit., p. 92.

[33]Lim and Fong, *op. cit.*, p. 94; Chi Schive, *The Foreign Factor: The Multinational Corporation's Contribution to the Economic Modernization of the Republic of China* (Stanford, California, Hoover Institution Press, 1990), chap. 6; Bohn Young Koo, "The role of direct foreign investment in Korea's recent economic growth", in Galenson, op. cit., p. 195.

[34]Schive, op. cit., p. 76-77.

[35]Lim and Fong, op. cit., p. 94.; see also Schive, *op. cit.*

[36]Hal Hill, *Foreign Investment and Industrialization in Indonesia* (New York, Oxford University Press, 1988).

[37]Lim and Fong, op. cit., pp. 87-89.

[38]For examples from the automobile industry, see Kurt Hoffman and Raphael Kaplinsky, *Driving Force: The Global Restructuring of Technology, Labor, and Investment in the Automobile and Components Industry. A UNCTC Study* (Boulder, Colorado, Westview Press, 1988); and James P. Womack, Daniel T. Jones and Daniel Ross, *The Machine that Changed the World* (New York, Macmillan, 1990).

[39]"As has been pointed out by many other studies in this and other volumes, the provision of capital through [FDI] is probably much less important than the supply of management skills, technology, market access, and access to finance." Mari Pangestu, "Foreign firms and structural change in the Indonesian manufacturing sector", in Ramstetter, op. cit., p. 48.

[40]For summaries of this literature see Caves, *op. cit.*, chapter 4; Rhys Jenkins, "Transnational corporations, competition and monopoly", *Review of Radical Political Economics*, vol. 21, No. 4 (Winter 1989), pp.12-32; Richard Newfarmer and Claudio Frischtak, "Introduction", in Richard Newfarmer and Claudio Frischtak, eds., *Transnational Corporations, Market Structure and Industrial Performance. United Nations Library on Transnational Corporations* (London, Routledge, forthcoming). Newfarmer and Frischtak include a number of articles relevant to the issue in their collection.

[41]Rhys Jenkins, "The impact of foreign investment on less developed countries: cross-section analysis versus industry studies", in Peter J. Buckley and Jeremy Clegg, eds., *Multinational Enterprises in Less Developed Countries* (London, Macmillan, 1991). For a state-of-the-art review of the literature on transfer pricing and a collection of the major writings in this respect, see S. Plasschaert, ed., *Transnational Corporations: Transfer Pricing and Taxation. United Nations Library on Transnational Corporations* (London, Routledge, forthcoming).

[42]Larry Wilmore, "Determinants of industrial structure: a Brazilian case study", *World Development*, vol. 17 (October 1989), pp. 1601-1617; Magnus Blömstrom, "Multinationals and market structure in Mexico", *ibid.*, vol. 14 (April 1986), pp. 523-530. Both articles are reprinted in Newfarmer and Frischtak, op. cit.

[43]Newfarmer and Frischtak, "Introduction", op. cit.

[44]Caves, op. cit., p. 102; Newfarmer and Frischtak, "Introduction", op. cit.

[45]Jenkins, op. cit.

Chapter VI

TRANSNATIONAL CORPORATIONS, TECHNOLOGY AND GROWTH

Technology plays an undisputed role in economic growth by increasing the productivity potential of all factors of production, both tangibles such as labour and capital and intangibles such as organization and quality control. As the economies of the world are becoming increasingly globalized, technology emerges as the most decisive factor in determining international competitiveness and hence growth prospects. The present chapter provides a brief overview of the relationship between technology and growth, evaluates the role of TNCs in that relationship and draws some policy implications relevant to strengthening the contribution of TNCs to growth through technology transfer.

A. Technology as a determinant of growth

1. Linkage between technology and growth

The concepts of technology and technological change encompass many dimensions. Technological progress in some cases involves process innovation, implying that new ways are found to produce existing goods and services, often involving less use of resources. In others, it involves product innovation, implying the introduction of new products or the improvement of quality. Technology comprises more than machinery and other forms of hardware embodied in physical goods. It can be considered as "the stock of knowledge (technical or management)" [1] used in production and marketing. A part of that knowledge is embodied in machines, but much of it is also embodied in human skills, management methods, organizational structures and work routines. Technology, therefore, takes different forms: "hardware", such as machinery and equipment; "software", such as blue prints and process specifications; and the "services" of technicians and professionals for tasks such as quality improvements, management and marketing know-how and process and product design. The software and service components of technology are becoming increasingly important in the international economy, with the emergence of information technology as the central element in the production of many goods and services.

The pervasive nature of the concept of technology, as indicated above, raises several problems in relating technology to growth. There is no single measure of the level of technology and the rate of technological change; it is not easy to separate the independent contribution of technology from other factors of production, particularly capital and labour, in which technology often becomes embodied; [2] and the impact of technology on growth depends on complex interactions between technological change, the structure of incentives confronting enterprises to apply, adapt and innovate upon available technologies, as well as institutional arrangements regarding, among other things, the flow of information and the functioning of markets. [3]

Despite those problems, analysts generally agree on the importance of technology as a determinant of growth. At the conceptual level, technology is considered to promote growth in several ways. First, advancements in technology enable a country to obtain a greater output from any given combination of inputs, which means that the productivity of factors of production is enhanced by technology. Second, technology can promote and sustain growth through the production of new products (including qualitatively superior products), with higher value-added and greater income elasticity. Third (related to the above but deserving of special mention), technology can foster growth through improved export performance, which often requires a shift in the composition of exports from primary commodities to manufactures, and within manufactures to more technology-intensive products.

2. Some empirical evidence on technology and growth

A substantial body of empirical evidence drawn from developed countries provides empirical support for the conceptual links between technology and growth. Empirical evidence for the central importance of product innovations in long-term growth was provided by S. Kuznets as early as 1930. [4] Based on the premise that old consumer goods typically suffer from low long-term income and price elasticity, he argued that a cost-reducing impact of technological change in old goods would have a small aggregative impact on growth. The long-term growth impulse, therefore, came from new products. Similarly, J. Schumpeter emphasized the role of "creative destruction" of old products and their replacement by new ones in the dynamics of growth. [5] Many subsequent studies at both the aggregate and sectoral levels have provided empirical evidence for the beneficial impact of technology on growth through increased productivity of factors of production. [6]

Recent empirical studies on developing countries also demonstrate a significant impact of technology on growth through higher factor productivity. According to one study on Latin America, for example, nearly 20 per cent of growth in output for that region for the period 1940-1970 was accounted for by growth in total factor productivity. [7] The findings of several studies on countries/territories in Asia are presented in table VI.1. Very recently, furthermore, one study based on a sample of 25 countries, comprising developed countries as well as six newly industrializing economies (Argentina, Brazil, Hong Kong, Mexico, Republic of Korea and Taiwan Province of China), has found that innovation and diffusion of technology exerted a significant impact on growth of GDP and productivity for the period 1960-1985. [8]

As was noted earlier, technology can promote growth through improved export performance, which often requires a change in the composition of exports in favour of manufactures. Available evidence shows that, within the manufactures group of exports, R&D intensive industries have been the most rapidly growing exporters. Thus, over the period 1980-1987, the rate of growth of imports into developed countries averaged 10 per cent for high R&D intensive industries, while that of low R&D intensive industries was only 5 per cent. [9] It follows that, in so far as exports exert an influence on growth, the technological content will determine the strength of (export-led) growth.

The studies cited above provide convincing empirical evidence of the significant contribution of technology to growth, which in recent decades appears to have assumed an even greater importance for growth. For example, from about the mid-1970s, per capita use of commodity materials (such as, energy, steel, copper, cement) declined or levelled off, while per capita world GDP continued its upward trend; the difference between the growth in the use of materials and the growth of GDP can be largely attributed to growth in the use of knowledge-intensive new technologies such as electronics, computers and new materials. [10] Consistent with that assertion, data show a generally declining trend in the intensity of raw materials per unit of GDP in developed countries (figures VI.1 and VI.2).

Table VI.1. Selected developing economies in Asia: growth of output and contribution of total factor productivity

(Percentage)

Economy	*Period*	*Growth rate in output*	*Contribution of total factor productivity*
Hong Kong	1955-70	9.3	46.5
	1970-80	9.6	21.3
India	1950-80	3.5	39.1
	1970-80	3.0	0.2
Indonesia	1970-80	7.7	31.5
Korea, Republic of	1955-70	8.8	56.4
	1970-80	8.5	41.2
Malaysia	1970-80	7.8	21.7
Philippines	1957-62	4.9	0.0
	1963-69	5.2	15.4
	1970-74	6.3	19.0
	1970-80	6.2	20.6
Singapore	1957-70	6.6	55.2
	1966-72	12.5	4.8
	1972-80	8.0	- 11.3
	1970-80	9.1	19.7
Taiwan Province of China	1955-77	8.0	53.6
	1970-80	8.5	50.0
Thailand	1970-80	6.9	19.7

Source: Yukio Ikemoto, "Technical progress and level of technology in 1970-1980: a translog index approach", *The Developing Economies*, vol. XXIV, No. 4 (December 1986), pp. 368-390.

Figure VI.1. Intensity of use of selected agricultural raw materials in developed countries

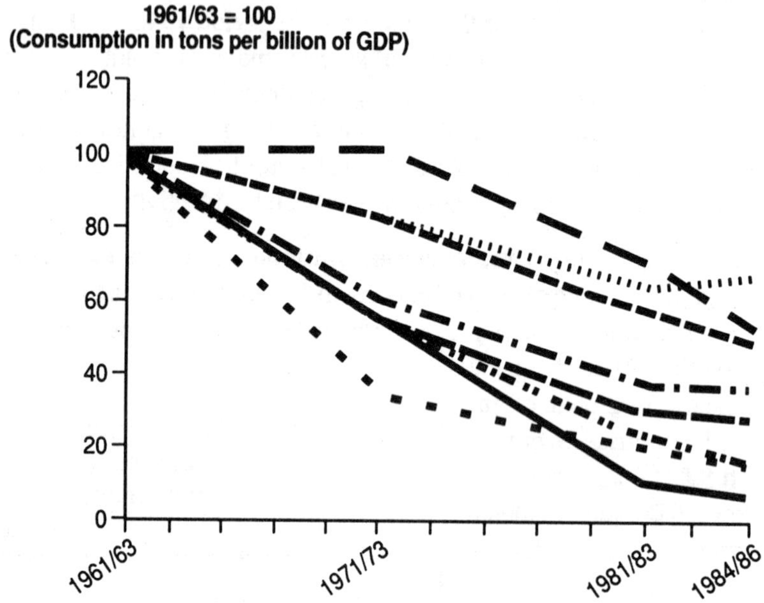

Source: UNCTAD, "Impact of technological change in patterns of international trade" TD/B(XXXV)/SC.I/CPR.2 (March 1989), p. 4.

Key: Rubber, Cotton, Jute, Sisal, Abaca, Wool, Wood, Sugar

B. Transnational corporations and technology development

As mentioned earlier, the common denominator linking technology to growth is that it permits production of a greater amount of, or new output from, a given amount of resources. That production requires new technological development that normally involves R&D efforts. Results of R&D, in turn, are often reflected in patents. The present section, therefore, deals with the role of TNCs in technology development, as indicated by R&D and patents.

1. Overview

In recent years, a notable shift has occurred in the perception of the process of technology development. The conventional view was that scientific innovation and discoveries are largely made in academic institutions and research laboratories. Once these are in place, firms seek to commercialize them. This view of technology development is no longer appropriate. With the emergence of information based technologies, the increasing globalization of enterprises and growing competition in the interna-

Figure VI.2. Intensity of use of selected minerals, ores and metals in developed countries

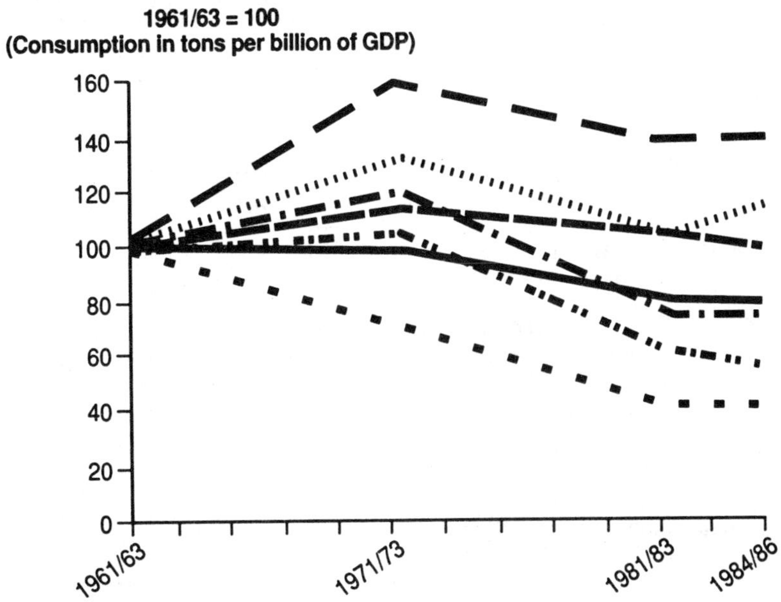

Source: UNCTAD, "Impact of technological change in patterns of international trade" TD/B(XXXV)/SC.I/CPR.2 (March 1989), p. 4.

Key: Manganese, Aluminium, Copper, Iron ore, Nickel, Phosphate, Tin

tional market place, science and technology have become more and more linked. It is being increasingly recognized that a large part of technological development occurs because of actions taken by enterprises.[11] Indeed, TNCs devote substantial resources to R&D, in addition to having a variety of institutional arrangements with universities, research institutions and other enterprises.

The role of private companies in R&D relative to overall national expenditure on R&D by major home countries of TNCs is illustrated in table VI.2. It is interesting to observe that the proportion of sales spent by these companies on R&D far exceeds the proportion of total national expenditure as a proportion of GDP. Furthermore, R&D expenditures of the limited number of companies for which data are presented in table VI.2 account for a significant share of total national expenditures. And most of these firms, in turn, are TNCs, which, recognizing the key importance of technologies, have undertaken extensive research programmes. Such TNCs as IBM, General Electric, Hitachi, General Motors and Siemens have allocated funds amounting to billions of dollars annually for R&D (table VI.3).

Research-and-development expenditures capture the resources devoted to technological development. They are, therefore, an *input* indicator. Results of R&D often find expression in patents, which can be viewed as an *output* indicator of technological development. Here, again, available data on patents registered in the United States clearly show the dominant role of corporations. Foreign-owned corporations together with those of United States origin account for over three-fourths of patents registered in the United States; the share of foreign-owned corporations has increased from the mid-1980s and is now larger than that of domestic firms (table VI.4). The top 50 TNCs accounted for more than one-fourth of all patents granted to corporations during the 1980s. Overall, the development of technologies appears to be increasingly undertaken by TNCs.

2. The internationalization of technological development and transnational corporations

Historically, TNCs have undertaken technological development mostly in their home countries. Foreign affiliates generally undertook modifications and adaptations to innovations, emanating mainly from the R&D establishments of their parent firms in home countries. That is still the predominant pattern. In recent times, however, there has been a marked growth in the internationalization of R&D. As TNCs become progressively more global and acquire a world orientation for their inputs, products and markets, a number of them are establishing

Table VI.2. Research-and-development expenditure of selected countries and top companies [a]

A. National R&D expenditure, latest available years

Country	*R&D expenditure (Million dollars)*	*Share of R&d expenditure in GDP*	
		Per cent	*Year*
Canada	7 250.6	1.3	1989
France	22 241.0	2.3	1989
Germany, Federal Republic of	34 234.0	2.6	1989
Italy	11 189.6	1.3	1989
Japan	82 853.1	2.7	1989
Netherlands	4 792.3	2.1	1989
Sweden	5 459.5	2.9	1989
Switzerland	3 899.6	2.9	1986
United Kingdom	18 356.3	2.4	1988
United States	144 867.0	2.7	1989

B. R&D expenditure of top companies

Country	*R&D expenditure of top companies (Million dollars)*	*R&D expenditure as percentage of sales*	*Number of companies*
Canada	2 069	4.6	6
France	6 997	4.2	17
Germany, Federal Republic of	14 086	6.1	19
Italy	2 640	4.2	8
Japan	27 295	4.9	74
Netherlands	4 208	3.0	7
Sweden	3 454	6.5	10
Switzerland	4 426	5.9	10
United Kingdom	7 570	2.1	33
United States	37 569	4.7	28

Sources: Calculations of the Transnational Corporations and Management Division, based on OECD, *Basic Science and Technology Statistics* (Paris, 1991), table 3; United Nations, *National Accounts Statistics: Analysis of Main Aggregates*, various issues; and *Business Week;* Quality 1991, pp. 171-172 and 176-208.

a Companies with the highest absolute amount of R&D expenditures.

integrated R&D systems, with overseas laboratories playing a significant role. The increasing importance of economies of scope, shorter product cycles and rapid obsolescence, all of which require closer interaction with customers, have necessitated such an internationalization. In some cases, internationalization has been motivated by the desire to take advantage of scarce scientific and technical personnel, in which particular host countries possess a comparative advantage. At the same time, the process has been facilitated by the development of transnational computer-communication networks and on-line systems that permit the smooth flow of data and information among remote sites and, indeed, the on-line conduct of R&D. [12]

Table VI.3. Research-and-development expenditure by top 20 transnational corporations, 1990

(Millions of dollars)

Ten non-United States TNCs	*R&D expenditure*	*Ten United States TNCs*	*R&D expenditure*
Siemens	4 132	General Motors	5 342
Hitachi	3 011	IBM	4 914
Matsushita Electrical Industrial	2 423	Ford Motor	3 558
Philips Electronics	2 411	AT&T	2 433
Alcatel Alsthom	2 237	Digital Equipment	1 614
Fujitsu	2 097	General Electric	1 479
Toshiba	1 864	Du Pont	1 428
Nippon Telegraph & Telephone	1 739	Hewlett-Packard	1 367
NEC	1 728	Eastman Kodak	1 329
Bayer	1 699	Dow Chemical	1 136

Source: Business Week, Quality 1991, p. 176.

No comprehensive data exist on the geographical distribution of the R&D efforts of TNCs by country of origin. But the sketchy evidence available from limited survey data lends support to a growing internationalization. In the case of United States TNCs, the proportion of R&D expenditure accounted for by foreign affiliates increased to 10 per cent in 1989, from seven per cent in 1966. [13] The data seem to indicate that European TNCs have reached a considerably higher degree of internationalization of their R&D expenditures. Some 23 per cent of the R&D expenditures by 20 Swedish TNCs were undertaken abroad in 1987, compared with 21 per cent in 1980. [14] In the case of TNCs from the Federal Republic of Germany, it has been noted that the growth of R&D employment abroad has risen much faster than the growth of total employment abroad. A survey of 33 major firms showed that 18 per cent of their total R&D employees in 1989 were employed in affiliates abroad. [15] In contrast, a survey of 11 large TNCs from the Federal Republic of Germany at the end of the 1970s revealed that 15 per cent of their R&D personnel were employed abroad. [16] Some of the leading European TNCs, such as Ciba Geigy, Royal Dutch Shell, Bull, Philips, Olivetti, ABB and Norsk Hydro, each spend more than a third of their total R&D expenditure in foreign locations. [17]

Available data on patents also generally indicate a rising importance of R&D in foreign locations (table VI.5). Between the early 1970s and mid-1980s, the share of patents filed in the United States by TNCs that are credited to research undertaken outside the home country of the parent company has increased in 7 of the 11 countries included in the table.

Table VI.4. Number of United States patents, by type of grantee,[a] 1980-1991

(Thousands)

	Year											
	1980	*1981*	*1982*	*1983*	*1984*	*1985*	*1986*	*1987*	*1988*	*1989*	*1990*	*1991*[b]
United States-owned												
Individuals	11.4	12.0	10.3	9.2	10.4	10.7	11.0	10.9	11.7	14.7	14.9	7.7
Corporations[c]	27.6	29.4	25.8	25.7	29.9	30.9	29.3	33.5	31.3	37.9	36.0	18.6
Top 50 United States-based TNCs[d]	9.2	10.1	8.7	8.8	10.1	10.3	9.6	10.8	9.5	11.2	10.5	9.2
Government	1.2	1.1	1.0	1.0	1.2	1.1	1.0	1.0	0.7	0.8	1.0	0.6
Foreign-owned												
Individuals	4.1	4.2	3.4	3.3	3.7	4.0	4.3	4.9	4.8	5.4	5.3	2.7
Corporations[e]	19.2	21.3	19.6	19.9	24.0	26.8	27.6	33.5	32.1	38.7	37.3	19.1
Top 50 non-United States-based TNCs[d]	6.3	7.2	6.9	7.0	8.6	9.5	9.4	11.6	11.3	13.6	12.5	6.2
Government	0.3	0.3	0.4	0.3	0.4	0.5	0.5	0.6	0.5	0.4	0.4	0.8
All corporations c	46.8	50.7	45.4	45.6	53.9	57.7	56.9	67.0	63.4	76.7	73.3	37.7
Top 50 TNCs[d]	11.6	13.2	11.8	12.1	14.2	15.3	14.8	17.6	16.5	20.2	19.1	10.0
All corporations as a percentage of total	73.4	74.2	75.2	76.8	77.4	78.0	77.2	79.4	78.2	78.3	77.3	76.2
Foreign corporations as a percentage of all corporations[e]	41.0	42.0	43.2	43.6	44.5	46.4	48.5	50.0	50.6	50.5	50.9	50.7
Top 50 TNCs[e] as a percentage of all corporations[e]	24.7	26.0	26.0	26.5	26.3	26.5	26.0	26.3	26.0	26.3	26.0	26.5

Sources: United States Patent and Trademark Office, OEIPS/TAF Program within the Office of Information Systems, *All Technologies Report, January 1963-June 1991* (Washington, November 1991), *Design Patents Report, January 1977-June 1991* (Washington, November 1991) and OEIPS/TAF Program Database (Washington, June 1991).

a Utility and design patents only.
b Figures up to June 1991.
c May also include non-corporate organizations.
d Inventor patents only.
e May exclude subsidiaries identified separately from parent organizations.

In sum, TNCs account for the bulk of R&D expenditures in their home countries, which, in turn, are the global leaders of technological development. A small but increasing share of those expenditures is being shifted to host countries, albeit primarily to developed ones.

Obviously, technology development is the pre-requisite for improved factor productivity and product innovations which, in turn, fuel growth. By virtue of their dominance in technological development, TNCs play a major role in the growth process, a role that is likely to become of greater importance in the future because of the increasing importance of technology as a determinant of growth.

C. Transnational corporations and the transfer of technology to developing countries

The preceding section has demonstrated the importance of TNCs in the development of technology at the global level. The focus of analysis in the present section is on their role in technology transfer to developing countries. [18] The rationale is that, as demonstrated in the preceding section, technology development by TNCs mostly takes place in the home countries of those firms or in other developed host countries. [19] Therefore, access to technologies for developing countries is largely a matter of acquiring technologies from TNCs in developed countries. The impact of technology transfer from TNCs on the

Table VI.5. The share of United States patents of the largest firms world-wide attributable to research in foreign locations (outside the home country of the parent company), organized by the nationality of parent firms, 1969-1986

(Percentage)

Country	*1969-72*	*1973-77*	*1978-82*	*1983-86*
Belgium	49.6	54.2	56.1	71.3
Canada	42.0	40.0	39.8	35.5
France	10.2	9.4	8.8	10.9
Germany, Federal Republic of	13.6	11.5	12.3	14.4
Italy	20.1	18.3	13.7	11.7
Japan	2.9		1.9	1.3
Netherlands	63.9	68.8	64.1	70.0
Sweden	20.9	17.8	25.9	31.3
Switzerland	45.0	44.3	44.1	42.6
United Kingdom	43.3	40.5	38.7	45.0
United States	4.3	5.5	6.0	7.4

Source: John H. Dunning, "Multinational enterprises and the globalization of innovatory capacity", Rutgers University GSM working paper No. 91-03 (January 1991), table 7, p. 18.

growth of the host economy, however, depends on how the various modes of technology transfer interact with the local technological capabilities, incentive structures and institutional arrangements.

The principal sources of technology acquisition are scientific and technical publications (typically widely accessible at low costs); trade (through the import of machinery and equipment); FDI (through both wholly-owned foreign affiliates and joint ventures); and non-equity links with TNCs through mechanisms such as patents, licenses, technical assistance agreements and other contractual arrangements, as well as strategic alliances. Transnational corporations play a major role in all those modes of transferring technology, particularly so in the latter three.

1. Transnational corporations and the supply of capital goods

The import of capital goods is a prime determinant of the productive capacities of developing countries. As table VI.6 shows, developing countries in Africa recorded a significant decline in the absolute value of capital-goods imports during the decade of 1980s; those in Latin America and the Caribbean achieved only a marginal increase; and those in Asia and the Pacific raised their imports by nearly three-fourths. That is undoubtedly a significant explanatory variable in the differential growth performance of those groups of countries.

Table VI.6. Capital goods [a] imports by developing countries, 1980-1989

(Billions of dollars)

Country group	*1980*	*1981*	*1982*	*1983*	*1984*	*1985*	*1986*	*1987*	*1988*	*1989*
All developing countries	115.3	130.5	122.4	106.2	105.9	101.4	112.4	126.1	143.9	155.2
Africa	23.5	26.3	22.5	18.2	17.6	16.7	16.5	16.5	17.2	18.2
Asia and the Pacific	56.7	65.1	68.2	65.3	62.4	56.7	63.7	74.0	87.2	95.8
Latin America and the Caribbean	31.1	35.8	29.0	20.3	23.6	25.3	28.5	31.8	35.0	36.3

Source: UNCTAD Secretariat.

a Includes SITC Rev. 1, Section 7, machinery and transport equipment, except 7194 domestic appliances non-electrical; 7241 television receivers; 7242 radio receivers; 7250 domestic electrical equipment; 7321 passenger motor cars; 7326 chasis for passenger motor cars; 7329 motor cycles; and 7331 bicycles.

The key issue in the present context is the role of TNCs in capital-goods imports. The non-availability of data does not permit a disaggregation of imports of capital goods from TNCs as compared with imports from other entities. Indirect evidence suggests, however, a major role of TNCs in the supply of capital goods. For example, in 1989, at least 80 per cent of United States foreign trade was undertaken by those corporations, including parent companies in the United States, foreign affiliates of United States TNCs and United States affiliates of foreign TNCs. It is, therefore, not unrealistic to assume that the proportion of capital-goods imports of developing countries from the United States accounted for by TNCs is quite high. The importance of TNCs in the supply of capital goods is also underscored by the high proportion of intra-firm trade in some capital goods items. For example, exports of non-electrical machinery by United States TNCs are substantially intra-firm; in 1989, 60 per cent of such exports were represented by intra-firm transactions. [20] The importance of intra-affiliate transactions in total capital goods imports of developing countries, however, would be considerably less (see chapter VIII).

2. Technology transfer through foreign direct investment

A TNC normally undertakes FDI when it possesses certain technological or other economic advantages over its competitors, which it finds in its best interest to exploit internally from a foreign location. [21] Technology forms an important part of the competitive advantage of a TNC, and many firms choose to service their foreign markets through FDI, not only to exploit that advantage but also to retain company control over their technology. Transnational corporations generally transfer their most recent technology to their affiliates, while selling or licensing older technology to locally-owned firms and joint ventures. [22] Hence, FDI may be the only way for many developing countries to gain access to the latest technology and especially to certain key technologies.

Foreign direct investment can promote technological change in developing countries—and, as box VI.1 shows, in developed countries as well—in a number of ways. The direct impact may occur through its contribution to higher factor productivity, changes in product and export composition, R&D undertaken by foreign affiliates, the introduction of organizational innovation and improved management practices, and employment and training (the last of these aspects is being dealt with in chapter VII). Indirect impacts occur through collaboration with local R&D institutions, technology transfer to local downstream and upstream producers, the effects of the presence of foreign affiliates on competition and on the efficiency of local producers and the turn-over of trained personnel.

(a) Direct effects

(i) Transnational corporations and factor productivity

An important contribution of technology to growth is through increased factor productivity. An evaluation of the contribution of TNCs to that process would require highly disaggregated data on the

Box VI.1. Foreign direct investment in developed countries and technology transfer

A good part of the discussion of FDI and technology transfer in developed countries focuses on the possibility that FDI may, in fact, reduce the technological capacity of the host economy and, hence, impair its growth prospects. For example, it has been argued that Japanese TNCs in the United States cause a drain of United States technology to Japan. More specifically, it is feared that, when Japanese companies acquire United States firms, especially in high-technology industries, they do so in order to capture innovative products and their technologies for the parent firm in Japan.[1] It is argued that, in the longer run, foreign investors will shift the bulk of R&D activities from the United States to their home countries and denude the United States of its innovative capacity by making the results of R&D unavailable to firms in the United States.

It is very difficult to assess the longer run impact of foreign investors acquiring or displacing United States firms on the development of technological capacity in the United States. However, if the concern is that foreign investors will shift R&D activities from their United States affiliates back to headquarters, the data show that, in fact, foreign affiliates in all industries taken together in the United States perform twice as much R&D per worker than United States firms (table 1). In the manufacturing sector, however, the differential is less pronounced and the amount of company-funded R&D expenditure per worker for United States firms is marginally lower than for foreign affiliates. Those figures do not give any indication of the type or quality of R&D undertaken by the two categories of firms, but they do not support the view that foreign firms are transferring large amounts of R&D from their United States affiliates to headquarters. Similarly, a study of royalties and licence fees found that transfer of foreign technology into the United States by foreign affiliates was more than five times larger than technology transferred out by them.[2] In fact, measured by royalties and licence fees, the largest proportion of technology transfer from the United States was accounted for by United States parents of foreign affiliates.

Many foreign investors may locate their R&D activities in the United States in order to take advantage of the technology centres in that country.[3] A study of Japanese entries into 297 United States industries showed that Japanese FDI predominated in R&D intensive industries in respect of establishment of new plants, but there is no indication that Japanese acquisitions are more frequent in high-technology industries.[4] Many Japanese companies pursue a strategy of vertical integration for their overseas activities. Fujitsu, for example, has constructed a $100 million R&D, manufacturing and service facility in Texas for the development of fiber optic transmission systems for the United States market, jointly by United States and Japanese engineers.[5] Like-

Table 1. Research and development by United States affiliates of foreign firms, 1988

	Foreign affiliates [a]	*United States firms*	
		Total [b]	*Company-funded*
All industries			
R&D (millions of dollars)	7 382	97 889	65 583
Employment (thousands of workers)	3 682	91 076	...
R&D per worker (thousands of dollars)	2.00	1.07	0.72
Manufacturing			
R&D (millions of dollars)	6 402	89 776	60 223
Employment (thousands of workers)	1 762	19 341	...
R&D per worker (thousands of dollars)	3.63	4.64	3.11

Source: Edward M. Graham and Paul R. Krugman, *Foreign Direct Investment in the United States* (Washington, D.C., Institute for International Economics, 1991), table 3.3, p. 73.

a Data are preliminary

b Includes federally funded as well as company-funded expenditure.

/.....

(Box VI.1, continued)

wise, in 1985, Honda established an R&D facility in Ohio, now employing 200 persons. Honda's goal is to employ 500 people in R&D centres in the United States by 1995. The strategy of the company is to develop and build cars in the areas in which they are sold.[6]

Foreign affiliates in the United States may also be helping to increase United States factor productivity by introducing new technology and management methods. This may particularly be the case in industries in which the United States is losing international competitiveness. In the automotive industry, the Japanese automakers in the United States are introducing new standards in the manufacturing and engineering of cars, which serve as models for United States automakers. For example, in 1990 the Ford Motor Company switched to the production of a new model without stopping the assembly line, by introducing reprogrammable machines that move on tracks. This is a practice Japanese automakers have developed, and used in the United States, to increase productivity.[7] In 1982, General Motors turned over a run down and inefficient auto plant in Fremont California to Toyota Motor Corp. as a part of a joint venture. By introducing new technology and a typical Toyota production system, with just-in-time delivery and a flexible assembly line, it only takes half of the previous work force to assemble the same number of cars.[8]

Japanese automakers in the United States also transfer technology indirectly, by providing technical assistance to United States suppliers. Since the surge of the yen made it more profitable for Japanese firms to source locally, they encourage United States car-part firms to adopt new methods to improve quality and lower production costs.[9]

In fact, Japanese FDI in the United States automotive industry has brought new investments and technology transfer to other declining industries in that country, like the steel and rubber industries. Faced with strong international competition and declining demand from the automotive industry, the United States steel industry verged on collapse at the beginning of the 1980s. However, many Japanese steel firms have invested heavily in the United States, building state-of-the-art plants for coating and preparing steel coils used by carmakers, and entering joint-ventures to modernize large integrated United States steel plants.[10] In this manner, the United States partners gain access to state-of-the-art Japanese technology, as well as the new market of Japanese automakers.

---

1 Marjorie Sun, "Investors' yen for U.S. technology", *Science*, vol. 246 (8 December 1988), pp. 1238-1241; Eduardo Lachicha, "Japanese firms the most active investors in U.S. high-tech concerns, study says", *The Wall Street Journal*, 14 May 1991; and Georgio Gilder, "American technology at fire-sale prices", *Forbes* (22 January 1990), pp. 60-64.

2 See Kan H. Young and Charles Steigerwald, "Is foreign investment in the U.S. transferring U.S. technology abroad?", *Business Economics*, vol. XXV, No. 4 (October 1990), pp. 28-30.

3 See Edward M. Graham and Paul R. Krugman, *Foreign Direct Investment in the United States* (Washington D.C., Institute for International Economics, 1991).

4 See Bruce Kogut and Sea Jin Chang, "Technological capabilities and Japanese foreign direct investment in the United States", *Review of Economics and Statistics*, vol. 73, No. 3 (August 1991), pp. 401-413.

5 In 1989, Fujitsu had seven R&D centres in the United States, mainly devoted to software and development of data storage equipment. See *Business International*, 23 October 1989.

6 See Martin Kenney and Richard Florida, "How Japanese industry is rebuilding the Rust Belt", *Technology Review*, vol. 94 (February/March 1991), pp. 24-33. Toyota also announced a major expansion of research facilities in the United States in 1991 (see *The Wall Street Journal*, 3 June 1991).

7 See *The New York Times*, 14 March 1990.

8 See *Business Week*, 14 July 1986.

9 See *The Wall Street Journal*, 12 April 1988.

10 See Kenney and Florida, op. cit.

use of factors of production and value-added, differentiated by ownership in different industries. Such data are not readily available.

There are case studies, however, that provide some evidence of the relative efficiency of the use of factors of production, as between foreign affiliates and domestic enterprises. For example, an analysis of 282 pairs of foreign and domestic firms of similar size drawn from 80 manufacturing industries in Brazil concluded that foreign firms have a significantly higher ratio of value-added to output than domestic ones. [23] A study on Thailand found that foreign firms had higher average productivity of both capital and labour in the manufacturing sector compared with domestic firms, and the difference was owing to the higher efficiency of foreign firms as measured by a technology co-efficient derived from production-function estimations. [24] Similarly, a study on the Republic of Korea observed that the marginal product of both capital and labour was higher in foreign firms compared with domestic firms, but the differential was much greater for capital than labour. [25]

All these studies, therefore, support the view that foreign firms can contribute to growth through the provision of technologies that make more efficient use of capital and labour.

(ii) *Transnational corporations and product composition*

As noted earlier, the introduction of new products or qualitatively superior old products is one of the ways by which technology promotes growth. Transnational corporations can play a role in this process. One way of assessing the role is to examine the performance of TNCs in the production of relatively more research-intensive products (table VI.7). The table shows that, for United States

Table VI.7. Shares of high and medium research-intensive industries [a] in total sales and manufacturing sales of foreign affiliates, 1982 and 1989

(Percentage)

Developing region	*1982* Share in total sales	*1982* Share in manufacturing sales	*1989* Share in total sales	*1989* Share in manufacturing sales
United States majority-owned affiliates				
Africa	3.5 [b]	59.2 [b]	3.1 [b]	23.0 [b]
Asia and the Pacific	15.7	..	50.7 [b]	..
Latin America	21.8	57.3	33.1	60.9
Japanese affiliates				
Africa [c]	17.1	42.4	10.8	40.9
Asia and the Pacific [d]	29.0	74.5	25.9	79.8
Latin America	20.1	66.0	19.4	74.3

Sources: United States, Department of Commerce, *U.S. Direct Investment Abroad: 1982 Benchmark Survey*, (Washington, D.C., United States Government Printing Office, 1985), table III.D.3, and *1989 Benchmark Survey*, Preliminary Results (Washington, D.C., United States Government Printing Office, 1991), table 32; Japan, Ministry of International Trade and Industry, *The Fourth Basic Survey on Japanese Business Activities Abroad* (Tokyo, Okurasho Insatsu-Kyoku, 1991), p. 12, and *Survey on the Overseas Activities of Japanese Companies*, No. 12-13 (Tokyo, Toyo Hoki Shuppan, 1984), p. 43.

a High and medium research-intensive industries include chemicals, machinery (except electrical), electrical machinery and domestic equipment, and transportation equipment.

b Part of data are suppressed by the source to avoid disclosure.

c Includes South Africa.

d Includes Australia and New Zealand.

TNCs, the expansion of the share of sales of high and medium research-intensive industries primarily occurred in Asia and the Pacific. In that region, United States affiliates also had the largest increase of R&D expenditure as percentage of sales, as noted later. Latin America shows a much slower growth in sales of high and medium research-intensive industries and Africa shows a decline. For Japanese TNCs, the picture is similar as far as Africa is concerned. And, again, there has been an increase in the share of sales of high and medium research-intensive industries in manufacturing sales in Asia and the Pacific as well as Latin America, with a slightly more pronounced growth in the latter region in terms of the share of manufacturing sales.

The creation of production facilities by TNCs in high and medium research-intensive industries can imply technology transfer not merely through a changing product composition, but also through the training of host country personnel in new technical skills and the introduction of new management methods and new ways of organizing the production process. The impact of FDI on the transfer of skills from host-country personnel, however, does not depend only on the degree of complexity of the technology employed; it is also a function of the methods used for transferring skills, the quality of in-house training programmes, the promotion policy for nationals through exposure to progressively higher levels of responsibility and the provision of off-the-job training.

As a note of caution, it should also be mentioned that the data in table VI.7 do not provide information on the value-added activities of the foreign affiliates. It could be that some TNCs locate only relatively labour-intensive, low value-added operations of those research-intensive outputs in the host country, and that the high value-added operations are located in the home country.

(iii) Transnational corporations and export composition

The technological content of exports can be an important determinant of growth performance. It is well known that R&D intensive exports generally have higher income elasticities; therefore, the growth of those exports is more sustainable over the long run. Besides, a rising share of such exports also carries the implication that the country concerned is in a position to take advantage of shifts in international demand (manifested in the growth of internationally competitive R&D intensive industries), rather than to rely exclusively on traditional exports based on natural-resource endowments or low labour costs. The role of TNCs in the export of R&D intensive products, therefore, deserves scrutiny.

The relevant data are presented in table VI.8. They show that, in the case of Japanese affiliates, the share of R&D intensive exports in total manufactured exports increased between 1982 and 1989 in Latin America and Asia, but declined in Africa, where an absolute decline of R&D intensive exports also occurred. In the case of United States affiliates, their share of R&D intensive exports increased somewhat in Latin America, declined slightly in Asia (though the share is still much higher than in Latin America) and remained very small in Africa. On the whole, affiliates have significantly increased R&D intensive exports.

Again, it is difficult to estimate the local value-added in the host country from export-oriented production. It should also be noted that the performance of TNCs in respect of R&D intensive exports is not necessarily better than that of local enterprises. In particular, local enterprises in certain Asian countries have clearly outperformed foreign affiliates. Total R&D intensive exports from Asia in 1989 were more than four times those recorded in 1982; [26] but the increase in R&D intensive exports by both United States and Japanese affiliates over the same period, though significant, did not reach a similar proportion. (See also the discussion on structural change of exports in chapter VIII.)

(iv) Research and development by affiliates

The evidence that an overwhelming proportion of the *foreign* R&D of TNCs is located in developed countries does not necessarily imply that such R&D is insignificant from a host-country perspective. In countries such as India, the Republic of Korea and Singapore, the share of aggregate R&D expenditure attributable to foreign firms exceeded 15 per cent in the 1970s. [27] Moreover, some evidence indicates that foreign affiliates may now be devoting more of their resources than before to R&D. In the case of the majority-owned foreign affiliates of United States TNCs, there has been a noticeable increase in their R&D expenditures as a proportion of sales in a number of developing countries (table VI.9). But there are some noticeable regional differences. Research-and-development expenditure by United States affiliates as a percentage of sales increased four times between 1982 and 1989 in Asia and the Pacific, while it stagnated in Latin America and remained insignificant for the developing countries in Africa.

The location of R&D activities in developing countries can be explained by locational advantages and the corporate

Table VI.8. Manufactured exports and research-and-development intensive [a] exports of foreign affiliates, 1982 and 1989

(Millions of dollars)

	United States majority-owned affiliates		*Japanese affiliates* [b]	
Developing region	*Manufactured exports*	*R&D intensive exports*	*Manufactured exports*	*R&D intensive exports*
Latin America				
1982	4 692	2 908	971	84
1989	10 176	6 794	815	165
Percentage increase	117	134	- 19	96
Asia				
1982	5 954 c	5 453 c	5 950	3 027
1989	13 861	12 176	11 560	7 230
Percentage increase	133	123	94	139
Africa				
1982	169 c	3 c	23	9
1989	566	9 c	30	5
Percentage increase	235	200	30	- 44

Sources: United States, Department of Commerce, *U.S. Direct Investment Abroad: 1982 Benchmark Survey*, op. cit., tables III.E.4. and III.E.5, and *1989 Benchmark Survey* tables 42 and 44; Japan, Ministry of International Trade and Industry, *Survey on the Overseas Activities of Japanese Companies*, No. 12-13, op. cit., pp. 90, 91 and 95 and No. 18-19, (Tokyo, Okurasho Insatsu-kyoku, March 1990), pp. 74-75, 78-79 and 82-83.

a Definition same as in table VI.7.

b The values may be substantially understated because of incomplete coverage of firms in the surveys.

c Part of the data is suppressed by the source to avoid disclosure.

strategies of TNCs. The decisions of corporations to locate R&D activities in certain host countries are very much dependent on factors, such as the availability of R&D facilities and of trained scientific and engineering personnel. Generally, countries with high expenditures for R&D are also the countries in which United States affiliates have a high proportion of R&D expenditure compared to sales.

Very little is known of the type of research undertaken by foreign affiliates. The R&D activities taking place within foreign affiliates are, most likely, typically confined to adapting the technology of the parent company to local conditions. In a sample of 218 Japanese TNCs, 57 per cent expressed the view that the main objective of their foreign R&D facilities was to develop products tailored to meet local demand.[28] The effect of TNCs on deeper indigenous research-and-innovation capabilities ("know-why") in developing countries is less evident. As TNCs can import all their "know-why" and need to perform only adaptive research in host countries, local firms may well conduct more research (as opposed to development) than do foreign affiliates.

Table VI.9. Research and development expenditures of selected developing economies as a percentage of GNP and research and development expenditures for United States majority-owned affiliates as percentage of sales

	R&D expenditure of countries as percentage of GNP				*R&D expenditure of United States majority-owned affiliates as percentage of sales*	
Developing regions/economy	*Percentage*	*Year*	*Percentage*	*Year*	*1982*	*1989*
Latin America					0.2	0.2
Argentina	0.2	1982	0.5	1988	0.4	0.25
Brazil	0.7	1982	0.4	1985	0.4	0.3
Mexico	..	..	0.6	1984	0.3	0.2
Africa					0.01	0.02
Middle East					0.1	0.4
Asia and the Pacific					0.04	0.2
Hong Kong	..	..	..	..	..	0.1
India	0.7	1982	0.9	1986	0.5	0.6
Indonesia	0.4	1983	0.2	1988	0.02	0.03
Republic of Korea	0.9	1982	1.9	1988	..	0.3
Malaysia			..	..	..	0.1
Singapore	0.3	1981	0.9	1987	..	0.3
Thailand	0.3	1985	0.2	1987	0.03	0.02
Taiwan Province of China	..	..	..	..	0.3	0.4

Source: UNESCO, *Statistical Yearbook,* various issues; United States, Department of Commerce, *U.S. Direct Investment Abroad: 1982 Benchmark Survey,* op. cit., tables III.H.3 and III.E.1; and *1989 Benchmark Survey*, op. cit., tables 40 and 76.

It may also be that a strong presence of TNCs can inhibit the development of an indigenous technological base beyond adaptive research.[29] When TNCs penetrate a host-country market, indigenous firms may be forced to cut back on research or to narrow their field of specialization, as they are confronted with declining market shares caused by competition with TNCs that possess much greater technological capacities. On the other hand, foreign competition could also induce domestic firms producing similar products to undertake R&D that otherwise would not have taken place, in order to improve their competitive advantage. In that case, FDI could advance local innovatory capacity in areas in which the host country and its firms are strongest and have a competitive market structure. In the case of greenfield investments, which do not compete with local industry, there is no displacement of local enterprises, and FDI will most likely lead to a net increase in the innovatory capacity of a host country, even through adaptive research.[30]

(v) Organizational innovation and management practices

Organizational innovation and improved managerial practices are being increasingly viewed as a major aspect of technological development for enhancing productivity and accelerating growth. The principal components of these aspects that have evolved over the last two decades or so can be summarized as follows:[31]

- The underlying philosophy of production has been altered: instead of producing to stock, goods are produced to order. That necessitates a demand-driven system capable of producing a variety of product types in much smaller volumes. Hence, lot sizes have been reduced dramatically.
- The efficient production of different products in small lot sizes requires minimizing downtime. That, in turn, requires quick line changeovers and tool setups. Machinery redesign becomes necessary but, more importantly, production-line workers must be trained to do changeovers rather than having them done by separate teams as in mass production.
- Production layouts need to be restructured, and changes made in the use and management of machines in order to create a smooth flow of smaller lot sizes.
- Inventories have to be reduced to a minimum "just-in-time" level rather than being stocked "just-in-case", so that the increased number of different product types can be accommodated without large carrying costs.
- Maintaining a smooth flow of production without inventories requires that components have zero defects or be of perfect quality, whether they come from suppliers or from in-house sources further back in the production line.
- Skill and craft demarcations among workers are eliminated and workers are trained to be multi-skilled; they are paid according to their skill level and the quality of their work.

The organizational changes involved extend throughout the firm: from design to marketing to production; from senior management to the shop floor; and from management's relations with its workforce to the firm's relations with its suppliers.

Transnational corporations from Japan, particularly those in the automobile industry, have been the pioneers of these developments. It was during the 1980s that these organizational techniques began to be introduced outside of Japan. In some cases this was a direct result of the operations of the Japanese affiliates themselves, especially in the electronics, automobiles, component and machine tool industries that had been established in North America and Europe. In other cases, non-Japanese suppliers of these Japanese foreign investors began to restructure to incorporate new patterns of organization in order to meet the requirements of their Japanese customers. A third source of innovation were the practices of those firms that had subsidiaries or joint ventures in Japan and which were learning through the operations of these subsidiaries - Bendix's production of auto components and Xerox's restructuring of the mid 1980s are cases in point. By the late 1990s, the central tenets of the new organizational paradigm had filtered through to the major non-Japanese TNCs and were being implemented at the plant level in various industrialized countries.

More recently, TNCs from Japan and elsewhere have started implementing organizational changes in developing countries. No systematic data are as yet available to document the extent of such technology transfer. However, available case studies show that some developing country firms have adopted these changes either as joint venture partners of TNCs or under licensing agreements (box VI.2); in other cases, similar changes have been introduced in TNC affiliates or subsidiaries in developing countries. Examples of the adoption of these technological changes can be found in such diverse countries as Brazil, the Dominican Republic, India, Mexico and Zimbabwe.[32]

(b) Indirect effects

Foreign direct investment can promote growth through several indirect mechanisms of technology transfer. For example, backward linkages to local firms, in the form of subcontracting the supply of parts, components and services, create additional demand for intermediate products. A supplier firm in a developing country that is in a subcontracting relationship with a foreign subsidiary can receive technical assistance to improve its product quality and production process or to undertake new product development. When upgrading the technological level of supplier industries, FDI often increases the local value-added and generates growth. The presence of foreign affiliates can increase competition and thereby force domestic enterprises to improve productive efficiency, which is growth-enhancing.

An earlier chapter has provided evidence that TNCs may be increasing their use of inputs from local sources. Local sourcing of inputs, particularly when done under subcontracting arrangements, is often associated with technological assistance to the local suppliers by TNCs. In a survey of the largest foreign affiliates operating in Mexico, for example, it was found that almost two thirds of them had local subcontracting relationships. Almost all of the foreign affiliates that subcontracted locally imparted some kind of training to their national subcontractors: 87 per cent provided training in quality control,

68 per cent gave technical assistance and 22 per cent offered financial assistance to their subcontractors.[33]

As to the spillover impact of TNCs on the technological capacity and productive efficiency of indigenous enterprises, several studies on developed countries provided mixed evidence.[34] The same is true of developing countries. A recent study on Mexico showed that the rate of productivity growth of local firms and their ability to reach the productivity standards of TNCs were positively related to the degree of foreign ownership of an industry.[35] That estimate was interpreted to imply that competition from foreign affiliates forced Mexican firms to increase productivity by investing in human capital and new technology. The study could not exclude, however, the possibility that the competitive pressure from foreign affiliates had simply forced out inefficient local firms, thus improving the average productivity performance of Mexican firms. In contrast, a study on Morocco did not provide any evidence that the presence of foreign firms resulted in increased productivity of domestically-owned firms.[36] Although

Box VI. 2. Transfer of organizational technology: the case of Escorts Ltd. in India

Escorts Ltd. is a large Indian firm which grew to prominence since the mid-1950s. It began by producing motorcycles, and diversified into tractors and automobile components. In 1985, following the general opening-up of the Indian automobile industry to TNCs, Escorts entered into a licensing agreement to manufacture Yamaha motorcycles in a new plant in Surajpur. This commenced production in 1986, manufacturing 100 cc motorcycles predominantly designed by Yamaha. Escorts' older Faridabad plant producing motorcycles of wholly Escorts design remained in operation. In early 1990, the two Escort plants accounted for 40 per cent of the Indian motorcycle market.

A key strategic decision was taken to build a new plant and to employ a young and skilled labour-force rather than to attempt a turnaround of the existing plant. The youth of the labour-force (average age of 25 years in 1990) was intended to facilitate training in radically new forms of work-organization; it was also designed to reduce pressure from workers and trades unions to "impose traditional workpractices".

Training has therefore been a priority for Escorts in its new plant. It began with senior managers, senior technical personnel and supervisors. Yamaha organized extensive training for these groups, including spells in Japan—from two weeks to six months, depending upon the tasks involved. Thereafter, training was extended to the direct work-force by teams of 10 Japanese and 10 Indian trainers. Workers received two weeks initial training before going on to the shop-floor. After approximately one month, they received training in new skills (off the shop-floor), with this cycle being repeated for a period of approximately six months, until workers were deemed to have reached a minimum acceptable standard. Thereafter, additional training was provided at regular intervals as the average skills of the labour-force were gradually increased, especially in the acquisition of multiple skills. This is reflected in the payments system, where basic wages are supplemented by increments for skill acquisition and are thus partly paid on the principle of what the workers can do, rather than what they actually do.

The plant is laid out on a cellular basis, with kanban carts moving work-in-progress between various stages of stamping, machining and assembly. Typically, each operator is responsible for a number of machines, unlike Faridabad where each machine tends to have a dedicated operator. Work-teams are responsible for each

/.....

foreign firms had higher levels of productivity, domestic firms showed faster productivity growth; but that could not be attributed to dynamic externalities from FDI.

In some cases, TNCs stimulate technology development by local R&D institutions. In India, for example, one TNC recently signed a letter of intent with a Government-funded telecommunications R&D facility—the Centre for the Development of Telematics—to use switches designed by the Centre in a new open-architecture cellular system. In addition, the TNC intends to sponsor research at nine leading engineering colleges.[37]

(Box VI.2, continued)

cell, and workers within each team are generally cross-trained to perform all the tasks in the cell (as well, in many cases, as tasks in other cells). Just-in-time production on work-in-progress is carefully observed. The result, as can be seen from table 1, is that changeover time in the Surajpur press shop is eight to sixteen times quicker than at Faridabad. Batch-sizes were less than half, and inventory components and raw materials were generally six times greater than at the sister plant.

Table 1. Comparison between the Surajpur and Faridabad plants of Escorts Ltd., 1990

Plant	*Annual output (Number of motor-cycles)*	*Number of workers*	*Output per worker (Number)*	*Change-over time*	*Batch size*	*Inventory inputs*
Surajpur	77 500	625	124	30-60 minutes	4 000	15-30 days
Faridabad	96 000	4 000	24	8 hours	8 000-10 000	3-6 months

The Surajpur plant has thus experienced considerable progress and is considerably more efficient than its sister-plant at Faridabad. Labour productivity was almost five times higher, with 625 workers producing 77,500 motorcycles (124 motorcycles per worker), compared with the 4,000 workers manufacturing 96,000 units at Faridabad (24 motorcycles per worker). Most of this superiority in performance was due to organizational factors, although the product design by Yamaha also played a role. The decidedly superior performance of the Surajpur plant clearly illustrates how transfer of organizational technology by TNCs can bring about major improvements in productivity.

Source: Transnational Corporations and Management Division, *Transnational Corporations and the Transfer of New Management Practices to Developing Countries* (New York, United Nations, forthcoming).

3. Transnational corporations and technology transfer through non-equity forms

Apart from wholly- or majority-owned FDI (usually known as internalized forms of transfer), TNCs also transfer technologies through a variety of externalized (primarily non-equity) forms, which include minority joint ventures, licensing, management and marketing contracts and international subcontracting. (Box VI.3 discusses transfer of technology through joint ventures in developed countries.) But data on such technology transactions between developing countries and TNCs are sketchy and difficult to interpret. Few developed countries disaggregate their technology receipts by country, type of transaction (for example, licensing or management contracts) or relationship between the receiving and the paying enterprise (an affiliate or an unrelated enterprise). Similar comments also apply to developing country-data on technology payments. Hence, it is a formidable task to assess the role of TNCs in technology transfer through such forms, and it is harder still to assess their impact on growth.

An earlier study by United Nations Centre on Transnational Corporations concluded that, during the 1970s, and up until the mid-1980s, the incidence of externalized forms of technology transfer seems to have increased.[38] Data on United States TNCs suggest a weak corroboration of that trend (table VI.10). Attention should be drawn, however, to the fact that technology receipts from unaffiliated enterprises in developing countries account for a very small proportion of total receipts.

Data for host countries tell a similar story. In the Republic of Korea, for example, payments for foreign licensing and technology contracts increased their share in total technology-transfer transactions (defined as FDI inflows plus payments for foreign licensing and technical consultancy plus capital-goods imports) from 1.2 per cent in 1972-1976 to 1.6 per cent in 1982-1986.[39] In Thailand, technology payments (comprising payments for royalties, trademarks, technical and management fees) increased from around 0.1 per cent of GDP during the 1972-1976 period to 0.2 per cent during the 1984-1987 period.[40]

Several points need to be considered to put the pattern into perspective:

- The first concerns the potential of non-equity forms for the future. It is well known that many factors—such as the age and sophistication of a technology, industry characteristics, corporate strategies within particular industries as well as the level of host-country entrepreneurial, technological and human-resources development—affect the choice of particular TNCs regarding externalized technology transfer. That form of transfer, however, may be even less favoured in the future than it was in the past. For one, recent developments in information technologies tend to increase the internalization advantages of TNCs. Those developments facilitate and cheapen the cost of intra-firm communication, coordination and control. The high costs of development and rapid obsolescence are likely to reinforce efforts of TNCs to secure a quicker pay-back through internalization. Furthermore, the internalization of the R&D expenditure noted earlier and the trend towards strategic alliances among TNCs in respect of the development and transfer of technologies limit the plurality of sources in the technology market. The

Box VI.3. Joint ventures in developed countries and technology transfer

A study of Japanese FDI in the United States showed that joint ventures were the preferred entry mode for Japanese firms in industries with high United States R&D expenditure, while Japanese R&D expenditures had no significant influence on the mode of entry.[1] However, before any conclusions can be drawn on the role of Japanese-United States joint ventures in technology transfer from the United States, it is necessary to distinguish between different types of joint ventures.[2] One type is related to barriers in the form of Governments encouraging joint ventures in disadvantaged national industries to maximize the gains for domestic partners. A second type involves voluntary joint ventures between partners with mutually beneficial strengths. Again, voluntary joint ventures can occur between a strong firm in a national declining industry and a relatively weaker firm from a foreign firm with a strong competitive advantage or between equally strong partners with specialized advantages.

It can be assumed that technology transfer between the partners will be highest within voluntary joint ventures, and that a strong firm in a declining industry will receive relatively more technology than the partner with the competitive advantage. The well known joint ventures in the automotive industry, like Chrysler's joint venture with Mitsubishi, General Motors' investment in Isuzu and Ford's joint venture with Mazda, are examples of firms in a declining industry gaining access to new technology (among other things, the production of compact cars). The relatively smaller Japanese firms with the competitive advantage gain access to the United States market. The reverse example is Fujitsu's joint venture with Amdahl, a small and innovative computer firm.[3] Fujitsu gained United States technology while Amdahl received financial support.

Joint ventures of the type were the partners have mutual beneficial strengths are also numerous between United States and Japanese firms. One such joint venture is the Toshiba-Motorola venture to manufacture microprocessors (Motorola's competitive advantage) and large memory chips (Toshiba's competitive advantage). The joint venture with Toshiba has allowed Motorola to gain access to technology in order to compete in advanced dynamic random access memory (DRAM) chips.[4]

It is difficult to determine who has benefited the most from technology-related joint ventures between Japanese and United States firms. However, a study of the industry distribution of joint ventures between Japanese and United States firms in 1987 showed that industries in which Japan has a clear competitive advantage (measured by market share in the OECD countries) account for the largest share of joint venture assets.[5] This indicates that the existing joint ventures in manufacturing presumably provide more opportunities for the transfer of technology from Japan to the United States than from the United States to Japan.

---

1 Bruce Kogut and Sea Jin Chang, "Technological capabilities and Japanese foreign direct investment in the United States", *Review of Economics and Statistics*, vol. 73, No. 3 (August 1991), pp. 401-413.

2 See Dorothy B. Christelow, "U.S.-Japan joint ventures: who gains?", *Challenge*, vol. 32, No. 6 (November-December, 1989), pp. 29-38.

3. Ibid.

4 See *Asian Business*, January 1991.

5 See Christelow, op. cit.

deceleration in the growth of external resource inflows through official development assistance and private flows other than FDI would limit the ability of developing countries to acquire unpackaged technology. Finally, recent policy changes in developing countries in favour of FDI tend to reduce the cost of internalization. Those factors are likely to increase the importance of FDI as an instrument of technology transfer.

- The second observation relates to the interrelationship between FDI and externalized technology transfer. With the exceptions of India and the Republic of Korea, the bulk of technology receipts of United States TNCs from unaffiliated enterprises in developing economies originates precisely in economies such as Argentina, Brazil, Hong Kong, Indonesia, Malaysia, Mexico, Philippines, Singapore, Taiwan Province of China and Venezuela, which are also among the largest FDI host economies. Thus, familiarity with the enterprises of a country and their capabilities gained through FDI may be a precondition for (or at least a facilitator of) externalized forms of technology transfer. In the case of India and the Republic of Korea, a combination of restrictive policies towards FDI, the availability of a substantial pool of well-trained human resources and the large market size encouraged externalized forms of technology transfer despite comparatively less FDI.

- Third, the growth impact of technologies transferred through externalized forms depends, as in the case of capital-goods imports, largely on the capacity of domestic entrepreneurs to make the right selection, use the acquired technologies effectively and adapt and innovate continuously. Relevant also to the growth-promoting im-

Table VI.10. United States and the Federal Republic of Germany: technology receipts, 1986-1990

(Millions of national currencies)

		Receipts from all unaffiliated enterprises		*Receipts from unaffiliated enterprises in developing countries*	
Year	*Receipts from all countries*	*Value*	*Percentage*	*Value*	*Percentage*
United States [a]					
1986	7 531	1 842	24.5	296	3.9
1987	9 419	2 171	23.1	364	3.9
1988	11 211	2 513	22.4	443	4.0
1989	12 404	2 814	22.7	563	4.5
1990	15 840	3 445	21.7	690	4.4
Germany, Federal Republic of [b]					
1986	1 690	134	7.9	10	0.6
1987	1 670	163	9.8	7	0.4
1988	1 892	129	6.8	9	0.5
1989	2 166	189	8.7	7	0.3
1990	2 360	157	6.7	..	..

Sources: United States, Department of Commerce, *Survey of Current Business*, vol. 71, No. 9 (September 1991), tables 4.1-4.5, pp. 74-78; and *Monthly Report of the Deutsche Bundesbank*, various issues.

a Includes royalties and licence fees.
b Includes receipts from patents, inventions and processes.

pact of technologies acquired through externalized forms is the capacity to negotiate reasonable terms. The many imperfections in technology markets give rise to a considerable scope for bargaining. If technology purchasers are not equipped with adequate knowledge concerning the availability of alternative sources of the same or similar technologies and their costs, transactions are very likely to be settled in terms more favourable to the sellers. In the case of Thailand, for example, it has been observed that no correlation existed between licensing fees and the complexity of technologies; fees were paid for technologies no longer covered by patents; and technical fees paid for similar technologies in the pharmaceutical industry ranged from 0.4 per cent to 20 per cent of sales. Even though many of the buyers were aware that the terms were disadvantageous, they did not have adequate information on alternative sources.[41]

4. Strategic alliances and technology transfer

High risks and rising R&D costs (especially in the area of new technologies) and the rapid obsolescence of new products have forced many TNCs to form technology-related strategic alliances to share development costs, acquire new technologies and make better use of scarce qualified personnel.[42] The substantial number of strategic alliances in existence now is a relatively new phenomenon, and it is very difficult to obtain precise data on its frequency and purpose. There are indications, however, of an emerging trend towards a very high proportion of agreements involving the development of and access to technologies.[43] The alliances of IBM with several other corporations for the purpose of developing its personal computer are an example: the Lotus Corporation provided the application software, and Microsoft wrote the operating system, for a micro-processor that was produced by Intel.[44] IBM (traditionally reluctant to conclude alliances) has now created alliances with more than 40 partners around the world, pooling technology and customer bases in the telecommunications and related fields. As a response to competition from IBM, the Japanese computer firm Fujitsu formed alliances with Texas Instruments, Siemens and Hitachi. Such alliances are often undertaken for the joint development of new generations of products and to set industry standards. Table VI.11 illustrates the geographical and industry breakdown of technology alliances among TNCs from the Triad. Transnational corporations from the United States and Europe are clearly the most active participants in strategic alliances, most of which take place in information technologies.

Technological alliances can be viewed as a way of providing collective protection to technological advances among a few partners. The increasing incidence of such alliances combined with the current pace and cost of technological development makes it more difficult for developing countries to acquire technology through traditional non-equity arrangements. Many alliances also involve common actions for setting international standards that increase the barriers to entry (including, for new products from developing countries) in the international market. Some developing countries, particularly the newly industrializing ones, have the potential and capability, however, to become partners in technology alliances. In the information-technology industry, for example, Taiwan Province of China, has made extensive use of alliances with TNCs to acquire technological capabilities. A typical example of that use is in the area of computer software, where the Government has set up two software engineering firms in cooperation with IBM.[45] Taiwan Province of China, provides good quality engineers at a relatively low cost while IBM provides experience in software research and development. Similarly, the Sony Group is to transfer advanced technology to the electronics industry in Taiwan Province of China. Sony has announced that it has entered into alliances with 130 electronics companies from that country working with a "technology development centre" to create a production base for export to Japan and affiliated companies of Sony world-wide.[46] Similarly, several firms in the automobile industry in the Republic of Korea have entered into alliances with TNCs from the Triad. Examples are those of Hunday with Mitsubishi and Chrysler; Daewoo with General Motors, Suzuki and Isuzu; and Kia with Ford and Mazda.[47]

These examples, however, represent only a small number of alliances that include developing countries. Indeed, only 2 to 3 per cent of technology alliances in the 1980s were between companies from the Triad and firms from newly industrializing economies, and less than two per cent included firms from other developing countries.[48] For most developing countries, then, the acquisition of new technologies is likely to rely—at least for the present—on intra-firm transfers by TNCs, rather than on inter-firm alliances between independent firms.

Table VI.11. International distribution of technology cooperation agreements in biotechnology, information technologies and new materials, cumulative 1989

(Number and percentage)

	Biotechnology		*Information technologies*		*New materials*	
Area	*Number*	*Per cent*	*Number*	*Per cent*	*Number*	*Per cent*
Japan	58	5	95	4	88	13
United States	428	35	707	26	139	20
United States-Japan	155	13	406	15	94	14
United States-Western Europe	245	20	599	22	133	19
Western Europe	223	18	509	19	118	17
Western Europe-Japan	38	3	177	7	49	7
Other	66	5	225	8	67	10
Total	1 213	100	2 718	100	688	100

Source: John Hagedoorn and Luc Soete, "The internationalization of science and technology (policy): how do 'national' systems cope?" in H. Inose, M. Kawasaki and F. Kodama, eds., *Science and Technology Policy Research: What Should be Done? What Could be Done?* (Tokyo, Mita Press, 1991), pp. 201-216.

D. Assessment

The present chapter has shown that technology is a key determinant of growth. It promotes growth by increasing factor productivity, enabling the introduction of new products with greater long-run income elasticities and bringing about shifts in the export composition in favour of research-intensive exports with higher growth potential. In recent decades, the importance of technology as a determinant of growth has been increasing.

Transnational corporations are responsible for the bulk of technological development. Therefore, in so far as growth is driven by technology, the growth and development of developing countries are closely linked to a variety of equity and non-equity links with TNCs that permit access to technologies.

One channel of access to technology is through the import of capital goods, in the supply of which TNCs play a dominant role. Because the choice of technologies acquired through that mechanism largely rests with domestic importers, the contribution of TNCs to growth through this mechanism is essentially indirect.

Foreign affiliates can promote technological change in developing countries—and thereby growth—through their own R&D. During the past decade, data for United States majority-owned affiliates in developing countries show that the share of R&D expenditures in sales, though small, has increased. The net impact on growth arising from increased R&D expenditure by foreign affiliates also depends on what effects such an increase has on the R&D capabilities of indigenous firms. In general, it appears that the effect is likely to be more beneficial where domestic firms are capable of undertaking R&D to meet the challenge of competition from foreign affiliates. Foreign affiliates generally appear to exhibit higher factor productivity, which contributes to growth. They also appear to have contributed to the growth of developing countries through increasing the share of R&D intensive products in their total sales and their manufactured exports, over the past decade. Domestic enterprises in Asia, however, outperformed TNCs in respect of R&D intensive manufactured exports.

Foreign affiliates also have contributed to the growth of developing countries indirectly by increasing their purchase of local inputs; but the level and nature of such purchases is conditioned by the level of the industrial development of the host country (see chapter V). In some cases, foreign affiliates have stimulated R&D by local institutions through collaborative arrangements. Sparse information on that aspect does not allow any conclusion of the overall effect of such a stimulation on growth.

In some cases, a growth stimulus has also been generated through significant technology transfer by TNCs via such non-equity channels as licensing and subcontracting. The countries that have benefited most from such transfers appear to be typically the largest host countries; but, sometimes, those forms involved unfavourable terms that imply an avoidable drain on domestic resources.

In recent times, there has been an upsurge of technological alliances among TNCs, particularly in respect of new technologies. The upsurge raises the concern that reduced competition in the international technology market and restrained access for developing countries could limit the contribution that the dissemination of new technologies can make to growth.

In sum, TNCs are making a worthwhile direct contribution to the growth and technological development of host developing countries through the R&D expenditure of affiliates, changes in their product and export composition and higher factor productivity. As to the indirect stimuli to growth through non-equity forms of technology transfer, integration with domestic economies, the stimulation of local R&D and technological alliances with developing country enterprises, the evidence is rather mixed. The beneficial impact of those mechanisms appears to be largely contingent on, among other things, the domestic capacity of the host country to generate and adapt acquired technologies; the competitive ability of domestic enterprises; and the availability of well-trained human resources. It can be concluded, therefore, that, as regards indirect stimuli to growth through a wider dissemination of technologies, TNCs can strengthen a national technological base where the above conditions already exist; but they are unlikely to create them.

E. Some policy implications

Several policy implications emerge from the findings in the present chapter. For one, R&D by foreign affiliates in developing countries appears to be mainly located in those countries that already possess some domestic technological competence and a reasonable supply of trained scientific and technical personnel. Policy measures directed towards inducing TNCs to undertake greater R&D in host economies should, therefore, be conceived in the broader context of the indigenous technological development policy of a country, encompassing, among other things, the creation of an adequate human-resources base for technological activities.

As noted earlier, FDI has made a notable contribution to technology transfer and thereby growth through changes in the composition of products and exports in favour of greater technological intensity. Here, again, performance variations of TNCs appear to be related to indigenous technological capacities of host economies; hence, the conclusion noted above with regard to inducing TNCs to undertake greater R&D in host economies is applicable here as well. In addition, it should be pointed out that, while FDI may be a useful means of quickly benefiting from the results of new innovations abroad through the transfer of production, it does not necessarily imply a dissemination of technological knowledge to domestic producers. That raises the question of the choice of mode of transfer as between FDI and externalized forms. There are contrasting experiences in respect of that choice, even though national-growth performances have been quite comparable. Singapore can be easily cited as a case of high reliance on FDI, while the Republic of Korea represents a greater reliance on externalized forms. That was facilitated in the Republic of Korea both by the creation of an ample entrepreneurial skill base and by governmental assistance to local enterprises that provides information and support in bargaining. Any country seeking to pursue a similar strategy would be well advised to evaluate carefully the level of human resources development of the country, the entrepreneurial capacity of domestic producers and the ability of the Government to provide appropriate information and guidance to domestic firms. Besides, it should be pointed out that restrictive policies towards FDI may severely limit access to sophisticated technology, as amply demonstrated by the experience of India. Furthermore, even the Republic of Korea chose to liberalize its FDI policy progressively since the early 1980s, as more modern technologies were needed to sustain international competitiveness and, as noted in chapter V, FDI contributed almost one half of the new capital in technology-intensive industries such as electrical machinery and transportation equipment.

In the context of the varying performance of TNCs in respect of linkages with the domestic economy, the question of performance requirements assumes relevance. Quite obviously, for example, if the objective is to promote efficiency in the use of resources in order to promote faster growth, the imposition of a local content requirement, in the absence of an internationally competitive supplier industry, would be counterproductive, at least in the short run. There may be a case for a highly selective use of such requirements, however, in cases with a high probability that local producers would be able to achieve quickly international standards with assured demand for their products.[49]

Even where TNCs are willing to transfer technologies in externalized forms, the terms of transfer may leave something to be desired, as the experience of Thailand (cited earlier) demonstrates. Excessive payments imply a drain on domestic resources and thus may inhibit growth. Technology purchasers should, therefore, be provided with adequate information regarding available alternatives, to enable them to make informed choices. An arbitrary imposition of limits on royalty payments or licence fees is likely to limit access to desired technologies.

A correlation appears to exist between FDI and access to externalized forms of transfer in most cases. Hence, highly restrictive policies towards FDI may also limit the scope to acquire technology through other channels, unless the country concerned has a strong bargaining position because of its large market size or its capacity to develop technologies independent of an association with TNCs. The link between FDI and externalized forms also raises a formidable technology barrier for the vast majority of developing countries that attract little FDI because of their structural constraints, no matter how liberal their national policies towards such investment.

The present chapter has also demonstrated that there is a marked tendency among TNCs to hold new technologies closely among themselves through strategic alliances. There have been, at the same time, some instances of such alliances with developing-country enterprises. Local enterprises, therefore, deserve encouragement to enter into such arrangements with TNCs from advanced countries, wherever possible, in order to gain access to new technologies, or to be able to apply them more widely in the interest of sustaining competitiveness and growth.

Finally, it should be emphasized that the growth-promoting impact of technologies acquired through FDI as well as other forms of association with TNCs ultimately depends on the incentive structure faced by both foreign and domestic enterprises in acquiring, adapting, innovating upon and diffusing technologies. The incentive structure is conditioned by a host of public policies, concerning physical infrastructure, human resources development, R&D, technology and FDI, competition, international trade, factor pricing, venture capital, subsidies etc. The formulation of such a holistic approach is, no doubt, immensely complex; but without such an approach the contribution of TNCs to growth through technology transfer will fall short of its potential.

Notes

[1]Francois Chesnais, "Science, technology and competitiveness", *STI Review*, No. 1 (Autumn 1986), pp. 85-129.

[2]OECD has published a major work dealing with these issues: *Technology and Productivity: The Challenge for Economic Policy* (Paris, OECD, 1991).

[3]Sanjaya Lall and George Kell "Industrial development in developing countries and the role of government intervention", *Banca Nazionale del Lavoro Quarterly Review*, No. 178 (September 1991), pp. 271-292.

[4]S. Kuznets, *Secular Movements in Production and Prices* (Boston, Houghton Mifflin, 1930).

[5]J. Schumpeter, *Capitalism, Socialism and Democracy* (New York, Harper and Row, 1942).

[6]See, for example, Robert M. Solow, "Technical change and the aggregate production function", *Review of Economics and Statistics*, vol. XXXIX, No. 3 (August 1957), pp. 312-320; Edward Denison, *The Sources of Economic Growth in the United States* (New York, Committee for Economic Development, 1962) and *Why Growth Rates Differ?* (Washington, D.C., The Brookings Institution, 1967); M. Abramowitz "Resource and output trends in the United States since 1870", *American Economic Review: Papers and Proceedings*, vol. XLVI, No. 2 (May, 1956), pp. 5-24; J. Kendrick, "Productivity trends: capital and labour", *Review of Economics and Statistics*, vol. XXXVIII, No. 3 (August 1956), pp. 248-257; Z. Griliches, "Hybrid corn: explanation in the economics of technological change, *Econometrica*, vol. 25, No. 4 (October 1957), pp. 501-522; W. Parker and J. Klein, "Productivity growth in grain production in the United States, 1840-60 and 1900-10", in Brady Dorothy, ed., *Output, Employment and Productivity in the United States after 1800* (New York, National Bureau of Economic Research, 1966).

[7]V. J. Elias, "Sources of economic growth in Latin American countries", *Review of Economics and Statistics*, vol. 60, No. 3 (August 1978), pp. 362-371.

[8]J. Fagerberg, "Innovation, catching up and growth", in OECD, *Technology and Productivity: The Challenge for Economic Policy* (Paris, OECD, 1991), pp. 37-43.

[9]UNCTAD, "Impact of technological change on patterns of international trade", TD/B(XXXV)/SC.1/CRP.2 (March 1989), table 3, pp. 8-9.

[10]William F. Miller, "Europe 1992: regionalism and globalism", *The International Executive*, vol. 33, No. 2 (September-October 1991), pp. 28-35.

[11]Paul M. Romer, "Endogenous technological change", *Journal of Political Economy*, vol. 98, No. 5 (1990) pp. S71-S102. For a state-of-the-art review of the role of TNCs in innovatory activity, and a collection of major writings in this respect, see J. Cantwell, ed., *Transnational Corporations and Innovatory Activities. United Nations Library on Transnational Corporations* (London, Routledge, forthcoming).

[12]Jeremy Howells, "The location and organization of research and development: new horizons", *Research Policy*, vol. 19, No. 2 (1990), pp. 133-146 and Karl P. Sauvant, *International Transactions in Services: The Policies of Transborder Data Flows* (Boulder, Colorado, Westview Press, 1986).

[13]John H. Dunning, "Multinational enterprises and the globalization of innovatory capacity", Rutgers University GSM working paper No. 91-03 (January 1991), mimeo., and United States Department of Commerce, *U.S. Direct Investment Abroad:*

1989 Benchmark Survey Preliminary Results (Washington, D.C., United States Government Printing Office, 1991), tables 76 and 91.

[14]Dunning, "Multinational enterprises", op. cit.

[15]Christoph Doerenbacher and Michael Wortmann, "The internationalization of corporate research and development", *Intereconomics*, vol. 26, No. 3 (May/June 1991), pp. 139-144.

[16]Quoted in Michael Wortmann, "Multinationals and the internationalization of R&D: new development in German companies", *Research Policy*, vol. 19, No. 2 (1990), pp. 175-183.

[17]John H. Dunning, *Multinational Enterprises and the Global Economy* (Reading, Massachusetts, Addison Wesley, forthcoming), chap. 11.

[18]For a recent state-of-the-art review of the subject and a collection of major writings in this respect, see E. Chen, ed., *Transnational Corporations and Technology Transfer. United Nations Library on Transnational Corporations* (London, Routledge, forthcoming).

[19]In this context, it should be noted that only 2 per cent of total R&D expenditures of 11 TNCs of the Federal Republic of Germany surveyed at the end of the 1970s were in developing countries (see Wortmann, op. cit.). In the case of United States TNCs, 5 per cent of foreign R&D expenditures were in developing countries in 1982, and that proportion declined to 4 per cent in 1989 (see United States, Department of Commerce, *U.S. Direct Investment Abroad: 1982 Benchmark Survey* (Washington D.C., United States Government Printing Office, 1985), tables III.H.3 and III.E.1, and *1989 Benchmark Survey*, op. cit., tables 40 and 76.

[20]United States, Department of Commerce, *U.S. Direct Investment Abroad: 1989 Benchmark Survey*, op. cit., table 85. For electrical machinery, 32 per cent of the exports were intra-firm. There are no separate data on the industrial distribution of exports by United States TNCs to developing countries. However, the intra-firm portion of exports to developing countries is generally lower than it is for developed countries.

[21]John H. Dunning, *Explaining International Production* (London, Unwin Hyman, 1988), p. 10.

[22]Magnus Blomström, "Host country benefits of foreign investment", Working Paper No. 3615 (Cambridge, National Bureau of Economic Research, 1991), mimeo.

[23]Larry N. Wilmore, "The comparative performance of foreign and domestic firms in Brazil", *World Development*, vol. 14, No. 4 (April 1986), pp. 489-502.

[24]Somsak Tambunlertchai and Eric D. Ramstetter, "Foreign firms in promoted industries and structural change in Thailand", in Eric D. Ramstetter, ed., *Direct Foreign Investment in Asia's Developing Economies and Structural Change in the Asia-Pacific Region* (Boulder, Colorado, Westview Press, 1991), pp. 65-102.

[25]Chung H. Lee and Eric D. Ramstetter, "Direct investment and structural change in Korean manufacturing", in ibid, pp. 105-141.

[26]Calculations of the Transnational Corporations and Management Division, based on United Nations Statistical Office, *Monthly Bulletin of Statistics*, various issues.

[27]John H. Dunning, "Multinational enterprises", op. cit., p. 16.

[28]Dunning, *Multinational Enterprises and the Global Economy*, op. cit., chap. 11.

[29]J. Cantwell, *Technological Innovation and Multinational Corporations* (London, Basil Blackwell, 1989), p. 178.

[30]John H. Dunning, "Multinational enterprises", op. cit.

[31]UNCTC, *New Approaches to Best-Practice Manufacturing: The Role of Transnational Corporations and Implications for Developing Countries* (United Nations publication, Sales No. E.90.II.A.13).

[32]Transnational Corporations and Management Division, *Transnational Corporations and the Transfer of New Management Practices to Developing Countries* (New York, United Nations, forthcoming).

[33]UNCTC, *Foreign Direct Investment and Industrial Restructuring in Mexico* (United Nations publication, Sales No. E.92.II.A.9).

[34]See, for example, Richard Caves, "Multinational firms, competition and productivity in host country markets", *Economica*, vol. 14, No. 162 (1974), pp. 176-183; S. Globerman, "Foreign direct investment and 'spill-over' efficiency benefits in Canadian manufacturing industries", *Canadian Journal of Economics*, vol. 12, No. 1 (1980), pp. 24-52.

[35]Magnus Blomström and Edward N. Wolf, "Multinational corporations and productivity convergence in Mexico" (1989), mimeo.

[36]Mona Haddad and Ann Harrison, "Are there dynamic externalities from foreign direct investment? Evidence from Morocco", in R. Newfarmer and C. Frischtak, eds., *Transnational Corporations, Market Structure and Industrial Performance. United Nations Library on Transnational Corporations* (London, Routledge, forthcoming).

[37]*Business Asia*, vol. XXIII No. 46 (18 November 1991), p. 14.

[38]UNCTC, *Transnational Corporations and Technology Transfer: Effects and Policy Issues* (United Nations publication, Sales No. E.87.11.A.4), p. 14.

[39]Calculated from table 2 in Lim Su Kim, "Technological transformation in Korea and its implications for other developing countries", *Development and South-South Cooperation*, vol. IV No. 7 (December 1988), pp. 19-29.

[40]The World Bank, Industry and Energy Department, *Technology Strategy and Policy for Industrial Competitiveness: A Case Study of Thailand* (Washington, D.C., The World Bank, April 1990), p. 16.

[41]Ibid.

[42]See Jonathan B. Tucker, "Partners and rivals: a model of international collaboration in advanced technology", *International Organization*, vol. 45, No. 1 (Winter 1991), pp. 83-120.

[43]See Lynn Krieger Mytelka, ed., *Strategic Partnerships: States Firms and International Competition* (London, Pinter Publishers, 1991), pp. 7-35.

[44]See Kenichi Ohmae, "The global logic of strategic alliances", *Harvard Business Review*, vol. 89, No. 2 (March-April 1989), pp. 143-154.

[45]See Gee San, "Technology, investment and trade under economic globalization: the case of Taiwan", in OECD, *Trade, Investment and Technology in the 1990s* (Paris, OECD, 1991), pp. 57-97.

[46]See *Financial Times*, 20 November 1991.

[47]*Asian Business* (January 1991), p. 26.

[48]The numbers are based on a total of 4,192 strategic technology alliances contained in the MERIT data bank, University of Limburg, Maastricht.

[49]For a discussion of issues related to performance requirements, see UNCTC and UNCTAD, *The Impact of Trade-related Investment Measures on Trade and Development* (United Nations publication, Sales No. E.91.II.A.19).

Chapter VII

TRANSNATIONAL CORPORATIONS, HUMAN RESOURCE DEVELOPMENT AND GROWTH

Human development is linked to economic growth through the relationship between human resources and production as well as the relationship between human welfare and consumption. Improvements in the quality of human resources through investments in health, education and training enhance the stock of human capital and increase the productivity of labour and other factors of production. Human resources are thus important determinants of economic growth. But human beings are not only "instruments for furthering commodity production...they are also ultimate ends and beneficiaries of the process." [1] While greater investment in human development as a factor input contributes to economic growth, the resultant improved quality of life of the people of a nation is also an end in itself. Economic growth can thus be viewed as dependent upon, as well as a means for, human development, which includes human resource development or the development of human beings as productive agents as well as the development of human beings as the final consumers of goods and services.

To a significant extent, activities contributing to the development of human resources fall within the domain of Governments, which is especially true of health and education, for which the public sector is responsible in many countries. Nevertheless, the private sector, including TNCs, has a role to play in several respects. The present chapter describes and analyses the contribution of TNCs to economic growth through their impact on human resource development, that is, human development from a productive capacity point of view. First, it briefly outlines the relationship between the development of human resources and economic growth and examines the linkages between the main areas of that development and growth. Second, it considers how the activities and operations of TNCs affect the development of human resources in host developing countries, drawing upon available empirical evidence. Third, it discusses the role of TNCs in the creation of employment opportunity, which is closely related to the development of human resources. Finally, the chapter assesses the role of TNCs in the development of human resources and considers some policy implications for strengthening the contribution of TNCs to that development.

A. Human resource development as a factor in growth

The development of human resources involves improvements in population quality through investments to make people more healthy, educated and skilled. Developing the quality of human resources through improved health, education and training raises the physical, mental and cognitive skills of the population and thereby enhances the productivity of human effort, which, in turn, contributes to economic growth. Improvements in population quality, which have economic value and can be augmented by appropriate investment, are investments in human capital. [2] A substantial body of empirical evidence now shows that such investment in human capital is a significant determinant of economic growth in developed as well as developing countries. [3] The contributions to growth arise not only from increased labour productivity, but also from improved entrepreneurial and managerial capabilities that enable the human agent to take better advantage of economic opportunities and to deploy resources more effectively.

More specifically, the main areas of human resource development are linked to growth in the following ways:

- *Health and nutrition.* While improved health and nutrition are certainly desirable ends from a consumption point of view, strong evidence exists that improved health and nutrition also have a positive impact on economic performance. [4] Additions to the quantity and improvements in the quality of food and medical services, while normally classified as consumption expenditure, have the attributes of investment in several respects, especially when the initial levels of consumption are low. Improved health and nutrition contribute to economic growth through their immediate effects on productivity as well as through the long-term effects of increased absorptive capacity for new knowledge. Immediate effects on productivity include increases in worker energy, reduction of illness and thus of work days lost through illness, and prolonged duration of working life. Improved health and nutrition affect absorptive capacity by enhancing the ability and motivation of both adults and children to learn. [5] Improved health and nutrition for children also have an immediate effect on adult productivity in that parents need not substitute "nursing time", caring for sick children, for "productive time".

- *General education.* General education refers to literacy, numeracy and general skills and knowledge usually transmitted during primary and secondary education. The links between education, labour productivity and economic growth are well established in a number of studies.[6] A recent study of the determinants of real GDP covering 58 countries over the period 1965-1980 suggests that an increase of one year in average years of education could lead to a 3 per cent rise in GDP.[7] Investments in human development through general education affect productivity by increasing the national level of willingness, as well as the capability to accept and adopt new techniques and knowledge. For example, it has been shown that the more educated workers are, the more willing and able they are to adopt new agricultural production techniques. The national level of general education of a people also affects the absorptive capacity for more advanced technical knowledge. Japan represents a classic example of a nation that succeeded in the rapid accumulation of technical knowledge based on a solid investment in the levels of general education of its human resources.[8] Similarly, much of the success of the newly-industrializing East Asian countries, most notably the Republic of Korea, has been attributed to their significant investments in improving secondary and higher education.[9]

- *Vocational training.* The productive use of capital and technology for economic growth requires an appropriate mix of complementary vocational and technical skills in the work force. Unlike general education, which yields a broad range of benefits only indirectly linked to productivity, the benefits of training in skills in specific occupations are immediately and directly tied to the economy.[10]

  Investments in vocational training succeed when workers use their skills efficiently and the returns are captured by enterprises in the form of increased efficiency and profitability and by workers in the form of increased wages.[11] For example, a study comparing vocationally trained workers with academically educated workers in a Chinese automobile factory showed that workers with vocational training have 6 to 11 per cent higher productivity than those with only academic education.[12] Specific vocational training in lieu of general secondary education can be positive for a young, growing workforce if such training leads to productive, remunerative employment, as has been observed, for example, in China, Egypt and Thailand.[13] In the absence of sustained growth in employment, however, vocational training alone has little impact on unemployment rates.

- *Managerial capability.* Three key areas of human resource capability, which are often defined in the literature as fundamental requirements for national industrial growth, are entrepreneurial, technological and managerial.[14] While the three capabilities may be separated conceptually, entrepreneurial and technological capabilities are essentially underlying components of general managerial capability. Human development in managerial capability has both cognitive and non-cognitive aspects. Cognitive aspects include the formation of competencies (such as reasoning and analytical abilities) and the transmission of information (such as technical knowledge, theories and facts).[15] Non-cognitive aspects refer to the values, attitudes and beliefs underlying such capabilities.

  Entrepreneurial ability includes the "skills needed to identify suitable investment opportunities, master the financial, technical and other resources necessary to mount projects ... at appropriate scale and with appropriate market orientation".[16] Entrepreneurs who perceive profitable opportunities, take risks and have the ability to manage businesses have played an important role in the rise of all modern societies, [17] and thus are critical for economic development. The 1989 World Bank Report on Sub-Saharan Africa, for example, called for an enlarged role for entrepreneurs and a correspondingly improved business environment, so that enterprises of all sizes could make a greater contribution to economic development of the region. [18]

Technological capability is necessary for a nation to develop its industrial and service sectors. It includes not only the ability to operate a plant or business, but also the ability to create new productive capacity and, most importantly, to innovate, or to adapt, modify and improve methods and products and to develop new ones. [19] The acquisition of technological capabilities by developing countries with access to imported technology chiefly depends on training possibilities for local personnel, including those needed to adapt such technology to local needs. [20] In the services sector, a significant part of technology consists of skills and knowledge embodied in human beings, and it is only through training that most of this "soft" technology can be transferred.

Tertiary education in universities and other institutions, which provides some of the skills mentioned above, has been growing in developing countries. Nevertheless, the development of managerial capability has often been identified as one of the most critical needs for economic development. The lack of effective organizations is a serious bottleneck to economic development in many developing countries. Failures in private enterprise as well as failures in publicly managed development programmes, have often been attributed to inappropriate organizational forms and procedures, inability to plan, implement and evaluate projects and inadequate management information systems. [21]

Finally, human resource development for growth is closely linked to the opportunity for gainful employment. Employment contributes to economic growth through human resource development in two fundamental ways. First, gainful employment generates income for the former unemployed and under-employed; increased personal income permits individuals to make greater personal investment in health and education, both for themselves and for their families. The personal investments result in high private rates of return through better job opportunities, further income increases and improved family nutrition and health. Increased private investments in basic human capital in the aggregate contribute to overall increases in national productivity as well. Second, employment not only increases personal income, but also is a means for professional training and development. Employment and skill development are therefore complementary: while employment requires and is dependent on skills being present in the labour force, it also generates skills in a process of learning by doing. Lack of employment leads to a deterioration of skills. Thus, unemployment is not only a loss of potential output in the present, but, if sustained, represents a loss of potential output in the future as well.

B. Transnational corporations and human resource development

1. Impact on health and nutrition

Transnational corporations in pharmaceutical, health-care, agricultural, biotechnology and food-products industries potentially influence health and nutrition levels in both developed and developing countries through major breakthroughs in health and medical research and the introduction of new food products and food-production technology. While most of the actual effects of the innovations in developing countries are the result of local government or private-sector action, TNCs can play some role through their production and trade activities in host countries.

Research and development by large transnational pharmaceutical corporations has been responsible for a multitude of discoveries that have improved the level of human development world-wide in terms of health. Those firms show high levels of R&D expenditure as a percentage of sales, ranging from 5 to 15 per cent. [22] Empirical evidence suggests that the R&D expenditure of pharmaceutical TNCs will remain steady or will increase in the future, as new products are their essential lifeline. In the past decade, none of the world's 30 largest pharmaceutical firms reduced R&D expenditures, even during periods of falling profits. [23] The actual benefits from the advances depend, of course, on the costs of improvements in health and nutrition in relation to the resources available. For example, drug prices in developing countries are very high in relation to wages and basic necessities. As a representative of the Belgian drug company Janssen pointed out: [24]

> "... far too often ... the drugs we found and developed after years of research, do not always reach the people who are most in need of them. It is often very difficult to reach the rural populations in developing countries. But the biggest problem for people who have to do with a strict minimum of existence ... remains the *price* of the drug".

In response to developing-country needs, many pharmaceutical TNCs have expressed interest in supplying essential drugs for public health-service use in poor countries at lower cost. [25] Transnational drug manufacturers can also contribute by becoming actively involved in providing consulting services to advise on improvements in national drug policies and the logistics of supply. One example is the Burundi Pilot Project, the result of a collaboration between the Ministry of Health of Burundi, the World Health Organization and three Swiss pharmaceutical TNCs: Hoffmann-La Roche, Ciba-Geigy and Sandoz. [26]

Transnational corporations may also engage in R&D in health-related fields within the developing countries in which they operate. Such activity can contribute to the professional development of indigenous researchers, and it can generate relevant knowledge locally about health issues. Although localization of R&D by large research-intensive TNCs takes place only rarely, [27] some exceptions to this trend have been noted. Four laboratories dedicated to research in developing new drugs to treat tropical diseases have been set up in developing countries by Wellcome, a British drug manufacturer. [28] And, in

1984, IBM established a regional health-industry centre in Singapore to design and develop applications software for health management. [29]

Where no new technology or innovation is involved, TNCs in the health-care industry may internationalize operations. Several health-care enterprises based in the United States and other industrialized countries have established affiliates in developing countries. [30] More recently, the momentum for the economic integration of the United States, Canada and Mexico is encouraging the relocation to Mexico of subacute and nonacute health-care facilities owned and operated by United States corporations. [31] Such a relocation enables health-care TNCs to benefit from the lower labour costs in Mexico. While the local population may not benefit from such centres as patients, the inflow of medical equipment and of more advanced health-care practices and standards potentially contributes to the development of local health-care practitioners. Training of health-care practitioners may also occur through autonomous programmes developed and supported by transnational corporations. Ciba-Geigy, for example, supports a programme to train general practitioners in epilepsy treatment that has been introduced in more than 15 developing countries. [32]

Another area of health on which TNCs have a potential impact relates to nutrition. Affiliates of TNCs produce approximately 12 per cent of the processed food in developing countries; in the more advanced developing countries, with a heavier investment in the food industry, the percentage can rise to over 25 per cent. [33] Transnational corporations in the food-processing industry are thus in a unique position to influence the nutrition levels of the developing countries in which they operate. The activities of the H.J. Heinz company, for example, illustrate the potential for food-processing TNCs to contribute to increased health and nutrition levels (box VII.1). The positive impact of Heinz in particular regions, however, is the result of specific corporate policy and philosophy; in general, the contribution of TNCs to increased health and nutrition must be considered on a case-by-case basis.

Box VII.1. Examples of contributions to health and nutrition through joint ventures in the food-processing industry

The H.J. Heinz Company formed a 51 per cent-owned joint venture with Olivine Industries in Zimbabwe. As part of the arrangement, Heinz offered the Government of Zimbabwe assistance in agriculture, food production and training in new product development. Heinz agronomists introduced the Michigan pea bean, a hardy crop that supplies the home market with a nutritious, inexpensive source of protein (and which has also become a valuable export commodity for Zimbabwe). Heinz also made direct contributions of $200,000 to build and run a medical clinic at Nyamatikiti, and $50,000 towards the construction of a hospital at the Kutama mission.

In China, Heinz holds a 60 per cent-owned joint venture with the General Corporation of Agriculture, Industry and Commerce and the United Food Enterprise (UFE), which is a cooperative of food manufacturers linked to the China National Food Industries Association. Through a $10 million baby-food plant employing 120 workers, Heinz introduced a highly nutritious affordable product to feed infants in the country—a need

/.....

The introduction of new food products and food-production technology by TNCs may, however, also have deleterious effects on local consumption patterns,[34] which could be negatively affected in terms of health and nutrition through strong TNC advertising programmes for alcohol, tobacco, soft drinks, less nutritious processed foods and infant bottle formula. For example, United States cigarette manufacturers have implemented aggressive advertising and promotion campaigns in a number of Asian developing countries, in addition to exerting pressure to open the markets to foreign competition.[35] The new consumer tastes promoted by TNCs may induce a switch to higher-priced, imported brand-name food products that may be less nutritious than traditional diet staples, or harmful to health, although the extent to which that happens would depend on individual choice as well as on public and private efforts to promote awareness of health issues.

2. Impact on general education

The impact of TNCs on primary or secondary education in host countries, through direct investment or financial contributions, is minimal. Education is an area that is typically and entirely the domain of the Government or other domestic societal groups; the role of external participants, to the extent that it exists, is primarily confined to financial and other contributions by foreign public and non-governmental organizations. It has been observed, however, that some TNCs include training in basic educational skills in their training programmes when local circumstances make it necessary; for example, Unilever and Mobil Oil France have provided teaching in reading, writing and arithmetic to workers with little or no formal education in their developing-country affiliates.[36]

(Box VII.1, cont'd.)

the Government of China had specifically identified. Along with the factory came a research programme into malnutrition in Chinese babies. Outcomes of the research programme include identification of regional variance in deficiencies of protein and iron; this research has been channelled through the China National Women's Foundation—a group which offers instruction on infant care and feeding to mothers throughout the country.

In Thailand, Heinz holds a 51 per cent-owned joint venture with Win-Chance Foods Company, Ltd., and built on the local company's flavoured milk powder line to introduce Heinz Infant Milk Cereals—a newly formulated, highly nutritious product aimed at decreasing malnutrition. A team of Heinz nutritionists worked with the faculty of Bangkok's Mahidol University on a research project to determine the effectiveness of a proposed four-month feeding programme to improve infant metabolism and nutritional well-being.

Source: Anthony J.F. O'Reilly, "Establishing successful joint ventures in developing nations: a CEO's perspective", *Columbia Journal of World Business*, vol. 23 (1988), pp. 65-71.

Transnational corporations could also have an impact on the relevance of a national education system. In an economy in which the rate and type of change of technology depend primarily on changes in the domestic economy itself, the degree of interface between the educational system and the economy is usually achieved with minimal effort. The knowledge and skills required for indigenous industries and organizations are generally institutionalized in national educational programmes. The presence of TNCs in a developing country, however, sometimes contributes to sudden technological changes. Such changes require new and rapidly-changing skills and knowledge that are often not synchronized with the knowledge and skills being provided by the local educational system: [37]

> "... when the rate of technological change becomes imposed ... by the sudden introduction of techniques of production that bear little resemblance to the emerging needs of the mass economy, educational relevance is somewhat undermined. How the educational systems and policy in the receiving economies adjust and respond to these strains has never been examined fully. It is believed that the adjustment processes are complex and difficult, and when, as is the case, the multinational corporation is the means for such transfers of technology, these difficulties could constitute serious constraints on the articulation and execution of educational-cum-manpower policy in the typically less-developed country."

In economies that face rapid technological change (whether developing or developed), the expansion of general education is an important policy task. [38] Enhancing secondary education increases the willingness of the population to accept the new technology in addition to ensuring a basic level of literacy and analytical ability on which individuals may build further capability. General secondary education also provides graduates with more labour market flexibility than narrow vocational training. [39] In the face of rapid industrial advancement, however, one typical response to educational policy in developing countries is to substitute formal vocational training for general secondary education. The implications of such a policy are discussed below.

3. Impact on vocational training

Private vocational training capacity in developing countries is often weak; thus, formal training in vocational skills is largely provided by government agencies and ministries. The efficiency of public vocational education and training, however, has often been questioned. Most new technology enters into a developing country through private foreign enterprise; thus ownership of the equipment, technical information and training methods needed to develop the skills required to work with the technologies reside within TNCs. An important channel for government agencies to increase, improve and update their vocational training efforts is, therefore, through collaboration with TNCs. The Economic Development Board of Singapore, for example, has collaborated with various TNCs to establish and improve training centres and institutes (table VII.1). While vocational training, however, may at times be beneficial for employment opportunities in general, such training is industry-based and usually tied to the specific needs of TNCs. Thus, a structure of dependence may be created in which local human resources are being supplied with skills suitable for employment in TNCs, but inappropriate for indigenous industrial or agricultural expansion.

Table VII.1 Contributions by transnational corporations to vocational training in Singapore

TNC	*Training provided*
Tata	Tool- and die-making; precision machining
Brown-Boveri	Tool and die production; toolroom machining; precision mechanics
Philips	Precision machining
Computervision Corporation	Mechanical design; drafting; numerical control; structural analysis; circuit board design
ASEA	Robotics applications; robotics programming; operating, maintenance and servicing; project engineering

Source: Hafiz Mirza, *Multinational Corporations and the Growth of the Singapore Economy* (London, Croom Helm, 1986), p. 68.

The most important aspect of vocational training by TNCs consists, however, of training provided to production workers in host-country affiliates and subsidiaries of TNCs. Most of the training is conducted to satisfy staffing requirements essential for the functioning of the enterprise. According to available studies of manufacturing TNCs, the volume and quality of such training is important and extends to all categories of personnel, although training efforts are uneven and vary according to production sector, length of involvement in the country, the qualifications of the available indigenous manpower and local training policies.[40] The training of manual (unskilled and semi-skilled) production workers represents the bulk of TNC training efforts in terms of numbers. But it is usually less developed than training provided to skilled workers and management staff; rather, it is geared towards complementing existing skills as required for the immediate performance of a specific production-line function in an enterprise. Such training is usually brief, on the job and conducted by the host-country affiliate. It is typically more specific than in local enterprises and sometimes of limited use in the wider national labour market.

The training of skilled workers is provided only to a small proportion of the labour force in a TNC, but is generally of a high quality. Training of the workers apparently absorbs the largest share of expenditure by TNCs on training. Apprenticeship training is also reported to be important in a majority of TNCs, meeting significant standards and often going beyond the immediate needs of the TNCs.

4. Impact on management capability

Investment in health and nutrition, general education and vocational training constitutes investment in the basic quality of the human capital of a nation. As mentioned earlier, the basic quality of human capital is a critical factor affecting the national absorptive capacity for more advanced technical and managerial knowledge. Those specific capabilities are probably the most important areas in which TNCs can make a contribution.

Foreign direct investment in developing economies can stimulate the development of managerial capability in various ways. Discussions in the current literature on human resource development via training commonly make a distinction between formal, non-formal and informal learning. [41] Formal learning refers to a planned and evaluated sequential programme leading to a certificate, degree or diploma. Non-formal learning is organized learning that is usually ungraded, non-sequential and/or part-time. Informal learning is a lifelong process by which people acquire attitudes and values through daily experience, observation and exposure to their environment. The impact of TNCs on the development of managerial, entrepreneurial and technological capabilities will be discussed below in terms of each of three channels: through formal institutions such as management schools and technical institutions; through non-formal on-the-job training and professional development, both within TNCs and through collaborative agreements with TNCs; and through the informal transmission of values, attitudes and beliefs embedded in the organizational culture of the TNCs.

(a) Formal learning

A wide gap exists in many developing countries between the demand for and the supply of knowledgeable and skilled indigenous managerial talent. The gap represents a major constraint to the development of entrepreneurial activities and the utilization of foreign direct investment. [42] For example, one study reporting on research in Latin America concludes that the "inability of Latin American managers to effectively utilize all factors of production, notably human resources, has been [an] ... important constraint on regional development". [43] One focus of transnational training institutions, therefore, has been on the development of management education in the developing countries. The potential for a substantial impact on management development through joint ventures between management schools based in developed and developing countries is considerable. Transnational business schools, to the extent that they are profit-seeking institutions, are transnational corporations (table VII.2). Even if otherwise, they remain important channels through which conventional TNCs contribute to human resource development in the developing world. The management-education programmes of North American universities are often influenced by large TNCs, which provide both direct financial assistance and input for curriculum development through executive advisory boards. As North American business schools develop linkages with developing countries, they transmit, in part, the strategies and philosophies of the TNCs that support them as well as provide much of the empirical base for their research and training activities.

Harvard University, for example, was instrumental in the development of INCAE (Instituto Centroamericano de Administración de Empresas) in Nicaragua and Costa Rica and maintains strong linkages with that institution. Both campuses offer graduate programmes (MBA) and executive MBA programmes patterned after the Harvard model, as well as numerous executive development programmes. Another example of extensive transnational linkages in management education exists between Canada and China (box VII.2). Several other North American and European business schools or universities have affiliates or joint ventures in various developing and Eastern European economies. Training in formal institutions such as those develops both the cognitive and non-cognitive components of managerial capability, even though both components are, to a certain extent, culture-bound. Western management schools, particularly those in the United States, concentrate on producing MBAs with the knowledge,

Table VII.2. Transnational affiliations of institutions of higher education, 1992

Parent university	*Home country*	*Name of associated institution*	*City of associated institution*	*Country of associated institution*	*Type of association* [a]
European University	Belgium	European University	Antwerp	Belgium	Subsidiary
		European University	Brussels	Belgium	Subsidiary
		European University	Paris	France	Subsidiary
		European University	Toulouse	France	Subsidiary
		European University	Munich	Germany	Subsidiary
		European University	Athens	Greece	Subsidiary
		European University	Thessaloniki	Greece	Subsidiary
		European University	Rome	Italy	Subsidiary
		European University	St. Vincent	Italy	Subsidiary
		European University	The Hague	Netherlands	Subsidiary
		European University	Lisbon	Portugal	Subsidiary
		European University	Barcelona	Spain	Subsidiary
		European University	Lisbon	Spain	Subsidiary
		European University	Geneva	Switzerland	Subsidiary
		European University	Montreux	Switzerland	Subsidiary
		European University	Sion	Switzerland	Subsidiary
EAP Paris	France	EAP Oxford [b]	Oxford	United Kingdom	Subsidiary
		EAP Madrid [b]	Madrid	Spain	Subsidiary
		EAP Berlin [b]	Berlin	Germany	Subsidiary
Ecole Européen de Gestion — Groupe EBS	France	Paseo del Pinto Rosales and European Business School	Madrid	Spain	Subsidiary
		European Business School	Milan	Italy	Subsidiary
		European Business School	Munich	Germany	Subsidiary
		European Business School	Brussels	Belgium	Subsidiary
		Escola Europea de Gestio	Andorra	Andorra	Subsidiary
		European Business Management School	London	United Kingdom	Subsidiary
European Business School	Germany	European Business School	Prague	Czechoslovakia	Subsidiary
		European Business School	Paris	France	Subsidiary
		European Business School	London	United Kingdom	Subsidiary
Luigi Bocconi University	Italy	St. Petersburg University	St. Petersburg	Russia	Joint venture
The Netherlands International Institute for Management	Netherlands	Debrecen Agricultural University [c]	Debrecen	Hungary	Joint venture
		National Productivity Association	Singapore	Singapore	Joint venture
		University of Trisakti	Jakarta	Indonesia	Joint venture
		Intercollege	Nicosia	Cyprus	Joint venture
		Centre for Management and Human Resource Development	..	Yugoslavia	Joint venture
		Malaysian Institute for Management [d]	Kuala Lumpur	Malaysia	Joint venture
		Intercollege [d]	Athens	Greece	Joint venture
St. Katherine's College, Oxford University	United Kingdom	St. Katherine's College	Kobe	Japan	Subsidiary
University of Hartford	United States	The University of Hartford Business School (UHBS)	Paris	France	Subsidiary

Source: United Nations Department of Economic and Social Development, Transnational Corporations and Management Division, 1992.

a In the case of subsidiaries, ownership is 100 per cent.
b Management learning centre.
c Agro-based industries management programme together with University College of Dublin and the Agricultural University Wageningen.
d Facilities are not yet fully operational.

skills and attitudes that enable them to achieve the profit-maximizing objectives of the corporations. Effective management for economic growth in other regions may require a different set of skills and attitudes. For example, it has been observed that organizations in Asia "place equally high importance on the Asian manager's intuitive and philosophical skills" and that "the Asian manager must be sensitive to the all-pervasive Asian value of familial relationships, which is evident across the range of Asian corporations". [44]

Box VII.2. Transnational management education: Canada and China

The Canada-China Management Education Program Phase II (CCMEP II) is designed to assist Chinese universities to meet the growing demand for management education in China. Under the auspices of the Canadian Federation of Deans of Management and Administrative Studies and China's State Education Commission, Phase II is an integrated network of approximately 25 Canadian and 25 Chinese schools. Since one of the primary strategies of the programme is to strengthen China's managerial training capacity (in addition to managerial capacity), doctoral programmes and in-China MBA programmes are important elements in the project. A National Executive Development programme responds to China's more immediate need to upgrade the skills of its line managers. Phase I of the programme began in 1983. Linkages were formed between 8 leading Chinese universities and 10 Canadian faculties of management. Phase II has also introduced a National PhD programme which grants a Chinese degree to 40 students jointly trained in China and Canada. Other activities include materials development, study tours and conferences. Additional linkages include the training of 145 visiting scholars, 50 master's students and 73 doctoral students in Canada and over 130 Canadian professors who will share their expertise by teaching in China.

Source: Canada-China Management Education Program II National Coordinating Office Bulletin (Montreal, December 1989).

In addition to differences in managerial values, countries differ in terms of institutional and economic environments. Western business schools primarily cater to the needs of the urban-based business community. In developing countries, however, managerial skill must also be developed for rural-based agricultural enterprises, for government agencies and state-owned enterprises and for cooperatives and non-profit organizations. Abilities and skills in the functional areas of management imparted through transnational business schools should therefore be made relevant to the actual environment of the students. If the goal of the transnational business school is to develop local capability, business cases and teaching materials used in developing countries should have a high level of local content and should emphasize the development of the particular managerial skills most needed for the region or country. INCAE, for example, has succeeded in doing so by developing a vast number of cases with Central American business structures and strategies, in Spanish.

In addition to the role played by transnational educational institutions in developing countries, TNCs in manufacturing and services also contribute to formal training of host-country nationals in management and technical skills. One avenue is the financing of university degree courses for senior employees and managers (from developed as well as developing countries). According to an ILO study based on responses from 15 major TNCs, such programmes were provided by Alusuisse, Unilever and Mobil Oil France. [45] Some TNCs establish formal training programmes of their own (leading to a degree or diploma) for students other than their own employees. Examples are the Philips International Institute or Alusuisse, both of which provide scholarships to students from developing countries, and the establishment of a training programme by German TNCs for managers in India.[46] Similar formal training is provided by transnational banks (TNBs) that develop the professional skills of their managers by sending a selected number to attend courses at business schools or management departments of universities.[47] Some TNBs have regional training centres outside their home countries, where they provide their staff with specialized training as well as more advanced and professional courses.

Furthermore, the direct operations of TNCs in developing countries can affect the national proportion of human resources that are induced to attend advanced formal training institutions. Transnational corporations draw on the existing pool of trained candidates, sometimes depriving local enterprises of competent personnel. The presence of TNCs offering relatively sophisticated employment opportunities can stimulate potential employees to invest in advanced training. A recent study in Brazil indicates that importation of foreign technology leads to an increase in university-trained personnel. By contrast, traditional industries based on established technologies with little foreign import did not substantially increase their technically trained personnel on their own.[48]

(b) Non-formal learning

The second broad component of training and development concerns the process of non-formal learning. Transnational corporations have their most substantial impact on the development of managerial capability via non-formal training and development activity. The principal channels for non-formal learning are, first, direct training and development programmes offered by TNCs; and, second, the indirect absorption of knowledge and practices by local firms that enter into joint ventures, strategic alliances and collaborative arrangements with TNCs.

(i) Non-formal learning through direct training and development

Training and development in foreign affiliates takes place in two steps: first, a foreign affiliate recruits and trains local workers in skills (technological and managerial) necessary to master and implement the technology used by the affiliate in its operations in that country; second, as local workers gain experience, they advance within the affiliate, replacing expatriates and taking on assignments of greater responsibility.

Transnational corporations have a potentially significant impact on the development of managerial capability through direct training of the local staff they recruit. There is, however, limited empirical work throwing light on human-resource management in foreign affiliates, including the selection, recruitment and training of host-country nationals.[49] It appears that affiliates generally expend at least as much, if not more, in resources to train local managers as do indigenous firms. For example, a study comparing executive training of host-country nationals in TNCs with executive training of nationals in local firms in Turkey concludes that TNCs spent twice as much on training (as a percentage of payroll) than did local firms (table VII.3). Other empirical research, including a major study by the ILO, supports the view that foreign affiliates train a substantial percentage of their employees, particularly in new industries, with emphasis on training programmes for high- and medium-level managerial staff and key technical personnel. Types of training provided include short internal and external courses at headquarters or in the host country, assignments to the parent company, study travel to keep abreast of products and techniques and deputation of trained personnel from the parent company.[50] In the services sector, which is now the principal recipient of FDI worldwide and of growing importance in developing as well as developed countries, TNCs are an important source of training in management and related skills, which is the main channel for the transfer of services technology (see box VII.3).

Table VII.3. Executive training programmes of transnational corporations and local firms in Turkey

Item	*TNC*	*Local firm*
Existence of standard executive training programmes (per cent)	72.4	54.8
Frequency of standard training programmes		
Once a year (per cent)	29.4	41.2
Twice a year (per cent)	70.6	58.8
Mean cost of training programme (thousands of Turkish Lira)	37 908	7 543
Mean total payroll of white-collar employees (thousands of Turkish Lira)	648 000	632 600
Ratio of costs of training programmes to total payroll of white-collar employees (per cent)	4	2
Cost of training per executive (thousands of Turkish Lira)	1 516	613

Source: D. Erden, "Impact of multinational corporations on host countries: executive training programs", *Management International Review*, vol. 28, No. 3 (1988), pp. 39-47.

The capabilities of employees are further enhanced through professional development and advancement within the firm. Expatriate employment is an important factor influencing such development, since opportunities for local employee advancement depend at least partially on the extent to which TNCs rely on expatriates. The importance of expatriate employees appears to vary according to the origin, the maturity of the investment and the organizational and technical complexity of the enterprise.[51] Recent evidence points to a noticeable replacement of United States expatriates by local (or third-country) nationals. In a major study of large United States-based TNCs (industrial companies and banks), half of the companies surveyed indicated a significant reduction in expatriates during the 1980s.[52] Other research reported that 80 per cent of United States firms surveyed employed a host-country national as head of a majority of country operations.[53] Such significant replacement of expatriates with developing-country nationals in the managerial ranks of TNCs may be regarded as a positive sign for the growing managerial and technical competence of the local labour force.[54] Aggregate data for the United States confirm the trend towards decreasing employment of home-country citizens by United States TNCs. Similar replacement has not taken place in Japanese TNCs, whose investments are relatively more recent (table VII.4).

Even though TNCs may expend substantially more resources training and developing their local staff than do indigenous firms, the impact on growth of the host economy depends upon whether the

Box VII.3. Investments in training by transnational service corporations in developing countries

Persons with technical training and cognitive and communication skills are of special importance in the service industries, where much of the technology is embodied in human beings. Transnational corporations in services rely heavily on the technical, administrative and managerial skills of local personnel in host countries to maintain company standards and contribute to innovations. For this reason, many of them have created extensive training programmes to develop these skills and further employee education.

A survey of the operations of its members in a sample of 15 developing countries by the Coalition of Service Industries, an organization of 17 major TNCs representing various service industries, indicated various forms of formal and non-formal training, including local programmes, developmental courses, fellowships and scholarships, regional and headquarters training centres, and support for outside academic and professional programmes. Some professions require a minimum number of hours of training each year, and one company indicated a strong commitment to training its suppliers and customers, as well as its employees. The average hours of training per year across the 15 countries in the respondent companies ranged from 26 to 103, with the average at 59.4 hours per year.

Eight companies maintained facilities in developing countries designed specifically for R&D or training. One firm built an Advanced Systems Center in the Philippines which provided state-of-the-art technology for computer systems development. This company also maintained a regional training centre for accounting and related services in Mexico.

Another company established a regional training centre in Indonesia for engineering and construction management, and another respondent maintained training facilities in Hong Kong and Singapore for information and telecommunications products and services. One company initiated the establishment of national institutes in Hong Kong, Taiwan Province of China and Thailand to stimulate professionalism and productivity of the local insurance industry.

In addition to training programmes for enhancing employee skills and management capabilities, service TNCs have implemented activities to improve the capabilities of local service providers. For example, in Thailand, an innovative training technique was developed to teach foreign currency trading skills to local financial institutions through the use of computer simulation of global exchange markets. In Malaysia, seminars have been organized and guides produced to improve management performance in restaurant and retail industries. In Mexico, the "Juntos Podemos" programme was established in cooperation with local tourist establishments to promote less well known regions of the country, to invoke local community awareness of the benefits of tourism and to train staff from local tourism and retail establishments.

An information centre was built in the Côte d'Ivoire by one of the respondent companies to aid African countries in maintaining a regional network for the exchange of news and data within the continent, and connecting to networks in Europe and the United States. The company provided the hardware for the facility and is responsible for training the local personnel.

Source: The Coalition of Service Companies, *Company Operations in Developing Countries* (Washington, D.C., The Coalition of Service Companies, 1989), pp. 4 and 7.

skills developed through TNC training are diffused and absorbed outside of the TNC, especially through the turnover of trained staff. In many cases, the training offered by TNCs is observed to be "incomplete, in the sense of enabling nationals to eventually run the industry successfully".[55] A survey examining the nature of training programmes for local managers by the subsidiaries of 21 TNCs operating in Turkey concludes that the training programmes provided successful results for the subsidiaries; however, the effect on the local industry as a whole was slight.[56] Thus, although the TNC effectively trains its own employees, thereby raising the level of employee expertise, the broader penetration of the expertise into the pool of human resources of the developing country can be relatively small. There is also some evidence, however, that, in more rapidly expanding developing countries, the turnover of trained technical and managerial staff in the host economy can be quite high. For example, poaching on trained engineers from TNCs by small or new enterprises, and job hopping, have become apparently quite common in Thailand.[57]

Table VII.4. Expatriate employment in foreign affiliates of United States and Japanese transnational corporations

(Percentage share of home country citizens in total employment)

Sector	*United States* [a]		*Japan*	
	1982	*1989*	*1982*	*1989*
All industries	0.8	0.4	2.0 [b]	3.0
Mining	5.3 [c]	2.6 [c]	1.2 [b]	2.5
Manufacturing	1.9	0.2	1.0 [b]	1.7
Services	1.3	0.5	..	..
Wholesale trade	0.6	0.4	10.2 [b d]	8.8 [d]
Other services	1.7	0.6	5.4 [e]	5.1

Source: United States, Department of Commerce, *U.S. Direct Investment Abroad: 1982 Benchmark Survey Data* (Washington, D.C., Department of Commerce, 1985), and United States Department of Commerce, *U.S. Direct Investment Abroad: 1989 Benchmark Survey, Preliminary Results* (Washington, D.C., Department of Commerce, 1991). See also Ministry of International Trade and Industry, *Kaigai Toshi Tokei Soran: Kaigai Jigyo Katsudo Kihon Chosa*, No. 1 (Tokyo, Toyo Hoki Shuppan, 1983), No. 3 (Tokyo, Kaibun Shuppan, 1989) and No. 4 (Tokyo, Printing Bureau, Ministry of Finance, 1991).

a Data are for majority-owned non-bank affiliates of non-bank United States parents.
b For 1981.
c Petroleum.
d Data are for "commerce".
e For 1986.

In spite of its variable impact, training remains one of the most important channels through which TNCs can contribute to human resource development in the countries in which they operate, particularly if the training activities of TNCs may be extended to include human resources beyond the immediate employees of a TNC. The provision of training beyond the basic needs of the firm, however, is not the operating norm of TNCs: given the potential loss of competitive advantage to indigenous or non-indigenous rival firms, TNCs may be unwilling to invest heavily in either the training of non-proprietary skilled workers or of managers beyond what is perceived to be the minimum necessary.[58]

In addition to government incentives for TNCs to invest in training beyond their own needs, which is discussed further in section E below, different mechanisms have been identified through which corporations can "train beyond capacity" to benefit the host nation as a whole. For example, a firm can train in excess of its own needs and absorb the additional cost as a contribution to human development in the countries in which it operates (an approach pioneered by Goodyear).[59] Or, as practised by Daimler Benz, a TNC may simultaneously train employees of other firms along with its own and be subsequently reimbursed by the other firms.[60] That practice may be a cost-effective strategy for smaller firms to have access to high-quality training programmes, and could also include the upgrading of skills of the non-employed. (Firms that later hired the "excess trainees" could reimburse the TNC for the initial training costs.) Another alternative is for TNCs to set up autonomous training institutions that supply skills to an entire industry, as Toyota Astra and National Gobel have done in Indonesia.[61] Finally, as box VII.4 shows, there are also possibilities of assistance through the cooperation of international institutions and TNCs, such as, between the Transnational Corporations and Management Division and a number of individual TNCs.

Training by TNCs can also extend beyond the firm through vertical linkages with local suppliers. For example, strong vertical linkages have been created by numerous TNCs in the electronics industry in Singapore.[62] One TNC, for example, has actively helped to set up and develop locally owned supporting industries. The TNC encouraged firms to become suppliers to it by offering technical training and advice from local and expatriate engineers and consultants flown in from Europe. Years of training are invested in some suppliers to enable them to improve the quality of products and develop cost-efficient practices. When new products or techniques are introduced, the suppliers are also retrained. The streamlining of the production methods of the supplier benefits both the TNC that offers the training (as the supplier becomes capable of producing cheaper inputs), as well as the supplier whose increased level of technological and managerial capability makes the local firm more competitive.[63]

(ii) Non-formal learning through collaborative arrangements

A second major channel for non-formal learning relates to the transfer of technological and managerial knowledge and practices through collaborative arrangements between local firms and TNCs. As noted in the previous chapter, contractual arrangements can be important vehicles for the transfer of technology by TNCs to developing countries, in addition to direct investments by TNCs.[64] Such arrangements allow for the transfer of embodied or disembodied know-how to a contracting partner in the host country, providing opportunities for training in technical and managerial skills.

In principle, collaborative arrangements are likely to provide good opportunities for human resource development, since the local firm retains control over operations and develops its own management systems, conducive to local industry and practice. Thus, it can benefit from the introduction of management systems and the provision of training that are usually a part of the technology-import package, without implying a continuing dependence of the local firm on the TNC. There is, in fact, considerable evidence that "unpackaged" forms of technology transfer and joint ventures may be preferable to FDI or majority-equity participation by TNCs, from the point of view of effective transfer of technology and the building up of local technological capacity.[65] But the unpackaged forms may not be a realistic option in the case of more sophisticated technologies, which TNCs are reluctant to provide except through FDI, or for countries at an early stage of development. Several studies have shown that

Box VII.4. Training with transnational corporations

The development of entrepreneurial capabilities is one of the most crucial bottlenecks in many developing countries. The following projects, undertaken by the Transnational Corporations and Management Division of the United Nations Department of Economic and Social Development, suggest how an international organization can, in cooperation with TNCs, make a contribution in this respect.

China management training

One of the factors slowing down China's economic modernization efforts is the shortage of personnel competent to establish joint ventures, manage Chinese affiliates abroad, conduct import and export business and guide domestic enterprises more efficiently. This bottleneck is particularly acute at a time when the country embarks on its new development plan, in which greater emphasis is being placed on the absorption of more FDI and on the expansion of China's international business. Existing management education suffers, however, from a shortage of experienced teachers and teaching materials and, in particular, opportunities to gain hands-on experience in modern enterprises.

To address this problem, the Transnational Corporations and Management Division, the Ministry of Foreign Economic Relations and Trade of China and UNDP launched a programme to improve practical managerial and business skills of managers working in state enterprises, joint ventures of small- and medium-size TNCs and government offices involved in dealing with TNCs. After a structured and merit-based selection process, the candidates (persons with key decision-making responsibility) enter a two-month formal management training programme in China. (It is envisaged that the curriculum specifically designed for this programme will eventually be transferred to Chinese universities.) The best qualified candidates will then be sent to TNCs for an on-the-job training experience of about one year. During that time, the participants in the programme will be involved in practical work in their host TNCs, with a view towards obtaining a better understanding of how modern, profit-oriented enterprises function in a competitive international environment.

Participating companies

AKZO	(The Netherlands)	Arthur Andersen	(Germany)
ASEA Brown Boveri	(Sweden)	Avon	(United States)
Cable & Wireless	(United Kingdom)	Coopers & Lybrand Deloitte	(United Kingdom)
Crédit Suisse	(Switzerland)	Ellicott Machine Corporation	(United States)
Ericsson	(Sweden)	Ivo International Ltd.	(Finland)
Lieberherr	(Switzerland)	Logitech	(United States)
Mobil	(United States)	Nestlé	(Switzerland)
Olivetti	(Italy)	Otis Elevator/United Technologies	(United States)
Ransburg/ITW	(United States)	Rauma-Repola	(Finland)
The Royal Bank of Canada	(Canada)	Sandoz Chemicals Ltd.	(Switzerland)
Sulzer Brothers Ltd.	(Switzerland)	Valmet Paper Machinery	(Finland)

/.....

(Box VII.4, cont'd.)

The programme is financed by UNDP and the Governments of China, Japan and Switzerland. The participating TNCs (see inset) contribute the training and the living expenses of the Chinese participants.

EMPRETEC

Entrepreneurial qualities have traditionally been regarded as innate or culturally derived, leaving little room for promotion other than broad measures to change the social environment or economic conditions. However, recent research has identified 21 personal entrepreneurial competencies consistently demonstrated by successful entrepreneurs. These consist of traits such as opportunity-seeking and initiative, risk-taking, persistence and goal setting. The research also concluded that the behaviour of successful entrepreneurs occurred invariably in the different countries in which the study was conducted.[1]

That research opened up the possibility for encouraging and developing entrepreneurship through training and business support programmes. Selection procedures and training workshops emphasizing the personal entrepreneurial competencies can be developed. Support centres can be designed to provide ongoing business education and consultancy to assist the entrepreneurs in realizing their business projects. Entrepreneur networks can be encouraged to provide peer support and stimulate national and transnational business. To provide a solid underpinning and ensure long-term viability, government/private sector coalitions can be organized to ensure community support. Transnational corporations can be enlisted by these initiatives to lend executives who provide hands-on expertise on specific business problems. Linkages with TNCs can also result in subcontracting, material and equipment financing, licensing and marketing arrangements.

One example of a programme pursuing those objectives is the EMPRETEC Entrepreneurship Development Programme launched by UNCTC. Started in Argentina in 1988, the programme has expanded to Brazil, Chile, Ghana, Nigeria, Uruguay, Venezuela and Zimbabwe. The programme has involved some 1,000 entrepreneurs. Over 150 new businesses were established and some 200 existing businesses have been re-focused and expanded. More than 60 intra-EMPRETEC national and regional joint ventures, sales agreements and technology transfers have been consummated. Businesses range from genetic plant breeding, computer programming and pollution control to plastics and textile manufacture and food products.

Transnational corporations have been central to the success of the programme. Training and executives have been provided by companies such as the Bank of Boston, Ogilvy and Mather, Siemens and Techint. Du Pont has provided materials and financing to new ventures. Licensing and technology transfer agreements for vehicle emission control have been negotiated with a Canadian company. IBM has been a source for subcontracting. Banca Nacionale de Lavoro has provided start-up financing.

The EMPRETEC entrepreneurs' associations, in cooperation with the EMPRETEC programme, have organized three regional business exchange meetings in Latin America in which nearly 500 of their members have participated and negotiated business arrangements. Several have formed joint ventures, making them mini-TNCs.

---

1 See Robert McBer, *Report on Entrepreneurship Training and the Strengthening of Entrepreneurial Performance* (Washington, D.C., USAID, October 1990). See also Albert Berry, *The Future Role of Small and Medium Industry in Latin America and the Caribbean* (Toronto, University of Toronto, October 1991).

active local efforts at the firm level, as well as through national policies for building up education (general, as well as scientific and technical), are necessary.[66] Thus, the impact of collaborative agreements on the development of technological and managerial capabilities depends on the specific conditions of the contractual agreements concerning access to information, the level of technology and know-how shared and the efforts by host-country participants.

With respect to the sharing of technology, the size of a TNC also appears to be an important factor. In particular, some of the smaller TNCs in developed countries have demonstrated a strong interest in helping developing countries industrialize, particularly through the mechanism of technology transfer. Swedish firms appear to have taken the lead in that area, while, in contrast, United States firms seem to guard their technology more closely.[67] It has also been observed that, for countries with weak domestic technological capability, TNCs from developing countries may have more to offer in terms of technology transfer and building up local capabilities, although their operations are generally concentrated in mature technologies.[68]

A final aspect of the impact of TNCs on capability development through non-formal training concerns the extent of R&D undertaken by TNCs in developing countries. As discussed in the previous chapter, TNCs engage in relatively little R&D, the major source of their competitive advantage, outside of their home countries and, especially, in host developing countries. Some exceptions to this general practice were noted. The extent of R&D by TNCs in developing countries, however, tends to be correlated with the level of development of the host country: TNCs are likely to carry out more R&D in countries with fairly well-developed scientific and technological infrastructures than in those that are at an incipient level of economic development. Thus, countries at an early stage of development are unlikely to gain in terms of human resource development from the R&D activity of TNCs.

(c) *Informal learning*

The third broad channel for the development of technological and managerial capability concerns the process of informal learning whereby values, attitudes and beliefs embedded in organizational cultures are transferred to the host country. As local staff members advance to higher levels of responsibility within a TNC, they may change cultural, social and psychological values and attitudes.[69] The development of the values, attitudes and beliefs—the non-cognitive components underlying technological, managerial and entrepreneurial capabilities—occurs through a process of socialization into the organizational culture of a TNC. Underlying values and beliefs of the culture of an organization are manifest in the tangible artifacts of the firm. For example, "evaluation criteria are a direct reflection of corporate values and norms. Items like press releases, interoffice memoranda...procedures for expenditures or decisions, policy statements, speeches by company officers, the physical layout of offices...and telephone manners each reflect the company's culture".[70]

Organizational culture is also embedded in the culture of the home country of a company and thus reflects its national socio-cultural values. Thus, TNCs operating in developing countries socialize employees into an organizational culture that reflects the values of their home countries. That may be of significance in host countries in which certain cultural values may be inconsistent with the values (non-cognitive components) underlying particular managerial capabilities that are required for economic growth. For example, entrepreneurship is the fundamental link between productivity and growth in a market economy. Entrepreneurship requires moderate risk-taking and the personal acceptance of responsibility. Most Western TNCs have organizational cultures that place a high value on individual (or group) achievement and responsibility and, to the extent that the values transmitted by TNCs correspond with the values underlying the particular managerial capabilities required for development within a host country, such acculturation may be considered growth-promoting.

The process of acculturation directly affects the local employees of a TNC; in addition, inculcation of corporate values and attitudes occurs through backward and forward linkages, thus affecting the local suppliers and customers as well. Furthermore, the development of entrepreneurial, technological and managerial capabilities is encouraged by certain modifications in values and attitudes in the general populace. For example, an increased national propensity of a people to accept new products stimulates innovation and the creation of new markets. [71] The presence of TNCs in a developing country contributes to such value-and-attitude modification through its stimulation of demand, through the provision of new products and services and through marketing efforts that enhance the perceived attractiveness of modern living and values. The stimulation of demand for Western consumer products, however, also encourages greater development of the luxury consumer-goods sector, rather than of products that benefit a broader base of the people of the nation. The "know-how" unique to TNCs that produce luxury consumer goods is also centred more on marketing and packaging than on production and technological innovation. As developing countries are more in need of building capability in the latter than in the former, the stimulation of demand for new products may not always be growth-promoting.

C. Transnational corporations and employment opportunity

Transnational corporations have three main impacts on the opportunities for employment in developing countries: directly through the provision of employment within TNCs: indirectly, through the creation of employment opportunities in other organizations; and qualitatively, through changes in employment policies and practices, allowing greater access to employment for particular groups, including women, who may experience discrimination in employment.

1. Direct effects

Direct employment by TNCs in host developing countries was estimated at approximately 7 million in the mid-1980s (out of a total of 22 million employed by TNCs outside their home countries), which represented less than 1 per cent of the economically active population of developing countries. [72] Thus, employment by TNCs, in its overall dimensions, is quite small; furthermore, it appears that its percentage-share in the world-wide economically active population may be declining. [73] The preliminary results of the 1989 benchmark survey of United States direct investment abroad confirm the trend: employment by (non-bank) foreign affiliates of United States TNCs on a world-wide basis remained virtually unchanged during the period 1982-1989, at a level of 6.6 million workers; by contrast, world-wide assets of those affiliates of TNCs grew by 78 per cent and world-wide sales by 34 per cent during the same time period. [74]

The overall magnitude and trends, however, conceal the importance of TNCs as providers of employment in industries that are of particular significance for the transmission of industrial and technological know-how. As shown in table VII.5, in more than half of the developing host countries for which data are available for the 1980s, foreign affiliates accounted for more than 25 per cent of paid employment in the manufacturing sector. Furthermore, the importance and influence of TNCs can be particularly significant in the modern and technologically advanced activities in manufacturing and services of host developing countries. [75]

The generation of employment by TNCs is a direct function of the amount of their capital investment and of the labour intensity of the production process. Trends and inter-host-country disparities in capital investment have been noted in chapter II. As regards the latter factor, TNCs in industries that bring advanced production technologies to developing countries may have a positive impact on the capability-development aspect of human resource development, but they have a small impact on employment when compared with TNCs in industries that use labour-intensive production processes which are less technologically advanced. For example, the decline in manufacturing employment of United States TNC affiliates between 1977 and 1986 reflected, in part, the adoption of labour-saving technologies. [76] Over the same time period, employment by United States foreign affiliates increased rapidly in services (excluding banking). The increase, however, was insufficient to offset the overall trend of declining employment of United States TNCs abroad, as the manufacturing sector accounted for a much higher share of affiliate employment (63 per cent of affiliate employment as compared with 30 per cent in affiliates in services in 1989). [77]

A substantial share of TNC employment in developing countries is provided by foreign affiliates in export processing zones (EPZs) and other offshore plants with EPZ-like conditions. About 2 million workers are employed in EPZs (excluding China), mainly in traditional labour-intensive manufacturing (such as textiles, clothing, electrical and electronic appliances), but also in services such as data-processing. Although some of this employment is in domestic enterprises, most of it is linked to equity, non-equity or subcontracting relationships with TNCs. [78] The direct employment contribution of EPZs is high, and growing relatively rapidly in newer recipient countries of export-oriented industrial production. It is generally agreed, however, that EPZs do not necessarily contribute significantly in terms of employment quality or stability. In most zones, TNCs have been observed to adopt "casual labour strategies", and to follow a distinctive pattern of employment in terms of gender, age and skill composition that has undergone few changes since the mid-1970s and involves primarily an exceptionally high share of young unskilled or semi-skilled women. [79] Overall, the pattern of EPZ employment seems to hold limited scope for training or for the development of skills.

Table VII.5. Employment in affiliates of transnational corporations, by host developing country

Economy	Year	All sectors: Number of employees in foreign firms (Thousands)	All sectors: Share of economically active population (Percentage)	All sectors: Share of paid employment (Percentage)	Manufacturing: Employees in foreign firms (Thousands)	Manufacturing: Share of economically active population (Percentage)	Manufacturing: Share of paid employment (Percentage)
Latin America							
Argentina[a]	1984	..	..	..	185	..	32[b]
Barbados[a]	1989	..	..	..	3	19	31
Brazil[c]	1977	..	..	..	909	14	..
Colombia[d]	1981	..	..	..	81	..	16[e]
Jamaica[a]	1988	87	10	12	36	26	..
Mexico[a]	1988	756	2	12	516	8	21
Panama[a]	1988	24	..	3	4	6	..
Uruguay[a]	1988	24	2	..	15	7[l]	..
Africa							
Botswana[a]	1989	35	8	..	6	..	35[f]
Cameroon[g]	1984	35	1	10[f]	34	..	..
Côte d'Ivoire[g]	1984	61	1	14[f]	29	..	42[f]
Mauritius[h]	1990	..	..	..	35	26	33
Rwanda[a]	1989	6	..	..	2	14	..
Senegal[g]	1984	41	1	..	26	..	..
Swaziland[h]	1990	..	..	..	3	..	30[f]
Zaire[g]	1984	67	1	30[f]	44	..	..
Asia							
China[h]	1989	2700	..	..	..	..	..
Hong Kong[a]	1989	..	..	..	100	12	14
Indonesia[g]	1985	..	1	..	400	7	24[i]
Malaysia[a]	1988	215[j]	4	..	134	16	27[k]
Philippines[a]	1988	156	1	..	124	5	20[e]
Republic of Korea[a]	1978	315	2	..	288	9	15[k]
Singapore[a]	1988	270	21	26	193	52	58[m]
Sri Lanka[h]	1990	..	..	..	71[n]	5	40[o]
Thailand[g]	1986	..	..	..	183	9	15

Source: Aurelio Parisotto, "Direct employment in multinational enterprises in industrialised and developing countries in the 1980s: main characteristics and recent trends", in G. Renshaw, *Employment and Multinationals in the 1990s* (Geneva, International Labour Office, forthcoming).

a Based on a comprehensive survey.
b Firms with 300 or more workers.
c John Dunning and John Cantwell, ed., *IRM Directory of Statistics of International Investment and Production* (New York, New York University Press, 1987).
d Based on data from the Economic Commission for Latin America and the Caribbean.
e Firms with 10 or more workers.
f Modern sector.
g International Labour Office estimate.
h Official estimate.
i Firms with 20 or more workers.
j Majority-owned foreign limited companies.
k Firms with 5 or more workers.
l 1987 Censos Economico Nacional.
m Private sector firms with 10 or more workers.
n Foreign firms in Greater Colombo only.
o Employment in foreign firms in Greater Colombo divided by 1986 paid employment in manufacturing firms with 5 or more workers.

2. Indirect effects

Transnational corporations may contribute substantially to indirect employment generation in several ways. First, TNCs may induce competition with other TNCs and with local firms in related industries and thereby stimulate employment in other firms, although they could also crowd out local firms or force them to rationalize and reduce employment. Second, as discussed in chapter V, TNCs have extensive backward and forward linkages and may generate employment among their suppliers, as well as distributors and service agents. Rough estimates derived from case studies of individual TNC subsidiaries by the ILO suggest that backward and forward linkages could each create employment two or three times higher than the number directly employed by TNCs, depending on the product. The overall assessment, however, after considering jobs displaced, is that indirect employment is at least of the same order of magnitude as the direct employment generated by foreign affiliates.[80]

3. Quantitative and qualitative changes in employment of women

The third main impact TNCs may have on employment opportunity is by effecting qualitative changes in employment by allowing greater access to employment for particular groups, especially women, who may experience systemic discrimination. The underutilization of women is a critical concern with respect to the effective deployment of the national human resources. The causes of such underutilization are not merely economic, but are also embedded in the social, cultural and political heritage of a nation. Transnational corporations may promote the greater utilization and involvement of women in developing countries, through direct employment and through acculturation processes whereby the values of the home country are transferred to the host country via the practices of TNCs.

Total direct employment of women by TNCs in developing countries is relatively small, amounting to about 2 million women in the mid-1980s.[81] As mentioned above, a large proportion of women are employed by TNCs in EPZs. A newly emerging trend in direct employment of women by TNCs in developing countries is the rapidly growing job market in offshore data processing and office administration services, facilitated by the growing tradability of those services over computer-communication lines. American Airlines and "up to 70 other firms" are now using offshore clerical workers in mainland China and in Barbados for data-processing work; American Airlines estimates that it saved in excess of $3.5 million per year, a figure that will surely encourage other TNCs to follow suit.[82] Jamaica, the Philippines and Singapore are other developing countries that have emerged as popular locations for "back office" jobs.[83] It is estimated that as many as 250 of the Fortune 1,000 companies may be using such off-shore employment.[84] Many data-processing and keyboarding jobs are held almost exclusively by women. Although such jobs are important sources of income, they are isolated from the organization, with minimal opportunity for advancement in the firm. Consequently, little development of skills takes place either through formal or informal learning processes.

Thus, most of the employment generated by TNCs for women is concentrated in the manufacturing and services sectors in low-skilled jobs. While it offers benefits in terms of income generation, with wages and working conditions, which are often above average, it provides little opportunity for training or skill development. Furthermore, such employment patterns do little to change the prevailing circumstances in developing countries that largely confine women to lower-paid, lower-skilled jobs.

Transnational corporations from industrialized countries, however, have the potential to influence the employment of women in developing countries through the more subtle effects of acculturation. In developing countries, the low levels of participation of women in paid economic activity mean that the incentives for poor households to invest their scarce resources in human resource development for their female members are often weak. By contrast, developed countries have less gender distinction in human resource-development investments and have absorbed many more women into the labour force (59 per cent) than the developing countries (49 per cent), including a greater proportion of women into managerial positions (see table VII.6). Exposure of the local workforce to women in managerial positions within a TNC can assist in breaking the constraints upon the participation of women in advanced education and in responsible positions within organizations. Unfortunately, however, few TNCs send female managers abroad. A survey of 686 North American firms revealed that only 3 per cent of the 13,338 managers sent to Asia were female.[85] A reason commonly cited for corporate resistance to sending female managers abroad is that foreign prejudice renders them ineffective.[86] Thus, the lack of development and acceptance of women in managerial positions in developing countries becomes a self-fulfilling prophecy because of the absence of female managerial precedents. Transnational corporations could potentially play a pioneering role in that respect.

Table VII.6. A cross-cultural comparison of the roles of women in management

Country	*Representation of women in management*
United States	Women hold approximately one-third of managerial positions.
Canada	Women hold approximately one-third of managerial positions.
Indonesia	Four times as many men as women hold managerial positions in the private sector.
India	Women have fewer opportunities for promotion than men.
Singapore	Women hold fewer than 18 per cent of positions in administration and management.
Philippines	Less than 3 per cent of working women have administrative or managerial positions in Government or business.

Sources: Nancy J. Adler, "Pacific basin managers: a gaijin, not a woman", *Human Resource Management*, vol. 26, No. 2 (1987), pp. 169-191; Nancy J. Adler and Dafna N. Izraeli, "Women in management worldwide", in Nancy J. Adler and Dafna N. Izraeli, eds., *Women in Management Worldwide* (New York, M.E. Sharpe, 1988); Virginia R. Crockett, "Women in management in Indonesia", in Nancy J. Adler and Dafna N. Izraeli, ed., *Women in Management Worldwide*, op. cit.; D. Singh, "Women executives in India", *Management International Review*, vol. 20 (August 1980), pp. 53-60; Audrey Chan, "Women managers in Singapore: citizens for tomorrow's economy", in Nancy J. Adler and Dafna N. Izraeli, eds., *Women in Management Worldwide*, op. cit., pp. 54-73; and B.F. Ople, *Working Managers, Elites: The Human Spectrum of Development* (Manila, Institute of Labour and Management, 1981).

D. Assessment

In assessing the overall impact of TNCs on economic growth via human resource development, it is important to note that the presence of TNCs affects the quality of human resources and their deployment through the regular operations of TNCs, as well as through specifically focused investments in human resource development beyond what is required for the standard operations of a TNC. In the area of health and nutrition, TNCs in the pharmaceutical, agricultural and food-and-beverage products industries have considerable potential for both positive and negative effects, although the actual impact depends upon host-country policies and conditions. The effects of the production and sales activities result in the introduction to consumers of new medicines, vaccines and certain nutritious food products that raise health and nutrition levels; however, they may also disrupt healthy indigenous consumption patterns which, in turn, lowers the quality of health and nutrition. By contrast, the specifically focused investments of some TNCs in those same industries have had a substantial and uniquely positive impact on health and nutrition in many developing countries. Transnational corporations in those particular industries also have specialized knowledge that may be directed to locally specific issues through R&D programmes, training and consultancy.

In the area of general education, TNCs have a small role to play. In vocational training, the effects of TNCs on human resource development through standard operations are somewhat mixed. On the positive side, TNCs introduce new technology and train their employees in the required skills. The new skills acquired, however, may be TNC-specific and not always readily applicable in local firms. Furthermore, the introduction of new technology by TNCs may influence local Governments to make changes in educational policy and programmes that may not necessarily be consistent with educational needs for the broader development of the national economy. For example, the substitution of vocational education and training for general secondary schooling may yield in the short term a larger pool of ready employees for TNCs, but excessive emphasis on such training could limit labour-market flexibility and the absorptive capacity of workers for more advanced knowledge. In terms of specifically focused investments in vocational training beyond what is required of their own employees and what is necessary for standard operations, several instances show that TNCs collaborate with local institutions to establish and improve training centres, and to extend their training to host-country nationals other than their own employees.

In the area of managerial capability, the contribution of TNCs to host-country human resource development is largely positive, but the potential is underutilized. Through standard operations, TNCs train and develop local employees in their management policies and practices. The scope of impact of managerial training on human resource development is thus dependent on the extent of direct employment by TNCs; as direct employment by TNCs is small, the effect on managerial capability through employee training is in the aggregate correspondingly low, although the indications of a declining share of expatriate employment in some TNCs are a positive sign. Given the larger role of TNC employment in more sophisticated industries, however, training effects are likely to be more significant in those industries. Spill-over effects to the industry and economy can materialize to the extent that there is job mobility between foreign affiliates and local firms. Moreover, the impact of TNCs is likely to be greater when collaborative agreements are taken into account, through which they indirectly impart both cognitive and non-cognitive aspects of competent management practices to the collaborating partners. Local capability is particularly enhanced in collaborative arrangements in which TNCs adapt their technology to local conditions and form strong linkages with the local infrastructure. In addition, TNCs can substantially increase their impact on local human resource development by opening their regular training activities to local people outside their firms.

Finally, in terms of providing employment opportunities, the aggregate impact of TNCs on human resource development is quite small. In economies with few other options for remunerative employment, or in which links to the world economy are very important, however, TNCs have had a substantial impact on the development of human resources through direct employment. That is also the case as regards modern manufacturing employment in a larger group of countries. In those cases, employment by TNCs not only enhances the material well-being and productivity of the employees concerned in the present, but also allows for greater private investments in health, nutrition and education for their families, thus having an even greater impact on the national productive capacity in the future.

In summary, the overall impact of TNCs on human resource development through their regular activities and standard operating procedures is, on balance, positive; their contribution through additional investments specifically oriented to local human resource development is positive, but the potential is underutilized. The extent to which individual host countries benefit from those contributions depends on the forces determining the complex relationship between TNCs, human resource development and economic growth. The literature on corporate strategies suggests that one of the critical challenges for TNCs in an increasingly global environment is to balance the competing requirements of global-scale efficiency of operations with locally responsive strategies. [87] The relationship between TNCs, human resource development and economic growth is characterized by a similar tension between the forces of globalization and local responsiveness. A TNC, in its efforts to operate efficiently on a global scale, is inclined to behave in a way that often competes with the requirements of the host-country for local human resource development.

The empirical evidence discussed earlier suggests, however, that many TNCs do engage in activities that correspond to the requirements for local human resource development in host developing countries. Generally, however, TNCs will not pursue such strategies unless they perceive a potential benefit for the firm, or unless they are encouraged to do so by the policies of Governments of host countries. Given that dynamic, it may be appropriate to consider a TNC as being simply a stock of resources, knowledge, technology, management practices and values. The impact of TNCs on economic growth via human resource development then depends on the extent to which that stock of resources is outwardly invested, and the extent to which such knowledge, technology, practices and values are disseminated in host countries and adapted to fit the particular needs of a given host country for economic growth. Most importantly, therefore, fuelling economic growth through human resource development requires policies of the Government of the host country that strike a balance between benefiting TNCs, extending global operations to the host country and ensuring that local human development goals are supported.

E. Some policy implications

Governments of host countries can affect the contribution by TNCs to human resource development in two ways: first, through policies that are directly related to human resource creation and deployment; and second, through policies that attempt to channel FDI into areas particularly relevant for human resource development, and to encourage specific investments by TNCs in human resource development.

Although an in-depth discussion of developing-country policies and programmes relating to health, education, vocational training and employment is beyond the scope of this chapter, it is important to understand the role that such policies play in the relationship between TNCs and economic growth through human resource development. Government policies can affect positively the creation and efficient deployment of human resources, whether through domestic firms and organizations or TNCs, by establishing an institutional framework that enhances incentives for investment in health, education and training that removes impediments to resource mobility and resource mobilization and that increases participation in decision-making. National programmes to increase the levels of health, education and skills of human resources not only increase labour productivity, but also raise the level of national absorptive capacity for more advanced knowledge. Such policies enhance the potential for human resource development through TNC activities in two ways. First, the quality of the labour force is an important determinant of the amount and type of FDI a country receives and the extent of FDI in higher value-added industries with greater scope for human resource development. Second, the extent of advanced knowledge and expertise that a developing country can acquire as a result of TNC investments largely depends on the national absorptive capacity in terms of the basic quality of the human capital. Enhanced national programmes to create a population that is healthy, literate and skilled thus enable the country to receive and take greater advantage of the investments of TNCs.

High levels of investment in human resource development by TNCs (or other entities) do not, however, necessarily lead to economic growth for a country, unless the "developed" human resources are deployed in a way that benefits the nation as a whole. The institutional framework that governs the labour market, including employment and wage policies, determines the income structure of a country that in turn determines how human resources will be deployed. If particular skills or professions are considered critical for development, the national income structure must encourage the native human resources to pursue such professions. Among other things, the income structure affects the "internal brain drain", of a nation, whereby human-resource movements take place across sectors or regions within the same country. Although internal brain drain may not constitute a net loss in human resources for the country as a whole, "it can cause serious dislocations and management problems leading to delays in development, especially in those countries where the government plays a leading role in the management of the economy".[88] Transnational corporations can exacerbate the internal brain drain by drawing local managerial talent away from the indigenous sector where it is needed to develop and modernize domestic firms. Yet, the hiring of local staff by TNCs represents a potentially important channel through which advanced knowledge may enter developing countries.

Capitalizing on the training potential of TNCs requires a concerted programme for the national diffusion of the increased capability resulting from TNC investment. Such a national diffusion of capability takes place through the movement of TNC-trained and experienced managerial and technical personnel to employ their acquired skills and expertise in starting new firms or modernizing existing organizations.[89] To increase the movement of TNC-trained staff to indigenous organizations requires, as mentioned earlier, an institutional framework that encourages labour mobility. Necessary also are cooperative efforts on the part of indigenous private- and public-sector actors to minimize salary and benefits differentials between TNCs and indigenous public and private organizations; to enhance career and professional opportunities within local organizations; to remove discriminatory employment policies and practices; to develop staff exchanges between TNCs and local organizations; and to institutionalize incentives for TNC-trained staff to enter the local public or private sector (that is, bonuses, pension plans, benefits packages etc.).

In addition to the policies discussed above that have direct effects on human resource development, Government policies of host countries on foreign direct investment may also encourage human resource development by TNCs. Policies performing that role may focus on human resource development arising from the normal effects of the standard operating procedures of TNCs, as well as those arising from investments by TNCs, which are specifically focused on local human resource development beyond the minimum required for standard operations.

Impacts on human resource development that occur normally through the standard operating procedures of TNCs include hiring local workers, training them in the basic skills required to perform the functions of a TNC within a given country and collaborating with local firms and institutions. The essential role of the Government of a host country in this respect is thus one of channelling the normal activities of TNCs into directions that enhance human resource development through appropriate policies and regulations on FDI. In order to derive the greatest human resource development benefits from the normal activities of TNCs, Governments of host countries must pursue policies that encourage TNC activity in the industries and in the forms that are most vital for importing knowledge, and for developing and diffusing skills and managerial capability for national economic growth. Policy measures could include fiscal, financial and other incentives and/or promotional measures. The effectiveness of such policies for human resource development depends, however, on the existing human resources pool of a country and on other factors influencing decisions of TNCs to invest, which are closely related to the level of national income and development. In particular, given the interrelationship between the prevailing stock of qualified human resources and the willingness of TNCs to invest in sophisticated manufacturing and service industries, countries at low levels of development are likely to be able to induce FDI only into low-technology activities with limited scope for developing human resource capabilities. Moreover, less developed countries are often able to absorb foreign technology only in the form of imported capital goods, whole production systems under foreign ownership, or the product technology contained in licences to use patents and brand names, all of which tend to offer a smaller scope for the development of local capabilities than joint ventures and other non-equity modes of TNC participation. In contrast, a number of developing countries with a relatively advanced level of industrialization have pursued a more active strategy for the management of FDI and the complementary development of local capability. [90]

Beyond the impacts that naturally occur as a result of standard operating procedures, TNCs also make investments that are more specifically dedicated to human resource development in the countries in which they operate. As discussed, such activities include specific research efforts for local health, nutrition and food-growing issues; financial contributions to and the provision of consulting services for health, research and educational institutions; and the provision of training and development programmes beyond what is minimally required by a TNC (that is, to members of other organizations or to the unemployed). Transnational corporations may make such investments for a number of reasons: to enhance their public image in the country of operations; to make an investment that will enhance their operations in the future (for example, building a school might ensure a future group of literate workers); or, as a result of host-government incentives or mandated performance requirements.

The role of the Government of the host country in increasing the potential contributions of TNCs through specific human resource development investments is primarily a negotiating role. Many developing as well as developed countries have established legal or administrative requirements for the provision of training for employees by national firms as well as by foreign affiliates. [91] Requirements for training and localization or increased participation of local personnel in management, over time, are also incorporated into contractual arrangements with TNCs, which is especially important in extractive and certain services industries in which non-equity arrangements are often more common than FDI. In addition, in return for increased investment areas such as health, education and training, Governments of host countries might offer TNCs certain incentives. Or, more directly, investments in human resource development beyond the basic needs of a TNC may be mandated by a Government as an essential performance requirement for the TNC to operate within its borders. For example, Malaysia has negotiated with United States electronics TNCs to produce in Malaysia on the condition that the companies provide education for a number of Malaysians who are *not* employed by the TNCs, but who would then have the competencies to work for Malaysian firms. [92]

Policies of Governments of host countries relating to FDI thus play a dual role in mediating the impact of TNCs on national human resource development: a channelling role, to draw investment into industries in which technical skills and managerial capability most need to be developed; and a negotiating role, to increase the levels of specific investments by TNCs in human resource development. By exercising the two roles, the Government of the host country would focus on the national long-term objectives for human resource development, without losing sight of short-term objectives. A proper policy mix can increase the potential contribution that TNCs can make to human resource development for economic growth.

Notes

[1]United Nations Development Programme, *Human Development Report 1990* (New York, Oxford University Press, 1990), p. 11. See also subsequent reports, including UNDP, *Human Development Report 1992* (New York, Oxford University Press, 1992).

[2]See, for example, Theodore W. Schultz, *Investment in Human Capital: The Role of Education and Research* (New York, The Free Press, 1971).

[3]See, for example, Robert J. Barro, "Economic growth in a cross section of countries", *Quarterly Journal of Economics*, vol. CVI, No. 2 (May 1991), pp. 407-443.

[4]See Giovanni Andrea Cornia, "Investing in human resources: health, nutrition and development for the 1990s", in Keith Griffin and John Knight, eds., "Human development in the 1980s and beyond", *Journal of Development Planning*, No. 19 (1989), pp. 159-188.

[5]See The World Bank, *World Development Report, 1991: The Challenge of Development* (Oxford, Oxford University Press, 1991), pp. 54-55.

[6]See, for example, T. W. Schultz, *Investing in People: The Economics of Population Quality* (Berkeley, University of California Press, 1980); N. Hicks "Economic growth and human resources", World Bank Staff Working Paper, No. 408 (Washington, D.C., The World Bank, 1980).

[7]G. Psacharopolos, as cited in *World Development Report, 1991*, op. cit., p. 80.

[8]*World Development Report, 1991*, op. cit., pp. 57-58; see also Ryokichi Hirono "The human role in the development process: experiences of Japan and Singapore", in Khadija Haq and Uner Kirdar, eds., *Human Development: The Neglected Dimension* (Islamabad, Pakistan, North South Roundtable, 1986).

[9]Carl J. Dahlman, "Technological change in industry in developing countries", *Finance and Development*, vol. 26, No. 2 (June 1989), pp. 13-15.

[10]John Middleton, Adrian Ziderman and Arvil Adams, "Making vocational training effective", *Finance and Development* vol. 27, No. 1 (March 1990), pp. 30-31.

[11]Ibid., pp. 30-31.

[12]As cited in United Nations Development Programme, "Education, productivity and income growth: the empirical evidence" (New York, UNDP, 1991), mimeo.

[13]Middleton, Ziderman and Adams, op. cit., p. 31.

[14]See Sanjaya Lall, "Human resource development and industrialization, with special reference to Sub-Saharan Africa", in Keith Griffin and John Knight, eds., "Human development in the 1980s and beyond", *Journal of Development Planning*, vol. 19 (1989), pp. 129-157.

[15]See Daniel Cotlear, "The effects of education on farm productivity", in Keith Griffin and John Knight, eds., "Human development in the 1980s and beyond", *Journal of Development Planning*, vol. 19 (1989), pp. 73-99.

[16]Lall, op. cit., p. 132.

[17]See P. Kennedy, *The Rise and Fall of Great Powers* (New York, Vintage Books, 1989).

[18]The World Bank, *From Crisis to Sustainable Growth: A Long-Term Perspective Study* (Washington, D.C., The World Bank, 1989).

[19]See, for example, Carl J. Dahlman, B. Ross-Larson and L. E. Westphal, "Managing technological development: lessons from the newly industrializing countries", *World Development*, vol. 15, No. 6 (1987), pp. 759-775; Carl J. Dahlman and Francisco C. Sercovich, "Exports of technology from semi-industrial economies and local technological development", *Journal of Development Economics*, vol. 16, No. 1-2 (1984), pp. 63-99; Carl J. Dahlman and L. E. Westphal, "The meaning of technological mastery in relation to transfer of technology", *Annals of the American Academy of Political Science*, vol. 458 (November 1981), 12-26.

[20]See, Lascelles Anderson, "The multinational corporation and educational relevance in developing countries", in Lascelles Anderson and Douglass M. Windham, eds., *Education and Development* (Lexington, Mass., Lexington Books, 1982), p. 92.

[21]See, for example, R. A. Fehnel, H. Freeman, A. Murray and L. Picard, "Interim evaluation of development support training project: USAID/Pakistan" (Washington, D.C., National Association of Schools of Public Affairs and Administration (NASPAA), Contract No. DAN 0000-1-00-5051-00, United States Agency for International Development, Bureau for Science and Technology, Office of Rural and Institutional Development, 1985); Moses N. Kiggundu, *Managing Organizations in Developing Countries: An Operational and Strategic Approach* (West Hartford, Conn., Kumarian Press, 1989); B. Z. Dasah and M. N. Kiggundu, *Report on the Briefing of the Canada-Kenya Business Forum* (Hull, Quebec, Canadian International Development Agency, 1985); F. A. Chenoweth, *Ministry of Agriculture and Water Development: A Study of the Organization and Planning Process of the Planning Division* (Hull, Quebec, Canadian International Development Agency, 1986).

[22]*The New Internationalist*, November 1986, p. 17.

[23]See J. H. Taggart "The pharmaceutical industry: sending R & D abroad", *Multinational Business*, No. 1 (Spring 1989), pp. 10-15.

[24]As cited in D. Melrose, *Bitter Pills: Medicines and the Third World Poor* (Oxford, OXFAM, 1982), p. 183.

[25]See Melrose, op. cit., p. 183, for an example.

[26]Melrose, op. cit.

[27]See, Taggart, op. cit.

[28]Melrose, op. cit., p. 183.

[29]Hafiz Mirza, *Multinationals and the Growth of the Singapore Economy* (London, Croom Helm, 1986), p. 65.

[30]See, UNCTC, *Foreign Direct Investment and Transnational Corporations in Services* (United Nations publication, Sales No. E.89.II.A.1), p. 28.

[31]K. Ramakrishnan and A. M. Weatherford "Internationalizing U.S. health care", *Business Forum*, vol. 15, No. 4 (1991), pp. 28-30.

[32]Klaus M. Leisinger, "Corporate responsibility in third world countries". Presentation to the Swiss Society of New York, 14 November 1991, mimeo, p. 3.

[33]UNCTC, *Transnational Corporations and Technology Transfer: Effects and Policy Issues* (United Nations publication, Sales No.E.87.II.A.4), p. 17.

[34]See, for example, Susan George, *Feeding the Few: Corporate Control of Food* (Washington, D.C., Institute for Policy Studies, 1979); R. Franke and B. Chasin, *Seeds of Famine, Ecological Destruction and the Development Dilemma in the West African Sahel* (Montclair, N.J., Allahold Osmun, 1980); F. Lappe and J. Collins, *Food First* (New York, Ballantine, 1979).

[35]See Dennis Joyce and Pamela Joyce, "U.S. cigarette manufacturers in Asia: the emerging battlefield", *Journal of Southeast Asia Business*, vol. 7, No. 2 (Spring 1991), pp. 15-35.

[36]See ILO, *Multinationals' Training Practices and Development* (Geneva, ILO, 1981), p. 31.

[37]Anderson, op. cit., pp. 75-76.

[38]Middleton, Ziderman and Adams, op. cit., p. 32.

[39]Ibid., p. 32.

[40]See, for example, ILO, *Multinationals' Training Practices and Development*, op. cit. The discussion in this paragraph and the next draws mainly upon this publication.

[41]See, for example, Canadian International Development Agency (CIDA), "Human resources development: working paper for the 4As" (Ottawa, Ontario, CIDA, 1989), mimeo.

[42]See J. E. Kerrigan and J. S. Luke, *Management Training Strategies for Developing Countries* (Boulder, Colorado, and London, Lynne Rienner Publishers, 1987).

[43]Farrokh Safavi, "Latin American management education in 1980: a growth inhibiting constraint upon regional development", *Journal of Business Administration*, vol. 7, No. 1 (1975), p. 158.

[44]P. M. Maher and A. Gupta, "The role of Canadian management schools in training managers for Asia", *Business Quarterly*, vol. 51, No. 2 (Summer 1986), pp. 48-51.

[45]*Multinationals' Training Practices and Development*, op. cit., p. 24.

[46]Ibid., pp. 24-25, and "German MNCs in India create programme to train managers", *Business Asia*, vol. 24, No. 10 (March 1992).

[47]ILO, *Multinational Banks and Their Social and Labour Practices* (Geneva, ILO, 1991), pp. 75-91.

[48]P. Ortiz Rocha de Aragao and R. Vanneman, "Technology transfer and managerial-professional employment: Brazilian manufacturing 1960-1975", *Latin American Research Review*, vol. 25, No. 1 (1990), pp. 87-101.

[49]D. Erden, "Impact of multinational companies on host countries: executive training programs", *Management International Review*, vol. 28, No. 3 (1988), p. 39.

[50]See UNCTC, *Transnational Corporations and Technology Transfer*, op. cit., p. 36. See also, ILO, *Multinationals' Training Practices and Development*, op. cit. and *Multinational Banks and their Social and Labour Practices*, op. cit. A number of country-specific studies by the ILO also throw light on training activities in developing countries. See, for example, A. Sibunruang and P. Brimble, "The employment effects of multinational enterprises in Thailand", Multinational Enterprises Programme Working Paper No. 54 (Geneva, ILO, 1988).

[51]Peter Enderwick, ed., *Transnational Corporations and Human Resources. United Nations Library on Transnational Corporations* (London, Routledge, forthcoming).

[52]See Stephen J. Kobrin, *International Expertise in American Business* (New York, Institute of International Education, 1984).

[53]R. E. Berenbeim, *Managing the International Company: Building a Global Perspective* (New York, The Conference Board, 1983).

[54]However, the reduction of expatriate managers may also be attributed to the low rate of success of North American expatriate managers, which has resulted in many TNCs preferring to hire local staff in order to minimize the high costs associated with failed expatriate assignments. For further discussion, see P. J. Dowling, "Human resource issues in international business", *Syracuse Journal of International Law and Commerce*, vol. 13, No. 2 (1986), pp. 255-271; M. G. Harvey, "The multinational corporation's expatriate problem: an application of Murphy's Law", *Business Horizons*, vol. 26, No. 1 (1983), pp. 71-78; Rosalie Tung, "Career issues in international assignments", *Academy of Management Executive*, vol. 2, No. 3 (1988), pp. 241-244; Rosalie Tung, "Expatriate assignments: enhancing success and minimizing failure", *Academy of Management Executive*, vol. 1, No. 2 (1987), pp. 117-126.

[55]UNCTC, *Transnational Corporations and Technology Transfer*, op. cit., p. 36.

[56]Robert W. Kerwin, "*Cokuluslu sirketlerin Turkiyedeki subelerinin yaptigi sevk ve idare teknolojisi transferi*", *Sevk ve Idare Dergisi*, vol. 10 (December 1975), pp. 21-27, as cited in S. T. Cavusgil and U. Yavas, "Transfer of management knowhow to developing countries: an empirical investigation", *Journal of Business Research*, vol. 12, No. 1 (1984), pp. 35-50.

[57]Mingsarn Santikarn Kaosa-ard, "A preliminary study of TNCs hiring and localization policies in Thailand", *TDRI Quarterly Review*, vol. 6, No. 4 (December 1991), p. 15.

[58]Anderson, op. cit., pp. 84-85.

[59]Charles T. Stewart and Yasumitsu Nihei, *Technology Transfer and Human Factors* (Lexington, Mass., Lexington Books, 1987).

[60]Ibid.

[61]Ibid.

[62]See Mirza, op. cit.

[63]Ibid.

[64]See also, S. Ozgediz, "Managing the public service in developing countries: issues and prospects", World Bank Staff Working Papers, No. 583, Management and Development Series, No. 10 (Washington D.C., 1983).

[65]See Frances Stewart, "Technology transfer for development", in Robert E. Evenson and Gustav Ranis, eds., *Science and Technology: Lessons for Development Policy* (Boulder, Colorado, Westview Press, 1990), pp. 301-323.

[66]Ibid., pp. 319-320.

[67]Gerry Gereffi, *The Pharmaceutical Industry and Dependency in the Third World* (Princeton, N.J., Princeton University Press, 1983), p. 249.

[68]Stewart, op. cit.

[69]See Stewart and Nihei, op. cit.

[70]Robert L. Craig, *Training and Development Handbook* (New York, McGraw Hill, 1987), p. 182.

[71]See Stewart and Nihei, op. cit.

[72]Aurelio, Parisotto, "Direct employment in multinational enterprises in industrialised and developing countries in the 1980s: main characteristics and recent trends", in G. Renshow, ed., *Employment in Multinationals in the 1990s* (Geneva, International Labour Office, forthcoming).

[73]UNCTC, *Transnational Corporations in World Development: Trends and Prospects* (United Nations publication, Sales No.E.88.II.A.18), p. 217.

[74]United States, Department of Commerce, *Bulletin* (30 September 1991), p. 2.

[75]Parisotto, op. cit.

[76]Jeffrey H. Lowe and Raymond J. Mataloni, Jr., "U.S. direct investment abroad: 1989 Benchmark Survey results", *Survey of Current Business,* vol. 71, No. 10 (October 1991), p. 33.

[77]Ibid.

[78]Parisotto, op. cit.

[79]See Otto Krueger, Jürgen Heinrichs and Folker Fröbel, *Export Processing Zones in Developing Countries: Results of a New Survey,* ILO Working Paper No. 43 (Geneva, 1988), mimeo, pp. 12, 17.

[80]Parisotto, op. cit, p. 39.

[81]UNCTC, *Transnational Corporations in the World Economy,* op. cit., p. 214.

[82]Robert O. Metzger and Mary Ann von Glinow, "Off-site workers: at home and abroad", *California Management Review,* vol. 30, No. 3 (1988), p. 109.

[83]"American firms send office work abroad to use cheaper labor", *The Wall Street Journal,* 14 August 1991.

[84]Metzger and von Glinow, op. cit.

[85]Nancy J. Adler, "Pacific basin managers: a gaijin, not a woman", *Human Resource Management,* vol. 26, No. 2 (1987), p. 176.

[86]Ibid.

[87]See, for example, C. Bartlett and S. Ghoshal, *Managing Across Borders: The Transnational Solution* (Boston, Harvard Business School Press, 1989); and C. K. Prahalad and Yves Doz, *The Multinational Mission: Balancing Local Demands and Global Vision* (New York, Free Press, 1987).

[88]Kiggundu, op. cit., p. 173.

[89]Stewart and Nihei, op. cit., p. 12.

[90]UNCTC, *Transnational Corporations and Technology Transfer,* op. cit., p. 33.

[91]ILO, *Multinational Banks and their Social and Labour Practices,* op. cit., p. 78.

[92]See L. Nadler and Z. Nadler, *Developing Human Resources* (San Francisco, Jossey-Bass, 1989).

Chapter VIII

TRANSNATIONAL CORPORATIONS, TRADE AND GROWTH

The preceding three chapters examined the role of TNCs in economic growth through an assessment of their contribution to the supply-side determinants of growth. In addition, the rate of growth is influenced by international trade. Though trade is not a factor input such as capital and labour, it has a significant bearing on economic growth because trade provides opportunities to expand and improve the production of goods and services. Accordingly, the impact of TNCs on growth through their role in international trade is addressed in this chapter. [1] This role is crucial since the growth of international production has made TNCs influential in terms of determining the volume, direction and composition of a substantial and increasing proportion of international trade.

A. The relationship between trade and growth

The conventional view of the relationship between trade and growth suggests that trade contributes to economic growth through its beneficial impact on resource allocation resulting from specialization. Trade also helps increase such inputs to growth as natural resources, capital goods and technology by exchanging those goods and services that a country can produce efficiently (that is, at a relatively lower cost) for others which the country either cannot produce, or can do so only at a relatively high cost.

In addition to increasing specialization, expanding the efficiency-raising benefits of improved resource allocation and providing access to critical inputs, trade (and particularly exports) also induces growth, by offering greater opportunities for economies of scale owing to an enlargement of the effective market and greater capacity utilization due to the addition of external demand. Besides, the competition faced in international markets for exports and in home markets through imports provides incentives for fostering more rapid technological change and better management in both tradable and non-tradable sectors, thus raising overall productivity and growth.

Despite the association between trade and growth, the causal relationship between the two is complex. Trade has been regarded by some as an engine of growth and, by others, as a handmaiden of growth.[2] In the engine-of-growth argument, trade was regarded as being a major source or having a dominant role in the growth of countries in the nineteenth century, owing to favourable demand conditions. It was "the tremendous expansion of Western Europe's, and especially Great Britain's demand ... for foodstuffs and raw materials" that provided the "basic inducement that caused them [especially the United States, Canada, Argentina and Australia] to develop. Trade in the nineteenth century... was above all an engine of growth".[3] However, trade as an engine of growth through external demand could not explain adequately the growth of all areas in the nineteenth century, nor differentiate between the growth of successful from that of unsuccessful countries. Those considerations gave rise to the view that trade expansion is a handmaiden of growth, rather than an autonomous engine of growth. In that view, trade and capital movements in their direct impact are supplementary to other factors that determine growth, with the mainsprings of growth being internal and based on the supply-side factors of growth: natural resources, human resources, the stock of capital goods and technology, as well as the system of social and economic organization. The same forces that stimulate a high growth of output (increasing technological capability, improving educational standards, the rise of local entrepreneurship and so on) also promote a faster growth of exports through a greater competitiveness of locally produced goods and services in world markets. Higher growth of exports, in turn, permits a higher growth of imports for such purposes as procuring raw materials and capital equipment that sustain growth. If the growth of international trade were curtailed under such circumstances, this would reduce the rate of growth of production. A slower growth of exports would reduce the growth in demand for domestically produced goods and also curtail the procurement of essential inputs to domestic production, both of which retard growth.

Whether or not it has acted as an engine or a handmaiden, it is clear that trade has played a critical role in world economic growth and integration in previous decades, particularly the 1950s and 1960s, when world trade in manufactured products grew in real terms at an annual average rate of 9 per cent, while world manufactured output rose at 7 per cent.[4] Experiences of several individual countries also underline the association between trade and growth, particularly between trade in manufactured products and growth in manufacturing output. For instance, the Asian newly industrializing economies -- Hong Kong, Republic of Korea, Singapore and Taiwan Province of China -- increased their shares of world trade in manufactured products between 1973 and 1988 from 4 per cent to 10 per cent. This matched their faster growth of manufacturing output, rising to 10 per cent per annum, between 1970 and 1989, in comparison with 3 per cent in the United States and just 2 per cent in the European Community.[5]

Numerous other empirical studies basically came to a similar conclusion, namely, that developing countries with higher than average export growth have also tended to experience higher than average growth in their output. [6] Exports are thus seen as a causal factor in growth. Several other studies, while broadly supporting the positive role of exports in fostering growth, have also pointed out that the direction of causality may run both ways. [7] In that view, exports and output growth reinforce each other. Hence, in those cases, trade tends to result from—but also to reinforce—internally generated growth.

While the growth-promoting effects of trade are often associated with exports, imports, too, can contribute to growth by relieving domestic supply constraints regarding goods and services, as well as technology. Although many developing countries have successfully built a capacity to produce non-durable consumer goods and some services, the domestic production of durable consumer, intermediate and capital goods and more complex services has not always proved feasible or efficient because of, among other things, limited opportunities for economies of scale due to the small size of domestic markets, inadequate resources and information, and a paucity of local expertise. In the absence of a substantial efficient domestic capacity to produce intermediate and capital goods as well as some producer services, imports are often the primary source of the machinery, equipment, services and other items essential to investment programmes and growth in many developing countries. [8] A number of empirical studies have, in fact, concluded that imports are a significant factor in explaining the growth performance of developing countries. [9] The economic rationale behind such findings is, precisely, that imports of intermediate and capital goods are crucial for domestic investment and output growth.

Finally, participation in international trade generates various externalities which contribute to growth. Access to the world's commercial knowledge base is one of the most important benefits in this regard. Trade plays an important part in the international exchange of information, as trade in tangible commodities facilitates the exchange of intangible assets necessary for growth. [10] A larger volume of international trade encourages contacts with foreigners leading to the exchange of information necessary to acquire novel perspectives on technical problems. Imported intermediate and capital goods enable local firms to inspect and use those goods, as well as to undertake reverse engineering, which eventually results in learning to produce some of those goods efficiently. The export of local goods may induce learning to effect improvements in manufacturing processes to meet the higher standards of foreign markets. [11] Similarly, competition in the domestic market from imports may act as an incentive for local enterprises to introduce technological improvements and upgrade the quality of their products, while the implementation of such improvements is facilitated by technology imports.

While, conceptually, those effects are clear, empirical evidence on the impact of trade on growth-promoting externalities is relatively scanty, in part because it is hard to measure such impact. Still, a number of studies have identified a positive correlation between export expansion and growth of factor productivity; [12] and, in the case of the Republic of Korea, it has been observed that export imperatives necessitated improvements in product standards and acquisition of greater expertise in production and marketing techniques. [13]

Overall, therefore, it is well established that for many developing countries, trade is an important element in their integration into the international economy which, in turn, helps stimulate their economic growth process. In the light of the above discussion, the principal mechanisms through which trade promotes growth can be summed up as follows:

- The growth of exports permits economies of scale and a degree of specialization that allow levels of production that could not be sustained by a country's domestic demand, thus enabling higher growth in the economy as a whole.
- The growth of imports alleviates potential growth-retarding supply shortages, especially of goods and services used in production, and leads to a slower rate of increase in the costs of goods, raw materials, capital equipment and services, thereby permitting an increase in locally-generated reinvested profits.
- Participation in international trade generates externalities, particularly with regard to learning, that can raise the efficiency of production and stimulate aggregate economic growth.

B. The impact of transnational corporations

International trade and FDI have become closely inter-linked, as shown by the increasing involvement of TNCs in international trade, a significant portion of which consists of intra-firm transactions. United States data are indicative for this: some 80 per cent of the country's external trade (exports plus imports) was undertaken by TNCs in 1989, including parent companies in the United States, foreign affiliates of United States TNCs and United States affiliates of foreign TNCs; one third of exports and over two fifths of imports were intra-firm transactions. In the case of Japan and the United Kingdom, intra-firm trade accounted for one third of the total value of their international trade in the early 1980s. [14] It is partly owing to the important interrelationships between FDI and trade, through both arm's-length and intra-firm transactions, that a close similarity has been found to exist between world-wide patterns in trade and FDI. [15] Given the important role of TNCs in international trade, they are able to exert a significant impact on the growth of developing countries, whether through exports, imports or externalities. These are analysed in the subsequent sections.

1. Exports

The expansion of the activities of TNCs, involving the establishment of world-wide affiliate networks, has created a considerable potential for those firms to contribute to the growth of exports from developing countries. The role of TNCs in growth through exports is examined here in terms of the share of foreign affiliates in total manufactured exports from developing countries, as well as their contribution to a change in composition in favour of those goods and services that offer greater potential for growth. Also examined are the contributions of TNCs in the growth of exports through non-equity links (which have been increasingly relevant in the case of South-East Asian countries) and the role of transnational trading companies. Finally, the role of TNCs in the export of services is discussed.

(a) Relative importance in exports of developing countries

The combined relative importance of the foreign affiliates of TNCs from the United States and Japan in the export of manufactured products from developing countries declined from 12 per cent in 1982 to 9 per cent in 1989 (table VIII.1),[16] despite the fact that the absolute value of their manufactured exports increased considerably. For Latin America and Africa, however, the export shares of United States affiliates increased from 11 per cent to 14 per cent in the former and from less than 2 per cent to more than 3 per cent in the latter, indicating that United States TNCs have been a positive element in the growth of exports of manufactured products from those regions. In contrast, the combined export share of United States and Japanese affiliates in Asia declined from, collectively, 13 per cent to 8 per cent over the same period. That decline is explained by the relatively faster growth of exports by domestic firms operating under national policies that place emphasis on greater outward orientation and economic growth

Table VIII.1. Manufactured exports by United States majority-owned and Japanese foreign affiliates in developing countries, 1982 and 1989

Country group	*Total manufactured exports by developing countries (Millions of dollars)*	*United States affiliates (Percentage)*		*Japanese affiliates* [a] *(Percentage)*	
		Share	*Export propensity* [b]	*Share*	*Export propensity* [b]
All developing countries					
1982	166 581	6.7	22.0	4.8	32.8
1989	451 986	5.7	33.1	2.9	39.2
Africa					
1982	10 579	1.6 [c]	..	0.2	8.2
1989	16 809	3.4	..	0.2	15.2
Asia and the Pacific					
1982	94 314	6.3 [c]	60.3	6.3	33.6
1989	332 120	4.2	56.2	3.5	40.2
Latin America and the Caribbean					
1982	44 814	10.5	11.9	2.2	18.6
1989	71 315	14.3	21.4	1.1	23.9

Source: Transnational Corporations and Management Division, based on data reported in United Nations, Statistical Office, *Monthly Bulletin of Statistics*, various issues; United States, Department of Commerce, *U.S. Direct Investment Abroad: 1982 Benchmark Survey Data* (Washington, D.C., United States Government Printing Office, 1985); *U.S. Direct Investment Abroad: 1989 Benchmark Survey, Preliminary Results* (Washington, D.C., United States Government Printing Office, 1991); Japan, Ministry of International Trade and Industry, *Wagakuni Kigyo no Kaigai Jigyo Katsudo (Survey of the Overseas Activities of Japanese Companies) 18th and 19th Surveys* (Tokyo, Okurasho Insatsu-kyoku, March 1990), and *12th and 13th Surveys* (Tokyo, Toyo Hoki Shuppan, September 1984).

a Figures cover April 1982 - March 1983 and April 1988-March 1989, and represent only a sample of affiliates in developing countries and hence may understate total exports by all Japanese affiliates.

b Export propensity is defined as the proportion of export sales in total sales by affiliates.

c Part of the data are suppressed by the source to avoid disclosure.

through export expansion; indeed, total manufactured exports of this region grew by more than threefold, much above the growth achieved by the other regions. Nevertheless, the role of TNCs through non-equity links may still be partly responsible for the faster growth of exports of domestic firms, as discussed later. Furthermore, it should be noted that the export propensity of TNCs has been generally increasing over the decade of 1980s, and has reached particularly high levels in Asia. In that region, United States TNCs had already reached a very high level of exports by the early 1980s (with over half of their sales being exported); they did not expand their share during that decade, partly because of strong domestic demand. In contrast, Japanese foreign affiliates in Asia rapidly increased their export orientation to about 40 per cent of their sales.

Data from individual host developing countries (annex table 9) confirm that, by the mid- and late 1980s, foreign affiliates have come to account for a significant proportion of exports, particularly in the manufacturing sector. Although the growth of exports by domestic firms in Asia has been significant, the role of foreign affiliates in exports is particularly important in some Asian countries. In Malaysia, the Philippines and Sri Lanka, for example, foreign affiliates accounted for over 50 per cent of manufactured exports over the past decade; in Singapore, their share was almost 90 per cent. [17] In addition, a recent survey of 777 firms in Thailand (which accounted for nearly one third of the country's total manufactured exports in 1990) found that nearly three fourths of their exports were undertaken by foreign affiliates and joint ventures. [18] Similarly, in Mexico and Paraguay, foreign affiliates accounted for 58 per cent and 46 per cent of total manufactured exports, respectively, in the late 1980s. For many developing countries, furthermore, the data show that the role of foreign affiliates in exports has not only been significant, but has also been increasing in importance since the late 1970s and early 1980s. This may be attributed to the fact that, in those countries, foreign firms have had higher export propensities than local firms, even controlling for industry-specific characteristics. [19]

(b) Structural change

The extraction and export of natural resources were the traditional areas of FDI in developing countries. They remain important in a number of resource-rich developing countries; in some cases, furthermore, TNCs played an active role in building processing facilities in host countries, especially where host country policies required that foreign firms engage in more local value-added activities. However, the relative importance of the role of TNCs in resource-extractive and resource-processing industries in developing countries has declined over the past two decades. Several reasons account for this: nationalisations leading to the withdrawal of TNCs from directly-owned production activities; tariffs on processed products in export markets; the often incremental nature of investment in processing operations that favour existing sites; lack of appropriate infrastructure; and the growth of local entrepreneurial capabilities. [20] Nevertheless, the role of TNCs in exports of natural resources or other primary commodities remains important, with their control of distribution systems and product branding; such is the case, for example, in the banana industry. [21]

The participation of TNCs in manufactured exports from developing countries, however, has become much more significant; in some cases, their activities have accelerated the pace at which shifts in competitive advantage have led to a changing pattern of exports. In particular, foreign affiliates have been in the forefront of generating shifts in the export composition of host countries towards technologically advanced products. Thus, developing-country locations account for a substantial share of the world exports of manufactured products by United States majority-owned foreign affiliates in such dynamic and technologically complex industries as electrical and electronic equipment and, to a lesser extent, non-electrical machinery, chemicals and other transport equipment (table VIII.2). Production by affiliates in some of these industries is often vertically integrated across countries, and there is wide scope for the relocation of many labour-intensive processes and components to developing countries. That has been the case in the production of automobile parts, electrical appliances and components and some machine tools and parts.

The share of developing countries has been most significant in electrical and electronic equipment, accounting for over one third of world exports of manufactured products by those affiliates in 1989. The Asian newly industrializing economies, in particular, have been important sites for the relocation of branches of the electrical and electronic equipment industry from the United States since the early 1970s. By the late 1980s, however, the relative share of Asia in world exports of electrical and electronic equipment by United States majority-owned foreign affiliates declined, and that of Latin America rose.

Similarly, limited evidence on exports of foreign affiliates of Japanese TNCs operating in Asia and Latin America during the past decade shows that those firms also play an important role in contributing to the growth of exports of machinery and transport equipment from these countries (table VIII.3). In both of those regions, the share of textile products in their total manufactured exports has dramatically declined; while the share of electrical and electronic products, particularly in Asia, increased significantly in importance from 39 per cent in 1980 to over 60 per cent in 1989. As with United States TNCs, this reflects, among other things, the strategies of Japanese TNCs to relocate to developing countries labour intensive processes and components in which Japan has no longer a comparative advantage.

Those data suggest that, under certain circumstances, foreign affiliates can contribute to a change in the composition of exports in favour of more capital- and technology-intensive products. Data on the composition of manufactured exports and inward FDI for six developing countries lend further support to that relationship (table VIII.4). In most of those countries, the increasing share of capital- and technology-intensive manufactured products in total manufactured exports between 1970 and the late 1980s has been accompanied by a rising share of inward FDI in those industries.

(c) Non-equity links

Apart from the role played by affiliates, TNCs also contribute to the growth of exports from developing countries through a variety of non-equity arrangements between them and producers in developing countries. By providing vital links to final buyers, those arrangements with local suppliers have been influential in expanding the volume of manufactured exports of a number of developing

Table VIII.2. Share of developing economies in world exports of manufactures of United States majority-owned foreign affiliates 1977, 1982 and 1989
(Percentage)

Year	Total manufacturing	Foods	Chemicals	Metals	Machinery: Non-electrical	Machinery: Electrical	Transport equipment	Other manufacturing
All developing economies								
1977	9.2	21.5	5.5	14.6	4.1	37.7	2.2	7.1
1982	12.2	16.8	7.5	15.4	7.4	49.9	3.7	8.2
1989	5.2	..	..	..	..	36.3	..	..
Africa								
1977	..	1.1	0.14	..	0	0.08	0	0.05
1982	..	..	0.02	..	0	..	0	..
1989	..	..	..	..	..	0.2	0	..
Asia and Pacific								
1977	..	5.5	..	..	1.6	..	..	3.6
1982	..	..	1.1	..	..	43.6	0.95	2.3
1989	5.0	..	..	..	..	23.5	..	..
Asian newly-industrializing economies [a]								
1977	2.5[b]	..	..	..	..	24.0[c]	..	..
1982	4.1[c]	0.2	0.7	0.2[d]	3.2[e]	24.7[c]	0.8[e]	0.8[d]
1989	3.4[c]	..	..	..	5.9[c]	13.9[c]	..	..
Latin America and the Caribbean								
1977	3.9	14.9	3.5	9.0	2.4	5.4	..	..
1982	5.1	13.8	5.9	9.2	3.7	5.9	2.7	5.2
1989	11.3	..	..	14.2	6.6	12.0	10.6	11.7

Source: Transnational Corporations and Management Division, based on data provided in United States, Department of Commerce, *U.S. Direct Investment Abroad, 1977* (Washington, D.C., United States Government Printing Office, 1981); *U.S. Direct Investment Abroad: 1982 Benchmark Survey Data* (Washington, D.C., United States Government Printing Office, 1985); *U.S. Direct Investment Abroad: 1989 Benchmark Survey, Preliminary Results* (Washington, D.C., United States Government Printing Office, 1991).

a Hong Kong, the Republic of Korea, Singapore and Taiwan Province of China.
b Excluding Hong Kong.
c Excluding some data on the Republic of Korea.
d Excluding some data on Taiwan Province of China and Hong Kong.
e Excluding some data on Taiwan Province of China.

countries, particularly in South-East Asia. The importance of non-equity modalities in fostering export growth may increase as domestic manufacturers in developing countries acquire greater capabilities and can be relied upon to meet export specifications of foreign-based TNCs. However, no systematic data are available to assess the role of TNCs in the promotion of exports from developing countries through non-equity links. The following discussion draws, therefore, on selected case studies.

Table VIII.3. Manufactured exports of Japanese affiliates in Asia and Latin America[a]
(Percentage of total manufacturing)

Area and year	*Textiles*	*Machinery*		*Transport equipment*
		Non-electrical	*Electrical*	
Asia and the Pacific				
1980	18.6	5.0	39.1	2.7
1989	4.6	5.6	61.0	4.4
Latin America and the Caribbean				
1980	13.4	1.4	3.3	0.2
1989	6.7	1.0	4.1	0.9

Source: Transnational Corporations and Management Division, based on Japan, Ministry of International Trade and Industry, *Wagakuni Kigyo no Kaigai Jigyo Katsudo (Survey of the Overseas Activities of Japanese Companies) 18th and 19th Surveys* (Tokyo, Okurasho Insatsu-kyoku, March 1990), and *10th and 11th Surveys* (Tokyo, Toyo Hoki Shuppan, 1983).

a Figures cover April 1979 - March 1980 and April 1988 - March 1989, and represent only a sample of foreign affiliates of Japanese TNCs that responded to the survey. In 1980, 32 per cent of the number of firms included in the survey responded, and in 1989, 47 per cent.

A major form of non-equity relationship is subcontracting. Several studies have shown that subcontracting arrangements with TNCs have been significant in the exports of garments from Hong Kong, Singapore, Thailand and Taiwan Province of China; and of bicycles and footwear from Taiwan Province of China and the Republic of Korea.[22] By contrast, until recently, TNC-related subcontracting arrangements have been less significant in the Latin American region, whose trade and investment policies were more inward-looking. However, the *maquiladora* (in-bond assembly plants) programme that was established by Mexico in 1985 has fostered subcontracting arrangements, particularly in the apparel industry.[23] Subcontracting arrangements also played a significant role in exports from Colombia where, during the period 1986-1990, the most rapid growth of exports was in such industries as apparel (53 per cent), footwear (34 per cent) and other leather products (25 per cent)—precisely the industries in which subcontracting was most prevalent.[24] In Morocco, subcontracting constitutes about 20 to 25 per cent of total exports.[25] The initial stages of subcontracting arrangements usually concentrate on low value-added components of export products. That changes, however, in many cases over time. For instance, in the shoe industry of Croatia and Slovenia, domestic firms have been able to increase the local material and value-added content of their subcontracting exports to such firms as Puma, Adidas, Bally and Salamander.[26]

Several developing countries have also been able to export relatively more sophisticated products through subcontracting. For example, several local firms in the Philippines and the Republic of Korea undertake subcontracting work for TNCs in the semi-conductor industry.[27] A large domestic firm in Thailand is supplying computer parts and is assembling hard disks for IBM. China has also been able to export some aircraft components under subcontracting arrangements with such companies as Boeing, McDonnell Douglas and Short Brothers; [28] and, for quite some time, the Republic of Korea has supplied high quality aircraft components to TNCs in the aviation industry. [29]

Table VIII.4. Share of capital-and technology-intensive manufacturing industries [a] in total manufacturing in selected developing countries, 1970, 1980 and 1988

(Percentage)

	1970		*1980*		*1988*	
	Exports	*Inward FDI*	*Exports*	*Inward FDI*	*Exports*	*Inward FDI*
Brazil	13.7	36.0	28.1	45.4	23.9	44.9
Korea, Republic of	26.4	36.0	32.4	38.8	47.4	57.9
Malaysia	6.9	--	27.8	--	47.3	20.8
Mexico	24.4	36.5	33.1	37.5	52.2	--
Thailand	8.9	16.2	18.3	36.2	25.7	48.4
Singapore	26.8	28.0	43.9	47.6	58.9	51.4

Source: Transnational Corporations and Management Division, based on data provided in UNCTC, *World Investment Directory* (New York, United Nations, 1992), and United Nations trade tapes.

a Defined as comprising mechanical equipment, electrical and electronic equipment, motor vehicles and other transport equipment.

In sum, the evidence suggests that non-equity links between TNCs and local enterprises, especially in Asia, play a significant role in the growth of exports and, hence, economic growth. The key assets that TNCs provide in this case are access to markets, product specifications and quality standards.

(d) The role of trading companies

Subcontracting and other forms of non-equity arrangements are of particular importance for trading companies which, given their role in world trade, deserve special attention. Trading TNCs can help exports of developing countries by providing marketing services and access to international distribution networks. In this function, trading affiliates typically do not directly produce goods and services, but rather organize a part of the exports of host economies. The importance of this function stems from the fact that many developing countries may have a comparative advantage in manufacturing certain products, but lack a comparative advantage in marketing those products abroad. Trading TNCs can enable developing countries to overcome marketing barriers in the form of product design, quality standards, packaging, presentation and access to consumers. They may also directly distribute goods purchased from developing countries manufacturers through their wholesaling or retailing networks and provide after-sales service and brand-name promotion. [30]

The trading function of TNCs in host developing countries has undergone a significant transformation. The activities of many TNCs, including their trading affiliates, in the primary sector of developing countries were phased out as a result of host Government intervention and the increasing competitiveness of private indigenous commodity traders in more advanced developing countries. As a result, the role of TNCs, including trading affiliates in the primary sector, declined, and shifted largely to the manufacturing sector where they perform a variety of functions, particularly in the initial stages of export-oriented manufacturing industries in developing countries. [31] Data for the United States show this shift (table VIII.5). The role of trading affiliates in total non-petroleum affiliates' exports from developing countries diminished between 1977 and 1988, but remained quite significant; they accounted for almost one quarter of total exports of United States majority-owned affiliates from developing countries in 1989. In contrast, about 90 per cent ($89 billion) of exports by affiliates of Japanese TNCs in developed countries and 54 per cent ($25 billion) in developing countries were handled by Japanese trading affiliates in fiscal year 1989. [32] To a certain extent, that reflects the different pattern of industrial organization in Japan, where trading firms in general play a more important role.

Not all trading affiliates are established by trading TNCs. Indeed, on a global basis, the majority of them are probably affiliates of industrial firms. This is certainly the case for the United States. Of the 3,986 trading affiliates of United States TNCs world-wide in 1989, only 691 were established by 191 parent trading companies. In terms of assets, non-trading parent firms owned about 80 per cent of trading affiliates; for developing countries, that percentage was 65 per cent. [33] In terms of absolute numbers, Japanese manufacturing TNCs established more trading affiliates (1,058) than trading TNCs (910) by March 1990, making the imbalance considerably less striking than in the case of the United States; [34] in developing countries, in fact, Japanese trading TNCs established more trading affiliates (381) than did manufacturing TNCs (248), indicating a more important role of Japanese trading TNCs in those countries.

The most remarkable among the Japanese trading companies are the *sogo shosha*. Those firms are not only large in size (as indicated by the fact that the world's five largest companies in terms of sales in 1991 were all *sogo shosha* [35]), but they are also highly sophis-

Table VIII.5. The role of trading affiliates of United States transnational corporations in exports of United States majority-owned foreign affiliates from host countries, 1977, 1982, 1988 and 1989

Origin of exports and year	*Total exports by all affiliates (Billions of dollars)*	*Share of trading affiliates in total exports*			*Share of other trading affiliates in non-petroleum exports*
		All trading affiliates	*Petroleum trading affiliates* [a]	*Other trading affiliates*	
All host countries					
1977	194	33	19	14	28
1982	252	39	20	19	30
1988	322	28	9	19	23
1989	318	25	6	19	22
Host developing countries					
1977	92	...	...	5	35
1982	84	...	...	7	24
1988	65	...	...	15 [b]	23
1989	68	...	...	17 [b]	24

Source: Transnational Corporations and Management Division, based on data contained in United States, Department of Commerce, *U.S. Direct Investment Abroad, 1977* (Washington, D.C., United States Government Printing Office, 1981); *U.S. Direct Investment Abroad: 1982 Benchmark Survey Data* (Washington, D.C., United States Government Printing Office, 1985); *U.S. Direct Investment Abroad: Operations of U.S. Parents and their Foreign Affiliates* (Washington, D.C., United States Government Printing Office, 1991).

a In the case of the United States, petroleum trading affiliates account for the overwhelming share of exports by trading affiliates in the primary sector.

b Including Israel.

ticated organizations involved in a broad spectrum of commercial activities world-wide. Through their large-scale communications networks, *sogo shosha* have access to and provide a wealth of information, expertise and contacts to their clients. In addition to assisting in marketing and distribution, those firms extend financial support by way of providing low interest-rate loans required for trade expansion, sometimes linking loan payment schedules to a plant's exports. The nine largest *sogo shosha* had, in 1990, more than 3,000 foreign affiliates, of which 55 per cent were located in developing countries. By March 1991, FDI by those firms amounted to $19 billion, [36] accounting for 6 per cent of Japanese FDI stock, of which a large part is export-oriented in nature. Some examples of the role of those firms in the promotion of exports from developing countries are provided below: [37]

- In Indonesia, a *sogo shosha* entered into the world's largest liquid natural gas (LNG) project with Pertamina and two United States oil and gas companies. This project involves a trading agreement to export nine million tons of LNG to Japan every year. The *sogo shosha* arranged financing of $4 billion and organized a team of engineering, construction and equipment companies to complete the project. In China, another *sogo shosha* was involved in the development of a state farm, Hong He, a part of whose products are exported to Japan.

- There are also examples of FDI by *sogo shosha* in the manufacturing sector that facilitates exports not only to Japan, but also to third countries. Marubeni Corporation and Nissho Iwai Corporation both financed the establishment of a $150 million methanol plant in Chile in 1985, whose products are solely exported to the United States. P.T. Kanebo Tomen Sandang Synthetic Mills, established in Indonesia by Tomen Corporation and Kanebo, Ltd., is increasing exports of synthetic fibre to the United States and Hong Kong. CPC-Cia. Petroquimica Camacari, a vinyl chloride maker, set up by Nissho Iwai Corporation in Brazil, began to export to third countries products amounting to $14 million in 1987. Similarly, Mados-Citoh-Daiken Sdn. Bhd., an affiliate of C. Itoh & Co. Ltd. in Malaysia, is exporting wood products to Japan through the network of the *sogo shosha.*

Since third-country transactions by *sogo shosha* amounted to $144 billion in 1988 (or 5-6 per cent of world trade), [38] developing countries need to pay special attention to the role of foreign affiliates of *sogo shosha* in their economies as promoters of exports world-wide.

In conclusion, the important role of TNCs in the exports from developing countries is not only reflected in the production, distribution and marketing activities of manufacturing affiliates and their parents (discussed earlier), but also in the activities of independent transnational trading companies, which include, in addition to the Japanese trading companies, agency houses, commodity traders, retailers and buying agents. During the mid-1980s, those independent trading companies handled approximately 20 per cent of global exports and imports. [39] While the role of trading TNCs dealing with natural resources (particularly petroleum) has become less important, that of trading affiliates dealing with manufactured products remains important. [40]

(e) The export of services

Since most services are non-tradable by nature, total world trade in services is much smaller than trade in goods, amounting to only one-quarter of the latter. [41] Foreign direct investment is, therefore, the predominant mode of delivering services to foreign markets. Accordingly, the role of TNCs in host country services trade is less significant in absolute terms than in the trade of goods; in addition, FDI in a number of easily tradable services is typically not permitted (for example, air transportation and telecommunications) and, hence, cannot create trade. Still, TNC exports from host countries, mainly in the form of sales of services to foreigners by TNC affiliates (classified as exports for balance-of-payments purposes), are quite important in a number of developing countries. Those include mainly tourism-related services, such as hotel accommodations and car rentals. In addition to direct exports of services, transnational service corporations may also exert an indirect impact on exports of goods by undertaking FDI in producer services, such as financial or market-research services supporting exports of goods from host developing countries.

The volume and range of services exported and the contribution of TNCs to service exports may, however, increase considerably in the near future, because of breakthroughs in data and communications technologies that render more services more transportable. The result is that it is becoming increasingly possible to relocate parts of the production process of services in a manner similar to that in export-oriented manufacturing. Many operations of this kind are already in place in developing as well as developed countries. A translation of potential export opportunities into realized competitiveness in exports of services from developing countries may initially be based on labour intensity, and many of these countries stand to benefit because of their ready supply of low-cost personnel. [42] When this occurs, the role of TNCs in the growth of host developing countries through the export of services may become more important in such service industries as engineering, financial services, various business services and data input and software production. Over the longer term, however, technological progress alters the relative importance of labour and capital inputs or directly reduces the labour intensity of particular tasks, thereby imposing limits on sustaining competitiveness fostered by TNC-related trade in labour-intensive services. [43]

2. Imports

As mentioned earlier, imports can facilitate economic growth by relieving domestic supply constraints, particularly of intermediate and capital goods. Transnational corporations play a role in that process in host developing countries through direct intra-firm imports and other channels. During the initial establishment of foreign affiliates, their imports may be more significant than at later stages of their operations. The reason is that foreign firms often have limited knowledge of market conditions in host countries and locally available inputs. Over time, as operations mature, foreign affiliates may switch to a greater use of domestic goods and services, assuming that these are available locally. However, a TNC may often favour foreign sources of supply over domestic ones, in order, among other things, to take advantage of bulk purchases for the firm as a whole, maintain greater control over quality and ensure the reliability of supply channels. Since little is known about the extent to which imports of capital goods by TNCs in host developing countries are constraint-relieving in nature, and the extent to which such imports are substitutes of domestic equivalents, any definitive conclusion regarding the role of TNCs in promoting growth through imports is difficult to draw. Nevertheless, the role of TNCs in imports of capital and intermediate goods is an important issue, particularly because the scope for the domestic availability of those goods in most developing countries is often limited.

(a) *Imports of capital and intermediate goods*

As noted in chapter VI, disaggregated data on the role of TNCs in the import of capital goods by developing countries are not available. However, data on imports of capital goods by affiliates of United States TNCs in developing countries provide some evidence of this role. Such imports have accounted for between 5 per cent and 6 per cent of total capital goods imports by developing countries between 1982 and 1989 (table VIII.6). Of all developing regions, the relative significance of United States affiliates as importers of capital goods is most evident in Latin America, where their share was 9 per cent in 1982 and 11 per cent by 1989. Asia is the second most important region in relative importance in terms of the role of United States affiliates as importers of capital goods; during the decade of the 1980s, those affiliates accounted for at least 5 per cent of total imports of capital goods in those countries.

The growing value of imports of intermediate products by United States affiliates in developing countries provides another indication of the role played by TNCs in the imports of those goods to

Table VIII.6. Imports of capital goods by United States affiliates in developing countries

Region	*Imports of capital goods [a] by United States affiliates (Billions of dollars)*	*Share of United States affiliates in total capital goods imports [b] into developing countries [c] (Percentage)*
All developing countries		
1982	6.3	5.2
1989	9.1	6.3
Africa		
1982	0.147	0.6
1989	0.008[d]	0.04[d]
Asia and the Pacific		
1982	3.1[e]	4.7[e]
1989	4.8	5.0
Latin America and the Caribbean		
1982	2.6	9.0
1989	4.0	11.1

Source: Transnational Corporations and Management Division, based on data contained in table VI.6 and United States, Department of Commerce, *U.S. Direct Investment Abroad: 1982 Benchmark Survey Data* (Washington, D.C.,United States Government Printing Office, 1985); *U.S. Direct Investment Abroad: 1989 Benchmark Survey, Preliminary Results* (Washington, D.C., United States Government Printing Office, 1991).

a Includes machinery and other transport equipment, but excludes road vehicles and parts.

b Items included are mentioned in table VI.6.

c The share of United States foreign affiliates in total imports of capital goods into developing countries may be over-estimated owing to the inclusion in the data of non-electric and electric consumer machinery.

d Does not include machinery; hence the share of United States affiliates may be under-estimated.

e Does not include other transport equipment; hence the share of United States affiliates may be under-estimated.

meet local production requirements. Between 1982 and 1989, the level of imports of those products by United States affiliates in developing countries increased from $4.3 billion to $7.8 billion. Almost three quarters of those imports were accounted for by affiliates in Latin America and the Caribbean. [44]

Individual country experiences also tend to suggest that TNCs play an important role in growth through imports, a major example of which is Brazil. [45] A sizeable proportion of Brazilian imports are capital goods, despite the impressive growth of the Brazilian capital-goods industry. Domestic production bottlenecks and a backlog of orders have often forced both foreign and domestic firms to look abroad for equipment. Foreign affiliates generally operate in capital- and technology-intensive industries, in which substitutes for imports for intermediate and capital goods required in production are often not available locally. Those affiliates fulfil a significant part of their production requirements through imports from parent firms. Hence, TNCs have relieved supply constraints in Brazil and expanded their local production by importing, in some cases through intra-firm transactions, needed intermediate and capital goods.

There are also examples of the contribution of TNCs to growth through imports at the industry level. For instance, the growth of the local textile industry in Hong Kong was spurred by imports of new machinery from foreign-based TNCs. [46] More recently, the imports that Hong Kong firms have sourced from foreign TNCs in the form of components, parts and intermediate products have helped to build their technological competitiveness. Other examples are found in the growth of firms in Taiwan Province of China, engaged in synthetic fibre production that has been sustained through the purchase of equipment from TNCs in developed countries. [47]

Apart from manufacturing affiliates, marketing affiliates of TNCs also import capital and intermediate goods. In the case of the United States, approximately 17 per cent of the total value of merchandise imports by affiliates of United States firms in 1982 and 1989 were directed to marketing affiliates located in developing countries. A considerable proportion (86 per cent in 1989) of those merchandise imports by marketing affiliates of United States TNCs in developed and developing countries consisted of intermediate and capital goods that are important for the growth of production in host countries, especially in developing countries. [48] Some of these imports represent either intra-firm trade or resale to domestically-owned firms in host countries. In both cases, marketing affiliates relieve growth-retarding supply shortages in production while, at the same time, increasing the range of products available in the host economy. They also fulfil an important function in the after-sale servicing of goods that they sell; this also puts them in a good position to communicate to their own suppliers changing requirements for product adaptation and development.

It should also be noted that TNCs can contribute to the growth of home countries, both developed and developing, through the integration of outward FDI and imports. That role is discussed briefly in box VIII.1.

(b) Imports of services

Transnational corporations also have an important role to play in relieving supply-bottlenecks in the services sector. This is especially the case where TNCs are the sole providers in developing countries of certain sophisticated business services that are not available locally but are necessary for efficient domestic production by both foreign affiliates and local firms. The provision of such unique services through imports is one of the most significant contributions that transnational service corporations can make to growth in host developing countries.[49] Such is the case, for example, in the provision of certain international banking services to domestic trading companies; the provision of certain insurance and

Box VIII.1. The impact of imports on growth in home countries and the role of transnational corporations

The growth of trade often reduces, or results in a slower increase in, the cost of imported materials, thereby enhancing and reinforcing the growth of importing nations. In the case of resource-scarce countries, whose growth is constrained by a lack of local natural resources, for example, imports of resource-related products provide a supply of raw-material inputs to sustain domestic industrial expansion. Similar advantages apply to the imports of intermediate or final products, even if, in principle, these could be produced domestically. Though these imports can be acquired through arm's-length transactions, TNCs play a major role in their acquisition, be it through equity or non-equity linkages. The phenomenon of international sourcing of labour-intensive intermediate and final products from developing countries by TNCs has also been increasingly associated with the rationalization of production by TNCs.

Evidence of the role of TNCs in growth through this import linkage can be found in the activities of United States and Japanese companies which established production facilities in ASEAN countries in 1970s to make use of the local availability of raw materials and cheap qualified labour.[1] A substantial part of United States and Japanese FDI in those countries had been geared to the production of labour-intensive components at the more competitive lower labour cost of ASEAN countries. The components were then imported by the respective home countries. The concurrent growth of FDI and trade ensured a slower rate of increase in the costs of production in Japan and the United States and led to a greater competitiveness of their products in world markets.

The case of the semiconductor industry provides an important example whereby the location of routine assembly operations in low-labour-cost locations became an important means in the 1960s and 1970s to reduce production costs of final outputs produced or consumed in home countries.[2] Transnational corporations are increasingly pursuing regionally integrated strategies in the production of semiconductors such that "integrated circuits may be fabricated in Japan, packed in Malaysia, tested in Singapore and assembled in Hong Kong and then finally exported to a consumer electronics company in the United States".[3] Similar strategies are also being pursued in other industries, for example, the automobile industry.[4]

/.....

re-insurance services to a wide range of local firms; in air transport and shipping, and in advanced data-processing and telecommunication services, where TNC-related imports can enable domestic firms to reduce costs and gain access to world-wide networks of TNCs.

The trend towards a greater tradability of many services, particularly information-intensive services, implies that host countries may increasingly be able to use imports, in addition to inward FDI, to obtain services that are required for efficient domestic production.[50] Increased tradability is likely to lead to a rise in the number of distribution affiliates that are service-specific and whose function is to act as a conduit through which services produced elsewhere, but needed for the growth of host countries, are distributed in those countries. As tradability increases, the cross-border import of services by and

(Box VIII.1, cont'd.)

Similar considerations apply to foreign production aimed at extracting and importing natural resources. The importance of resource-based outward investments for resource-scarce countries has always been particularly high. The problem of resources required for domestic industrial development became apparent in the second half of the nineteenth century for Japan, the United Kingdom, France and Germany. Those countries were unable to compete commercially with others that availed themselves of cheaper resources outside their own borders.[5] In the case of Japan, the rapid development of heavy industries made resource-scarce Japan the most resource-consuming nation (relative to its GNP) among the industrialized countries. Foreign direct investment related to the import of natural resources from elsewhere in Asia helped to alleviate supply shortages that might otherwise have arisen in the course of growth of Japan's resource-consuming industries.[6]

Extractive investments to gain access to raw materials and natural resources have also been important to the Republic of Korea. That country is similar to Japan in terms of insufficient supplies of indigenous natural resources. Until recently, therefore, outward FDI by the Republic of Korea was concentrated in mining and natural resource-based activities. Similar objectives apply to FDI in resource-based activities by firms from Taiwan Province of China.[7]

---

1 Ulrich Hiemenz, "Expansion of ASEAN-EC trade in manufactures: pertinent issues and recent developments", *The Developing Economies*, vol. 26, No. 4 (December 1988), pp. 341-366.

2 David B. Yoffie, "Foreign direct investment in semiconductors". Paper prepared for the National Bureau of Economic Research conference on Foreign Direct Investment Today, Boston, Massachusetts, 15-16 May 1992.

3 Peter Dicken, *Global Shift: The Internationalization of Economic Activity* (London, Paul Chapman, 1991).

4 See UNCTC, *World Investment Report 1991: The Triad in Foreign Direct Investment* (United Nations publication, Sales No. E.91.II.A.12).

5 C. Fred Bergsten, Thomas Horst and Theodore H. Moran, *American Multinationals and American Interests* (Washington, Brookings Institution, 1978).

6 Terutomo Ozawa, "A newer type of foreign investment in third world resource development", *Rivista Internationale di Scienze Economiche e Commerciali*, vol. 29, No. 12 (December 1982), pp. 1133-1151; "New forms of investment by Japanese firms", paper prepared for the OECD research project on new forms of foreign investment in developing countries, April 1984.

7 Paz Estrella E. Tolentino, *Technological Innovation and Third World Multinationals* (London, Routledge, 1992).

from TNCs is likely to become a more important contribution that transnational service corporations can make to growth.[51]

However, for the time being, most services necessary for growth remain non-tradable and can only be obtained through FDI rather than trade. Thus, developing countries that had previously imposed restrictive policies towards FDI in services have more recently liberalized such policies in selected services industries precisely to relieve bottlenecks and increase the overall efficiency of their development efforts.

3. Externalities

The activities of a TNC may have effects on the economy that are not reflected in its own costs or revenues and are therefore called external. Those may be negative, as when a polluting industry is not obliged to pay for the damage it inflicts on the environment, or positive, as when a producer undertakes the training of employees who later move to other firms or start their own. One important kind of such

Box VIII.2. Acquisition of export marketing skill from transnational corporations: the case of garments exports from Bangladesh

The phenomenal success of garments exports from Bangladesh vividly illustrates the positive impact of learning through trade in association with TNCs. Starting from virtually zero in 1978, export earnings from garments reached $560 million in the fiscal year 1989-1990 and may have been higher still in the fiscal year 1990-91 (data for the whole year are not available). The average growth rate in garment export-value was over 120 per cent in the 1980s; during that period, the absolute value of exports of garments surpassed that of jute manufactures, traditionally the highest foreign exchange-earning item of the country. The contribution of garment exports to foreign exchange earnings, a vital but scarce resource for the economic development of Bangladesh, was enormous, amounting to 40 per cent of the total by the fiscal year 1989-1990.

The process started in 1979 with a non-equity arrangement with a developing country TNC, the Daewoo Corporation of the Republic of Korea.[1] That company signed a five-year collaboration agreement with the Desh Garment Company of Bangladesh, under which Daewoo provided: six months of training for Desh workers in the Republic of Korea (later extended to seven months); assistance in start-up activities, including the installation of machinery purchased from Daewoo; supervision of production managed by Desh; and marketing services. In December 1979, 130 Desh workers trained by Daewoo in the Republic of Korea returned to Bangladesh, along with three Daewoo engineers assigned to assist start-up activities. In April 1980, production of garments began with 500 employees and 450 machines. Desh exported its first products in 1979-1980, amounting to about $56,000.

It was initially impossible for Desh to sell garments in the international market without Daewoo's expertise. A so-called "triangular trade" arrangement was established: first, Daewoo received a letter of credit from an overseas buyer; second, it opened a back-to-back letter of credit addressed to Desh; and, finally, Desh

/.....

externalities occurs in the case of an expanding industry, which induces the emergence of specialized suppliers of inputs, spare parts, maintenance and financial services, lowering costs and spreading skills and technical knowledge. Such processes have characterized the historical rise of industrial regions and economies. They imply that the social returns to investment in a core industry may exceed those received by companies. The effects involved, however, are difficult or impossible to measure.

Exports are often the basis of the initial growth that spurs positive externalities. As noted earlier, subcontracting arrangements typically involve product specifications and technical assistance to ensure that export requirements are met by host country enterprises. In such cases, TNCs contribute to the growth of exports which, in turn, often necessitates the transfer of hard and soft technologies. Transnational corporations can also impart valuable marketing skills to domestic enterprises by way of assisting them in breaking into new export markets (see box VIII.2).

On the import side, a large portion of imports by foreign affiliates consists of technology imports, embodied in intermediate and capital goods. To the extent, therefore, that local enterprises derive spill-over benefits from the presence of TNCs in their own technological development (see chapter VI), such benefits can be largely attributed to technology imports by TNCs. There are several case studies

(Box VIII.2, cont'd.)

shipped its garments under the Daewoo brandname directly to the overseas buyer, while it received payment from Daewoo. In this triangular trade, Daewoo assured product quality through production line supervision and quality inspection, while Desh could fully utilize the established marketing networks of Daewoo and learn the necessary marketing techniques.

The speed of learning was so rapid that Desh cancelled its collaboration agreement in June 1981, after only about one-and-a-half years of factory operation, long before the expiration of the agreement. Export performance following the cancellation was impressive, as Desh acquired the ability to handle all its export marketing and to purchase all its inputs from abroad, including from non-Daewoo sources. Its exports reached $10 million in 1987-1988.

Meanwhile, 115 of the 130 Daewoo-trained workers left Desh to set up their own, or to join other newly established, garment companies. Those workers were major agents for imparting export skills throughout the whole garment industry, leading to its dramatic success in foreign exchange earnings. Indeed, many new garment companies did not need the expertise of foreign companies because of the existence of those workers. The remarkable speed with which the ex-Desh workers transmitted their production, marketing and management know-how to hundreds of other factories demonstrates the potential for learning through initial exposure to trade in association with a TNC. It should also be noted that the spread of learning was facilitated by government policies that permitted automatic access to inputs at world prices, provided adequate trade financing at reasonable costs and exempted the industry from investment licensing.

---

1 Yung Whee Rhee, "The catalyst model of development: lessons from Bangladesh's success with garment exports", *World Development*, vol. 18, No. 2 (February 1990), pp. 333-346.

that provide evidence concerning such beneficial externalities. For example, a study of United States TNCs concluded that technology imports by affiliates induced, in some cases, local competitor firms to imitate the behaviour of affiliates.[52] Similarly, imports of new production techniques by foreign affiliates forced domestic competitors to improve their technologies in some industries in Kenya.[53]

It must, of course, also be expected that in some cases domestic firms are forced out of business, which results in increased average productivity. There is also the risk that a TNC or a large domestic firm acquires an excessively dominant position in the domestic markets of host countries which may thwart the process of dynamic externalities. Despite such caveats, it seems clear that learning through trade has been an essential feature of industrial catching-up and the transfer of technology, and that TNCs have had and continue to have an important role in that process.

C. Assessment

The preceding analysis shows that TNCs are important agents in fostering developing countries' growth through trade. They play this role through their direct organization of the international division of labour and their participation in a substantial proportion of the trade of those countries.

The impact of TNCs on the linkages between trade and the growth of production can be conceptualized at the macroeconomic level, the industry level and the company level. On the macroeconomic level, the trade promoted by TNCs helps facilitate a higher growth rate by raising the demand for domestically produced goods through host-country exports, by easing supply constraints of both host and home economies through imports, and by facilitating a dynamic learning process. At the industry level, TNCs facilitate trade by fostering a deeper international division of labour which involves the location of production of components and final products across different countries. That, in turn, facilitates a more efficient utilization of each country's resource and skill endowments, thus lowering production costs and promoting growth. At the company level, the organization of international networks of TNCs, including those of trading affiliates, can increase world trade and, in this manner, influence the growth and development of trading nations.

It should be stressed that the analysis in the present chapter has focused on the principal trade linkages in isolation from one another for the sake of analytical convenience. In theory and practice, however, TNC activities have multiple effects that permeate two or three of the trade linkages in interaction with one another. For example, labour-intensive investments in resource-rich countries or low labour-cost countries contribute to the growth of host countries through increased exports, while helping to sustain industrial expansion, fulfilling a tutorial role for local firms in host countries and maintaining the international competitiveness of home countries through cheaper imports. Clearly, the potential role of TNCs as an agent of growth through trade can only be fully appreciated in terms of their impact on the principal linkages and mechanisms acting in isolation as well as in interaction with one another.

D. Some policy implications

The role of TNCs in trade has major implications for both FDI and trade policies. If there are restrictions on inward investment in conjunction with an emphasis on exports, the influence of TNCs on the relationship between trade and growth would be more indirect, taking the form of licensing and contractual agreements in place of investment. That has been the case of Japan and the Republic of Korea, where the role of TNCs in fostering trade and growth has been significant, but not as much through FDI *per se*, as through licensing and other contractual forms. On the other hand, economies such as Hong Kong and Singapore and, recently, Mexico, have grown with open policies towards FDI as well as emphasis on exports. Such contrasting experiences suggest that different approaches may be pursued by different countries in relation to TNCs, trade and growth. It should be noted, however, that a high degree of cooperation between Government and the domestic private sector, the level of entrepreneurial and human resources development and the overall macroeconomic policy framework, which provided a strong stimulus to domestic growth, are among the unique features of the experiences of Japan and Republic of Korea that may not be easily replicable in other developing countries; in addition, the economic growth of those countries took place when world trade was expanding rapidly, a performance that may not necessarily be sustained. Besides, as noted in chapter VI, the trend towards an internalization of technologies by TNCs, particularly in high-technology industries with greater trade and growth potential, would limit the scope for restrictive policies towards FDI, while simultaneously pursuing an export-oriented growth strategy. This underscores the need for attention to improved co-ordination between trade and FDI policies.

A central concern of trade policies in developing countries is to increase exports. Apart from the structural benefits that are generated by new exports, prospects for a significant acceleration in other sources of foreign exchange (for example, official development assistance and bank credit) are currently not bright. Transnational corporations can contribute to those efforts by increasing their export propensity which, in turn, is significantly influenced by the structure of incentives of the host countries' trade regime, in addition to such other macroeconomic variables as inflation and exchange rates. Where the enabling framework is favourable, TNCs are clearly at an advantageous position to promote exports along the lines discussed earlier. The significant improvement of the export performance of foreign affiliates in Mexico in recent years illustrates this potential role of TNCs and suggests the need for a regime that has the proper mix of FDI, trade and macroeconomic policies. It is, of course, also crucially important to ensure that developing countries do not face protectionist barriers in their export markets in both developed and other developing countries.

Another concern of special importance for developing countries that currently specialize in labour-intensive processes and component production is that further export growth of those products may be threatened by shifts of production by TNCs to more competitive foreign locations or to alternative subcontractors. In such cases, trade and FDI policies should be aimed at increasing the competitiveness of existing exports to the extent possible and at providing incentives to both domestic and foreign firms to develop new areas of comparative advantage.

The role of TNCs in relieving domestic supply constraints of intermediate and capital goods could be enhanced if TNC imports were complemented by competitive domestic production, either by foreign affiliates or local firms. In so far as the import propensities of TNCs are driven by cost and quality considerations, government policies need to encourage linkages between foreign affiliates and domestic firms, with a view to developing efficient local industries. A country's stage of industrial development and the success of its policies to promote efficient industrialization would, therefore, have an important influence on the role of TNCs in growth through trade. This requires support to domestic enterprises, such that they can become competitive producers and suppliers without requiring prolonged protection from competing imports.

As to the beneficial externalities resulting from TNC participation in the trade of host countries, those can be enhanced and spread to the extent that the capacity of domestic enterprises to learn, imitate and adapt TNC practices can be increased. Domestic policies, including trade and FDI policies, that foster the growth of entrepreneurship and competitive spirit play a crucial role in this process. A policy regime that offers prolonged protection against imports or subsidy to exports would reduce incentives to compete and, therefore, the potential externalities of TNC activities.

Finally, an overarching policy question concerns the role of TNCs in a country's use of strategic trade and FDI policies to foster growth. More specifically, the issue is whether TNCs can make a contribution to selective import substitution and export augmentation, particularly through a combination of incentives and performance requirements. This is a difficult option, even for those developing countries with large domestic markets and other specific locational advantages (such as availability of low-cost skilled labour relative to productivity and high-quality infrastructure) that confer strong bargaining leverage (see chapter XI). Broadly speaking, there may be a justification for highly selective use of a combination of investment incentives and performance requirements in a limited number of activities which promise strong positive externalities, for example, by opening new markets or introducing new technologies.

Notes

[1]The relationship between international trade and transnational corporations is examined in detail in H. P. Gray, ed., *Transnational Corporations and International Trade and Payments. United Nations Library on Transnational Corporations* (London, Routledge, forthcoming).

[2]Trade as an engine of growth has been discussed, among others, by Ragnar Nurkse, in G. Haberler and R.N. Stern, eds., *Equilibrium and Growth in the World Economy* (Cambridge, Massachusetts, Harvard University Press, 1961). Trade as a handmaiden of growth has been discussed by Irving B. Kravis, "Trade as a handmaiden of growth: similarities between the nineteenth and twentieth centuries", *The Economic Journal*, vol. LXXX, No. 320 (December 1970), pp. 850-872.

[3]Nurkse, op. cit., pp. 242-243.

[4]Based on P. Armstrong, A. Glyn and J. Harrison, *Capitalism Since 1945* (Oxford, Blackwell, 1991).

[5]GATT, *International Trade, 1988-89*, vol. II (Geneva, GATT, 1989), table 4.3; and United Nations, *National Accounts Statistics, 1989* (New York, United Nations, 1992).

[6]See, for example, Anne O. Krueger, *Foreign Trade Regimes and Economic Development: Liberalization Attempts and Consequences* (Cambridge, Massachusetts, Ballinger Publishing Company, 1978); Bela Balassa, "Export and economic growth: further evidence", *Journal of Development Economics,* vol. 5, No. 2 (June 1978), pp. 181-189; Bela Balassa, "Exports, policy choices, and economic growth in developing countries after the 1973 oil shock", *Journal of Development Economics,* vol. 18, No. 1 (May/June 1985), pp. 23-35; Gershon Feder, "On exports and economic growth", *Journal of Development Economics,* vol. 12, Nos. 1/2 (February/April 1982), pp. 59-73; Jong H. Park, "Export performance and economic growth in Latin America", paper presented at the annual meeting of the International Trade and Finance Association, 3-5 January 1992; Tain-Jy Chen and De-piao Tang, "Export performance and productivity growth: the case of Taiwan", *Economic Development and Cultural Change,* vol. 38, No. 3 (April 1990), pp. 577-585; C. Michalopoulos and K. Jay, "Growth of exports and income in the developing world: a neoclassical view", AID Division Paper 28, United States Agency for International Development, Washington, D.C., 1973.

[7]See, for example, Woo S. Jung and Peyton J. Marshall, "Exports, growth and causality in developing countries", *Journal of Development Economics,* vol.18, No. 1 (May/June), pp. 1-12; Y. Chow, "Causality between export growth and industrial development: empirical evidence from the NICs", *Journal of Development Economics,* vol. 26, No. 1 (June 1987), pp. 53-63; Dominick Salvatore, "A simultaneous equations model of trade and development with dynamic policy simulations", *Kyklos,* vol. 36, No. 1 (1983), pp. 66-90; Park, op. cit.; and Krueger, op. cit. These studies on the causal relation between exports and output growth in developing countries also show that the results are sensitive to the choice of sample size and composition, time-periods, estimation techniques and proxy variables included in the study.

[8]James Love, "Export instability, imports and investment in developing countries", *The Journal of Development Studies,* vol. 25, No. 2 (January 1989), pp. 183-191; Magnus Blomström, *Transnational Corporations and Manufacturing Exports from Developing Countries* (United Nations publication, Sales No. E.90.II.A.21).

[9]See, for example, Manuel Agosin, "Trade policy reform and economic performance: a review of the issues and some empirical evidence" (Geneva, UNCTAD, 1991), mimeo; Hadji S. Esfahani, "Exports, imports and economic growth in semi-industrialized countries", *Journal of Development Economics,* vol. 35, No. 1 (January 1991), pp. 93-116.

[10]Gene M. Grossman and Elhanan Helpman, "Trade, knowledge spillovers and growth", *European Economic Review,* vol. 35, Nos. 2/3 (April 1991), pp. 517-526.

[11]Gene M. Grossman and Elhanan Helpman, *Innovation and Growth in the Global Economy* (Cambridge, Massachusetts, MIT Press, 1991).

[12]See for example, Mieko Nishimizu and Sherman Robinson, "Trade policies and productivity change in semi-industrialized countries", *Journal of Development Economics,* vol. 16, Nos. 1/2 (September-October 1984), pp. 177-206; David Dollar and Kenneth Solzoloff, "Patterns of productivity growth in Korean manufacturing industries", *Journal of Development Economics,* vol. 33, No. 2 (October 1990), pp. 309-327.

[13]Yung Whee Rhee, Bruce Ross-Larson and Garry Pursell, *Korea's Competitive Edge: Managing the Entry into World Markets* (Baltimore, Maryland, Johns Hopkins University Press, 1984).

[14]See UNCTC, *World Investment Report 1991: The Triad in Foreign Direct Investment* (United Nations publication, Sales No. E.91.II.A.12), pp. 67-74.

[15]David Gold, Persephone Economou and Paz Estrella Tolentino, "Trade blocs and investment blocs: the Triad in foreign direct investment and international trade". Paper presented at the Annual Meeting of the Academy of International Business, Miami, Florida, 17-20 October 1991.

[16]Comparable data on exports of foreign affiliates other than those of Japanese and United States firms for the same time-periods are not available. Some indications for 1986 are available for Swedish majority-owned foreign affiliates, which accounted for 0.44 per cent of total manufactured exports of Latin America. See Blomström, 1990, op. cit.

[17]For similar findings, see Seiji Naya and Pearl Imada, "Trade and foreign investment linkages in ASEAN", in Soon Lee Ying, ed., *Foreign Direct Investment in ASEAN* (Kuala Lumpur, Malaysian Economic Association, 1990).

[18]Atchaka Sibunrang and Peter Brimble, "Export-oriented industrial collaboration: a case study of Thailand" (New York, United Nations Centre on Transnational Corporations, 1990), mimeo.

[19]See, among other studies, Sanjaya Lall and Sharif Mohammad, "Foreign ownership and export performance in the large corporate sector of India," in Gray, op. cit. Those studies indicate that foreign ownership has a positive correlation with export propensity. Other empirical studies covering other countries, however, indicate that firm-ownership does not influence export

propensity in any consistent direction. See UNCTC, *Transnational Corporations and International Trade* (United Nations publication, Sales No. E.85.II.A.4) for the case study on Brazil.

[20]See, among other studies, Marian Radetzki, "Where should developing countries' minerals be processed? The country view versus the multinational view", in Bruce McKern, ed., *United Nations Library on Transnational Corporations: Transnational Corporations and the Exploitation of Natural Resources* (London, Routledge, forthcoming).

[21]See R. A. Read, "The banana industry: oligopoly and barriers to entry", in McKern, op. cit.

[22]Carl Goldstein, "Marketing: brand of hope", *Far Eastern Economic Review*, vol. 154, No. 40 (3 October 1991), pp. 52-54; Brian Levy, "Transactions costs, the size of firms and industrial policy: lessons from a comparative case study of the footwear industry in Korea and Taiwan", *Journal of Development Economics*, vol. 34, Nos. 1-2 (November 1990), pp. 151-178; Charles M. Galbraith, Jr., "Offshore sourcing—Hong Kong: a world apparel player", *Bobbin*, vol. 29, No. 10 (June 1988), pp. 106-107; Steven Feldman, "Offshore sourcing: the open door to the Far East", *Bobbin*, vol. 29, No. 10 (June 1988), pp. 100-112.

[23]Andrew Daniels, "Bordering on opportunity", *World*, vol. 22, No. 3 (Summer 1988), pp. 4-5.

[24]Lewis E. Salcedo, "Export oriented industrial collaboration: a case study of Colombia" (New York, United Nations Centre on Transnational Corporations, 1991), mimeo.

[25]Monkid Mestassi, "La collaboration industrielle tournée vers l'exportation: le cas du Maroc" (Geneva, UNCTAD, 1991), mimeo.

[26]Marjan Svetlicic and Matiga Rojec, "Export-oriented industrial collaboration in Yugoslavia" (Geneva, UNCTAD, 1991), mimeo.

[27]See United Nations Centre on Transnational Corporations, *Transnational Corporations and the Electronic Industries of ASEAN Economies* (United Nations publication, Sales No. E.87.II.A.13), and Alden M. Hayashi, "The new shell game", *Electronic Business*, vol. 14, No. 5 (1 March 1988), pp. 36-40.

[28]See Michael Westlake, "Aviation and aerospace '88: China—Joint ventures and joint opportunities", *Far Eastern Economic Review*, vol. 139, No. 5 (4 February 1988), pp. 50-56.

[29]John D. Morocco, "Korean aerospace firms seek greater role in world market", *Aviation Week and Space Technology*, vol. 130, No. 24 (12 June 1989), pp. 201-206.

[30]For a discussion of marketing barriers faced by developing countries, see, Sanjaya Lall, "Marketing barriers facing developing country manufactured exports: a conceptual note", *The Journal of Development Studies*, vol. 27, No. 4 (July 1991), pp. 137-150.

[31]UNCTAD/GATT, *Structural Change in Export Marketing Channels for Developing Countries* (Geneva, International Trade Centre, 1988).

[32]Japan, Ministry of International Trade and Industry, *Dai Yon-kai Kaigai Jigyo Katsudo Kihon Chosa: Kaigai Toshi Tokei Soran* (Tokyo, Okura-sho Insatsu-kyoku, 1991), tables 2-25-1 to 2-25-12, pp. 210-211. All data contained in this survey underestimate the true value of operations of Japanese TNCs as the survey is based on the companies that responded to the questionnaire of MITI. In this survey, only 47 per cent of TNCs responded. Data include retail trading affiliates.

[33]United States, Department of Commerce, *U.S. Direct Investment Abroad: 1989 Benchmark Survey* (Washington, D.C., United States Government Printing Office, 1991), tables 2, 4 and 5.

[34]Japan, Ministry of International Trade and Industry, op. cit., tables 2-90-1 to 2-90-12, pp. 475-480. Data include retail trading affiliates.

[35]In fact six of the world's ten largest companies in terms of sales are *sogo shosha;* see "The global 1000", *Business Week*, 15 July 1991, pp. 52-105.

[36]Data compiled from Toyo Keizai Shimposha, *Kaisha-betsu Kaigai Shinshutsu Kigyo, 1991/1992* (Tokyo, 1991). On *sogo shosha* in developing countries generally, see Kiyoshi Kojima and Terutomo Ozawa, *Japan's General Trading Companies* (Paris, OECD, 1984).

[37]See A. K. Young, *The Sogo Shosha: Japan's Multinational Trading Companies* (Boulder, Colorado, Westview Press, 1978); *Nihon Keizai Shimbun*, 8 November 1985, p. 8; 28 April 1988, p. 9; and 14 October 1989, p. 8.

[38]*Ekonomisuto*, 12 July 1988, p. 96.

[39]ESCAP/UNCTC, *Transnational Trading Corporations in Selected Asian and Pacific Countries* (Bangkok, ESCAP/UNCTC, 1985).

[40]UNCTC, *Transnational Corporations and World Development: Trends and Prospects* (United Nations publication, Sales No. E.88.II.A.7).

[41]GATT, *International Trade, 1990-91*, vol. I (Geneva, GATT, 1992) p. 5.

[42]Kenneth Heydon, "Developing country perspectives", in World Bank and UNCTC, *The Uruguay Round: Services in the World Economy* (Washington, D.C. and New York, The World Bank and United Nations Centre on Transnational Corporations, 1990), pp. 159-165.

[43]Heydon, op. cit.

[44]The data on intermediate products have been estimated on the basis of data on crude materials, inedible, except fuels; petroleum and products; coal and coke; chemicals; road vehicles and parts; and metal manufactures.

[45]Paul A. Natke, "Foreign ownership and firm-level import performance in Brazilian manufacturing industries", *Atlantic Economic Journal*, vol. 15, No. 4 (December 1987), pp. 39-48.

[46]Louis T. Wells, "Foreign investment from the Third World: the experience of Chinese firms from Hong Kong", *Columbia Journal of World Business*, vol. 13, No. 1 (Spring 1978), pp. 39-49.

[47]This was particularly the growth path of Tuntex Fiber Company. See W.L. Ting and C. Schive, "Direct investment and technology transfer from Taiwan", in K. Kumar and M. G. McLeod, eds., *Multinationals from Developing Countries* (Lexington, Massachusetts, D.C. Heath and Company, 1981), pp. 101-114.

[48]Data obtained from United States, Department of Commerce, *U.S. Direct Investment Abroad: 1982 Benchmark Survey Data* (Washington, D.C., United States Government Printing Office, 1985); *U.S. Direct Investment Abroad: 1989 Benchmark Survey, Preliminary Results* (Washington, D.C., United States Government Printing Office, 1991).

[49]Robert Lipsey and Zbigniew Zimny, "Impact of transnational service corporations in developing countries", in Karl P. Sauvant and Padma Mallampally, eds., *Transnational Corporations and Services. United Nations Library on Transnational Corporations* (London, Routledge, forthcoming).

[50]Karl P. Sauvant, "The tradability of services," in World Bank and UNCTC, op. cit., pp. 114-122.

[51]UNCTC, 1988, op. cit.

[52]Edward Mansfield and Anthony Romeo, "Technology transfer to overseas subsidiaries by U.S.-based firms", *Quarterly Journal of Economics*, vol. 19, No. 4 (December 1980), pp. 737-750.

[53]R. Jenkins, "Comparing foreign subsidiaries and local firms in LDCs: theoretical issues and empirical evidence", *Journal of Development Studies*, vol. 26, No. 2 (January 1990), pp. 205-228.

Chapter IX

TRANSNATIONAL CORPORATIONS, ENVIRONMENTAL QUALITY AND SUSTAINABLE GROWTH

Transnational corporations, in addition to affecting economic growth in host countries through the channels described in the four preceding chapters, also influence the *quality* of the physical environment, with implications for the long-run sustainability of growth. The relationships of TNCs, environmental quality and economic growth to each other are complex. The present chapter identifies the principal relationships, presents evidence on the environmental role of TNCs and outlines some policy implications.

Section A traces the relationship between economic growth and environmental quality, which has given rise to the concept of sustainable development, arguing that in some areas a tradeoff exists but in other respects the two are mutually reinforcing. The section also points out some deficiencies of the conventional national income accounting system due to incorrect inclusion or exclusion of items relating to costs and effects of environmental protection or degradation and of natural capital depletion, and notes that steps are being taken recently for the incorporation of environmental externalities into the measurement of growth. In section B the role of TNCs—positive and negative—in determining environmental quality is examined, with special attention to their role in developing countries. The final section contains a discussion of policy issues arising from the intersection of TNCs and environmental concern and emphasises the importance of coordinating efforts among national Governments, the international community and TNCs.

A. Economic growth and environmental quality

1. Conceptual linkages

The early theoretical view of the relationship between economic growth and environmental quality was of a simple trade-off between growth and the environment. Rapid economic growth increased environmental stress. Conversely, environmental protection slowed economic growth. Two mechanisms were at work. Economic growth, that is, growth of production, created environmental stress in the extraction of natural resources (evident in agriculture, mining and forestry) and multiplied pollution (that is, waste-disposal) problems. Environmental protection diverted real and financial resources from the production of conventional goods and services and hence slowed GDP growth. The implication of that simple view appeared clear. Industrial countries, burdened by the "effluents of affluence" and enjoying high incomes, could and should trade off some economic growth for higher environmental quality. Developing countries, burdened by poverty, should strike a different balance, with more attention to growth and less to environmental protection.

There remains an important kernel of truth to this simple trade-off view. But it is deficient in four important respects. First, the attributes of poverty themselves—unsanitary water supplies, endemic disease, overcrowding, urban squalor—are now considered environmental problems, whose existence restrains economic growth. [1] In that sense, the trade-off collapses, and environmental improvement and economic growth are reinforcing, provided that the economic growth is equitably distributed and reaches the poor. Second, and perhaps more important, environmental resources are inputs into conventional production and must be conserved for sustained economic growth. The environmental resources—land, water, forests, fisheries—play a larger role in economic production in developing countries, and hence their conservation is essential for long-term growth. [2] Again, the simple trade-off dissolves. Third, it has become apparent that poor people, at the margin of survival and with worsening ratios of natural resources to population, frequently undermine the productivity of the resource base itself. In technical economic terms, their personal time preferences heavily discount future versus present consumption. The examples are frequently drawn from agriculture, where population pressures and poverty force the cultivation of marginal lands and result in erosion and exhaustion of soil nutrients. Again, strong economic growth may contribute to improved resource conservation, modifying the growth-environment trade-off. Finally, there is today a greater appreciation of the need for strong economic growth to provide the real financial resources for environmental protection. Available evidence suggests that the demand for environmental quality is income elastic, and rising per capita income translates into effective political demand for environmental protection, again modifying the earlier simple view of a trade-off.

The concept of "sustainable development", while not subject to a single precise definition, captures the newer, more sophisticated understanding of the relationship between growth and the environment, taking into account the various elements discussed above. It modifies the conventional view of economic growth as GDP growth to incorporate a new balance between economic growth and environmental quality; it also recognizes that environmental quality and economic growth can be mutually reinforcing at all income levels.[3]

2. Sustainable development and the measurement of growth

Traditional measures of aggregate economic activity and economic growth—the national income and national product accounts—are deficient as measures of sustainable development.[4] There are three principal sources of error. First, national income and product statistics include certain expenditures that defend against environmental damage (that is, pollution control and pollution cleanup), but that do not contribute to improving productivity. Second, the statistics fail to account for certain welfare reductions from residual environmental damages. Both the incorrect inclusions and exclusions tend to overstate national income and economic growth. Finally, and most serious for developing countries that rely heavily on natural resources in production, conventional national-income accounting fails to include the depletion, depreciation or degradation of natural capital. That failure can substantially overstate real income and economic growth, and can contribute to a poor resource-management policy.[5] Those accounts are used as management tools in policy formation. If they do not accurately measure what they purport to measure, serious mistakes in resource-management decisions can result.

There has been some progress in modifying conventional national-income accounting systems.[6] Two approaches to adjusting for natural capital depletion have been proposed. One would parallel current treatment of man-made capital. In essence, it would calculate a monetary value for the change in natural capital, and subtract that value from GNP to derive an adjusted figure for net national product and net national income. The second approach, called the user-cost method, separates receipts from depletable asset sales into two components, a user cost and a true income component.[7] In that fashion, gross and net product are adjusted for capital consumption, but still include true (sustainable) income from asset sales. Empirical applications of the adjusted measures of growth are now being undertaken.

3. The role of policy

Increased understanding of the interrelationship between economic growth and environmental quality highlights the role of policy in sustainable development. Environmental deterioration is now seen as the consequence of pervasive externalities in the extraction, processing, transport, consumption and disposal of goods and services. Externalities are simply costs not borne by agents engaged in economic activity—consumers, businesses and Governments. It is now generally accepted by all, including the business sector, that Governments have a major role to play in improving social welfare by correcting the distortions in the price/market system arising from the externalities. In some instances, the role involves the use of either command-and-control environment regulations and/or "market-friendly" type government measures in order to improve social welfare. It follows that regulation of externalities, and the search for efficient policy measures, are also central elements of sustainable development.

At the same time, there is an increasing recognition that inappropriate government policies themselves are a serious source of environmental deterioration. The effect is most visible when government subsidies distort the price of environmental and natural resources. Examples can come from both industrial and developing economies. The Government provides subsidies for energy, water, pesticides, land, livestock and below-market charges for grazing and timber-harvesting, all of which can lead to excessive use. [8] Sustainable development suggests very sparing use of government subsidies that have incidental, adverse environmental effects. In that connection, some observers have argued that a liberal trade and investment policy itself may contribute to environmental degradation. [9] Others feel that the problem lies not with trade and FDI, but with the failure of Governments to regulate externalities and to scale down abusive environmental subsidies as described above. Obviously, if Governments fail to correct externalities and distortive subsidies, any production, whether for domestic or international markets, will involve environmental damages.

B. Transnational corporations and environmental quality in host countries

1. The extent of transnational corporation involvement and influence

While all firms—domestic private, state enterprises and TNCs—affect and are affected by environmental quality, TNCs possess certain characteristics that support specific analysis:

- First, TNCs tend to be more mobile and to have greater discretion in the location of production than domestic firms, [10] which suggests the possibility that TNCs have greater leverage in negotiating favourable environmental regulations, permits and exemptions with host countries.
- Second, TNCs are extensively involved in environmentally significant activities. According to a recent UNCTC study that focused on six major areas that contribute significantly to global environmental problems and account for roughly 80 per cent of anthropomorphic greenhouse-gas generation, TNCs have a large influence, direct or indirect, in those areas. Among other things, they are the primary producers and intermediate consumers of chlorofluorocarbons, which are the principal cause of stratospheric ozone depletion and account for at least 15 per cent of greenhouse-gas emissions. [11] One chemical company alone, E. I. DuPont de Nemours and Company, accounted for 25 per cent of world production of CFCs. It has also been estimated that the 20 largest international pesticide manufacturers accounted for 94 per cent of world agrochemical sales in 1990. [12] Furthermore, TNCs are reported to have extensive involvement in most pollution- and hazard-intensive industries as measured by environmental control costs. [13]
- Third, many TNCs tend to have financial, managerial and technological resources superior to those of local firms. The superior position both raises expectations and allows TNCs to exercise

leadership in environmental protection. The importance of technology, in particular, is self-evident; not only do TNCs generally have access to clean technology, developed in response to stringent environmental protection among industrial countries, but they possess skills in the safe handling, transport, storage, use and disposal of hazardous materials, and in the development of pollution-abatement technology itself. The technology advantage is reinforced by sophisticated management skills, again refined by long experience with environmental and resource management in highly regulated industrial countries.

- A fourth characteristic of TNCs that bears on their environmental performance is their relatively greater visibility and vulnerability, which takes two forms. On the one hand, TNCs are guests in the host country and, compared to local firms, often must strive harder to maintain good relations with host governments and local communities. On the other hand, large TNCs have a global image to protect and tend to be quite conscious of public and stockholder opinions, and of the potential for restrictive home country regulation, even for their foreign operations.

It is, however, not easy to evaluate the impact of TNCs on the environmental quality in host countries, and this impact cannot be easily gauged from their direct role in aggregate economic production (box IX.1). As noted in chapter II, the direct role of TNCs in total investment in host countries is quite modest, especially as it concerns investment in developing countries. The average ratio of FDI inflows to gross domestic capital formation was 4.1 for developed countries and 4.4 for developing countries for the period 1986-1989 (chapter II). Investment inflows accounted for less than 5 per cent of gross domestic capital formation in more than half of the countries for which data are available (annex table 6). The implication of those figures is that the challenge of maintaining environmental quality and securing sustainable development is principally a domestic task, although it may need to be supplemented by international assistance and co-ordination.

To rest the case on such aggregate data alone, however, would be misleading. For one thing, the significance of FDI varies considerably among host countries; some of the differences among developing countries, by region and by income group, have been highlighted in chapter II. Further, in many host countries, FDI is concentrated in a relatively few industries, which may be the most important in terms of their impact on the environment. Finally, TNCs have many non-equity relationships and various backward and forward linkages in host countries that give them additional opportunities to influence the environmental quality of growth.

2. Assessing the environmental impact of transnational corporations

To assess the impact of TNCs on environmental quality in host developing countries, it is necessary to examine the extent to which TNCs are involved in environmentally significant activities outside their home countries, and in developing countries in particular. One approach towards gauging the environmental effects of TNCs in host countries is by establishing a ranking of environmentally sensitive industries in each country and looking at the importance of FDI in each industry.

At a very general level, one might argue that the primary and secondary sectors, which roughly correspond to the extractive and the manufacturing sectors, involve greater environmental risk than the tertiary sector, involving services. By that indicator, the environmental impact of FDI should be decreasing, at least in relative terms. As the data in table I.3 show, the tertiary sector increased significantly its relative share in FDI outward stock of major home countries for the period 1975-1990, whereas the share of the primary sector fell over the same period. The correlation, however, between the importance of the primary, secondary and tertiary sectors in FDI and the extent of environmental stress is far from perfect. For example, construction and tourism, which fall in the services sector, often involve significant environmental degradation.

Two approaches have been taken to measure the pollution intensity of industries within the manufacturing sector, a far narrower question than determining the environmental sensitivity of all

Box IX.1. Transnational corporations and tropical deforestation

Tropical deforestation provides a good example of the difficulties in assessing the importance and performance of TNCs in environmental problems. That tropical deforestation is a serious environmental concern is widely acknowledged, with the annual rate of deforestation estimated to range from 2.2 per cent for Brazil to 0.1 per cent for Gabon.[1] The proximate causes of deforestation are conversion to agricultural and livestock production, fuelwood demand, commercial logging and mining. But the relative contributions of the different activities are not clear. It has been estimated that 18 per cent of deforestation may be attributed to commercial logging and mining.[2] Even if correct, the 18 per cent may not accurately reflect the direct and indirect effects, as logging can create serious environmental damage without deforestation.[3] Moreover, logging increases access to remote areas, opening them to agricultural conversion and associated environmental degradation.

Assessing the role of TNCs in commercial logging presents further difficulties. The available evidence from a 1981 study suggests that, by the early 1980s, United States TNCs had almost totally withdrawn from direct forest management and harvest, and their activities affected only about 7300 hectares (or 0.1 per cent) of total tropical forests logged per year. The same study concluded that United States and Canadian firms operating in the tropics followed generally good practice in forestry where ownership and concession agreements permit.[4] In contrast, the involvement of European firms in logging tropical forests, mainly in Africa, appears to be extensive, at least recently. It was estimated that foreign interests controlled 90 per cent of logging in Gabon (1982), 77 per cent of logging in the Congo (1984), virtually all logging concessions in Liberia and, together with joint venture partners, 88 per cent of concessions in Cameroon (1970s).[5] Other evidence shows a considerable involvement of Japanese firms in South-East Asia, with sometimes considerable negative environmental effects.[6] Another study found that, in earlier years, two types of firms dominated logging in Indonesia - large TNCs based in industrial countries and smaller firms based in neighbouring Asian developing economies (for example, Malaysia and Hong Kong); larger TNCs showed somewhat greater concern for environmental and resource-conservation issues, but not to the degree which the size difference between them and the small TNCs might have suggested; in any event, the larger TNCs were held to a higher implicit standard owing to their superior financial and technological capabilities.[7] Even if not directly involved in logging, TNCs often participate in processing, distribution and trade.

/.....

categories of economic production.[14] One involves ranking industries by the measured release of toxic substances after an effort has been made to control pollution. Table IX.1 is an example. While useful, the approach does not measure environmental damage, which is a function of the time, place, concentration, composition and disposal method of the released materials. Nor do the data on release reflect the quantity of pollution that has been successfully abated.[15] A second approach is to rank industries within the manufacturing sector by pollution-abatement expenditure, taking these expenditures as an indication of the pollution-intensity of an industry. Table IX.2 is an example. There is a reasonable correlation between the two methods of ranking, and they contain few surprises.[16] Chemicals, petroleum products, petrochemicals, pulp and paper and metals, for instance, are highly polluting industries.

Turning to FDI, data on the share of four pollution-intensive industries (chemicals, petroleum and coal products, metals and pulp and paper) in total inward FDI stocks, in both developing and developed

(Box IX.1, continued)

While further, updated research on the role of TNCs in deforestation would be useful, it can tell only part of the story. Transnational corporations operate within a policy framework set by Governments. As was shown in a study of deforestation in Brazil and Indonesia, national policies matter.[8] In Brazil, Government fiscal and financial incentives have encouraged deforestation in the Amazon region. In Indonesia, the Government log export tax and subsequent log export ban induced local processing and inefficient use of logs, leading to excessive rates of harvest. Thus, the experience of both countries shows that tropical deforestation is the outcome of the interaction between Government policy and the operations of TNCs and domestic firms.

---

1 World Resources Institute, *World Resources 1990-1991* (New York, Oxford University Press, 1990), table 19.1. Deforestation estimates are controversial. For details, see Carlos Alberto Primo Braga, "Tropical forests and trade policy: the case of Indonesia and Brazil", in Patrick Low, ed., *International Trade and the Environment*, World Bank Discussion Paper, No. 159 (Washington, D.C., The World Bank, 1992), pp. 175.

2 Brian Johnson, *Responding to Tropical Deforestation: An Eruption of Crisis - An Array of Solutions* (London, Conservation Foundation, 1991).

3 Napier Shelton, "Logging vs. the natural habitat", *Ambio*, vol. 14, No. 1 (1985), p. 39. A Malaysian logging operation can reduce canopy from nearly 100 per cent to an average of about 50 per cent for the concession.

4 James Bethel, et al., "The role of U.S. multinational corporations in commercial forestry operations in the tropics". Report submitted to the United States Department of State, March 1981, by the College of Forestry Resources, University of Washington.

5 Francois Nectoux and Nigel Dudley, *A Hardwood Story: Europe's Involvement in the Tropical Timber Trade* (London, Friends of the Earth, 1987).

6 Francois Nectoux and Yoichi Kuroda, *Timber from the South Seas* (Gland, Switzerland, World Wildlife Fund International, 1989).

7 Malcolm Gillis, "Multinational enterprises and environmental and resource management issues in the Indonesian tropical forest sector", in Pearson, ed., *Multinational Corporations, Environment and the Third World* (Durham, North Carolina, Duke University Press, 1987), pp. 64-89.

8 Braga, op. cit., pp. 173-193.

Table IX.1. Toxic release intensities by manufacturing industries

Industry	*Total pounds per million output in 1987 dollars after abatement*	*Risk factor weighted exponential*
Other industrial chemicals	52 260.3	96 660.0
Basic industrial chemicals	32 254.6	609 770.9
Leather and leather products	15 380.7	268 922.3
Synthetic resins	14 002.9	544 602.8
Plastic products n.e.c.	9 335.0	175 559.9
Non-ferrous metals	9 334.3	151 219.2
Other paper products	8 741.7	61 291.0
Iron and steel	7 642.8	349 897.7
Printing, publishing	7 513.9	109 252.0
Pulp, paper	6 225.9	98 109.5
Furniture, fixtures	5 366.8	61 291.0
Metal products	4 592.5	166 930.2
Wood products	4 399.4	137 294.6
Drugs and medicines	3 966.7	42 819.7
Non-metal products, n.e.c.	3 853.8	349 897.7
Petroleum refineries	3 757.9	78 634.6
Pottery, china etc.	3 614.5	29 164.7
Other chemical products	3 563.8	58 049.0
Other textile production	3 502.2	51 086.7
Spinning, weaving	3 106.7	154 381.3
Rubber products	2 934.2	26 305.2
Other industries	2 706.8	42 682.7
Shipbuilding, repair	2 546.5	17 426.9
Petroleum and coal products	2 544.1	29 444.3
Footwear	2 277.7	11 695.0
Radio, television etc.	1 808.3	29 207.4
Other electrical machines	1 797.3	38 967.4
Wearing apparel	1 744.8	17 515.8
Other machinery, n.e.c.	1 596.2	39 165.8
Glass and products	1 481.2	43 583.8
Transport equipment	1 007.8	28 055.7
Professional goods	887.6	16 127.0
Food products	781.6	20 776.7
Motor vehicles	669.9	15 733.1
Tobacco	489.0	5 308.9
Office and computing machines	303.3	3 163.4
Beverages	205.1	4 647.5

Source: Adapted from Robert E. B. Lucas, David Wheeler and Hemamala Hettige, "Economic development, environmental regulation and the international migration of toxic industrial pollution: 1960-1988", in Patrick Low, ed., *International Trade and the Environment*, World Bank Discussion Paper, No. 159 (Washington, D.C., The World Bank, 1992), p. 70.

Note: The first column reports total release of 320 toxic substances (atmospheric, effluent and solid) per million output in 1987 dollars; it was originally derived from the United States Environmental Protection Agency's Toxic Release Inventory for 1987. EPA uses a four-category ordinal ranking of toxic pollutants (1-mild; 4-very serious); the final column assumes exponential risk weights (1, 10, 100 and 1000) so that one pound of category 4 release is weighted 1000 times as heavily as one pound of category 1 release. The abbreviation "n.e.c." means "not elsewhere classified".

host countries, indicate that for a number of countries, the share has decreased somewhat during the 1980s (annex table 12). Data for the outward FDI stocks of major home countries confirm the trend during the 1980s (table IX.3). But the decline largely reflects the slower expansion of FDI in the industrial, as opposed to the services sector, during the 1980s. If only the shares of pollution-intensive industries in total manufacturing FDI are considered, no clear trend emerges. It is noteworthy, however, that the share of pollution-intensive industries in total manufacturing FDI has been relatively high, and remains at 20 to 50 per cent in developing countries and 30 to 60 per cent in developed countries. Furthermore, while developing countries experienced a declining share of those industries during the 1970s and a somewhat rising share during the 1980s, developed countries observed the opposite pattern, except for the United Kingdom (annex table 12). At the same time, the share of pollution-intensive industries in outward manufacturing FDI stock did not exhibit a clear pattern between the mid-1970s and the end 1980s: in the cases of the Federal Republic of Germany, Japan and Sweden, it declined; in the cases of France, the United Kingdom and the United States, it increased. In the area of trade, however, there was a 5 percentage point shift towards developing countries in the origin of pollution-intensive trade for the period

Table IX.2. United States pollution abatement costs, by industry, 1988

Industry	*Millions of dollars*		*Abatement costs as percentage of output value*
	Total gross abatement costs	*Total industry output*	
Petroleum and coal products	2 005.5	131 414.8	1.53
Primary metal industries	1 809.0	149 079.8	1.21
Chemicals and allied products	3 074.9	259 699.1	1.18
Paper and allied products	1 343.3	122 556.2	1.10
Stone, clay and glass products	438.5	63 059.4	0.70
Fabricated metal products	761.9	158 833.8	0.48
Electric and electrical equipment	659.3	186 950.8	0.35
Lumber and wood products	236.1	72 065.4	0.33
Food and kindred products	1 160.1	351 514.9	0.33
Furniture and fixture	118.4	39 226.1	0.30
Rubber and miscellaneous plastic products	278.0	94 200.2	0.30
Transportation equipment	974.5	354 047.8	0.28
Textile mill products	177.0	64 767.9	0.27
Leather and leather products	23.1	9 663.7	0.24
Miscellaneous manufacturing industries	76.7	34 869.4	0.22
Machinery, except electrical	429.7	243 260.8	0.18
Instrument and related products	197.7	114 528.4	0.17
Tobacco manufactures	37.6	28 831.8	0.16
Printing and publishing	206.4	143 906.8	0.14
TOTAL	14 008.6	2 617 476.9	0.54

Source: United States, Department of Commerce, *Manufacturers' Pollution Abatement Capital Expenditures and Operating Costs* (Washington, D.C., Government Printing Office, 1988), as cited in Patrick Low, "Trade measures and environmental quality: the implications for Mexico's exports", in Patrick Low, ed., *International Trade and the Environment*, World Bank Discussion Paper, No. 159 (Washington, D.C., The World Bank, 1992), p. 107.

1975-1988 (table IX.4). No information is available to attribute that shift to either TNCs or domestic firms. Although further data and analyses are needed to draw any general conclusions regarding the environmental role of FDI and TNCs in host developing countries, the data presented above do not suggest any systematic trend towards an increasing pollution intensity of FDI.

A number of studies have attempted to throw light on the location of pollution-intensive FDI by TNCs. An early study on United States FDI in pollution-intensive industries (chemicals, metal, pulp and paper, petroleum refining) found that such investment went mainly to other industrial countries, suggesting that United States FDI in developing countries was not mainly in pollution-intensive industries.[17] A study on "pollution havens" in Asia did not support the hypothesis that the growth of

Table IX.3. Share of pollution-intensive industries [a] in outward investment stock
(Percentage and millions of local currency)

Economy and year	*Total FDI*	*Total FDI in manufac-turing*	*Chemicals*	*Pulp and paper*	*Petroleum and coal products*	*Metal*	*Total (1) [b]*	*Share of (1) in total FDI*	*Share of (1) in total FDI in manu-facturing*
France									
(French francs)									
1975	15 159	5 786	730	--	--	2 609	3 339	22	58
1980	55 120	22 699	2 670	--	--	11 549	14 219	26	63
1989	433 131	116 615	28 989	4 774	--	39 682	73 445	17	63
Germany, Federal Republic of									
(Deutsche marks)									
1976	49 081	23 711	8 928	316	187	1 973	11 404	23	48
1980	84 485	40 175	14 921	557	207	3 229	18 914	22	47
1989	206 555	86 223	32 244	1 802	137	4 765	38 948	19	45
Japan									
(United States dollars)									
1975	15 943	5 164	887	512	--	782	2 181	14	42
1980	36 497	12 573	2 626	758	--	2 619	6 003	16	48
1989	253 896	66 128	8 649	2 654	--	9 261	20 564	8	31
Sweden									
(Swedish kroner)									
1977	26 782	10 429	400	1 148	--	1 717	3 265	12	31
1988	153 000	115 980	10 710	16 830	--	--	27 540	18	24
United Kingdom									
(Pounds sterling)									
1974	10 436	6 936	1 153	451	--	273	1 877	18	27
1981	28 545	16 167	4 533	884	--	321	5 738	20	35
1987	86 727	29 860	8 172	2 507	--	636	11 315	13	38
United States									
(United States dollars)									
1977	147 206	70 045	11 864	3 178	8 026	4 626	27 269	19	39
1980	220 178	107 801	18 877	4 301	18 509	6 322	48 009	22	45
1990	423 183	187 403	38 754	11 590	19 183	9 776	79 303	19	42

Source: Transnational Corporations and Management Division, *World Investment Directory: Developed Countries* (New York, United Nations, 1992).

a The coverage of data for different industries may vary from country to country.
b Total FDI in the industries shown only.

pollution-intensive industries in that region was a result of an environmentally-induced relocation; rather, it was market expansion that explained the growth of such industries.[18] Another study found that pollution-abatement costs did not explain the sectoral composition of *maquiladora* activity in Mexico, which is largely comprised of FDI.[19] Evidence of industrial relocation does exist in certain selected industries (for example, asbestos, heavy metals and leather tanning),[20] but the balance of the research suggests that environmental cost differences have not been a major determinant of FDI, and that major shifts through FDI have not occurred because of differences in national standards. That is also the general conclusion of six major empirical studies of industrial relocation owing to environmental cost differences, although some relocation in high control-cost industries cannot be ruled out.[21]

Table IX.4. Sources of pollution-intensive products in world trade

(Percentage)

Source	*1965*	*1975*	*1988*
Developed countries	78	78	74
Central and Eastern Europe	5	6	4
Developing countries	17	17	22
Total	100	100	100

Source: Adapted from Patrick Low and Alexander Yeats, "Do 'dirty' industries migrate?", in Patrick Low, ed., International Trade and the Environment, World Bank Discussion Paper, No. 159 (Washington, D.C., The World Bank, 1992), p. 94.

It is important to note, however, that the direct involvement of TNCs in the production process of pollution-intensive industries, even if adequately measured, provides only an incomplete description of their role in determining environmental quality. Transnational corporations exercise considerable influence on environmental variables through a wide variety of non-equity relationships, which include turnkey and plant-leasing operations, management contracts, subcontracting, supplier relations, franchising, licensing etc. As in direct production, the non-equity relations of TNCs have positive or negative impacts. For example, TNCs may choose to avoid responsibility by using subcontractors for hazardous operations. Conversely, they can insist that subcontractors and suppliers adhere to high environmental standards, and provide them with technical and managerial help in that respect. Finally, TNCs exercise a major influence on the innovation of new products, including the packaging, use and disposal characteristics of such products. Environmental stress occurs not only through production, but also through the use and disposal of products and services. The dominant position of TNCs in product design and development provides an additional important channel for determining environmental quality.

There have been very few studies that compare the environmental performance of TNCs with that of state enterprises or domestic firms. In principle, such comparisons should be made by pairing TNCs and domestic firms in the same industry, controlling for the age structure of plants, and then measuring various dimensions of environmental performance such as energy use, materials recycling, pollution discharge, workplace standards etc. Two studies on Asia found that, although TNCs adopted lower environmental standards in their operations in developing countries than in developed ones, they maintained a better track record in environmental management than local firms, using their superior technological, financial and managerial resources.[22] The findings are consistent with two earlier studies on Malaysia and the Philippines.[23] The general impression is that, because of their visibility, resources and access to clean "off-the-shelf" technology, large TNCs may have better environmental records than local firms, that they may be more interested in environmental protection than their local joint-venture partners and that small- and medium-size firms, whether foreign or local, have the worst record.[24]

Considering their direct role in production, the sectoral and country concentration of their activities, their dominant role in the development of technology, their non-equity links and their product-development roles, one can conclude that TNCs exert considerable influence in many aspects of environmental quality and hence on sustainable growth in host countries. On the whole, there is little evidence of a shift in the international pattern of FDI owing to variations in national environmental regulations. The principal reasons are that, for most industries, factors other than environmental control costs are much more important in determining locational decisions of TNCs, and that such costs typically account only for a small share of total production costs. (As table IX.2 shows, the weighted average pollution-abatement costs as a percentage of output value for a number of high-pollution industries is 0.54 per cent.) Another explanation is that TNCs sometimes anticipate stricter regulations and fear possible liabilities that may arise later. For a number of TNCs, adopting high environmental standards in home and host countries is therefore the least-cost approach to deal with those possibilities, apart from other considerations that might make the world-wide introduction of environmentally sound practices throughout the corporate system advisable.

In fact, the relatively greater vulnerability of TNCs noted earlier appears to have improved their environmental performance in their world-wide operations, at least for large firms. Transnational corporations with a vice-president for environment, health and safety (generally the larger firms) spent more time on environmental policy tasks in their foreign operations than did TNCs without such a position, although in all categories of environment, health and safety activities, firms spent more time in their home (United States) operations than in their foreign operations.[25] Attention to environmental auditing and inspection of foreign facilities was also positively related to the size of environmental staff, a proxy for TNC size. In the UNCTC *Benchmark Corporate Enviromental Survey*, three fourths of corporate respondents stated that they had corporate environmental policies that went beyond those required by national legislation in foreign operations; it also found that the largest firms were most likely to have environmental, health and safety programmes.[26] The *Benchmark Survey* did note a regional difference between TNCs. In general, Japanese TNCs reported greater details on policies and procedures than did North American firms, while EC firms generally ranked below the other regions in that regard. Anecdotal evidence tends to confirm the importance that large TNCs attach to public opinion of their environmental performance. For example, it has been observed that TNCs are more open to closer scrutiny by national politicians and journalists than domestic firms, and tend to respond faster when asked to correct environmental problems.[27]

C. Some policy implications

The preceding discussion raises a number of policy questions and provides the basis for outlining several policy implications. The main task is to devise a framework within which market-based solutions can be pursued and which, specifically, encourages approaches that compensate for market failures and maximize the positive contributions that TNCs can make towards sustainable growth.[28]

That task has to be accomplished largely on the basis of national policies. At the macroeconomic level, sustainable development needs to be supported by sound polices that aim at promoting economic growth and eliminating poverty; a reduction of poverty, in particular, would contribute considerably to the preservation of the environment.[29] But since TNCs operate within a price and market system, they cannot afford to override price signals and incur large environmental protection costs on their own, unless that is being done on the basis of a regulatory framework applicable to all firms. Moreover, as shown above, an essential element of environmental deterioration consists of externalities which, if left unregulated, represent a potent example of the failure of private markets to achieve socially optimal growth. Thus, Governments have a leadership role in guiding TNC activities towards sustainable development (see box IX.2 for a list of some of the challenges for Governments). In general, the responsibilities of Governments are fourfold: to eliminate subsidies to natural resource users that encourage overuse and abuse; to internalize environmental externalities through market reform (including appropriate combinations of pollution taxes and abatement-subsidy schemes); to establish effluent and emission standards; and to institutionalize a liability and compensation system. Put somewhat differently, prices must reflect the full social costs of production (including on-site and off-site environmental effects), if TNCs are to conduct their activities in accordance with sustainable development. If TNCs confront an efficient set of prices, they tend to engage in socially efficient production, and to reorient technology and product development towards sustainable growth.

Many developing countries now have regulatory frameworks for environmental protection. Many of them, however, lack the scientific infrastructure, the administrative arrangements and the staff for an efficient operation of their legal framework. In that context, two points are relevant. First, the transparency and stability of environmental regulation is often more important than the strictness of the regulation itself.[30] For example, Singapore, which is well known for strict but stable environmental regulations, has had no difficulty in attracting large flows of FDI. In contrast, uncertainty and delay in acquiring environmental permits, and the possibility of subsequent revisions of environmental standards, can inhibit investments.[31] Second, corporate environmental impact statements, if properly prepared, are a very useful tool for improving the environmental performance of TNCs. Such statements can not only form the basis for subsequent environmental monitoring, but also convey important cost and technology information to regulators and, if publicized, put a valuable public check on government-TNC agreements regarding environmental protection. Many host Governments now have some formal review of the environmental aspects of new foreign investments;[32] it might be useful to examine the effectiveness of such reviews in order to strengthen policy implementation. This might involve, among other things, an expanded use of environmental impact-assessment procedures and the use of environmental performance bonds.

A major issue for host countries in that context relates to the appropriate environmental standards to which TNCs should be held. The traditional arguments for nondiscrimination, or national treatment,

Box IX.2. Selected tasks for Governments to support the transition to sustainably managed corporations[1]

As part of the preparations for UNCED, a review was made of the tasks necessary for Governments to implement in order to guide and encourage corporations to adopt management practices conductive to sustainable development.

Managerial tasks for Governments and international organizations include:

- Make sustainable development objectives and aims as clear, stable and understandable to corporations as possible; adopt sustainable developments criteria and guidelines in government regulatory requirements and incentive programmes; devise regulatory and/or incentive frameworks in order to encourage a "cradle-to-grave" product life-cycle approach;
- Remove price distortions arising from governmental programmes affecting land, water, energy and other natural resources;
- Remove existing accounting and reporting regulations and develop new ones that require more transparent reporting; and
- Develop methods and rules for accounting for sustainable development, including the "polluter-pays" principle.

Capacity-building tasks for Governments and international organizations include:

- Assist small- and medium-size enterprises in developing countries in the education and training of management and employees in sustainable development issues;
- Support practical research for the development of new prototype statements and methods for valuing all environmental resources;
- Encourage the retaining of auditors in environmental accounting and reporting so that they can verify that the financial statement gives a true and fair view of the activities of the enterprise and reflects the environmental costs of production;
- Develop incentives which encourage corporations to adopt sustainable development policies and programmes; and
- Enforce environmental laws and regulations, regardless of forms of ownerships.

Source: UNCTC, "Transnational corporations and sustainably managed corporations: recommendations of the Executive Director" (E/C.10/1992/2, 16 December 1991).

1 A complete list of tasks is contained in the source.

of FDI are relevant with respect to environmental practices as well. There is little reason to hold TNCs to strict standards, while permitting domestic firms or state enterprises to operate under lesser requirements. In principle, the determination of the appropriate level of environmental protection in a country for all investment, domestic and foreign, should proceed from a careful assessment of benefits and costs, taking into account national assimilative capacity as well as industrial structure, income levels and environmental preferences. That does not mean, however, that the appropriate standards for developing countries are inevitably less stringent; as mentioned earlier, environmental damages to productive resources and the degradation of renewable resources undermine sustainable development and can slow long-term economic growth. At the same time, specific environmental regulations should be tailored to the particular circumstance of each developing country. For example, generally lower levels of worker training and lesser attention to equipment maintenance suggest that additional safeguards for worker health and safety need be in place for hazardous operations in developing countries. Examples are the Bhopal incident (in which training and supervision were apparently insufficient), and the need for special labelling and use-instructions for pesticides where literacy levels among farmers is low.

Several innovative measures have been devised by Governments to implement regulatory measures to control pollution and other negative impacts, and to maximize positive environmental contributions by domestic firms as well as TNCs. Among others, the measures include marketable permits and investment offsets. In the case of the former, permits are initially allocated by auction or by assignment on the basis of "grandfathering", with (polluting) firms receiving allocations on the basis of a predetermined set of criteria. The permits so allocated then command a market price and can be sold or leased. Such a system has been in effect in the United States since 1975. In principle, marketable permits could also be traded internationally. [33] An offset investment is a financial arrangement in which an industrialized country foregoes a domestic investment in environmentally sound technology to finance a more environmentally cost-effective programme in another country whose harmful technology undermines the anti-pollution effects of the industrialized country. [34]

Finally, while appropriate national policies in host countries have the most important role to play in ensuring that investments by TNCs are environmentally sustainable, home-country policies can also contribute to that end. Home-country Governments that encourage and assist FDI can take the environmental aspects of an investment into account. For example, the United States Overseas Private Investment Corporation, a quasi-governmental agency, has had for many years procedures for ensuring the sound environmental performance of the projects it assists.

An appropriate national regulatory framework for all firms, which compensates for imperfections in market mechanisms, provides an enabling framework within which TNCs can establish environmental practices conducive to sustainable growth. Regardless of the regulatory framework, however, TNCs undertake environmental protection in their self-interest. Many TNCs rely directly or indirectly on the natural-resource base and conserve renewable resources for future production needs. New energy and resource-sparing technology is also likely to be less pollution-intensive, and may be introduced by TNCs to save direct costs. Recycling and resource recovery have been shown to be commercially attractive in many instances. Above all, TNCs can make a very important contribution in the development and transfer of environmentally sound technologies (box IX.3). The development of such technology will, in any event, become more important for many TNCs in response to the heightened environmental awareness in most home countries. Transnational corporations may benefit from the introduction of this technology,

Box IX.3. Examples of the transfer of environmentally sound technology

Asea Brown Boveri in Poland

Asea Brown Boveri (ABB), an electro-technical equipment, energy and transportation TNC headquartered in Zürich, Switzerland, is a major supplier of combustion technologies for energy generation and of environmental-control technologies. It initiated a joint venture in Poland in 1989 which converted a former state-owned operation into a privately owned company, ABB Zamech.

In a large turnaround programme, restructuring projects retrofitted new combustion and power generation technologies and know-how, providing simultaneous productivity gains and pollution abatement. The total quality management practices of ABB were transferred, together with environmental management practices and extensive functional training of staff. The venture has been very successful so far. Results for the first operating year gave a return on sales of 5.2 per cent and a return on equity of 43.7 per cent.

Du Pont in Thailand

Having sold crop protectives in Thailand since the 1960s, by the 1970s Du Pont was dependent on bulk imports packaged by a local company in a fast-growing and competitive market. This was limiting Du Pont's ability to meet customer needs, and the corporation was not satisfied with local contractor fire and occupational health protection. It could not contract with other TNCs in the area because proprietary information would be put at risk; Thailand lacked patent protection until 1979. Thus, Du Pont decided to build its own plant, to respond to customers more quickly, and to adapt products to local humidity and temperature conditions. Bangpoo, an industrial estate near Bangkok, which was a joint venture of the Government of Thailand and the private sector, was chosen as the site.

The Bangpoo plant started up in 1982, with a Thai woman who had been one of the project planning group as the plant manager. The determinants of safety, health and environmental protection were Du Pont's internal corporate standards, because Thailand's regulations were weak. Plans included processes for recycling and an in-plant incinerator, because there were no incinerators or landfill sites satisfying Du Pont's requirements. The contractor, however, reduced costs by building at close to cost in exchange for learning Du Pont's design and construction approaches. Du Pont was able to recreate its United States technology and its corporate culture at the site.

Safety and environmental stewardship extends to product distributors and farmers, teaching application methods and supplying protective clothing at cost. Through the Thai Pesticides Association, Du Pont has shared its safety and health practices. Bangpoo won the national first prize in the small industry category for occupational safety and health in 1986.

Source: Adapted from Business Council for Sustainable Development, "Report on technology cooperation" (Geneva, BCSD, 1992), pp. 8 and 31.

not only in their home country operations, but also in their host-country ones, for example, because of economies of scale, especially to the extent that technology developed under the imperative of home-country requirements is of a customized variety. The greater environmental consciousness in many developing countries and the potential adverse consumer reactions are also likely to persuade firms to avoid using less environmentally-friendly technology in host countries, including developing ones. Beyond that, the need for TNCs to maintain long-term good relations with host and home governments, local communities, stockholders and consumers is likely to encourage additional environmental protection measures, at least among larger firms. Thus, many TNCs have adopted policies for managing corporate growth in an environmentally safe and sustainable manner (see chapter III). They lead their industries and provide important examples, particularly for other corporations that have not yet implemented such policies.[35] It is on such positive contributions that one should build further.

Although many firms have taken significant steps to bring their activities into conformity with sustainable development objectives, much remains to be done at the level of the firm. Transnational corporations need to accelerate the establishment of corporate environmental protection and natural-resource conservation programmes. That requires a strong public commitment by chief executives, and the necessary procedures and staffing within firms for compliance and monitoring; a redirection of corporate R&D towards resource conservation, pollution abatement and the development of products whose use and disposal do not create environmental damages; and the development and implementation of internal, corporate, environmental and resource-auditing procedures for tracking natural resource use, waste-disposal flows, toxic materials etc.

As industry leaders, TNCs also have an opportunity to assist in improving the environmental performance of firms with which they have direct business relations: joint-venture partners, suppliers, subcontractors and licensees. The specific channels include technology transfer, technical training, product specifications and, in some cases, the provision of joint waste-disposal services. At a broader level, corporate policy could include some responsibility for and monitoring of the resource-use and pollution-abatement practices of direct business partners (for instance, in the case of lending practices of banks). The divestment of hazardous operations to subcontractors is not desirable.

The relations of TNCs with host government regulators, non-governmental organizations and local communities are a third area in which significant progress can be achieved.[36] Transnational corporations can be an important source of technical and cost information that is badly needed by regulators, especially in developing countries, and they should be forthcoming in supplying non-proprietary information. Transnational corporations could also work with government authorities of host countries in areas such as developing joint waste-disposal facilities and in applied research on, for example, product safety and toxicity. A cooperative relationship with non-governmental organizations and local communities is likely to pay dividends for firms. It also implies much greater transparency in environmentally sensitive decision-making, including siting and emergency preparedness plans. Finally, TNCs have educative outreach possibilities. They range from support for local technical schools to support for national environmental-protection campaigns.

None of those steps—establishing strong internal policies, assisting their direct business partners or improving relations with regulators, non-governmental organizations and local communities—need be of great expense to a firm. But all of them require an explicit commitment by TNCs and an active, not passive, search for sustainable corporate practices (box IX.4).

In addition to firm-level measures, TNCs have also cooperated internationally, including through the adoption of common guidelines and codes for environmental protection. As discussed in chapter III, environmental performance has been a major focus of self-regulation by industry at the international level.

But here, too, international self-regulation by business needs to be embedded in firmer frameworks. In particular, the possibility of pernicious competition in attracting FDI on the basis of lax environmental regulations (or, more likely, lax implementation and enforcement) suggests a need for internationally agreed codes and guidelines. It also suggests the need for some efforts at international harmonization of environmental regulations to preclude major production-cost discrepancies, a step which major corpo-

Box IX.4. Corporate steps towards sustainable development management

The United Nations Centre on Transnational Corporations (now the Transnational Corporations and Management Division of the Department of Economic and Social Development of the United Nations), responding to a request by the Economic and Social Council during its July 1989 session, elaborated a set of "Criteria for sustainable development management" [1] to strengthen the participation of large industrial enterprises in efforts for environmental preservation and protection. The Criteria incorporate a new management approach that has the potential to strengthen and direct efforts towards a stable and balanced relationship between business activity and the environment and make a positive contribution to sustainable development by maintaining economic growth while reducing environmental risk and resource over-exploitation. The Criteria conclude with 10 short initiatives that might guide a firm in beginning the implementation of practices consistent with sustainable development:

- Establish and publish a transnational, corporate, sustainable development policy statement emphasizing sustainable growth, environmental protection, resource use, worker safety and accident prevention. Translate the policy statement into all the working languages of affiliate enterprises.
- Review strategic planning, resource acquisition plans, and operating procedures so as to align them with the sustainable development policy. Announce significant efforts to reduce the use of natural resources and minimize the generation of wastes.
- Review and modify corporate structure, lines of responsibility and internal reporting mechanisms to reflect the sustainable development policy. Encourage overseas affiliates to modify procedures in order to reflect local ecological and social realities.
- Educate staff on the ways in which sustainable development affects their firm and how they can utilize these criteria in their specific tasks. Reward employees who discover and report environmental problems or who recommend new, environmentally sound products and processes.

/.....

rations themselves appear to support. Two recent UNCTC surveys of TNCs indicate that corporations would prefer the establishment of international standards, presumably to forestall competitors from exploiting production-cost differences arising from different national environmental standards. [37]

Uniform international standards, however, could override legitimate differences among countries in the supply of, and demand for, environmental services and would oblige countries to take on unwarranted cost burdens. Transnational corporations with the bulk of their production in industrial countries could find uniformly high standards attractive in so far as their competitors in developing countries are forced into higher cost structures. The preferable approach would be to establish national environmental-protection standards, adhering to minimum international standards, but reflecting national conditions and objectives.

International cooperation at various levels is, therefore, essential for directing the activities of TNCs towards more sustainable growth patterns. Both the involvement of TNCs in critical global-environmen-

(Box IX.4, continued)

- Prepare sustainable development assessments of all major upcoming investment and operating decisions. Distribute them to affiliate offices as models for their own sustainable development assessments.
- Perform an environmental audit of ongoing activities, particularly those in developing countries, to verify that the criteria have been adequately considered. Establish a comparative scale for identifying affiliates with strong and weak environmental track records.
- Report publicly on the enterprise's most hazardous products, processes and toxic emissions. Distribute widely information on the methods in place to reduce these potential hazards and to cope with unanticipated emergencies.
- Institute research and development work on the reduction and/or elimination of industrial products and processes which generate greenhouse gases. Arrange for environmentally safer technologies to be available to affiliates in developing countries without extra internal charges.
- Inform joint venture partners and subcontractors about the corporate sustainable development policy. Establish ground rules for discontinuing business relationships with associated firms which operate with disregard for basic health and environmental concerns.
- Disseminate these criteria to other firms in relevant trade associations, local areas, or affiliated companies. Share the experiences with these criteria with local governments, national authorities, and the United Nations.

Source: UNCTC, "Criteria for sustainable development management", in *The CTC Reporter*, No. 30 (Autumn 1990), pp. 1-3.

1 The Criteria are set forth in *The CTC Reporter*, cited above.

tal interdependencies and the limitations of national frameworks underscore the need for international action on environmental issues. Among others, such cooperation and action could take the form of multilateral or regional agreements, guidelines or codes of conduct (binding or non-binding) negotiated by Governments. During the past decade, such international environment regulation has increased significantly, at both the global and the regional levels, with global regulation oriented towards combating specific threats such as ozone depletion.[38] Further progress in that direction would strengthen the role of TNCs in environmentally sustainable growth.

Notes

[1]*Development and Environment: Report and Working Papers of a Panel of Experts Convened by the Secretary General of the United Nations Conference on the Human Environment* (Founex Report) (Paris, Mouton, 1972).

[2]In technical terms, environmental services enter directly into utility functions as they are directly consumed, but also enter production functions, supporting conventional economic output.

[3]For an in-depth discussion, see The World Bank, *World Development Report 1992: Development and the Environment* (Washington, D.C., The World Bank, 1992); see also Patrick Low, ed., *International Trade and the Environment,* World Bank Discussion Paper, No. 159 (Washington, D.C., The World Bank, 1992).

[4]Yusuf Ahmad, Salah El Serafy and Ernst Lutz, *Environmental Accounting for Sustainable Development* (Washington, D.C., The World Bank, 1989); Kirit Parikh, "Toward a national resource accounting system" (Bombay, Indira Gandhi Institute of Development Research, 1991), mimeo.

[5]For example, Robert Repetto, et al., estimated Indonesia's adjusted real growth rate to be 4.0 per cent annually, not the recorded 7.1 per cent for the 1971-1984 period. Robert Repetto, et al., *Wasting Assets: Natural Resources in the National Income Accounts* (Washington, D.C., World Resources Institute, 1989).

[6]Relevant work is being done at the World Bank, the United Nations Statistical Office and at various private research groups.

[7]The user cost is that fraction of current receipts from the sale of depletable assets which, if set aside and invested, would cumulate to an amount sufficient to yield a permanent income stream, when the resource is exhausted, equal to the true income component.

[8]See for example Robert Repetto, *The Forest for the Trees? Governmental Policy and the Misuse of Forest Resources* (Washington, D.C., World Resources Institute, 1988); Robert Repetto, *Paying the Price: Pesticide Subsidies in Developing Countries* (Washington, D.C., World Resources Institute, 1985).

[9]See, for example, Charles Arden Clarke, "The General Agreement on Tariffs and Trade, environmental protection and sustainable development" (Gland, Switzerland, WWF International, June 1991), mimeo. For a discussion on trade and the environment, see General Agreement on Tariffs and Trade, *International Trade 90-91*, vol. 1 (Geneva, GATT, 1992), pp. 19-39.

[10]But not all investment is mobile. For instance, investment meant to jump trade barriers or to obtain access to domestic markets is not mobile. Also, once investments are made, they become fixed costs, and mobility diminishes.

[11]UNCTC, *Climate Change and Transnational Corporations; Analysis and Trends* (United Nations publication, Sales No. E.92.II.A.7).

[12]UNCTC, "Contribution of the Commission and the United Nations Centre on Transnational Corporations to the work of the Preparatory Committee for UNCED" (E/C.10/1991/3, 31 March 1991).

[13]Electric utilities are an exception. UNCTC, *Environmental Aspects of the Activities of Transnational Corporations: A Survey* (United Nations publication, Sales No. E.85.II.A.11).

[14]Pollution is only one form of environmental damage; serious environmental disruption also occurs outside the manufacturing sector in, for example, the extractive, transport and utilities industries.

[15]If abatement is 100 per cent effective, the industry would exhibit no toxic release.

[16]Robert E. B. Lucas, David Wheeler and Hemamala Hettige, "Economic development, environmental regulation and the international migration of toxic industrial pollution: 1960-1988", in Low, ed., op. cit., pp. 67-86.

[17]H. Jeffrey Leonard, *Are Environmental Regulations Driving United States Industry Overseas? An Issue Report* (Washington, D.C., The Conservation Foundation, 1984).

[18]ESCAP/UNCTC Joint Unit on Transnational Corporations, *Transnational Corporations and Environmental Management in Selected Asian and Pacific Developing Countries,* ESCAP/UNCTC Publication Series B, No. 13 (ST/ESCAP/608, 1988).

[19]Gene Grossman and Alan Krueger, "Environmental impacts of a North American Free Trade Agreement", National Bureau of Economic Research Working Paper No. 3914 (Cambridge, Massachusetts, November 1991), mimeo.

[20]See Barry Castleman, "Workplace health standards and multinational corporations in developing countries", in Charles S. Pearson, ed., *Multinational Corporations, Environment and the Third World* (Durham, North Carolina, Duke University Press, 1987), pp. 149-172; Jeffrey Leonard, "Environmental regulations, multinational corporations and industrial development", *Habitat International,* vol. 6, No. 3 (1982), p. 9.

[21]The studies have been reviewed in UNCTC, *Environmental Aspects,* op. cit., Charles S. Pearson, "Environmental standards, industrial relocation and pollution havens", in Pearson, ed., *Multinational Corporations,* op. cit., pp. 113-128, and Judith M. Dean, "Trade and the environment: a survey of the literature", in Low, op. cit., pp. 15-28.

[22]ESCAP/UNCTC Joint Unit, *Transnational Corporations,* op. cit., and ESCAP/UNCTC Joint Unit on Transnational Corporations, *Environmental Aspects of Transnational Corporation Activities in Pollution-Intensive Industries in Selected Asian and Pacific Developing Countries,* ESCAP/UNCTC Publication Series B, No. 15 (ST/ESCAP/857, 1990). The two studies are summarized in ESCAP/UNCTC Joint Unit on TNCs, "Environmental aspects of TNC activities in the ESCAP region", *The CTC Reporter,* No. 30 (Autumn 1990), pp. 4-6 and pp. 21-22.

[23]Michael Royston reported two surveys conducted in Malaysia and the Philippines which suggested that TNC performance was somewhat better than that of local firms. Michael Royston, "The role of multinational corporations in environment and resource management in developing countries". Paper prepared for the World Resources Institute Conference on "The role of multinational corporations in environmental and resource management in developing countries", Washington, D.C., 14-16 June 1984.

[24]"Natural allies? The roles of business and Government in environmental management in Asia and Pacific". Report of a conference sponsored by the World Resources Institute, the East-West Center and UNEP, Asia-Pacific Regional Office, Bangkok, January 1986, mimeo.

[25]Margaret Flaherty and Ann Rappaport, *Multinational Corporation and the Environment: A Survey of Global Practices* (Boston, Center for Environmental Management, Tufts University, 1981). The study found that firms in the United States responded most to laws and regulations; in South-East Asia and Japan, consumer influence dominated community opinion in firms' decisions; and in Africa, firms exhibited strong concern for high visibility accidents.

[26]UNCTC, *Benchmark Corporate Environmental Survey* (New York, United Nations, forthcoming).

[27]Foão Carlos P. Pimenta, "Multinational corporations and industrial pollution control in Sao Paulo, Brazil", in Pearson, ed., *Multinational Corporations,* op. cit., pp. 198-220.

[28]See The World Bank, op. cit.

[29]To quote the Development Committee of the International Monetary Fund and The World Bank: "At the national level, developing countries will require a threefold strategy. First, the mutually-reinforcing roles of sustainable development and environment must be vigorously exploited through sound macro-economic policies which will promote growth and reduce poverty. The fight against poverty helps to preserve the environment. Second, such policies must be supplemented by an incentive structure which will discourage overuse of natural resources; developing countries will need external support for technology transfer and for capacity-building in the environmental area. The top sectoral priorities for direct national action are clean water and sanitation, air quality, soil, water and agricultural productivity, and natural habitats. Thirdly, people and institutions (in

public and private sectors alike) should be motivated to adopt less damaging behavior by bringing environmental considerations into their decisions -- wherever possible by the use of market-based instruments which have the advantage of allowing reduction of environmental damages in the most cost-effective way." *Communiqué*, 28 April 1992, p. 3.

[30]See Charles S. Pearson, *Down to Business: Multinational Corporations, the Environment and Development* (Washington, D.C., World Resources Institute, 1985).

[31]This plays a role, for instance, in Central and Eastern Europe. Uncertainties concerning environmental standards and future liabilities concerning environmental damages are one of the reasons only TNCs hesitate to invest in the country of that region. See Marlise Simons, "Pollution blights investment, too, in East Europe", *The New York Times*, 13 May 1992.

[32]UNCTC, *Transnational Corporations and Industrial Hazards Disclosure* (United Nations publication, Sales No. E.91.II.A.18).

[33]For details, see UNCTC, "Draft papers on options to facilitate transfer of environmentally sound technologies to developing countries on favourable terms" (New York, UNCTC, 1991), mimeo.

[34]Ibid, p. T-13, provides examples, including those of offset investment by Finland (in Murmansk, Russia), Norway and Sweden.

[35]See UNCTC, *Benchmark Corporate Environmental Survey*, op. cit.

[36]The successful Japanese experience of curbing pollution is discussed in the World Bank, op. cit., box 4.5, p. 92.

[37]UNCTC, *Benchmark Corporate Environmental Survey*, op. cit., and Flaherty and Rappaport, op. cit.

[38]See Transnational Corporations and Management Division, *Emerging Trends in International Environmental Regulation at the Regional and Global Level: Implications for Transnational Corporations* (New York, United Nations, forthcoming).

Chapter X

TRANSNATIONAL CORPORATIONS AND GROWTH: AN INTEGRATED ASSESSMENT

A. The dynamics of transnational corporations and growth

The preceding chapters in Part Two established that transnational corporations (TNCs) have an impact on the factors that determine the process of economic growth in developing countries, by influencing the amount and quality of new capital formation, the transfer of hard and soft technology, the development of human resources, the expansion of trade opportunities and the long-term sustainability of growth. The analysis was based on a growth-accounting framework (briefly outlined in chapter IV), within which the impact of TNCs on each of the key determinants of growth was examined separately. Those separate contributions of TNCs stimulate economic growth. While the effect may be small for the host economy as a whole, it can be substantial in certain industries. For example, in many host countries, the contribution of TNCs to capital formation is largest in technology-intensive manufacturing industries. In all cases, prevailing conditions in the host country––including the policy environment, the level of human resources development and the capacity of domestic enterprises to benefit from the presence of TNCs—are important determinants of the impact of TNC activities on growth.

While this separate analysis of the contributions by TNCs to the individual growth determinants is important, it should be stressed that most of these determinants are interrelated. These interrelationships appear strongest between new capital formation, technology and trade. The relationship between those channels of growth is typically interactive in that gains in one may stimulate improvements in one or more of the others; the growth stimulus is thus potentially magnified. Capital formation often takes the form of new capital equipment which frequently incorporates new technologies. Indeed, one of the most important direct impacts of TNCs is on the availabity of technology, which in turn can stimulate gains in productivity, enabling firms to upgrade the technological capabilities of the host economy and to raise the quality and quantity of goods produced and exported. Exports, in turn, are associated with positive learning effects that can be translated into product and process innovations. Trade itself encourages economies of scale and specialization, improves efficiency and releases resources that can be put to more productive uses, thus stimulating further capital formation by domestic firms and foreign affiliates. This process is also helped by the fact that TNCs often bring with them production methods developed abroad, which are sources of competitive advantage in many industries. Indeed, as the creation of technology is increasingly internalized by TNCs and their networks, the scope for the technological development and growth of developing countries through means other than by some form of association with TNCs is likely to shrink. More generally, the increasing complexity of the interlinkages among the various activities undertaken by TNCs and the intangible nature of some of these activities (for example, organizational methods, informal training) imply that the possibilities to unbundle the elements of TNC contributions are becoming more limited.

An assessment of the overall contribution of TNCs to growth, therefore, needs to take into account not only the direct impact of TNCs via each individual channel, but also the existence of interrelationships between the various channels of economic growth (figure X.1). In other words, improved performance in more than one channel—investment, technology, trade and human resources—can occur simultaneously. Those interrelationships suggest that the various aspects of the activities of TNCs support each other, strengthening the overall contribution of TNCs to economic growth in host developing countries, in a manner that may not be directly evident from an assessment of their contributions to the individual determinants of growth. Thus, TNCs deliver a package of assets to a host economy, some tangible (such as new investment), others intangible (such as improved organizational practices), and those assets interact with each other in many ways. By linking together the various elements that determine growth, TNCs can contribute to a virtuous cycle of investment, technological progress, human resource development and trade which, together, stimulate economic growth. Thus, the overall impact of TNCs on the various factors determining growth may be greater than the sum of the individual effects, that is, it is likely to be synergistic. [1]

In addition to the direct impact of TNCs on growth via the various interlinkages described above, interactions between TNCs and the local economy can also enhance the growth stimulus indirectly. For instance, a good deal of soft and hard technology is transferred as part of FDI. The benefits of such transfers are not necessarily limited to foreign affiliates, but may be diffused to the local economy through backward and forward linkages (for example, through subcontracting and domestic licensing), through human resource development or through demonstration effects. Indeed, the positive growth impacts of TNCs through technology transfers or capital formation would become more pronounced the deeper these linkages are. Furthermore, the presence of TNCs in host countries also has an interactive effect on unrelated domestic firms. For instance, foreign affiliates can force domestic firms (including those

Figure X.1. Transnational corporations and the growth process

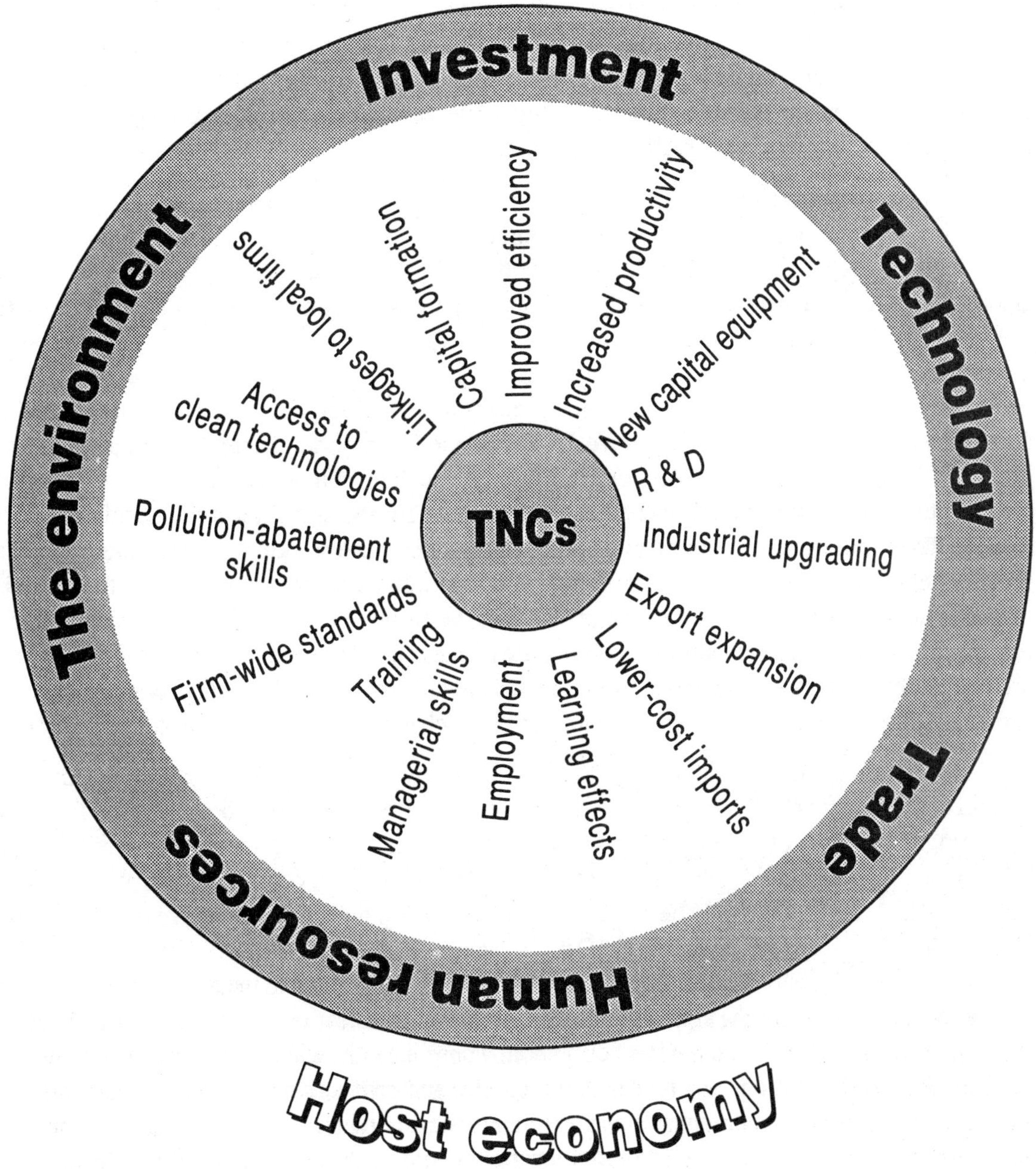

Source: United Nations Department of Economic and Social Development, Transnational Corporations and Management Division.

associated with them via non-equity arrangements) to compete more actively in both the domestic and international markets, which in turn could encourage product innovation by domestic firms and lead to new investment and an upgrading of the labour force. The evidence indicates that the presence of foreign affiliates creates opportunities for domestic entrepreneurs to become suppliers, and for employees to become entrepreneurs. In addition, the potential exists for TNCs to yield beneficial externalities and spillover effects for the host economy that are not transmitted through any particular direct channel. Such externalities include, for example, learning through observation (demonstration effect) of marketing and promotional methods by domestic firms not linked to TNCs.

It is quite clear from the preceding discussions that the *quantity* of FDI undertaken by TNCs in host economies—measuring, as it does, only one component of the package of assets brought by TNCs to host countries—is a very incomplete indicator of the full range of impacts that these firms can have on growth through the direct contributions they can make to individual growth determinants, the synergistic interrelationships between these individual contributions and the interlinkages between foreign affiliates and domestic enterprises. In fact, the role of TNCs in growth has to be seen in the wider context of these firms integrating input and output production structures both within domestic economies and between domestic economies and the rest of the world. Transnational corporations mobilize goods and services produced in the domestic economy and transform them into outputs for domestic or international consumption; in the process, they often utilize various tangible and intangible inputs from abroad. In that respect, TNCs differ from domestic companies in that they have a wider choice, more options and a broader perspective regarding the location of production, the sourcing of inputs and the servicing of markets for goods and services. The role of TNCs in the growth process of host countries is, therefore, best described as one of integrating, organizing and managing various productive activities. [2] It is, above all, this integrating, organizing and managerial capacity of TNCs that makes them engines of economic growth within an enabling policy framework and conducive structural conditions in the host economy.

However, certain considerations should be borne in mind when making an assessment of the overall contribution of TNCs to growth in developing countries. First, this contribution is likely to vary according to the stage of development of the host country. In particular, the impact may be greater for middle- and high-income developing countries than for low-income countries at early stages of development. This is the case not only because low-income developing countries receive little attention from TNCs, including very low amounts of FDI; it is also a result of the fact that growth in low-income developing countries may depend on processes that tend to be marginal to the activities of TNCs, that is, raising the productivity of the agricultural sector, improving basic infrastructure and raising the educational and nutritional standards of the population. Those areas in which TNCs can make the greatest contribution, such as introducing modern technologies and production methods, increasing exports of manufactured goods and improving the performance of service industries, are more important in countries that have already reached a more advanced level of economic development. Not surprisingly, at very early stages of development, countries rely more heavily on official aid than on FDI to raise living standards; chapter II has shown a pattern whereby the mix of foreign capital inflows to developing countries shifts as countries develop, from a concentration of aid flows to low-income countries to a larger share of FDI as GNP rises. While TNCs can certainly make a contribution to the economic performance of low-income countries, it is likely that their greatest impact will be in countries that can most effectively absorb the investment, technology, training and trade opportunities that TNCs offer. It is therefore probably necessary for a threshold level of domestic economic development to exist in order to benefit most from the potential for greater growth that TNCs can create.

Second, there can be circumstances in which TNC activity may not contribute to sustained growth in the long-term, although in the short term output may rise as a result of FDI. Transnational corporations are extensively involved in activities which may have adverse environmental impacts, though evidence suggests that these are not being shifted dispropotionally to developing countries. Nevertheless, to the extent that TNCs are involved in natural resources (for example, mining and logging) and pollution-intensive industries (for example, chemicals), either directly or through non-equity linkages with domestic firms, their activities have implications for long-term growth. In addition, FDI that remains concentrated in enclaves with few linkages to the rest of the economy may lead to dualistic economic structures within a country, a situation that may make growth difficult to sustain in the long term. Furthermore, transfer pricing might adversely affect host countries, thus reducing the growth potential of TNCs via the trade channel. Similarly, if TNCs reduce competition through an abuse of market power, long-term growth prospects may be harmed by stifling the activities of local entrepreneurs. In this regard, it is important to look at the quality, as well as the rate, of economic growth, and to ask whether the growth path made possible through FDI is not only sustainable in the long run, but also more beneficial, from a socio-economic perspective, than other possible growth paths.

Finally, the synergistic nature of TNC activities, their concentration in a limited number of industries and the complexity of the interlinkages between the different growth channels mean that it is difficult to establish a statistical relationship between TNC activities and growth. The variable most easily quantified is FDI, as measured by balance-of-payments flows. While data may show a direct correlation between the relative importance of FDI in an economy (for example, as measured by FDI inflows as a share of domestic output) and its growth rate for a cross section of developing countries, [3] or for some particular countries (box X.1), such a relationship is not always obvious for all countries. A few economies, including Hong Kong and Singapore, show consistently high shares of FDI and high growth rates. Some economies have experienced high growth with relatively low shares of inward FDI in total investment (for example, the Republic of Korea and Thailand), while still others with very high shares of FDI in total investment have experienced relatively slow growth (for example, Nigeria). In some cases, those overall relationships mask the high concentration of FDI in industries that have a disproportionately high impact on growth. Even in cases where regression analysis establishes a link between FDI and growth, caution needs to be exercised in the interpretation of the results. A positive relationship between FDI and growth does not mean that the direction of causality is necessarily from the former to the latter. In fact, several empirical studies on the determinants of FDI have found that growth in host countries is important for attracting TNCs. [4] On the other hand, data on FDI flows do not capture the package of growth stimuli embodied in the activities of TNCs or the conditions within host economies that are most conducive to utilizing this package.

Box X.1. The relationship between foreign direct investment and growth: some empirical evidence

The Transnational Corporations and Management Division of the United Nations Department of Economic and Social Development has embarked on an empirical investigation of the impact of FDI on the growth rate of developing countries, utilizing data from the *World Investment Directory*. First, a single-equation model was developed to examine the relationship between FDI and the growth of real domestic output for a number of developing countries. As a next step, a simultaneous equation model was developed (not shown here) to capture direct effects of FDI on growth, indirect effects via linkages with capital formation, technology, human resource development and trade and the possible simultaneous relationship between growth rates and FDI. Early results of the single equation model for Taiwan Province of China, using regression analysis and data for the period 1964 to 1990, are presented in the following equation:

$$(1) \quad Q_t = 3.998 + \underset{(0.31)}{0.0556I_t} + \underset{(2.12)}{1.5137F_t} + \underset{(3.50)}{1.3430L_t} + \underset{(2.50)}{1.1123E_t} + \underset{(2.13)}{0.0788O_t}$$

$R^2 = 0.48$ $\quad \bar{R}^2 = 0.34$ $\quad$ SEE = 2.37 $\quad$ D-W = 2.09 $\quad$ N = 27

(The numbers in parentheses below the estimated coefficients refer to t values)

Where:

Q_t = growth of real GDP in year t;
I_t = gross domestic fixed capital formation in year t as a percentage of GDP in the previous year;
F_t = FDI in year t as a percentage of GDP in the previous year;
L_t = growth of the labour force;
E_t = growth in the percentage of the labour force with secondary education;
O_t = exports plus imports of goods and services as a percentage of GDP.

This single-equation model hypothesizes that the growth of real domestic output is a function of domestic investment, FDI, the growth of the labour force, the share of the labour force with secondary education and the openness of the economy. The equation uses annual inflows to measure FDI. The stock of FDI, the preferred proxy for TNC activity in host countries, was not utilized because such data do not exist for Taiwan Province of China (though they can be estimated as cumulative inflows), and because comparable data on the stock of fixed domestic capital were not available. Although the stock of fixed domestic capital could be estimated, such an estimate would be more imprecise than stock estimates for other variables in the equation. Thus, while the use of the stock of both domestic and foreign direct investments is theoretically appealing, it is more consistent to use flow data related to both of those variables, rather than the flow of the former and the stock of the latter.

In the single-equation model, all estimated coefficients have the expected sign and, with the exception of domestic fixed capital formation, are statistically significant at the 5 or 1 per cent levels of significance. The statistical insignificance of domestic fixed capital formation might raise doubts regarding the results obtained by this exercise, although it is not an uncommon finding in the estimation of growth equations for developing countries.[1] While there is a positive association between fixed investment and growth, the inclusion of other variables may render the estimated coefficient insignificant or negative. One possible explanation is that domestic fixed investment contains elements that do not contribute to growth or that overwhelm any positive effects of an increase in domestic investment or output. This issue deserves further investigation.

/.....

(Box X.1, cont'd.)

The results reported here are similar to those recently obtained using a cross section sample of 69 non-oil producing developing countries by M. Blomström, R. Lipsey and M. Zejan. [2] The authors found a positive significant impact of FDI inflows averaged over the period 1965-1985 on real GDP per capita for middle-income developing countries. Other independent variables included in this single-equation model, such as the degress of enrollment in secondary education, were also significant and with a positive sign. In concurrence with the results reported here, the domestic investment variable was only marginally significant.

A great deal of growth in developing, as well as in developed countries, remains unexplained after the growth of capital and labour have been taken into consideration. [3] Such a residual is usually attributed to improvements in education and technology. The former is included by the variable E, which is statistically significant at the 1 per cent level. While expenditures on R&D would be a good proxy for technology, such data were not available for a sufficient number of years for Taiwan Province of China, to be included as an additional explanatory variable in the equation.

The degree of openness of an economy would also be expected to be directly related to growth, since open economies are more exposed to competition and are therefore less likely to undertake inefficient investments. The simplest and most commonly used proxy for openness is the value of exports plus the value of imports of goods and services as a percentage of GDP. The equation shows that this variable is also positively related to growth and it is statistically significant.

Other versions of equation (1), not reported here, used the level of industrialization as a proxy for the shift from the primary to the secondary sector (and ultimately to services), a process that underlies economic growth. This variable had the correct sign and was statistically significant at the 5 per cent level. However, when both the industrialization and the openness variables were included in the same equation, they were both statistically insignificant, reflecting multicollinearity. Thus, while the inclusion of both variables is theoretically justified, simple regression analysis does not permit the separation of the independent effect of each on growth. However, this line of investigation merits further analysis and more sophisticated estimation procedures.

It should also be pointed out that the value of R^2 for the equation is below .50, while the adjusted R^2 is even lower. While these appear to be low, this is not an unusual phenomenon in the growth literature, especially with the inability to measure technology. The value of the Durbin-Watson statistic indicates the absence of serial correlation in the residuals, which further strengthens the results of this model. Thus, while the results obtained in this simple exercise are preliminary and refer to only one economy—and a special one at that—they provide a justifiable basis for an investigation of the relationship between FDI and growth for other host developing countries.

---

1 For example, Dominick Salvatore and Thomas Hatcher, "Inward oriented and outward oriented trade strategies", *Journal of Development Studies*, vol. 27, No. 3 (April 1991), pp. 7-25.

2 Magnus Blomström, Robert E. Lipsey and Mario Zejan, "A cross-country study of growth in developing countries". Paper prepared for the conference on historical perspectives on the international convergence of productivity, New York University, New York, 23-24 April 1992.

3 Such a result is common in the growth-accounting literature. See the work of Denison, in this area, for example, E. F. Denison, *Trends in American Economic Growth, 1929-1982* (Washington, D.C., The Brookings Institution, 1985).

B. International production

1. Characteristics of the international production system

The package of assets, described earlier, is delivered to host countries by some 35,000 TNCs through more than 150,000 foreign affiliates plus numerous non-equity linkages. Since FDI, by definition, involves the establishment of lasting managerial control, it creates networks of ongoing relationships between parent firms and foreign affiliates and, increasingly, among foreign affiliates. That raises the question of whether those networks, in their aggregation and their interrelationships, are the nucleus of an emerging international production system. Such an international production system would be a form of international economic integration at the production level (see chapter I), organized by firms that coordinate and integrate their cross-national operations with a view to making the most efficient use of their resources.

While international production has existed for decades, changes in its magnitude and nature can be expected to have far greater implications for growth in host countries than before.

- Concerning its magnitude, FDI flows had reached unprecedented levels by the beginning of the 1990s. But what is more important is that these flows have built up stocks of productive assets amounting, in 1990, to some $1.7 trillion measured at book value. (Book value represents the value of an investment at the time when it was made, with adjustments for depreciations; it is typically considerably lower than market value, that is, the current value of an investment. In the case of the United States—which cannot be easily generalized because the FDI of that country is relatively mature compared to, for example, that of Japan—the book value of outward stock of FDI was $421 billion in 1990, while the current market value is estimated between $600 billion and $700 billion.[5]) Those assets represent a substantial amount of productive capacity which, as discussed in chapter II, is often concentrated in key manufacturing and services industries and, overall, is accounting for an increasing share of the economic activities of countries.

- As regards its nature, international production in the past was often characterized by stand-alone affiliates, typically aimed at producing final products for host country markets. This was (and still is) particularly true in the services sector, because of the limited tradability of many services. In its goods sector, FDI in natural resources has always been largely export-oriented. As regards manufacturing, though a large part of the production of affiliates continues to be sold to domestic markets, there has been an increase in export orientation (see chapter VIII). Progress in communication and transportation technologies (outlined in chapter IV), coupled with a far-reaching liberalization of national regulations of trade as well as outward and inward FDI (see chapter III), have created the technical and regulatory conditions for greater specialization of the various parts of a transnational production system and, hence, for the emergence of an intra-firm, international division of labour. It appears that the economics of production and the pressures of competition are leading TNCs to take advantage of these new conditions, thus reaping the benefits of country, product and process specialization. Foreign affiliates are increasingly becoming parts of networks in which they are closely linked with their parent firms and each other through intra-firm flows of trade, technology and training and through the common utilization of a host of services (for example, design, marketing, accounting, R&D, finance) available to the corporate system world-wide, precisely as part of an intra-firm division of labour (box X.2). It should be underlined that these networks not only find their expression in intra-firm trade but, perhaps even more importantly, in the intra-firm utilization of various intangible assets, all subject to a common organization and governance.

Thus, the international production system is characterized by a complex, closely knit web of interrelationships, as TNCs take an increasingly global view of investment, production, sourcing and marketing decisions and organize and manage value-adding activities in an integrated manner across national borders. The regional core network strategies of TNCs, discussed elsewhere, [6] are the most concrete and furthest developed expressions of the emergence of an international production system. But the magnitude of the stock of FDI and the number of foreign affiliates show that, for many TNCs, their international networks are in place, even if the integration of production is still rudimentary for many of them; for these firms, the issue is therefore no longer primarily the establishment of networks, but rather their maintenance, expansion and, most importantly, the integration of the various units of the networks into single production structures. As this process continues, an international production system is emerging.

International production has so far advanced primarily in selected industries in the manufacturing sector. However, a striking new characteristic of the emerging international production system is that it is beginning to involve the services sector as well. As of now, the production of services is taking place largely within domestic borders, even though consumption has in some cases become internationalized (for instance, in the case of global financial markets). Because of the intangible nature of most services, they have to be typically produced when and where they are consumed; their transportability, and hence tradability, is therefore limited. Because of this, internationalization in this sector has taken place mainly through FDI. Non-tradability means that foreign services affiliates operate independently of one another and the parent firms, as stand-alone miniature versions of their parent firms that replicate their activities on a smaller scale for foreign markets. [7] In this sense, the production of services has been internationalized to some extent; but as yet foreign service affiliates are not as integrated into international networks as are foreign goods-producing affiliates.

But two recent trends have begun to allow a greater integration of international services production. First, the service intensity of the goods sector is high and growing, such that industrial production, particularly of high-value and high-technology goods, is increasingly services-intensive. Second, and more importantly for international production, technological progress is increasing the tradability of services. [8] This makes it possible to deliver services across national borders, to specialize in the production of services or their components and hence to integrate the production of services on an international basis. Advances in telecommunications technology and its fusion with computer technol-

Box X.2. Asea Brown Boveri: an international production network

There are probably only a few TNCs in the world today which could be called truly global firms, and that own, organize and manage an international production network. Among those few firms is Asea Brown Boveri (ABB), which was formed in a 1987 merger of the Swedish firm Asea with the Swiss firm Brown Boveri. Following a massive restructuring, involving investments of some $3.6 billion in 60 newly-acquired or merged companies, ABB is now the world's leading supplier of power and railway equipment, with sales of $29 billion and 214,000 employees in 1991.

The structure and management practices of ABB place it among the few truly global corporations operating in the world economy: it comprises 1,300 companies located throughout the world, 130 of them in developing countries; its eight corporate board members are from five different countries; it has adopted an official language (English) for major transactions; and its 5,000 profit centres report all financial information in United States dollars to a single location, to allow for cross-border analysis. The firm is organized into a matrix structure, in which businesses are responsible to both a global leader as well as a national president. Leaders of the 50 Business Areas of ABB are based throughout the world and manage their operations on a global basis, devising overall strategies as regards exports, capacity and employee development; the leader of the power transmission business, for instance, is a Swede based in Germany, managing 25 factories in 16 countries. At the same time, the 1,300 individual companies that make up the 50 Business Areas each belong to a national company, and must prove themselves competitive on a national basis. This structure, which the company's president and CEO characterizes as "multidomestic", allows ABB to compete as if it were a national company in industries where local presence is important (such as locomotives), while at the same time drawing on the corporations' global resources in such areas as core technologies, design, component manufacturing, managerial expertise and finance. The management strategy of combining the advantages of globalization (economies of scale in both production and purchasing), along with the responsiveness of a national firm (ABB has companies in 140 countries), has led to the emergence of a globally integrated production and distribution system which involves extensive cross-border flows of goods and services, people, technology and know-how.

The operations of ABB reflect many of the trends of the new world economy, in which TNCs account for an increasing share of the world's trade, technology, financial and knowledge flows; in which economic distances are being shortened by new communication and information technologies; and in which regional integration is leading to the emergence of regional TNC-controlled production networks. From very low levels in 1989, the exports of ABB have grown to $1 billion and are expected to double in the next few years, particularly as North American and Eastern European operations achieve targeted export levels; its 1991 R&D budget totalled $2.3 billion; it has created its own private satellite networks to communicate with affiliates in countries with poor communications infrastructure; it manages its own Business Information Center; its World Treasury Center mobilizes financial resources for its global operations; and it makes large investments in management training for its newly-acquired personnel. Economic integration in both Europe and North America has led to a restructuring of operations in both regions. In North America, the combination of the emerging free trade area, relatively low United States wages and the specialized capabilities of United States-based affiliates of ABB will make the region an important export base for the company's global distribution network. In Europe, fewer production sites will serve larger markets to meet growing competition in the unified market, and current operations are being supplanted with a newly-acquired network of manufacturing facilities in Central and Eastern Europe and the former Soviet Union, where ABB currently employs about 21,000 people (half of which are in the former German Democratic Republic). Incorporating those affiliates into the global network of ABB has led to substantial transfers of modern capital equipment (from Western European facilities of ABB), finance, technological know-how and intensive management training in Western-style techniques (reportedly the costliest component of its Eastern European investments). Its Central and Eastern European network, composed

/.....

(Box X.2, cont'd.)

of some 41 companies and poised to grow as more firms are privatized, will not only serve the needs of local markets for infrastructure and capital goods, but will also form the basis of a regional core network, by serving as a high-volume, low-cost export base for the company's global operations. Indeed, turbine components produced by ABB affiliates in Poland and Hungary are already being exported to Western markets, and Central and Eastern Europe is due to become the centre for the company's welding and forging operations. Developing countries, where ABB employs some 34,000 employees and which account for its $6 billion in revenues, currently serve mainly as markets for ABB exports from North America and Europe as well as sites for local-market production. ABB has targeted the Asian region, which currently accounts for about 15 per cent of revenues, for major growth in the next few years. Selected developing countries, such as Brazil, are also emerging as important export bases for the global distribution network of ABB.

In addition to cross-border flows of goods, capital equipment and training, technology and know-how are important resource flows within the ABB network. Business Areas regularly rotate personnel to share expertise. After restructuring, the firm brought 11,000 R&D employees to three centres at Vasteras, Heidelberg and Baden to encourage economies of research by pooling talent from all of its affiliates. Moreover, a corporate R&D organization regularly combines resources from several parts of the organization, to centralize efforts that promise to yield company-wide benefits. At a less formal level, ABB consolidates research data, knowledge and experiences from various affiliates to be utilized in product development throughout the firm. For example, cooperation and pooling of technology and information of Drives and Process Automation divisions led to a greenfield paper mill investment in South Carolina (United States).

Finally, flows of goods, technology, information and management are complemented by movements of capital and services within ABB. The firm's Financial Services business, offering a full range of services including finance, treasury operations and insurance, is managed as a separate profit center which competes with outside financial service providers for the financing of ABB operations. As such, its relations with ABB's industrial operations are carried out on an arms-length basis, with the goal of maximizing synergies within the organization. A commercial bid by the power plant business segment for $136 million project in New Zealand illustrates the extent of intra-firm cooperation: ABB Project Finance raised finance for the proposal, ABB Credit arranged equipment leasing, ABB Credit B.V. procured interim financing, the World Treasury Center acted as lenders, while Sirius, another ABB company, provided credit risk insurance. In another example of cross-border, intra-firm cooperation, regarding a gas and steam turbine project in Bahrain, ABB Project Finance arranged and negotiated a financing package involving six different countries, and ABB Trading negotiated and managed required investments in local industries.

The structure of ABB and the geographical scope of its activities point are at the forefront of a relatively small number of companies whose operations may be characterized as "global". To the extent to which other companies adopt similar strategies, they lay the foundation for a global production system, integrating both industrial as well as service activities. Under such a system, countries are integrated into the international economy through the activities of TNCs, involving not only investment but also cross-border flows of goods and services, information, technology, personnel and finance.

Sources: Asea Brown Boveri, *Annual Report 1991;* "Asea Brown Boveri: power play" and "ABB in Eastern Europe: showing promise", *The Economist*, 28 May 1988, pp. 19-22, and 29 June 1991, pp. 61-62; "Asea Brown Boveri: a model for global management", *R&D Magazine*, vol. 33, No. 13 (December 1991), pp. 30-34; Roger Cohen, "The very model of efficiency", *The New York Times*, 2 March 1992, p. D1; Jonathan Kapstein and Stanley Reed, "The Euro-gospel according to Percy Barnevik", *Business Week* (23 July 1990), pp. 64-66; William Taylor, "The logic of global business: an interview with ABB's Percy Barnevik", *Harvard Business Review*, vol. 69, No. 2 (March-April 1991), pp. 90-115; Neil Wilson, "Capital markets: miracle of miracles", *The Banker*, 138 (December 1988), pp. 26-27.

ogy, as well as the rapid diffusion of those technologies to a wide number of countries, are of particular importance in this regard. The electronic linkages being built between countries increasingly allow the emergence of an international division of labour in the production of services, in a manner similar to that in the industrial sector. Thus, the international production system that is emerging is becoming more complete and pervasive, comprising both goods and services sectors.

Box X.3. Asia: an illustration of foreign direct investment, dynamic restructuring and growth

Achieving sustainable growth implies that countries need to be able to adapt to changing competitive conditions at the international level as well as in their domestic economies through a process of dynamic restructuring. In this context, development may be stylized as a series of stages through which countries pass, moving to higher-value, more skill- and technology-intensive activities as they proceed from one stage to the next. For example, the growth path of many developing countries is similar, in that many began by increasing the share of the manufacturing sector in their economies and exporting labour-intensive light manufacturing goods which built on their comparative advantage in abundant, low-skilled labour. As wages rise and domestic savings accumulate, there may be pressures for a structural upgrading of the economy into more capital-intensive activities, such as chemicals and machinery. A few developing countries have entered the latter stage, and are now competitive in such industries as automobiles, business equipment and consumer electronics, and producer and consumer services. This illustrates a process of continuous restructuring of the economy into higher-productivity activities—of continually upgrading the activities in which the country has a comparative advantage. As countries move from one stage to the next, their growth rates may accelerate, as productivity of both human and physical capital increases and as rising incomes boost domestic demand.

Transnational corporations in developing countries can accelerate this process of moving up the ladder of comparative advantage, by helping to effect a reallocation of resources to higher productivity industries. Often, this is accomplished by transferring to the host country activities that may no longer be productive in the home country, but which add significantly to the marginal productivity of the host country. In other words, TNCs can facilitate the shift of factors of production to higher-productivity activities, both within and across industries.

The Asian region provides an illustration of many of the concepts outlined above. Within that region, one finds countries at different stages of the development process, with Japan in the lead, followed by the newly-industrializing economies (Hong Kong, Taiwan Province of China, the Republic of Korea and Singapore) and, finally, their neighbours, including Indonesia, Malaysia, the Philippines, Thailand and the Guangdong Province of China, many of whom have experienced very rapid growth rates in recent years. The pattern of growth of these economies is, to a large extent, a regional phenomenon, with growth being promoted through a process of structural upgrading in a complementary fashion.

International production plays a central role in this process. Foreign direct investment has come from both within and from outside the region, although in recent years intra-Asian FDI has dominated inward FDI in the region, and is likely to have the most pronounced impact on the dynamic restructuring of Asian economies.[1]

/.....

Elements of such an extended international production system are gradually emerging as a result of the strategies of TNCs. In that sense, international production can be thought of as performing a role wider than trade, that is, one of moving not only goods and services across borders, but also moving factors of production and organizational methods, skills and technologies under a unified management structure. Thus, TNCs act as integrating agents by incorporating within a single organizational structure the many linkages to the world economy that can contribute to the economic growth of host countries. In that sense, they play a crucial role as direct coordinators of international economic activity. As a result

(Box X.3, cont'd.)

In this process, Asian TNCs—including those from Japan as well as the newly-industrializing economies—transmit to other Asian countries through FDI activities in which the home country is no longer internationally competitive, but which represent large potential gains for the host country. Over the long run, development stages may be staggered in the Asian region in such a way that countries at different stages of development follow one another in the process of dynamic restructuring. Foreign direct investment can thus be seen as channelling economic growth impulses from home to host countries. To illustrate, Japan made early export-oriented investments in what are now the Asian newly-industrializing economies in labour-intensive activities in which it no longer had a comparative advantage, such as textiles and toys. Those investments, many of which were made by small and medium-sized Japanese firms, helped to expand those sectors in the host economies and assisted them in capturing large shares of world markets for light manufactures. As those countries grew, rising wage rates and trade surpluses which led their currencies to appreciate undermined their comparative advantage in labour-intensive sectors, and they themselves transferred those activities through FDI to the less-developed Asian economies, enabling the latter to begin a path of structural upgrading. At the same time, new FDI from Japan in services industries and higher-value manufacturing goods in the newly-industrializing economies are enabling the latter to re-structure into those activities. Foreign direct investment is thus acting as a channel in the region not only for trade and technology transfer, but for the transfer of sequential stages of comparative advantage.

While the above depiction is no doubt simplified, it underlines how FDI, under a particular set of conditions, can facilitate a process of dynamic restructuring. A few other important points may be drawn from the example. In many cases, Japanese FDI in the region took the form of joint ventures with local partners, thus helping create positive spillovers into the local economy, and technologies which were no longer state-of-the-art in Japan were transferred to foreign affiliates. Furthermore, TNCs have created strong trading networks both within and between countries, such that much of the trade in the region is driven by TNC networks. Host-country policies to encourage exports and local entrepreneurs were essential in helping to create the growth dynamic of intra-regional FDI; indeed, in cases where industries were protected or FDI was kept in isolated enclaves, the growth impact of FDI appears to have been constrained. Finally, deliberate host-country policies to transform their economies through re-structuring are key elements in the contribution of FDI to growth in the region.

1 See, for instance, Terutomo Ozawa, "The dynamics of Pacific Rim industrialization: how Mexico can join the Asian flock of 'flying geese'", in Riordan Roett, ed, *Mexico's External Relations in the 1990s* (Boulder & London, Lynne Rienner, 1991); Hal Hill, "Foreign investment and East Asian economic development", *Asian Pacific Economic Literature*, vol. 4, No. 2 (September 1990), pp. 21-58; and Eric D. Ramstetter, ed., *Direct Foreign Investment in Asia's Developing Economies and Structural Change in the Asia-Pacific Region* (Boulder, Colorado, Westview Press, 1991).

of that organizational effort, the world economy is being transformed qualitatively: trading and other linkages are being complemented, if not supplanted, by linkages at the production level. In an international production system for goods and services, it is increasingly firms—transnational corporations—that play this coordinating role and that determine participation in the international division of labour, rather than arms-length transactions.

The evolving pattern of the international production system increasingly defines the conditions and potential for countries to grow. Indeed, the growth potential of developing countries will increasingly depend on their ability to participate in the process of international production, whether on an intra-regional or cross-regional basis. The active participation of TNCs in host countries, under an appropriate domestic policy framework, has become a primary means of integrating developing countries into the emerging world economy. Presently, however, the more advanced elements of international production are confined to developed countries and a small number of developing countries in selected industries.

2. Determinants of international production

At the heart of the international production system is the combination of the ownership-specific advantages of TNCs, the locational advantages of host countries and competitive pressures for TNCs to internalize a wide range of value-adding activities rather than rely on arms-length transactions. Transnational corporations possess advantages that may in part be derived from their home countries, but which are specific to the firm itself. Such advantages may be in the form of proprietary knowledge and/or technology, superior management techniques relative to rivals, established trade and distribution networks or brand names and patents. Indeed, it is these very firm-specific strengths that allow TNCs to compete effectively against local firms, which have the advantage of familiarity with and a direct presence in the domestic market. Sometimes, specific developments of the home country of TNCs influence the nature of their advantages. Japanese automobile TNCs, for instance, may be relatively advantaged in introducing new production and organizational methods geared towards high-quality output because these were pioneered in Japan; United States TNCs in the consumer products industry may have special marketing capabilities; and Italian textile firms may bring value in terms of their design capabilities—all reflections of their particular home country conditions. For their part, host countries possess locational attributes, such as natural resources, low-cost skilled labour, technical competencies, large domestic markets and policies favourable to FDI, that make it advantageous for TNCs to locate production in those countries. Together, the ownership-specific advantages of TNCs and the locational advantages of host countries interact to promote the competitive position of the investing firm and improve economic performance in the host country. In particular, TNCs often provide the host country with the ability to realize its own comparative advantage in the world economy, through an international re-allocation and integration of resources (box X.3).[9]

As an example, a country with an abundance of relatively inexpensive labour may lack the capital, both physical and managerial, with which to employ that labour in productive activities. Transnational corporations, attracted by a large labour pool, can provide the capital, know-how and export markets that enable the country to gain from its locational advantage in low-cost labour. When such a process succeeds, TNCs contribute to a further strengthening of the country's locational advantage by providing formal and informal training which upgrades the quality of the labour force, thus expanding the potential for the host country to grow. In addition, the transfer of soft and hard technology by TNCs can enable the host country to shift its locational advantage gradually towards specialized skill-intensive and high-technology production. Alternatively, TNCs may deliver high-quality inputs to host countries that possess a strong demand for such inputs, but lack the know-how or assets to produce or import them. By supplying the host country with such inputs, TNCs can contribute towards a more efficient utilization of the host country's resources. In addition, by generating shifts in the composition of exports towards technologically advanced goods and by assisting in the development of new lines of production in host countries, TNCs allow countries to realize their comparative advantage in exports and production. Thus, combining the competitive advantage of TNCs with locational advantages of host countries increases the ability of the latter to expand their growth potential.

3. Implications for developing countries

The strategies of TNCs in the context of the emerging international production system are a key determinant of the role of developing countries in that system, and of the potential benefits countries may derive from it. Integrated international production implies that, more and more, the foreign activities of TNCs will form an integral part of the whole company's operations, rather than a discrete adjunct to its domestic operations. Increasingly, competitive conditions in one market determine the activities of foreign affiliates in all countries, as all of a firm's operations are potentially available to enhance the ability to compete on a firm-wide basis. To the extent that such globally-integrated strategies grow in importance, developing countries may gain in leverage in relation to TNCs, as each part of a firm's activities becomes a more important component of its overall strategy, and as competition among TNCs for favourable locations intensifies; at the same time, to the extent that specialization increases, each part has little value in and by itself. Other developing countries may find themselves relatively marginalized if they do not offer the locational advantages required by globally-integrated firms, such as a skilled labour force, an open trading and investment environment, a developed communications and transport infrastructure and networks of local suppliers on which TNCs can draw.

The objectives of policy makers and the strategic objectives of TNCs are often different. For example, a country may look to TNCs to provide it with export opportunities. If, however, it has a large domestic market, TNCs might be more interested in domestic sales than exporting. The experience of China in attracting FDI is instructive in that regard. Countries may also consider it desirable to develop vertically-integrated, stand-alone domestic industries, whereas—in the context of international production—TNCs may wish to locate only a discrete value-adding activity in the host country, in order to integrate it with activities of affiliates located elsewhere. In those cases, host countries will have to determine whether it is to their advantage to try and develop complementary capabilities through domestic investment, or to specialize in a segment of an internationalized industry. While these choices may not be mutually exclusive, at least for large countries, they might be for small developing countries with limited local resources. In any event, the different perspectives of firms and Governments require that efforts are often needed to ensure that a balance acceptable to both in the longer run is found.

C. The role of host country policies

The preceding chapters emphasized the role of host country conditions, including policies, in enhancing the growth impact of TNCs. Many of those policies are not, however, FDI-specific. Clearly, an enabling environment for FDI is necessary as a minimum policy requirement for inward FDI. However, once investments are made, the most important policies from a growth perspective are likely to be in the areas of macroeconomic management, industrial, trade, technology and education policies. While an open FDI regime may be important in attracting TNCs, it is the overall policy framework of the host country and, more significantly, the interlinkages among policies which ought to be considered when seeking to strengthen the growth-promoting contribution of TNCs. In addition, policies to strengthen the locational advantages of host countries in order to attract FDI are also those which will themselves affect the potential of TNCs to affect favourably domestic growth. For example, policies to raise the quality of human capital or improve infrastructure will affect both the attractiveness of the host country to TNCs and its ability to benefit from their activities.

The interaction between those policies is instrumental in providing an enabling framework as regards the growth-promoting impact of TNCs. In particular, a well-managed macroeconomic environment is important both as a condition for deriving benefits from TNCs and for attracting FDI. Exchange rate policies, for example, are important insofar as they determine the amount of profits that will be reinvested by the affiliate and also affect the production costs perceived by TNCs wishing to invest there. Trade and industrial policies aiming to promote those industries in which a country has a comparative advantage in world markets would need to take into account not only the FDI regime, but also the potential contribution of TNCs to export promotion and technological development. It would therefore be necessary to coordinate aspects of trade, industrial and FDI-specific policies in order to not only attract the type of FDI that would be most growth-promoting for a given country, but also to enhance the contribution of TNCs that have already invested there. In that regard, trade and industrial policies will increasingly have to take into account the role of FDI in promoting growth; at the same time, FDI policies will have to consider the growth-promoting impact of TNCs via trade, technology and other channels in formulating appropriate regimes.

As a specific example of the interplay between FDI and national policy frameworks, policies designed to promote new industries through restrictive trade and FDI regimes may come under increasing pressure, given the rapidity of technological change and the rising costs of technological development (leading to a greater internalization of technologies, particularly advanced technologies, by TNCs), the entry of many countries into the international FDI market-place (for example, Central and Eastern Europe) and the deepening of global and regional production systems led by TNCs. Those factors may induce countries to modify FDI policies in an effort to improve their economic performance through greater participation in the international economy. But the success of a modification in FDI policies in achieving the desired results may well be predicated on trade-policy reforms. The presence of TNCs may actually bolster a host country's ability to nurture domestic industries, which otherwise might not be able to withstand intense international competition, including competition from imports. From that perspective, a relaxation of protectionist policies and allowing greater inflows of FDI may together contribute to the growth of domestic industries that may not be achievable through either FDI or trade-policy reforms alone. Similarly, a closer interplay between education and technology-related policies can enhance the competitiveness of a host country by enabling it to absorb the technology generated and transferred by TNCs. Government policies aimed at improving the quality of human capital in host countries through education (for example, minimum standards of education and vocational training programmes) are key elements in the process of assimilation and development of technology.

In the past, domestic policies in developing countries did not always take into account policy interlinkages in order to adopt an integrated framework aimed at maximizing the potential contribution of TNCs to growth. However, the growing awareness of the growth-promoting potential of TNCs through their impact on trade, technology and investment, combined with a decreasing potential for unbundling each of these activities, points to the need for an integrated policy package, with policies dealing with FDI at its heart. The policy regimes of many countries would benefit from greater coordination, to ensure that the host country takes advantage of the contributions of TNCs.

The Asian region provides a useful illustration of the fact that a country's integrated policy framework is more critical than its FDI regime per se, and that countries with open policies may benefit from TNC participation. Several Asian countries adopted export promoting policies, macroeconomic policies that encouraged savings and domestic investment and human resource development policies that produced a skilled labour force; at the same time, however, there was great variation in the degree to which these countries allowed FDI to enter their economies (although, in recent years, most of them have opened up significantly to FDI). The interplay of these policies contributed a great deal to the dynamism of certain Asian economies, particularly in the areas of trade and investment. In many cases, the growth impact of TNCs in Asia was magnified by the presence of a dynamic local economy, which often surpassed the performance of TNCs in terms of exports and capital formation. Critical in shaping the contribution of TNCs to economic growth in the Asian region was an integrated policy framework, mainly macroeconomic, trade and overall investment policies, rather than the FDI policies *per se*.

In summary, the policies of host countries play an important role in shaping the contribution of TNCs to economic growth: they establish the enabling framework within which the contributions of TNCs can be utilized and enhanced. While TNCs can be engines of growth, it is the Governments of the host countries that lay the tracks and provide the signals which, as part of an entire system, determine both the speed with which the engines can travel and the direction in which they do so. It is therefore the interaction between Governments and TNCs, and their relations with the domestic private sector, which shape the pattern of growth and development of host countries.

Notes

[1]For a state-of-the-art review of the literature on TNCs and economic development and TNCs and industrialization, as well as a collection of major writings in these areas, see S. Lall, ed., *United Nations Library on Transnational Corporations: Transnational Corporations and Economic Development* (London, Routledge, forthcoming); D. Chudnovsky, ed., *United Nations Library on Transnational Corporations: Transnational Corporations and Industrialization* (London, Routledge, forthcoming).

[2]For a review of a number of central issues in this respect, see G. Hedlund, ed., *United Nations Library on Transnational Corporations: Organization of Transnational Corporations* (London, routledge, forthcoming); D. Lecraw and A. J. Morrison, eds., *Transnational Corporations and Business Strategy. United Nations Library on Transnational Corporations* (London, Routledge, forthcoming); and, A. I. Stonehill and M. H. Moffett, eds., *United Nations Library on Transnational Corporations: International Financial Management* (London, Routledge, forthcoming).

[3]For example, such a relationship was found by M. Blomström, R. E. Lipsey and M. Zejan, "A cross-country study of growth in developing countries", paper prepared for the conference on historical perspectives on the international convergence of productivity, New York University, New York, 23-24 April 1992. Other efforts to examine this relationship include: Gustav Papanek, "Aid, foreign private investment, savings, and growth in less developed countries", vol. 81, No. 1 (January/February 1973), pp. 120-130; Pradumna B. Rana, "Foreign direct investment and economic growth in the Asian and Pacific region", *Asian Development Review*, vol. 5, No. 1 (1987), pp. 100-115; V. Bornschier, C. Chase-Dunn and R. Robinson, "Cross national evidence of the effects of foreign investment and aid on economic growth and inequality: a survey of findings and a reanalysis", *American Journal of Sociology*, vol. 84, No. 3 (1978), pp. 651-683; Eric D. Ramstetter, ed., *Direct Foreign Investment in Asia's Developing Economies and Structural Change in the Asia-Pacific Region* (Boulder, Colorado, Westview Press, 1991); Denis O'Hearn, "TNCs, intervening mechanisms and economic growth in Ireland: a longitudinal test and extension of the Bornschier model", *World Development*, vol. 18, No. 3 (1990), pp. 417-429; Chinyere Emmanuel Egbe, "The impact of foreign private investment on the growth of GNP and investment in Nigeria" (unpublished PhD dissertation, Washington State University, 1984); Volker Bornschier, "Multinational corporations and economic growth: a gross-national test of the decapitalization thesis", *Journal of Development Economics*, vol. 7, No. 2 (1980), pp. 191-210.

[4]UNCTC, *The Determinants of Foreign Direct Investment: A Survey of the Evidence* (United Nations publication, Sales No. E.92.II.A.2); Pan-Long Tsai, "Determinants of foreign direct investment in Taiwan: an alternative approach with time-series data", *World Development*, vol. 19, No. 2/3 (1991), pp. 275-285; and Steve Chan, Cal Clark and David R. Davis, "State entrepreneurship, foreign investment, export expansion and economic growth", *Journal of Conflict Resolution*, vol. 34, No. 1 (March 1990), pp. 102-129.

[5]Russel B. Scholl, "The international investment position of the United States in 1990", *Survey of Current Business*, vol. 71, No. 6 (June 1991), pp. 23-35. Stock data have not been adjusted for the finance (except banking), insurance, and real estate industry of the Netherlands Antilles.

[6]UNCTC, *World Investment Report 1991: The Triad in Foreign Direct Investment* (United Nations publication, Sales No. E.91.II.A.12).

[7]UNCTC, *Foreign Direct Investment and Transnational Corporations in Services* (United Nations publication, Sales No. E.89.II.A.1), p. 128.

[8]Karl P. Sauvant, "The tradability of services" in World Bank and UNCTC, *The Uruguay Round: Services in the World Economy* (Washington, D.C. and New York, The World Bank and UNCTC, 1990), pp. 114-122.

[9]See also Terutomo Ozawa, "Foreign direct investment and economic development", *Transnational Corporations*, vol. 1, No. 1 (February 1992), pp. 27-65.

PART THREE

POLICY IMPLICATIONS

Chapter XI

INTERNATIONAL PRODUCTION AND GOVERNANCE

The analysis in the present report documents the rising importance of foreign direct investment (FDI) in the world economy. Investment flows have grown considerably in both absolute terms and relative to a number of key economic indicators, with, for instance, sales of foreign affiliates being larger than world exports (Part One). Foreign direct investment, and the flows of capital, technology, training and trade that are part of it, has become the primary means by which a growing number of countries are integrated in the international economy. As a result, transnational corporations (TNCs) have become the principal private actors in the world economy.

This also means that TNCs play an important role in the growth process of countries. The analysis in Part Two has shown that those firms can make significant quantitative and qualitative contributions to the growth of developing countries. This contribution takes the form of providing additional investment resources, facilitating technological change, improving the quality of human resources and opening up new opportunities for trade. In all these areas, the catalytic qualitative role that TNCs can play in accelerating the growth process is perhaps even more important than its quantitative dimension by way of making investments in outputs with higher growth potential, introducing new products and technologies that contribute to structural change in a country's economy, raising productivity through the provision of training for workers and managerial staff, and changing the composition of exports and imports in a manner that permits a more sustainable integration in the international economy. Thus, TNCs invest a package of tangible and intangible assets in their foreign affiliates. Those, in turn, are linked to domestic enterprises through various forward and backward linkages, while, at the same time, being part of the global affiliate networks of their parent firms.

The growth of such cross-national networks is beginning to give rise to an international production system for goods and services, organized and managed by TNCs. If anything, the characteristics of the new world economy (outlined in chapter IV) further underline the centrality of TNCs and encourage the development of an international production system. Against this backdrop, the Report also documented that the share of developing countries in global FDI continues to decline, even though those countries have introduced many policy changes to facilitate FDI inflows into their economies, and most of them run the risk of being marginalized in the emerging international production system.

Those developments require that the conventional approach to international economic transactions, which focuses on trade and finance, be revised to take into account explicitly investment flows. More specifically, in a world in which the book value of FDI has reached $1.7 trillion, undertaken by some 35,000 TNCs through some 150,000 foreign affiliates, in which the total volume of goods and services delivered to foreign markets through the foreign affiliates of TNCs is larger than that delivered by exports; in which a good part of trade, technology and finance flows is associated with FDI; in which FDI is a mechanism through which economies are linked together at a deeper level of integration than at the trade level; and in which TNCs have a central impact on economic growth, international economic transactions ought to be viewed from the perspective of foreign direct investment and transnational corporations.

Thus, with the ascendancy of TNCs, the international economic reality has changed fundamentally. Economic theory, policy-making and institutional arrangements must follow suit, lest they lose their relevance.

Some of the implications that follow from seeing the world economy from the perspective of foreign direct investment and transnational corporations are outlined in this chapter. Section A contains an illustrative examination of two sets of policy measures that recently have received attention in international discussions or negotiations: measures that distort international flows, and measures taken at the national level to increase, under certain conditions, the benefits that accrue to the country taking them. But, in distinction to the conventional approach, the discussion here is not conducted from a trade perspective, which would focus on, respectively, trade related investment measures (TRIMs) and strategic trade theory; rather, the discussion is conducted from the perspective of FDI and, therefore, focuses on investment related trade measures (IRTMs) and strategic FDI policy.

Section B, then, turns to the principal actor of international production, the transnational corporation. The question is asked: what consequences does the failure of a TNC have, and how does the international community deal with such an occurrence in a world of multiple jurisdictions? Given the great number of TNCs, such incidents are likely to occur from time to time, and provisions have to be made sooner or later to deal with them in a cooperative manner.

The implications of viewing the world economy from the perspective of FDI would reach, of course, into the institutional sphere. Section C deals, therefore, with FDI-supporting mechanisms. Trade-supporting measures are quite common at the national level and, at the international level, had found their expression in the establishment of the United Nations Conference on Trade and Development (UNCTAD) in the 1960s. In the FDI area, however, such supportive measures are fairly limited and, at the international level, furthermore, quite dispersed. An appropriate mechanism in that respect would be particularly important to accelerate the flow of FDI to developing countries and enhance its growth-promoting role in those countries. That need alone calls for concerted efforts by host countries, home countries and the international community.

A more comprehensive approach, moreover, would also aim at increasing the transparency of national FDI regimes and introduce a measure of review of FDI policies—mechanisms that have become accepted and valued features of the multilateral trading system. Such mechanisms do not yet exist in the FDI sphere. Section D outlines, therefore, a multilateral approach to increase the transparency of national FDI regimes and to review national FDI policies, focusing particularly on the benefits such an approach would have for countries and firms.

A. A new policy perspective

1. Investment related trade measures

(a) Relevance

Transnational corporations have come to be responsible for a substantial share of world exports and imports. As mentioned in chapter VIII, in the case of the United States, for example, some 80 per cent of the country's trade was undertaken by TNCs in 1989, including parent companies in the United States, foreign affiliates of United States TNCs and United States affiliates of foreign TNCs. If only trade that passes through foreign affiliates of home-country TNCs is considered, the role of those firms is still quite important. To use again the example of the United States, in 1989, approximately half of the merchandise trade passed through either the foreign affiliates of United States TNCs or the United States affiliates of foreign TNCs. At the same time, more than a third of United States trade represented intra-firm transactions, between foreign affiliates and their parent corporations.

Such a symbiotic relationship between FDI and trade establishes the potential for the volume, sectoral composition and geographical distribution of FDI to be affected by trade measures with attendant consequences for the world at large and for the distribution of gains among countries. For example, if tariffs on imports imposed by one country attracts FDI, that may be at the expense of FDI in another country, and so the distribution of benefits associated with FDI is altered. It is also possible that such tariff-jumping FDI can reduce, under some circumstances, the welfare of the tariff-imposing country as well, and thus reduce overall global welfare.

Accordingly, in consideration of the importance of FDI, one has to explore investment related trade measures (IRTMs)—trade measures that are not specifically aimed at affecting FDI flows but, in the final analysis, do so—in the same spirit that underlies international negotiations on trade related investment measures (TRIMs). In view of the symbiotic relationship between FDI and trade, IRTMs carry significant policy implications, since investment diversion could arise from a variety of trade measures, just as trade diversion can result from investment measures. The spirit underlying the discussion of TRIMs is to review measures related to investment that have the effect of causing a pattern of trade different from what would be obtained from the operation of market forces in the absence of those measures. TRIMs have become a subject of discussion despite the recognition that the operation of market forces in the real world, with all its structural imperfections and multitude of interventions in product and factor markets, by no means guarantees that the elimination of TRIMs would bring about a pattern of trade conceived in a world of perfect competition with the same welfare consequences. The issue is essentially the deviation from the pattern of trade that emerges owing to interventions aimed at affecting investment. In the same vein, it is logical to consider the deviation from the pattern of FDI that emerges owing to interventions aimed at affecting trade. In each case, the concern is that such intervention affects national and global welfare.

(b) How do investment related trade measures work?

It would require considerable research to identify all trade measures that fall in the category of IRTMs, and to quantify their impact on FDI flows. However, considering that virtually all countries in the world adopt tariff and non-tariff measures to affect exports and/or imports and that much FDI involves international trade, it would appear that a very large part of FDI is affected by trade measures. The principal objective here is to identify possible IRTMs, without any claim to being exhaustive, and to indicate briefly how they might affect FDI. Table XI.1 contains a suggestive list of IRTMs and their likely impact on FDI flows.

Table XI.1. A suggestive list of IRTMs

Trade measure	*Possible impact on FDI*
Tariffs and quantitative restrictions on imports	Induces import-substituting FDI
Sectorally managed trade, including voluntary export restraints	Induces import-substituting FDI
Regional free trade agreements	Promotes FDI in the member countries
Rules-of-origin policies	Induces FDI in component production
Export processing zones	Induces export-oriented FDI
Export controls (security and foreign policy)	Induces export-replacing FDI
Export financing	Increases export-oriented FDI
Non-monetary trade arrangements (coproduction; buy-back)	Depends on the nature of specific arrangements
Safety, health, environment, privacy and other national standards	Induces import-substituting FDI

The most obvious trade measure—one that has received considerable attention by researchers—is the imposition of *tariffs* or *quantitative restrictions on imports*. Both of those measures affect the volume of trade. If the market of the country imposing that trade restriction is considered to be of significant interest to foreign firms, they might seek to engage in FDI in order to maintain their participation in that market. Foreign direct investment in this case, known as tariff-jumping investment, is therefore a response to restrictions on trade. As is well-known, many developing countries have pursued import-substituting development strategies, using protective tariff walls and other import restrictions. This was particularly true for such industries as automobile, steel and selected consumer electronics. A considerable amount of FDI took place in those and other industries in which restrictions were imposed on imports; often the foreign affiliates operating under those conditions are not efficient and, hence, not competitive in world markets. Given these inefficiencies, such FDI might not have occurred in the absence of trade restrictions.

Another significant trade measure that has proliferated in recent years involves an increase in structured *managed trade* arrangements, centred on particular sectors. Sectoral arrangements have included automobiles, textiles, semiconductors, steel, aerospace and construction projects. Such arrangements may take various forms. In the case of trade between the United States and Japan in automobiles, trade has been managed principally through voluntary export restraints by Japan. Since the United States auto market is considered important by Japanese producers, they have responded by undertaking FDI in the United States to protect or enhance their market share. Similarly, the Multi-fibre Arrangement (which provides the framework for managing trade in textile products) permits importing countries to assign quotas on exporting countries selectively. In consequence, countries whose quota on exports had been reached have undertaken FDI in other countries whose quota remained under- or unutilized or were not subject to quota. A considerable portion of FDI by Asian newly industrialized economies in other developing countries of Asia has been undertaken for that purpose. Here, again, FDI has been made in response to specific trade restrictions.

The creation of *regional free trade areas* can have considerable effects on FDI flows. Although regional arrangements may envision an eventual reduction of trade barriers *vis-à-vis* non-member nations, their typical immediate effect is to implement significant and advantageous trade liberalization measures exclusively within the free trade area. Such arrangements may draw in FDI from enterprises based in non-member countries. The impact is most pronounced for enterprises whose exports lose their relative competitiveness to local producers benefiting from the trade agreement, essentially forcing outside firms to invest within the region in order to maintain their market share. This effect can be seen in the case of the European Community (EC), when, after the announcement of the EC 1992 Single Market programme, FDI by firms based outside the Community increased considerably.[1] Investments were motivated both by the desire to take advantage of the expected market growth and to protect against exclusion from the EC market. Neither objective could be reached as effectively, if at all, from outside the regional trade zone. A parallel movement appears to be occurring in anticipation of a North American Free Trade Agreement, particularly in terms of FDI in Mexico (see chapter I). A similar effect could also arise sectorally in response to related efforts to create exclusive, regionally-assisted R&D or manufacturing programmes such as Esprit, Eureka and Sematech, which often incorporate an important trade-related element; currently, however, that type of IRTM probably exerts only a low impact on FDI flows.

One instrument of regional integration arrangements that can be a particularly important IRTM are *rules of origin*, especially their *local content* components; local content requirements can also be imposed independently of integration agreements. The investment impact of such trade measures is obviously to encourage investment and production in the consuming market, presumably at the expense of economies from which exports are displaced. For example, if country A decides that it would allow imports from country B only under rules of origin that require a minimum local content (that is, country A plus B's combined content), then all the countries that have been exporting inputs and components to the region may be forced to produce directly those inputs and components in A, B or both. In the evolving North American Free Trade Agreement, a key negotiating issue concerns rules of origin and local content, which set the minimum amount of North American value-added to qualify for duty-free status. As mentioned in chapter I, the three United States car manufacturers, all of whom already operate in Mexico (General Motors, Ford and Chrysler), are promoting local content requirements of 60 to 70 per cent for goods in that industry to qualify for duty-free access to other NAFTA countries. This would place most European and Asian car manufacturers in a disadvantaged position because they would not be able to rely on sourcing from their home countries in order to qualify for duty-free status in NAFTA. Clearly, local content requirements on imports and rules of origin significantly affect investment decisions.

The flow of FDI is also affected by *export processing zones* introduced by many countries, particularly developing countries. Using very liberal trade rules (and other incentives), the specific purpose of those zones is to attract FDI flows to them in order to boost exports and employment. During the past two decades, the number of such zones (also known by various other names, such as special economic zones and free economic zones), has increased significantly. By early 1989, there were about 200 export processing zones in operation in the developing world, and more than 150 under construction or at the planning stage. The operational zones employed over 1.5 million workers, and their exports were of the order of $15 billion. [2] A large part of investment in export processing zones is by TNCs.

Export controls and *export credits* can also influence FDI flows. The imposition of national export controls (applied for security or foreign policy reasons) over time can lead corporations to invest in areas outside the jurisdiction of control-prone Governments or prevent FDI flows into particular industries. For example, a prohibition of the export of technologies with potential military uses may discourage FDI in activities that make use of those technologies in their civilian applications. Export credits by developed countries are subject to an OECD agreement that seeks to limit the effective subsidization of trade through publicly assisted export-financing mechanisms. Although not comprehensive nor entirely effective, that agreement has reduced the level of competition among export-financing programmes. Differentials in the export financing support available in various nations can still affect corporate decisions to invest. Export-oriented investors would have an incentive to choose locations that offer more favourable export financing, which has the effect of subsidizing exports.

Rebates of indirect taxes on exported goods and services as an export incentive can also affect investment flows. Even if indirect tax rebates may be a step towards correcting a distortion of trade flows, that decision could nevertheless affect investment patterns. Export-oriented investors can often choose between alternative production sites. A country whose taxation system is based heavily on indirect taxes would be in an advantageous position over a nation using primarily a direct taxation structure for export-oriented investment projects that could benefit from the sanctioned rebates.

Since the debt crisis of the early 1980s, a growing proportion of world trade (estimated to range between 8 per cent and 30 per cent) has been conducted through such *non-monetary trade transactions* as barter arrangements or more sophisticated forms of countertrade, clearing provisions, co-production, buy-back agreements and other such mechanisms. In the case of buy-back agreements, for example, an enterprise setting up a plant in another country agrees to buy back all or part of the output of that plant. Thus, a host country permits FDI in exchange for guaranteed exports.

An impact on FDI might arise from *trade standards* that define appropriate and acceptable policy measures dealing with safety, health, the environment, privacy protection or cultural concerns. Countries sometimes adopt measures that may appear to be based on legitimate domestic policy concerns, but which, in practice, may erect discriminatory non-tariff trade barriers. For example, requiring health and safety inspections to be carried out by national inspectors can have the effect of a non-tariff barrier against imports and may favour import-substituting FDI.

Finally, trade measures undertaken by subnational Governments in the United States, Canada and several other nations with federal government structures also can act as IRTMs. For instance, many United States state agencies and many cities offer a variety of fiscal and non-fiscal incentives to promote exports with potential interactive effects on FDI flows. A trend towards economic decentralization in other countries, coupled with the growing appeal of federal structures in Europe, may further increase the importance of subnational government policies over the remainder of this decade.

(c) Conclusions

These examples provide a broad picture of how a variety of trade measures adopted by Governments can influence FDI flows. In fact, a significant part of global FDI flows is likely to have been influenced by trade measures in one way or another. Obviously, not all measures are equally potent in this respect. Trade interventions in the form of import tariffs, sectorally managed trade, regional trading arrangements and export processing zones are likely to be of greater significance than others. The purpose of this discussion is not to pass judgement on IRTMs; as in the case of TRIMs, positive and negative (intended and unintended) effects of each measure need to be weighed. The purpose is, rather, to point out that, in view of the increasing importance of FDI in the world economy, the international allocation of FDI and policy interventions that have the effect of changing the pattern of its allocation should be matters of great concern. Thus, the impact of IRTMs and their effects on efficiency and welfare need to be examined and, if need be, made subject to policy action.

Some of the IRTMs identified above are sanctioned by GATT, while others lie outside current multilateral agreements. GATT-actionable trade measures presumably either eliminate distortions or reduce them to their lowest practicable political level (which may be reduced further through periodic negotiations). However, a reduction of trade distortions does not necessarily mean a similar and accompanying reduction of investment distortions. Some measures that promote freer trade may have an adverse impact on investment flows from the viewpoint of global welfare. Where trade policies have a differential effect on investment flows, a new negotiating approach may be required.

Since FDI has emerged as a critical structural determinant of the international economy, its increased importance in shaping trade flows requires a policy analysis that reverses the historical concentration on trade policy and the more recent focus on investment issues only as they distort trade flows. Both policy analysis and political negotiations might be better served by examining also the impact of trade and other policy measures on investment flows, rather than simply concentrating on the reverse relationship. An investment analysis would help to inform public officials better about the impact of trade-policy choices. Such discussions could also contribute towards the acceptance of broad FDI principles to promote and guide global economic relations into the next century.

2. Strategic foreign-direct-investment policy

Few countries, developed or developing, pursue a policy of complete non-intervention in the area of FDI. The extent of intervention, of course, differs between countries and take various forms: closure of certain sectors to FDI; limitations on the share of foreign ownership; performance requirements, such as requiring foreign investors to meet some pre-determined levels of exports, or to use a minimum proportion of locally produced inputs; and a host of fiscal and non-fiscal incentives applied either to FDI generally or in particular sectors. Those and other measures, adopted by Governments with varying degrees and coverage, have as their objective to increase the benefits of FDI to host economies or to minimize negative economic or non-economic impacts. As has been documented in chapter III, however, the recent trend in policy changes has been unmistakably in the direction of progressively greater liberalization and significantly reduced intervention. This in turn raises the question as to whether there is any scope for "strategic FDI policy". The purpose of such a policy would be to increase the long-run benefits of FDI to an economy, both economic and non-economic, for example, through learning-by-doing, the development of an indigenous technological capability or attaining self-sufficiency in certain selected industries, even if such a policy were to impose some short-run cost (for example, by reducing FDI inflows or causing a fiscal drain).

Another reason why some attention should be paid to strategic FDI policy is that, during the past ten years or so, there has been considerable discussion of what is termed "strategic trade policy". This discussion usually deals with two aspects: one dealing with policies of Governments towards specific industries or sectors that might be termed "strategic" in that they confer certain special benefits on the economy; and the other with rent-transfer behaviour by Governments. [3] In both cases, the treatment of imperfect competition is at the heart of the new thinking, that is, the presence of firms that behave as monopolists or oligopolists in their relevant markets. Imperfect competition might result from economies of scale (including those resulting from fixed costs, such as R&D expenditures), economies of learning, product differentiation combined with economies of scope, or other factors that create barriers to entry to an industry. At the same time, the growth of FDI and the role of TNCs in host economies are, in turn, largely attributable to the presence of monopolistic or oligopolistic competition. Therefore, strategic FDI policy deserves the attention of policy makers owing to the same considerations which underline strategic trade policy.

The preceding discussion suggests that the rationale behind strategic FDI policy falls into one of two broad categories: the realization of long-term benefits (even with some short-term costs) and transferring rents from foreigners. Investment policies usually adopted by Governments of home and host countries to achieve either long-term benefits (including minimizing negative impact) or rent transfer include (i) the offering of subsidies or other investment incentives to TNCs to induce them to locate operations to territories within the offering Government's jurisdiction; (ii) the imposing of performance requirements (or, as termed in the GATT negotiations, "trade related investment measures" or TRIMs) on local operations of TNCs to induce them to take measures that are consistent with host nations' goals and objectives; and (iii) closure of the domestic market to, or restrictions on, FDI. Often, host countries link the first two sets of policies, that is, they mandate performance requirements as a condition for the receipt of investment incentives.

(a) Policy instruments to increase long-term benefits

(i) Investment incentives and performance requirements

Investment incentives and performance requirements can be fairly general, implemented with the objectives of enhancing the flow and increasing the long-term benefits from FDI. Alternatively, they can be geared to specific industries considered to be strategic for economic or non-economic reasons. The discussion below examines both aspects, though, in practice, the distinction between them may be rather blurred. The use of general investment incentives can be effective in some situations by inducing TNCs to place their operations in one geographic location rather than another. However, if the firms' choice of location in the absence of any such incentive is different from the choice they would make given the incentive, there must be some reason why firms prefer the former location over the latter; for example, the former location might offer lower operating costs, or have higher expected profitability than the latter (and, hence, from a global perspective, the former would be more efficient). To be induced to locate in the latter location, TNCs must, therefore, be offered incentives large enough to compensate for the reduced efficiency (lower profits) at the latter site.

As noted before, Governments often offer investment incentives in conjunction with performance requirements. These are designed to ensure that TNCs do in fact bring benefits to the local economy, often by specifying that TNCs meet certain goals and objectives, such as creating employment, generating exports, expanding domestic value-added and the like. If TNCs accept those performance requirements, it can be assumed that the value (to the firms) of the incentives or other concessions granted to them exceeds the costs (again, to the firms) of meeting the performance requirements. Otherwise, TNCs would locate elsewhere because they are capable of recognizing any performance requirement that acts as a hidden tax.

From the point of view of host countries, the relevant question is whether they can secure long-term net gains from an investment incentive/performance requirement package. There might be situations in which both the Government of the host country and TNCs might gain from the package. An example is when a performance requirement is linked to an incentive in the form of preferential access to the local market. This preferential access, in effect a monopoly or semi-monopoly right, acts as an inducement to the firm to accept performance requirements. Such linkages of local monopoly rights to performance requirements were quite common in larger developing countries such as Mexico during the 1970s; the local automotive industry, a major Mexican exporter controlled in effect by four TNCs, was built on this sort of arrangement. However, the nature of this arrangement has changed significantly due, in part, to policy changes.

The benefits that might be captured by the local economy from this type of arrangement vary. Some gains might come in the form of the realization of returns from a potential but unexploited comparative advantage in the production of certain goods or services. Such returns are of value to the host country; if a strong case can be made that, without the investment incentive/performance requirement package, the economy would never have achieved these or would have taken a considerably longer time to do so, the Government of the host country might feel justified in adopting those measures. Further gains might come from externalities, especially in the case of developing countries. For example, these might result from technology transferred to suppliers of local affiliates of TNCs, which, in turn, are able to use the technologies to benefit other customers. They might also take the form of infrastructure created by TNCs that is useful to agents other than those firms alone.

However, while investment/performance-requirement packages might be advantageous from the perspective of both TNCs and Governments in the case of a particular host country, they might well be disadvantageous from the perspective of other countries, especially smaller and poorer developing countries. The packages are most likely to be successfully implemented by those countries that are relatively large and prosperous; but smaller and poorer countries that can offer little in the form of incentives to TNCs as an inducement to accept a performance requirement are not likely to be able to implement packages that are of net benefit to their economies.

There are other considerations that need to be taken into account in relation to generalized investment incentives and performance requirements. For the country implementing such measures, there may be a loss of potential tax revenues that would be earned from FDI that could have taken place even in the absence of incentives. Furthermore, performance requirements may deter FDI that might otherwise be beneficial to a host economy. In addition, the offering of incentives may lead to a bidding war between host countries, to the detriment of all host countries.

The situation may, however, be different in the case of industries that are considered to be of strategic importance. If a Government has identified specific activities in which TNCs can offer certain special long-term benefits (for example, by opening export markets or producing products for export with proprietary technology), there may be a case for differentiated incentives. Incentives geared to such activities function as production or export subsidies *for those specific activities* and form part of the panoply of policy tools of a Government implementing a strategic FDI policy. However, those inducements should be moderate, their economic rationale should be clear and they should be offered only to a small number of activities.

That kind of industry-specific incentive may also be appropriate in order to encourage certain kinds of activities (beneficial to the host economy) by specific companies, for reasons of externalities. In those cases, the company and activity in question are usually identifiable. The investors are normally international oligopolies that have proprietary technologies and products whose introduction into the domestic economy can have effects that go far beyond the benefits accruing to the factors of production directly engaged by the company. That is the case of most manufacturing goods produced with complex technologies, and particularly those using information technologies.

Industry and activity-specific inducements to FDI can be usefully accompanied by performance requirements. For example, incentives can be made conditional on the export of a certain proportion of output or on training programmes for domestic employees or managers. An interesting example of this kind of approach is the agreement between the Government of Mexico and IBM whereby, in exchange for being allowed to set up an affiliate with 100 per cent ownership, IBM agreed, among other things, to establish facilities to train Mexican computer programmers. In many cases, performance requirements can be implicit, since foreign firms have to apply for special incentives not offered to all foreign investors and, in the process, will have to modify the nature of their operations in the host country. The more desirable a country is as a location and the fewer the locational alternatives, the greater will be the possibility that the Government of a host country can induce TNCs to contribute towards specific long-term development objectives through a combination of activity-specific incentives and performance requirements.

(ii) Restrictions on foreign direct investment in strategic industries

There are many cases in which Governments prohibit or regulate FDI in particular industries—not in an effort to capture rent, but to obtain some long-term benefits, usually non-economic in nature. These often have to do with national security; Governments are uncomfortable if the provision of certain goods and services deemed essential to national security is under the control of foreign nationals. But other goods and services are often affected as well. For example, almost all nations place some limits on foreign ownership or control of domestic broadcasting operations, the provision of telecommunications services and other public utilities and railroads and other common carriers. Similarly, many developing countries that are major suppliers of petroleum or minerals have taken steps to put the extraction of natural resources under national control and, in many cases, national control extends to at least some downstream operations as well. In many countries, both developing and developed, certain industries are deemed to be essential to economic security, and restrictions have been placed upon foreign ownership and control of firms undertaking those activities.

In all of these cases, the arguments for and against foreign ownership and control are intellectually complex as well as often emotionally charged. Also, the policy climate is subject to periodic change; in many countries, policies towards industries in which local ownership and control once was seen as a vital national goal are being re-evaluated at the present time in light of the economic cost of maintaining such policies. And in some countries in which such costs are seen as too high, the policies have been changed to allow a greater role for FDI. [4]

One of the arguments for restricting foreign ownership or control of activities that are deemed strategic concerns avoidance of dependence on foreign TNCs in a situation of defence emergency. That consideration is a special case of trade-off faced by all nations between self-sufficiency and efficiency. In the extreme case, countries might argue that national security considerations demand that they be self-sufficient in the production of all goods and services. But the cost of self-sufficiency in terms of inefficiencies is very high for most countries. Even large and advanced nations such as the United States have found themselves increasingly dependent upon foreign firms for a wide range of goods and services, including some that are militarily sensitive.

Another argument relates to the fear of Governments of host countries that foreign affiliates in their territories might not receive the latest and best technologies from parent firms, which might limit the diffusion of those technologies in order to gain advantages for the home country. There are, in fact, many goods and services for which firms (rather than nations *per se*) control the latest and best technologies or the latest and best product and process designs, and hence such fears might be justified. Indeed, it is widely recognized that firm-specific ownership advantages are among the key determinants of the ability of a firm to operate transnationally. If a TNC under foreign control is the sole or dominant supplier of products or services that are deemed necessary to a country's security, that country must often decide between accepting some degree of dependence on the TNC, or making its own efforts, with the risk of incurring gross inefficiency or technological inferiority. [5] Faced with that choice, many countries have concluded that admitting FDI is a more desirable option because a local foreign affiliate involves less dependence on the outside world than, for example, relying on a domestic supplier who must import products embodying critical technologies through arm's-length transactions from a foreign TNC.

Some arguments are also advanced in favour of restrictions on FDI in strategic industries for economic reasons. It is also argued, for example, that some activities are so critical to the economy of a nation that, although perhaps not sensitive for military reasons, they must none the less be under domestic ownership or control for considerations of "economic security" or "economic sovereignty". Typically, however, it is difficult to determine what exactly is meant by those considerations. In addition, countries risk costly errors when singling out specific activities and reserving them for domestically controlled enterprises on grounds of economic security (for example, building domestic steel mills that may never be cost-efficient). For those reasons, countries might be well advised to make sure that there are strong economic reasons for such policies before implementing them.

Another economic reason which is sometimes cited to exclude foreign ownership and control in specific activities is R&D. Since most TNCs concentrate their R&D activities in their home countries (see chapter VI), it is sometimes felt that, to encourage local R&D, it is necessary to limit foreign ownership or control of R&D-intensive activities. Research and development generates benefits that are captured by three sets of actors: the firms that undertake R&D, if that R&D leads to the creation of new products or processes that earn rents for the innovating firm; customers of the firm who are users of those products or processes and hence either benefit from lower prices or new or improved products; and the society at large, if new knowledge created by R&D can be useful in applications apart from those controlled by the innovating firm or its immediate customers. The benefits captured by society at large are one example of "externalities"—benefits that are captured by not only producer or the consumer of a product or service, but also by others. The preceding section discussed policies designed to *attract* FDI in order to capture externalities; thus, the discussion here is the opposite, namely to *exclude* FDI in order to capture externalities, a special case of which is R&D.

Two things would have to take place simultaneously for this strategy to be successful. First, if the Government of the host country were to exclude FDI in a certain industry, locally-controlled entities would have to undertake R&D that would otherwise have been performed by a foreign TNC. And second, if the R&D were to be performed by local firms, externalities would have to be generated that could not have been captured if the same R&D had been undertaken by a TNC and located elsewhere.

The key issue is whether both of these are, in fact, likely to happen simultaneously. Research and development doubtlessly does create externalities; but there appears to exist no strong basis to argue that externalities associated with R&D cannot be captured if R&D is performed by TNCs. In fact, in recent times there has been an emphasis on the benefits to one organization locating its R&D activity in close proximity to R&D activities of rival organizations, precisely in order to capture externalities. That partly explains why R&D activity is often clustered in one locality, for example, in California's "Silicon Valley", a cluster of related activities located in a region around the southern shores of San Francisco Bay. This would suggest that Governments might indeed wish to take positive measures to encourage locally-controlled firms to perform R&D, without necessarily excluding foreign-controlled firms. The presence of foreign affiliates might, in fact, serve to stimulate local R&D, precisely by creating the kernel of a potential cluster of related activities.

If FDI is excluded, it is possible that local entities would then perform the R&D that would otherwise have been undertaken by TNCs. But that possibility is much higher in developed than in developing countries. In this context, the cases of Japan during the 1950s and 1960s and of the Republic of Korea during the 1970s and 1980s are instructive. The past policies of those two countries were to restrict inward FDI and to encourage the local development of technology. But Japan, especially during the period 1959-1975, largely used this policy as a means of inducing non-Japanese holders of technology to license their technology to Japanese firms, rather than to induce Japanese firms to create equivalent technologies independently. The Government of Japan simultaneously encouraged Japanese firms to develop R&D activities needed to absorb and improve upon the technology acquired from abroad. Over time, those activities moved away from absorption and improvement and towards *de novo* development of technology; but that did not happen quickly. In effect, then, Japan used access to its internal market as an incentive for non-Japanese firms to *license* technology, by denying those firms access via other channels. Whether or not many other countries could successfully pursue a similar strategy is open to serious doubt; in high-technology industries, even the Republic of Korea—the country that has come the closest to emulating the Japanese model in that regard—has adopted relatively liberal policies towards FDI, as noted in chapter VI.

None of this is to suggest that Governments of developing countries should not promote technological innovation. Virtually all countries that are home to technologically dynamic firms have experienced governmental involvement in high-technology industries, and there are many ways in which Governments support technological innovation. But selective exclusion of foreign ownership from high-technology activities with the hope that such exclusion will foster local entities to do R&D that otherwise would be done by TNCs is not likely to be particularly fruitful.

Overall, therefore, it appears that, in general, the arguments for an exclusion of foreign ownership from selected activities on strictly economic grounds tend to be weak, even for high-technology industries. Rationales based on national security might be somewhat stronger, but they are open to abuse. The relevant criteria in either case are how important strategic considerations are and at what cost self-sufficiency is achieved. In the case of exclusions based on national security, the cost can be very high: efforts to be self sufficient in specific military-related technologies might not only raise costs (and hence reduce national income, the effect of which by itself is to weaken national security), but also threaten the local military with technological inferiority.

(b) Policies to transfer rents

One aspect of strategic trade policy concerns policies pursued by Governments that enable local agents to earn rents, where the rents in the absence of these policies might be captured by foreign rather than domestic agents. In most cases, the relevant agent is a local producer and exporter of a good or service.The major premises behind rent-seeking strategic trade policies are that, first, imperfect (oligopolistic or monopolistic) competition in an industry creates opportunities for firms supplying the industry to appropriate a rent from world markets for the relevant product; and, second, intervention by a Government can enable domestic firms to capture those rents from foreign producers such that the value of the rents captured by domestic residents exceeds the cost to the domestic economy of the intervention. The interventions might be, among other things, in the form of a subsidy to domestic producers [6] or trade protection for these producers. [7]

As regards the applicability of rent-seeking logic in the area of FDI, the overall conclusion that emerges from the literature on the analysis of the closure of markets to FDI as a means to appropriate rent from foreign markets is that some rent might, in fact, be gained by an enterprise based in a country closing its internal market to inward FDI, but that any such gain can easily be outweighed by efficiency losses within the same market. Inward FDI can increase efficiency by stimulating competition and enabling inward technology transfer. Lack of the latter can be especially serious in industries in which domestic and foreign firms possess technological complementarities. The only situation in which a strong case might be made for market closure on rent-transferring grounds is where the industry is marked by strong economies of learning.

Taxation is one means by which host countries can obtain a share of any rents garnered by TNCs. But it should be noted that taxation is not a rent-snatching policy tool *per se*; taxes can only be used to gain rents from TNCs if they are, in fact, established and are showing profits. Further, if a Government abuses the use of taxes as a means of rent-snatching, it could induce TNCs to relocate their operations elsewhere.

It is clear also that a Government cannot offer subsidies (incentives), on the one hand, and simultaneously try to capture a net rent via taxation, on the other. The latter would tend to offset the effects of the former, and the firm would judge an incentive/tax programme in light of its net subsidy or tax. Thus, it is difficult to imagine how an investment incentive can be effective as a rent-snatching device for a host country beyond what the country would normally have obtained. The reverse is more likely to occur, namely, that, after all costs of investment incentives are added up, TNCs extract rent from host countries.

This last possibility is especially likely in cases in which Governments engage in bidding contests against each other in efforts to offer the most attractive incentive packages to TNCs in order to lure FDI into their territories. The likely outcome of a bidding contest is that rents that might normally accrue to host countries from FDI would be bid away and, hence, would be captured instead by the foreign investors or their home countries. None the less, Governments might elect to offer investment incentives to attract FDI, if they believe that benefits other than rents (discussed earlier) will accrue from FDI.

The conclusion that emerges from the above discussion is that there is little scope for FDI policies by way of closure of markets or tax-subsidies to be successful in transferring rent.

(c) Some policy implications

In assessing the overall policy implications of the discussion of the two previous sections, a few points stand out. First, if countries pursue policies that exclude FDI from certain industries, and they make wrong choices, they largely hurt themselves. (If countries reduce their own national incomes as a result of such policies, other nations will suffer some indirect losses, but those are likely to be second-order losses at most.) But, second, if countries pursue policies designed to attract FDI in order to capture benefits that they might not otherwise have obtained (for example, externalities), they may actually obtain those benefits, but they do risk hurting other countries both through redistribution effects (one nation's gain might be another nation's loss) and in the aggregate (world welfare can be reduced as the result of TNCs responding to incentives to locate activities in localities that are not globally optimal). Similar considerations would also apply to performance requirements. Aggregate losses to host countries can be magnified if they are induced to retaliate against other countries' strategic FDI policies. There may be some gain captured by home countries as a result of such policies, if TNCs are able to capture rents from host countries and transfer these to home-country shareholders or treasuries. Third, it is clear that strategic FDI policies must be implemented unilaterally; otherwise, the gains of one country can be nullified by countervailing measures adopted by other countries. Furthermore, special care needs to be taken that strategic FDI policies are not merely short-term protectionist policies.

With regard to the desirability of specific investment inducements (such as tax rebates, outright cash grants, or production or export subsidies), the effects will depend on a variety of factors, not least on what other competing countries are offering. In order not to engage in bidding contests that benefit only the foreign investors or their home countries, it is important that countries exchange information on their FDI policies as a first step towards harmonizing them. Furthermore, investment incentives should be moderate and industry-specific, because of both budgetary considerations and in order not to shift the rents accruing from FDI to foreign investors. In addition, all such incentives should be open to domestic investors. Only in specific cases where TNCs make a contribution to the economy that domestic investors are unable to make, it may be justified economically to offer foreign firms encouragements that are better than those available to domestic investors. In any event, the economic rationale for such incentives should be carefully reviewed, to avoid unnecessary and costly incentives. Moreover, foreign investors with an orientation towards world or regional markets are more likely to be interested in the overall macroeconomic environment, the general policy framework for FDI and trade policies than in investment incentives *per se*.

B. International cooperation on issues arising from the failure of a transnational corporation

As more and more firms transnationalize, the likelihood increases that some of them will fail. The actual failure rate among TNCs is not known. Some national figures may, however, be indicative. In Germany, Japan, Sweden and the United States, the failure rate (primarily bankruptcies) of national firms is approximately 1 per cent.[8] Even if one were to presume that the world-wide failure rate of TNCs is lower than 1 per cent, one might still expect some 200 to 300 failures per year, given the total number of TNCs of about 35,000. In other words, failures by TNCs are not exceptional occurrences. While the overwhelming number of TNCs is small in size, some large TNCs fail as well—witness the 1991 failures of the Bank of Credit and Commerce International (BCCI) and the Maxwell Communication Corporation. Those two occurrences highlighted some of the consequences of major TNCs suspending their operations world-wide for reasons of insolvency and, possibly (but not necessarily so), going into liquidation. For example, BCCI operated in 73 countries, with over 400 offices and some 14,000 employees of 83 nationalities; the collapse of that bank reportedly affected 1.3 million persons world-wide.[9] In those cases, national action alone is not sufficient to address adequately the problems and issues resulting from TNC failures. In the emerging international production system, TNC failures are yet another aspect of governance for which more international cooperation is needed.[10]

1. Who may be affected by a transnational failure?

The failure of a TNC may affect a large number of persons in many countries. Most national bankruptcy laws establish a ranking of protection for creditors who are affected by the liquidation of an enterprise. With some variations among national regimes on the degree of protection or the ranking of credits, the following persons are considered to be among the most directly affected by the failure of an enterprise, though not necessarily in the same order:

- *The State.* Under most national bankruptcy laws, the State has a preferred claim, as tax collector, over any other creditor (secured or unsecured) in the liquidation of the assets of an enterprise.
- *The enterprise's employees.* Employees are obviously directly affected by failures because of the resulting loss of jobs and, therefore, for many, their only means of livelihood. Moreover, if a failing enterprise is in default of pension payments, retired employees could also see their pension funds affected by a failure.
- *Suppliers and contractors.* As a result of a failure, payments for supplies of goods and services sold and delivered may not be made and contractors may not receive full payment of their fees.
- *Lenders.* In the normal course of business, a corporation may borrow from a number of sources for a variety of purposes, including mortgages, secured and non-secured loans, bonds, commercial credits and overdrafts. Many creditors (particularly the non-secured ones) may never be able to recuperate their advances, principal or interest in full.
- *Shareholders of the company.* In the case of a company with limited liability, shareholders are liable up to the unpaid amount of capital subscribed for any financial responsibilities of the corporation. In the case of a failure, they would be called upon to pay up to the outstanding amounts in order for the failing corporation to meet its financial responsibilities, which might include criminal or civil penalties and damages. Where there is fraud or other wrongdoing, shareholders may not be protected by limited liability provisions in the applicable company law; officers and directors may be personally liable.

But the impact of a failure by a major TNC may extend also to a number of other individuals and corporations in a number of countries which, in many ways, depend on the failing enterprise for industrial and trade financing, imports and exports, raw materials and transfer of technology, skills, capital, goods and services. A failure could have destabilizing effects in a specific economic sector, and it could undermine consumer confidence (for example, of depositors, insurance policy holders, utility users). Those problems can acquire serious proportions in small developing countries for which the failing enterprise may be one of the main sources of essential capital, technology, skills, goods, services and employment. The failure of BCCI provided an instructive illustration of the consequences of a transnational failure for a large number of industrial and commercial enterprises and projects, mainly in developing countries, that relied on that bank for international financing.

The economic and social costs of a transnational failure inevitably reach the consumer and taxpayer. It is not uncommon to see the prices of insurance policies increase as a result of major failures of enterprises. Similarly, major rescue operations by Governments are likely to be financed from public resources. The multi-billion dollar rescue effort to protect uninsured depositors in the savings and loans failures in the United States is an example of the kind of massive public disbursements that may be needed to mitigate the consequences of major failures.

2. Shortcomings of unilateral actions

In general, bankruptcy laws are national in scope and aim at protecting the interests of the State, employees, creditors, contractors and shareholders within the jurisdiction to which they apply. Transnational bankruptcies present a number of problems that are not addressed by such legislation.

Box XI.1. The United States Bankruptcy Code

Bankruptcy cases in the United States are administered under the Bankruptcy Reform Act of 1978, as amended (11 U.S.C. Chapters 101 et seq., effective since 1 October 1979) (the "Bankruptcy Code"). Prior to its enactment, bankruptcies were administered under the so-called Bankruptcy Act of 1898, as amended. The current Bankruptcy Code seeks to provide greater flexibility for debtors in the reorganization and rehabilitation of their businesses.[1] For example, in the so-called Chapter 11 (reorganization) case under the Bankruptcy Code, debtors are normally left in possession of their property and business, and no receiver or trustee is appointed to take over the debtors' affairs. During a reorganization, the "debtors-in-possession", as the debtors are called, may continue to operate the business, needing specific court authority only for certain statutorily enumerated functions and for activities not in the ordinary course of business. A debtor-in-possession can reject unduly burdensome executory contracts (including labour agreements in certain circumstances) and leases. Moreover, debtors-in-possession have virtually all of the powers of a trustee (allowing them to avoid and recover preferential and fraudulent transfers, compel turnovers of their properties and challenge the claims and security interests of their creditors). At the same time, the creditors are held at bay by operation of the automatic stay, preventing enforcement of their claims during the reorganization case. Moreover, under the so-called "cramdown" provisions of the Bankruptcy Code, debtors-in-possession can obtain bankruptcy court approval of their plans of reorganization, notwithstanding the objection of one or more secured and unsecured creditors. Indeed, that shift in favour of debtors under the Bankruptcy Code has promoted the use of bankruptcy as a "business tool", prompting such well-known bankruptcy cases as those filed by some major United States airlines, including Continental Airlines, Eastern Airlines, Braniff Airlines and PanAmerican Airlines; major retailers such as R. H. Macy & Co., Federated Department Stores and Allied Department Stores; and other large United States corporations and businesses, such as Texaco, LTV Corporation and A. H. Robins.

Section 304 of the Bankruptcy Code

Section 304 of the Bankruptcy Code is best summarized, perhaps, by quoting pertinent parts of its legislative history:

"This section governs cases filed in the bankruptcy courts that are ancillary to foreign proceedings. That is, where a foreign bankruptcy case is pending concerning a particular debtor and that debtor has assets in this country, the foreign representative may file a petition under this section, which does not commence a full bankruptcy case, in order to administer assets located in this country, to prevent dismemberment by local creditors of assets located here, or for other appropriate relief. The debtor is given the opportunity to controvert the petition.

/.....

National laws usually provide for the appointment of liquidators to determine the liabilities, realize the assets and distribute assets equitably among those creditors of bankrupt firms who have proved their claims. As a result of a company's transnationality, however, the assets in one national jurisdiction may not match the liabilities in that jurisdiction, so that one State may find more than enough assets to satisfy the claimants and another can have a shortfall. Hence creditors in one country could be fully paid, while those in another country might receive much less than the full amount of their claims, or might not even be paid at all. Furthermore, most bankruptcy laws give priority in distributions to the Government for

(Box XI.1, cont'd.)

"Subsection (c) [of Section 304] requires the court to consider several factors in determining what relief, if any, to grant. The court is to be guided by what will best assure an economical and expeditious administration of the estate, consistent with just treatment of all creditors and equity security holders; protection of local creditors and equity security holders against prejudice and inconvenience in processing claims and interests in the foreign proceeding; prevention of preferential or fraudulent disposition of property of the estate; distribution of the proceeds of the estate substantially in conformity with the distribution provisions of the bankruptcy code; and, if the debtor is an individual, the provision of an opportunity for a fresh start. Those guidelines are designed to give the court the maximum flexibility in handling ancillary cases. Principles of international comity and respect for the judgements and laws of other nations suggests that the court be permitted to make the appropriate orders under all of the circumstances of each case, rather than being provided with inflexible rules."[2]

There was no comparable provision to Section 304 in the former Bankruptcy Act of 1898. One section of the former Act authorized the bankruptcy court to exercise, withhold or suspend exercise of jurisdiction when a bankrupt had be adjudged bankrupt by a court outside of the United States.[3] Before Section 304 was enacted, a foreign representative seeking relief involving assets located in the United States had to resort to litigation in state or federal non-bankruptcy courts or had to subject the debtor's estate to a full bankruptcy case.

The administration of ancillary cases under Section 304 has shown that Section 304 is far from perfect. The flexibility given to the bankruptcy courts under Section 304 has led to some inconsistent and confusing results.[4] In brief, Section 304 embodies a strong departure of historical United States policy towards foreign bankruptcies. Section 304 has been utilized in the BCCI case in the Bankruptcy Court in the Southern District of New York; its use in this case and others has undoubtedly increased awareness of its availability among bankruptcy practitioners. This, coupled with the increasing globalization of business, should invoke its more frequent use in the future.

---

1 See, for example, Thomas Hollanger (1981), *Bankruptcy Reporter*, vol. 15, No. 19 (Minnesota, West's Publishing Co., 1982), p. 35. ("There is an express Congressional policy in favour of rehabilitating debtors and maintaining the equity in their property"), p. 48.

2 H. R. No. 95-595, 95th Congress (1977), 1st Session, pp. 324-325; S. Rep. No. 95-989, 95th Congress (1978), 2nd Session, p. 35.

3 See, Comment to Section 304 of the Bankruptcy Code, *1991/1992 Collier Pamphlet Edition* (New York, Matthew Bender & Company, 1991), p. 97.

4 For further discussion, see, Jay L. Westbrook, "Theory and pragmatism in global insolvencies: choice of law and choice of forum", *American Bankruptcy Law Journal*, vol. 65 (1991), pp. 471-483; and Richard A. Gitlin and Evan D. Flaschen, "The international void in the law of multinational bankruptcies", *Business Lawyer*, vol. 42 (1987), pp. 317-325.

taxes owed and to employees for their wages. But a priority in one country may not be recognized in ancillary liquidation proceedings in another.

In other words, there is no mechanism to provide for the fair distribution of the assets of a bankrupt firm on a transnational basis. An example of legislation allowing liquidators to file a petition in another jurisdiction's bankruptcy proceedings in order to prevent dismemberment by local creditors of local assets is Section 304 of the United States Bankruptcy Code (box XI.1). But those examples are rare. As a consequence, in a transnational bankruptcy the liquidators may try to find and keep as many assets as possible in their jurisdiction—a kind of "ring fencing". That can lead to inequities and, furthermore, make it impossible to realize the true value of the assets of a TNC , which could be greater as a going transnational concern than the sum of its national parts.

The matter becomes even more complex in situations in which a TNC operates in some countries through branches and in others through locally incorporated subsidiaries. Within a group of companies, some subsidiaries may be only partially owned, making the determination of assets and liabilities more intricate.

Intra-group transactions further complicate the distribution of assets and liabilities as transactions result in debit and credit balances that can be quickly altered between jurisdictions when financial difficulties or collapse is expected. Transfer pricing at more or less than fair market values can serve the same purpose. Moreover, there may be some time-lags between the failure of individual units of a TNC located in different countries. The "timing" of individual failures may be manipulated by the enterprise concerned to favour certain creditors, or protect certain assets.

It may be difficult for liquidators in a transnational bankruptcy to locate and identify certain assets because of the confidentiality and secrecy laws of some jurisdictions that have been used to hide or protect assets from creditors. Such information is necessary to determine what assets could be salvaged and how to value them. There are very few international or bilateral agreements that require cooperation or the exchange of information in such circumstances. Furthermore, in certain jurisdictions, some assets may not be convertible or realizable at real market value owing, for example, to the non-convertibility of certain currencies, exchange control regulations or to restrictions on the transfer of land.

Those problems illustrate a fact found in many transnational failures that the interests of creditors of TNCs as a group may be similar, but the differences in the laws of national jurisdictions can lead to different treatment and, consequently, to inequities and conflicts. The law favours those countries that are in possession of assets rather than assuring the fairness of multinational claims.

Moreover, while there are procedures and mechanisms that are set in motion at the national level to avoid the liquidation of a failing enterprise and thus prevent some of the negative consequences of a closure of a major enterprise, they do not have any counterparts at the international level. The aim of such mechanisms is to protect the interests of creditors, beneficiaries, shareholders, employees, subcontractors, clients and other innocent parties who stand to be adversely affected if the liquidation were allowed to proceed. Public interest calls for maintaining confidence in the economic and social system and thus can justify the rescue of financial institutions as well as basic utilities and vital industries. The multi-billion dollar rescue effort to protect uninsured depositors, including the establishment of the Resolution Trust Corporation to guarantee the savings and loan associations in the United States, is a recent example of such mechanisms. Indeed, the vigorous implementation of such rescue mechanisms at the national level may even impede the resolution (especially the fair resolution) of the problem at the international level.

In summary, the potential costs of the current state of affairs for transnational business can be considerable. An analyst summarized the status quo as follows:

> "There are two categories of costs imposed by the current punitive regime. The most important is the inability to predict the results of defaults, which adds to the costs of every international transaction, especially international financing.....The second type of cost arises in the insolvency process itself. The present incoherent system destroys values that would otherwise be available to claimants in the enterprise, including commercial creditors, employers, tort victims, customers and shareholders. The destruction of values affects both reorganization and liquidation. The use of reorganization to maintain going concern values is almost impossible..." [11]

3. Possible international approaches

In the case of the failure of a TNC, liquidation under one or more national jurisdictions is not likely to produce satisfactory results - either to preserve the firm, or to realize the maximum value of the assets or to protect the interests of innocent parties in an equitable manner. Conventional approaches to preserving the viable portions of a TNC require that there be going concern values, at least in part. They also require information about what can be preserved and what is beyond recovery. All of this becomes more difficult in a transnational situation.

In those situations, increasing cooperation among national authorities would be an initial step forward towards avoiding some of the problems outlined above, while other, more comprehensive approaches, are being explored. Such cooperation could take several forms. Firstly, cooperation along sectoral lines may allow the utilization of existing networks and agreements between countries and institutions (as in the cases of banking and insurance). Secondly, cooperation on a non-strictly binding basis (as in the case of banks) may be useful. Thirdly, disclosure to appropriate national authorities of a TNC's activities and problems in other countries may help prevent ultimate failures.

Especially where the going concern values are substantial, international cooperation, based on a global approach, offers the best opportunity to preserve those values and, hence, minimize losses to all concerned.

Effective international cooperation on those matters may require the conclusion of an international agreement to fill the international void in this area. Indeed, to date, there have been few treaties dealing with bankruptcies or insolvency questions. Among these are the Bustamante Code of Private International

Law (1928), [12] ratified by 15 Latin American countries, and the Scandinavian Convention, adopted in 1933 and ratified by Denmark, Finland, Iceland, Norway and Sweden. [13] The European Community has yet to ratify a bankruptcy instrument. Some States, however, may accede to the draft Strasbourg Convention, a proposal for international cooperation in insolvency matters (including a provision allowing a liquidator appointed in one member country to act as such in another). Similarly, the draft Benelux Bankruptcy Convention has not yet been ratified. The United States is not yet a party to any treaties concerning bankruptcy, though there have been some sporadic attempts to conclude one with Canada. [14]

An international instrument could build upon the existing efforts while bringing them up to date to match the complexities of the emerging international production system. It could provide for, among other things, the exchange of information (thus overriding secrecy provisions under national legislation) on the firm's assets and liabilities, operations, branches, affiliates, shareholders, creditors etc., and the coordination of activities regarding the protection of assets and going concern values. In addition, the instrument could include provisions concerning the allocation of primary and secondary jurisdictions among the countries concerned; the notification of legal actions; judicial assistance with respect to claims, proceedings, the execution of settlements and their implementation between the countries involved. Such provisions would help to avoid a multiplicity of legal proceedings (and their high costs), as well as "ring fencing" and similar defensive actions by local authorities in transnational failures. Such an instrument could also prescribe the creation of such mechanisms as joint teams of experts to assess the overall situation; a joint executive body to design, where feasible, a scheme for the restructuring of an enterprise and, where that is not the case, to determine equitable distribution; a supervisory board to supervise a rescue operation; and mutually agreed dispute-settlement mechanisms to deal with conflicts arising from a restructuring. An international agreement to deal with such matters could be concluded at the bilateral level (based on mutual obligations and reciprocity) or at the multilateral level, or both. Given the fact that major TNCs tend to operate globally, however, a multilateral treaty may provide the most appropriate format for dealing effectively with all the parties concerned in a TNC failure.

The harmonization of standards at the multilateral level to ensure that the same meaning is ascribed to the key terms and concepts used could be another important aspect of intergovernmental cooperation. Harmonization of accounting and reporting standards could result in easier and clearer analysis and interpretation of financial information. International cooperation among external auditors could be required, along with timely communication with primary and other regulatory authorities. Information and disclosure requirements, as well as auditing standards, need to be improved.

Those are some options available in order to deal with failures of TNCs in a world of multiple jurisdictions. It would be worthwhile to examine those and others in order to arrive at mechanisms that would allow Governments to deal more effectively and equitably with failures of TNCs.

In conclusion, the same need and desire for commercial certainty that prompts international cooperation in the areas of trade, finance and FDI applies with equal force to the area of business insolvency. [15] However, relative to progress made in recent years in other areas, efforts to coordinate rules in the area of insolvency lag far behind. As one author put it: "At present the legal treatment of troubled multinationals is primitive and chaotic...[T]he development of sensible and efficient management of commercial default is a crucial element of the integration of the world economy".[16] The emergence of an international production system, with TNCs as its central actors, underlines the importance of action in this area.

C. Mechanisms to support foreign direct investment

In the past few years, developing countries have made great efforts to attract FDI by liberalizing and simplifying their FDI regimes, including, among other things, opening virtually all their industries to foreign investors, instituting privatization programmes that permit the participation of foreign investors, increasing fiscal incentives, relaxing performance requirements, guaranteeing the repatriation of profits, expediting screening and approval and providing one-stop services (see, for example, annex table 11).[17] Yet, for many of these countries, those efforts have not led to increased FDI flows and, for developing countries overall, their share in global FDI flows is still declining.

There are a few specific home country programmes aimed at encouraging TNCs to invest in developing countries.[18] Many of those relate to the protection of FDI, especially in the form of guarantees to foreign investors (that is, home country TNCs) concerning nationalization and expropriation and the conflicts associated with such actions. Those were important issues at a time when relations between TNCs and host countries were antagonistic, and nationalizations occurred frequently. However, circumstances have changed entirely, and much of the tension between TNCs and host countries has disappeared, as evidenced by the sharp drop in the number of expropriation acts from a peak of 83 in 1975 to 1 in 1985; since then, barely any nationalizations have taken place.[19] Apart from guarantees, a number of home countries offer some information and promotion services to their TNCs, some fiscal incentives (mostly in the framework of double taxation treaties) and some financial assistance (through public development finance corporations) for feasibility studies, co-financing or loan-guarantees. However, resources devoted to such purposes are generally quite small. At the moment (and with some exceptions), such support is given only to small and medium-size enterprises investing abroad.[20]

A number of international organizations such as the International Finance Corporation, the Multilateral Investment Guarantee Agency of the World Bank, ICSID, UNIDO and the Transnational Corporations and Management Division of the United Nations Department of Economic and Social Development, also participate in activities involving the co-financing of joint ventures, feasibility studies, investment guarantees or the provision of information-, promotional- or technical-assistance services. Yet, as noted before, the share of the developing countries in FDI flows continues to decline.

Thus, it may be useful to review the current national, bilateral and multilateral efforts to examine whether they could be re-directed in a more pro-active manner towards augmenting the flow of FDI and creating a more appropriate investment environment in developing countries. For instance, the national agencies in developed countries dealing with outward investment could pay more attention to the financing of feasibility studies, tax breaks for FDI infrastructure, the establishment of service parks for basic business services etc. Similarly, bilateral investment treaties for the protection and promotion of investment, which typically focus on the protection aspect, could pay more attention to the promotion of FDI flows to developing countries (box XI.2). Perhaps national FDI facilities need to be established which, similar to various programmes aimed at the promotion of exports, could dedicate themselves to the promotion of outward FDI to developing countries.

While all encouragement should be given to strengthen the current mechanisms at the national, bilateral and multilateral levels, a new impetus to multilateral efforts may be needed in the light of the crucial role of FDI as an engine of growth.

More specifically, one could consider establishing a multilateral FDI facility with a view to providing loans to developing countries to promote development through FDI (see box XI.3 for some of the types of activities that could be supported in this way). Such a facility, distinct from a multilateral ODA facility, would have to be geared specifically to FDI issues. While the objectives of ODA are of a general nature and aim at improving the overall infrastructure and policy environment of developing countries (particularly in the least developed coun-

Box XI.2. How bilateral investment treaties could be made more promotional

In principle, bilateral investment treaties deal not only with the protection, but also with the promotion of FDI. But many questions arise in connection with the promotional aspects of these treaties. An initial question is that regard is whether it is the host country, the home country or both that have an obligation to encourage investment. In current treaty practice, the obligation seems to fall more heavily on the host country. But, even then, bilateral investment treaties are not clear about the types of promotional measures that should be adopted to promote investment from the other country (whether it refers simply to laws and policies, or may include also the improvement of physical conditions, such as infrastructure, power supplies etc.). One may also ask whether bilateral investment treaties impose a reciprocal obligation on the home country to encourage its nationals and companies to invest in the territory of the treaty partner. Generally, the capital-exporting countries have taken the position that encouraging their nationals to invest in the other country is not their responsibility under the treaty.

Nevertheless, in the spirit of reciprocity, which forms the basis of bilateral relationships, capital-importing countries could seek to obtain some commitment that the capital-exporting country will take positive steps to encourage investment in the other country. In that respect, the Fourth Lomé Convention between African, Caribbean and Pacific (ACP) countries and the European Community provides a useful example of the type of promotional efforts that may be incorporated in bilateral investment treaties. Those include encouraging the flow of information on investment opportunities and the nature and availability of investment guarantees; providing assistance to small and medium-size enterprises in designing and obtaining equity and loan financing; exploring ways of overcoming or reducing the host-country risk for individual investment projects; providing assistance in strengthening the host country's capacity to improve the quality of feasibility studies and project preparation so that the appropriate economic and financial conclusions might be drawn; producing integrated management mechanisms covering the entire project management cycle within the framework of the development programme of the host State; and institutionalizing periodic discussions between any interested private investors and the host country. Alternatively, a cross-reference in particular bilateral investment treaties to relevant provisions of the Fourth Lomé Convention or other similar interregional or multilateral schemes would be a helpful reminder of the type of promotional measures that capital-exporting countries could take to promote investment in their partner countries.

Box. XI.3. Supporting foreign direct investment

Elements of an FDI facility—albeit in a regional context—already exist in some multilateral institutions. One noteworthy example is that of the Inter-American Development Bank (IDB) which is in the process of implementing two related programmes in response to the Enterprise for the Americas Initiative: the Investment Sector Loan Program and the Multilateral Investment Fund. Another is the European Community's Investment Partners facility.

Coinciding with reforms already under way in countries of Latin America and the Caribbean to increase economic growth and international competitiveness, the Enterprise for the Americas Initiative proposes to harness and strengthen those trends through encouraging trade, investment and the reduction of debt. The investment component of the Initiative, which continues to be defined in greater detail, seeks to create a competitive environment for attracting new capital and the return of flight capital to the hemisphere. To stimulate economic reforms and the liberalization of investment regimes, the Initiative gives a specific mandate to the IDB to implement the two programmes mentioned above, namely, the Investment Sector Loan Program and the Multilateral Investment Fund.

The Investment Sector Loan Program provides adjustment loans to countries committed to removing impediments to investment and fostering open investment regimes. Specific investment reforms encouraged by the loans include:

- adoption of clear and transparent investment regimes hospitable to all investors;
- measures to encourage the return of flight capital;
- opening of the financial sectors to competition, and modernization of financial services and markets to facilitate private investment;
- privatization of state-owned enterprises;
- adoption of international dispute settlement procedures to arbitrate investment disputes.

The IDB has already negotiated investor sector loans totaling $485 million with the Governments of Bolivia, Chile, Colombia and Jamaica.

In a parallel effort, the *Multilateral Investment Fund* (projected to reach $1.5 billion over five years) is meant to facilitate the adoption of comprehensive investment reforms by providing grant and loan financing for the following three purposes:

- technical assistance to identify and implement policy changes needed to transform the climate for investment;
- human resource development to meet the needs of an expanded private sector;
- credit and equity financing and technical assistance to small enterprises.

Twenty-one countries signed the Multilateral Investment Fund agreement in February 1992, pledging a total of $1.2 billion to the Fund. The United States has expressed its intent to contribute $500 million to the Fund over a five-year period. The other major contributors to the Fund are Japan ($500 million), Spain ($50 million), Canada and Germany ($30 million each).

/.....

tries), an FDI facility would focus solely on FDI issues. If that is done, caution should be exercised that such a facility does not merely subsidize TNCs wishing to invest in developing countries. In addition, there should be a clear demarcation line between the use of an FDI facility for FDI-supporting activities and the traditional uses of development funds, such as improving infrastructure, which will have an indirect impact on FDI promotion.

(Box XI.3, cont'd.)

To promote mutually advantageous economic cooperation between the members of the European Community (EC) and the countries of the Mediterranean, the *European Community's Investment Partners* (ECIP) facility was created. Launched in September 1988 on an experimental basis, ECIP is designed to enable participating developing countries to realize the potential of FDI in their development process. To that end, ECIP offers financial support covering:

- grants to financial institutions, chambers of commerce, professional associations and public agencies for the identification of potential projects and partners;
- interest-free advances for feasibility studies and other actions to firms intending to set up joint ventures or to invest;
- capital requirements of a joint venture or a local company with licensing agreements, in order to meet investment risks peculiar to developing countries, through participation in the provision of equity, or by equity loans;
- interest-free advances for training, technical assistance or management expertise of an existing joint venture, or joint ventures about to be set up, or a local company with licensing agreements.

One innovative aspect of ECIP is its largely decentralized functioning through a network of financial institutions (official development banks, private sector investment banks or multilateral institutions) which promote the instrument with their clientele, receive and evaluate project proposals and requests for financing, intervene as financial intermediaries between the EC and the final beneficiaries, act as partners in projects and ensure the follow-up and monitoring of the projects. At the end of February 1992, the network included 54 financial institutions located in EC member States and the participating developing countries.

The total financial support provided by ECIP to a single investment project is ECU 1,000,000. As of 31 December 1991, 285 projects had been approved for financial assistance. Over half of the financing requests concerned feasibility studies and pilot projects.

In light of the potential of ECIP to realize economic cooperation objectives, the EC Parliament, in a resolution adopted on 3 February 1992, proposed to continue, extend and improve the functioning of ECIP for a further three-year period starting 1 January 1992.

Sources: United States, Department of Commerce, *Enterprise for the Americas Initiative*, February 1992; *The IDB*, November 1991; *LA/C Business Bulletin*, March 1992; *Business America*, March 1992; and Commission of the European Communities, *E.C. International Investment Partners*, Directorate of External Relations, Brussels, 1991.

Perhaps, such a facility could consist of a capital-investment fund and of a fund through which other activities are financed. The capital-investment fund could provide credit to developing countries for the establishment of export-processing zones, science parks, service parks and similar facilities that would help attract FDI to a country. Finance for other activities could cover, for instance, technical assistance, information activities, the preparation of country assessment studies and the establishment of contacts between potential foreign investors and host country firms (including potential joint venture partners). What is critically important is to provide adequate resources for such a facility and to entrust it to an agency that can operate it effectively and provide a range of integrated services in harmony with the perspectives of developing countries, home countries, as well as TNCs.

A special window of the facility could be devoted to the promotion of outward FDI by TNCs from developing countries, enabling those firms to become more competitive in the world economy. Although cumulative outward FDI from developing countries for the period 1970-1990 reached $35 billion, this represented only 3 per cent of global FDI outflows and originated mainly from a small number of Asian and, to a lesser extent, Latin American developing countries. Increases in outward FDI by developing countries have several potential benefits, such as securing supplies of raw materials, providing access to new technologies and markets and, generally, making developing country firms more competitive in the world market.[21] A proposed FDI facility could therefore also be used to promote outward investment from developing countries.

In sum, a multilateral FDI facility, especially if established as a tripartite venture between host and home countries and TNCs, could give a new impetus to FDI flows to developing countries and, in that manner, contribute to their overall development.

D. Transparency and policy review

Policies on FDI affect the overall level, sectoral composition and direction of capital flows and the trade, technology, training and financial flows associated with them, as well as the degree and type of production integration effected between countries.[22] As a result, national FDI policies in one country affect economic performance in other countries, especially given the importance of FDI in the world economy and the role of TNCs as integrating agents of various international economic flows. Various measures, including trade measures and measures aimed directly at FDI, can divert FDI flows from one country to another; this is likely to become more important in the future, as many countries are viewing TNCs in a more positive light and are increasing their efforts to attract FDI. Where countries form part of an integrating region, their separate FDI policies are important determinants in the allocation of FDI within the region, while their common policies can cause FDI to be diverted from other locations.[23] In addition to FDI, other variables are also affected by policies relating to TNCs. For instance, export-performance requirements affect the trade balances of a country's trading partners (by increasing imports and/or reducing exports), as well as possibly leading to disinvestment from those countries. Requirements related to the local sourcing of technology can cause a reduction of R&D activities in other locations.

Home-country policies to encourage outward FDI in particular regions or sectors also influence the distribution and composition of FDI. Policy-making in the area of FDI thus carries international, as well as national, implications.

In order to construct effective policy frameworks, policy makers require information about a wide variety of interactions at both the national and the international levels. In the context of increasing international production, both Governments and TNCs rarely have access to all the information needed to understand the complex processes by which such integration is taking place. Hence they are often unable to evaluate properly the potential consequences of a given policy decision and its interrelation with policies in other countries. Furthermore, deep integration effected through FDI involves a degree of convergence of national policies that impact national sovereignty to a far greater degree than integration effected through trade liberalization. Thus, improved access to information about international investment policies and the analysis of those policies is critical to effective policy-making that promotes an efficient international production system for Governments and TNCs alike.

1. International transparency of investment policies

(a) The rationale

An important step in creating a more cooperative, open environment for FDI is to increase international transparency in the area of FDI policies. [24] Currently, no notification and verification mechanism exists through which Governments make their FDI policies, laws and regulations readily, and in an authoritative manner, available to each other and to foreign investors. In part, this reflects the fact that FDI is not governed by an international framework of rules that would necessitate international notification and reporting as a means of ensuring that the signatories are adhering to their commitments. Despite the absence of such a framework, however, there is still a need to increase international transparency in the area of FDI, by providing information regarding FDI policies of both home and host countries to a wide range of parties.

Currently, international transparency is required in the area of trade, where the contracting parties to GATT are obliged to inform the Secretariat about their trade policies on a regular basis. Other international organizations, such as IMF, the World Bank and OECD, routinely collect information regarding policies in their relevant areas of responsibility; however, none of them provides a mechanism for international transparency for all countries in the area of FDI.

A mechanism is therefore needed through which information on policies relating to both inward and outward FDI can be collected and disseminated in an authoritative manner. It certainly would be desirable if a large number of countries would participate in such a process in order to provide a comprehensive overview of prevailing policy regimes. Policy instruments that could be subject to greater international transparency would include, at a minimum, those that directly bear upon the activities of TNCs, in particular, FDI policy statements, laws, regulations and administrative guidelines (including those relating to incentives and performance requirements), bilateral investment treaties, double taxation treaties and instruments dealing with technology transfer and the repatriation of earnings. In addition, policies that significantly impact the locational decisions and activities of TNCs could also be made more transparent; those might include, for instance, certain laws and regulations regarding employment, the environment and intellectual property rights. While transparency could not extend to cover contracts and agreements between Governments and TNCs (since most of them are not in the public domain), those contracts that are published in official gazettes could be included. In sum, it would be helpful if a country's overall FDI regime could be made more transparent, and could include those policies that might apply most directly to TNCs.

(b) The benefits of increased transparency of investment policies

Increasing international transparency in the area of investment policies carries a number of benefits for multilateral agencies, for home and host countries and for TNCs, especially small- and medium-size ones and those from developing countries. Increasingly, FDI matters are at the heart of international and bilateral policy discussions on issues such as trade and technology. The growth of Japanese FDI in the United States and Europe, for example, is likely to influence any future discussions in the area of trade with Japan; similarly, European Community technology policy, which promotes joint research programmes, will increasingly have to consider the implications of the growing numbers of non-European TNCs active in high-technology industries in the Community.

Given those interlinkages, it is important to monitor the FDI policies of countries. Otherwise, the international community is likely to encounter increasing difficulties in constructing policies to promote a stable and efficient functioning of the international economic system. As outlined above, such transparency would encourage efforts to create a more favourable environment for FDI flows, and would also support multilateral efforts in related areas, such as trade and technology. In brief, greater transparency would contribute to a better functioning of the international market mechanism.

Host countries would also benefit from increased access to information on FDI policies. By disseminating information about their regulatory frameworks that govern FDI, countries facilitate the decision-making processes of TNCs, especially those of small or medium-size and those from developing countries, which may have limited capacities to obtain relevant regulatory information. In the current environment of increased liberalization, many host countries are instituting policy regimes that are more favourable towards FDI than they were in the past; in order for such policy shifts to have their desired effect, it is necessary for them to be made public in a systematic and unbiased manner. Furthermore, by having ready access to information concerning home-country policies, host countries may be able to tailor their inward FDI policies more effectively. Increased international transparency also relieves host countries of the need to convey legal information to foreign investors on a one-to-one basis.

Greater international transparency of FDI policies would also be beneficial to host countries by improving their bargaining position *vis-à-vis* foreign investors. If information about the regulatory regime for FDI is easily available, it may be less likely that foreign investors could encourage competition among potential host countries for a given investment through the granting of ever-more generous concessions. While increasing transparency would not eliminate competitive bidding for FDI—Governments and TNCs are free to negotiate and enter any agreement of their choice—it would at least take place in a more open environment. In addition, greater transparency allows host countries to judge more accurately the costs and benefits of agreements with TNCs, and hence to make better decisions regarding their contributions.

From the perspective of TNCs, increased transparency of investment laws would enable them to make better FDI decisions in an overall improved policy environment for their international activities. Many large TNCs have the resources to access the information they need concerning investment policies. Thus, among TNCs, the primary beneficiaries would be those that lack the means to engage in large-scale information-gathering, that is, small and medium-size TNCs and those from developing countries.

Even for larger TNCs, one of the ways in which increased transparency would improve the climate for FDI is by providing TNCs with readily accessible information about a large number of host countries, presented in a standardized format by a neutral party. Currently, there is no such authoritative mechanism available, and it is possible that incomplete information is, in some cases, resulting in an allocation of FDI that favours a limited number of developing countries which engage in extensive investment-promotion activities.

Other important reasons why transparency improves the investment climate for TNCs is that it helps promote the stability of investment policies (countries are less likely to resort to frequent rule changes if such changes are consistently recorded), and it lessens the power of special interest groups to influence domestic policy. Both factors are important elements in facilitating an objective assessment by TNCs of host-country regulatory frameworks.

(c) Options for implementation

To increase the international transparency of regulatory frameworks for FDI, Governments could undertake to inform an international agency of their policies, laws, regulations and administrative guidelines that bear directly upon the activities of TNCs. Information could also be provided on instruments that have significant impact on the locational decisions and activities of TNCs. Every effort should be made to encourage all countries to participate in the process.

The designated agency would compile the submissions in a standardized format, organized by a reporting country, and supplemented by information obtained from other sources. The presentation of each country's regulatory framework would be sent by the agency to the competent official authorities of the country for verification or, to facilitate the process, to one national contact point designated by the Government. The agency could also send the presentation to other interested parties for comments; such parties could include other international organizations, Governments of other countries and private entities (for example, chambers of commerce).

After verification, the information would be published and disseminated widely in the form of an authoritative catalogue. The publication would contain, on a country basis, the names and sources of the policy statements, laws, regulations and administrative guidelines comprising the FDI framework. As a further service, the catalogue could also highlight important regulatory instruments through brief descriptions and include selected statistics about the country's FDI position (both inward and outward) to present a more complete picture of the investment climate of a given country. The reports could be updated regularly and disseminated widely to Governments, business organizations and TNCs.

2. Foreign-direct-investment policy review

(a) The need for a review mechanism

The above discussion outlined measures to improve transparency in the area of FDI. If implemented, those measures would result in an authoritative catalogue of the policy statements, laws, regulations and administrative guidelines that comprise a country's FDI framework. While a reporting system of this type is, in and of itself, a desirable objective for both Governments and the private sector, it also provides the basis for improving investment policies through policy reviews. Such reviews would take into account the long-term, indirect consequences of a given policy, which are often greater than the direct, short-term impacts. This process, in turn, requires information about the policy in question, as well as about others which may have influenced its outcome. Unlike tariffs, which are highly visible, or subsidies, which appear in national budgets, investment measures often involve revenues foregone which are not easily traceable in national accounts; their evaluation thus depends on access to information concerning the application of relevant laws and regulations that may influence FDI flows. Furthermore, the actual implementation of a given policy may differ from its original objective, as countries pursue initiatives that differ from their regulatory framework. In addition, Governments may implement policies which, for various reasons, do not yield their desired results. Hence, in order to meet national policy objectives, it is necessary to go beyond the "raw" information contained in a catalogue of FDI measures, and to provide careful analyses and evaluations of those measures. In the long run, a strengthened policy-review system could lead to an increase in the amount and quality of FDI inflows, as a result of more effective, informed policy-making.

Another important aspect of a policy-review mechanism for home and host countries could be to promote not only an evaluation of the policy framework, but also the design of policies that are the most efficient from the viewpoint of national welfare. Often, there is an imbalance in the influence held by different economic actors on the policy-making process; for instance, producers frequently exert a disproportionate influence on policy as compared to consumers, as do urban areas compared to rural ones. In the area of FDI policy-making, domestic producers often press for limitations on the activities of TNCs, even if such limitations could be detrimental to national welfare. The result may be implicit protectionism. Conversely, Governments—whether knowingly or unknowingly—may provide special benefits to TNCs that may be unnecessary or damaging to domestic producers. Such imbalances have in some instances led to an unfavourable economic climate for investment, both domestic as well as foreign.

In such situations, the best way of ensuring that the wider national interest is being served is to open up the decision-making processes to public scrutiny and debate. International transparency of investment policies as outlined above is a necessary (though not sufficient) step in this direction. With proper information to weigh the costs and benefits of particular policies, Governments are in a better position to evaluate the choices they confront, including the weight to be attached to non-economic factors. Public choices made in this way are also likely to attract wider confidence and support in the community at large, which increases the stability of the policy framework. In order for the objectives of greater international transparency to be realized fully—increased investment flows to developing countries, a stable policy environment for FDI and the promotion of effective, equitable public policies—it is probably necessary to extend the process to include a multilateral policy review mechanism, similar to that performed by GATT in the area of trade.

The recently established GATT policy review mechanism involves systematic, periodic reviews of the trade policies of States that are parties to GATT. Such reviews are not meant to enforce specific GATT obligations or dispute settlements, nor are they intended to impose new policy commitments on member States. Rather, the review process is intended to foster greater transparency in trade policies and practices, to analyse their effectiveness against the broader context of domestic economic and development objectives and to examine the impact of such policies on the multilateral trading system.

A similar practice in the area of FDI could greatly support the efforts of countries to maximize the benefits of FDI, both inward and outward, to their economies. A review mechanism would provide to those countries requesting it an evaluation of their FDI policies, laws, regulations and administrative guidelines. The goal of the review process would be to assist countries in achieving national objectives in the specific area of FDI, as well as in related areas, such as trade performance and employment, which may be influenced by FDI policies. The review process could also promote a harmonization of national FDI policies in areas in which this is desired.

The reviews could consist of an analysis of the role of FDI (both inward and outward) in the participating country; an examination of the country's FDI regime (highlighting recent trends in the policy environment); an evaluation of the country's potential for FDI at the country, industry and perhaps major projects levels; options for realizing this potential (including through an improvement of the regulatory framework for FDI); and an outline of a comprehensive technical assistance programme aimed at assisting the country in improving its capacity to attract and benefit from FDI. The focus should be to provide an analysis of, and outline options for, the use of relevant policies and policy instruments in light of national policy objectives. Overall, the reviews should contain an objective, authoritative assessment of the participating country's FDI climate, with specific options of how to improve its FDI policy framework and realize its potential for greater investment.

Few multilateral commitments exist in the area of FDI. Reflecting this, the reviews should be carried out primarily from an economic standpoint with a view to improving policy-making through informed analysis in order to further domestic objectives, for both developed and developing countries. While an implicit objective of the review process could be to maximize the benefits of FDI while minimizing potentially negative impacts, no particular point of view regarding FDI should be promoted; rather, policies ought to be judged in light of the country's own objectives. The review process itself could be undertaken on a voluntary basis. This has the advantage of encouraging countries under review to participate actively in the process, and to benefit from outside discussions of their policy frameworks.

(b) Ways and means of implementation

A feasible investment review mechanism could be patterned on the trade-policy review mechanism of GATT. Accordingly, it could consist of the preparation of two reports, one by the Government of the country that has volunteered for a review, and the second by a competent international organization. If so desired by the Government of the country reviewed, the reports could perhaps be discussed by the United Nations Commission on Transnational Corporations, to benefit from the experiences of other countries. The reports, together with a report of the proceedings of the review meeting, could then be published and disseminated widely.

The national report could be prepared by the Government of the country concerned, and could focus principally on a description and explanation of its policies and its objectives. Governments of some countries, for example, the least developed countries, may require some technical assistance in the preparation of their own reports. To the extent possible, however, Governments should prepare their reports by themselves; it has been found in the trade-policy review mechanism of GATT that Governments learn more from the preparation of their own reports than if they use outside experts.

The second report could be prepared by a competent international agency. The contents would be based on the agency's own research, with the use of one or more questionnaires to be completed by the Government of the relevant country, and supplemented by field missions. The mission team could consist of staff of the international agency, international experts, as well as representatives from TNCs with substantial experience in the country. Alternatively, only one report could be prepared, by a team consisting of staff of the international agency, international experts, representatives of the Government and representatives of TNCs active in the country. In any event, every effort would have to be made to ensure that the report is based on careful research, is accurate and objective and presents an impartial view of the investment environment in the country.

A credible report, in turn, could become the basis of follow-up action by the Government of the country, in terms of improving its regulatory framework for FDI and realizing its investment potential. Additionally, it could become the basis of a comprehensive programme of technical cooperation aimed at assisting the country in the area of FDI. Finally, the report could also become the basis for locational decisions of foreign investors, especially small and medium-size TNCs that have only limited capacities to conduct thorough FDI assessment studies of countries in which they may wish to invest.

Notes

[1]See UNCTC, *Regional Integration and Transnational Corporations in the 1990s: Europe 1992, North America, and Developing Countries,* UNCTC Current Studies, Series A, No. 15 (United Nations publication, Sales No. E.90.II.A.14); and Transnational Corporations and Management Division, *The implications of EC economic integration on FDI to, from and within the EC,* Vol. 1 (New York, United Nations, forthcoming).

[2]UNCTC, *The Challenge of Free Economic Zones in Central and Eastern Europe: International Perspectives* (United Nations publication, Sales No. E.90.11.A.27), p. 2.

[3]This distinction is emphasized and expanded upon in Richard Pomfret, "The new trade theories, rent-snatching, and jet aircraft", *The World Economy,* vol. 14, No. 3 (September 1991), pp. 269-278.

[4]In the United States, however, the Exon-Florio provision of the Defense Production Act, enacted originally as part of the Omnibus Trade and Competitiveness Act late in 1988, grants to the President new power to block foreign takeovers of domestically-owned firms. While this new power has to date been used sparingly, there is a debate within the Congress as to whether it should be used more widely. See Edward M. Graham and Michael E. Ebert, "Foreign direct investment and United States national security: fixing Exon-Florio", *The World Economy* vol. 14, No. 3 (September 1991), pp. 245-268.

[5]This risk is not to be minimized. During the 1970s, for example, the United Kingdom attempted to develop the NIMROD, an alternative to the United States-developed air early warning system, or AWACs. The system developed by the United Kingdom was initiated in part to implement national industrial policy goals, and the effort was made to use all indigenous components. (The United States system was developed using substantial foreign content, by contrast.) One result was that the system developed by the United Kingdom was more costly than that of the United States; but, perhaps more important, the implementation of the system was delayed repeatedly. A case history is contained in Theodore H. Moran, "The globalization of the defense industry", *International Security,* vol. 15, No. 1 (Summer 1990), pp. 57-99.

[6]See, for example, J. A. Brander and B. J. Spencer, "Export subsidies and international market share rivalry", *Journal of International Economics,* vol. 18 (1985), pp. 83-100.

[7]See, for example, Paul R. Krugman, "Import competition as export promotion: international competition in the presence of oligopoly and economies of scale", in H. Kierzkowski, ed., *Monopolistic Competition and International Trade* (Oxford, Clarendon Press, 1984), pp. 180-193.

[8]See, Statistisches Bundesamt, *Statistisches Jahrbuch 1990 fuer die Bundesrepublik Deutschland* (Stuttgart, Metsler-Poeschel Verlag, 1990); Statistiska Centralbyran, *Statistik arsbok for Sverige 1989: Sveriges Officiella Statistik* (Stockholm, Norstedts Tryckeri, 1988); United States, Department of Commerce, *Survey of Current Business,* vol. 71, No. 1 (January 1991); Statistical Bureau, Management and Coordination Agency, *Japan Statistical Yearbook,* No. 41 (Tokyo, Management and Coordination Agency, 1991) , pp. 136-137; and *Japan Statistical Yearbook,* No. 40 (1990), pp. 386-387.

[9]See John M. Kline, "Testimony before the Joint Economic Committee of the United States Congress, 13 May 1992" (Washington, D.C., Georgetown University, 1992), mimeo, pp. 10-11.

[10]This section draws partly on UNCTC, "New issues for international cooperation in transnational banking" (New York, UNCTC, 1992), mimeo.

[11]See Jay L. Westbrook, "Theory and pragmatism in global insolvencies: choice of laws and choice of forum", *American Bankruptcy Law Journal,* vol. 65 (July 1991), pp. 460-461.

[12]*League of Nations Treaty Series,* vol. 86 (Geneva, League of Nations, 1929), p. 362.

[13]Ibid, vol. 155 (1935), p. 136.

[14]See Richard A. Giltin and Evan D. Flascher, "The international void in the law of multinational bankruptcies", *Business Lawyer,* vol. 42, No. 2 (February 1987), p. 487, pp. 307-325.

[15]See, for example, Report of the Insolvency Law Review Committee, *Insolvency Law and Practice,* 1982, Command Paper No. 8558, chaps. 49 and 50.

[16]Westbrook, op. cit., p. 458.

[17]On the factors influencing FDI flows, see UNCTC, *The Determinants of Foreign Direct Investment: A Survey of the Evidence* (United Nations publication, Sales No. E.92.II.A.2).

[18]See UNCTC, *Foreign Direct Investment, Debt and Home Country Policies* (United Nations publication, Sales No. E.90.II.A.16), pp. 25-41.

[19]UNCTC, *Transnational Corporations in World Development* (United Nations publication, Sales No. E.88.II.A.7), p. 314. See also Michael Minor, "Whatever happened to expropriation?" (Edinburg, Texas, The University of Texas, 1992), mimeo. For a more cautionary view for the future, see Charles R. Kennedy, Jr., "Relations between transnational corporations and Governments of host countries: a look to the future", *Transnational Corporations*, vol. 1, No. 1 (February 1992), pp. 67-92.

[20]Transnational Corporations and Management Division, *Small and Medium-sized Firms as Suppliers of Productive Resources to Developing Countries* (New York, United Nations, forthcoming).

[21]Transnational Corporations and Management Division, *Transnational Corporations from Developing Countries: Impact on Home Countries* (New York, United Nations, forthcoming).

[22]Factors besides government policies, such as market size and firm-specific advantages, are also very important (and may be even more important than policies in specific circumstances) in determining FDI flows. See UNCTC, *The Determinants of Foreign Direct Investment*, op. cit.

[23]See UNCTC, *Regional Integration and Transnational Corporations in the 1990s*, op. cit.

[24]There is a concurrent need to improve disclosure of information by TNCs, an issue that is being dealt with in the framework of the Intergovernmental Working Group of Experts on International Standards of Accounting and Reporting (ISAR) of the United Nations Commission on Transnational Corporations.

Chapter XII

A LOOK TO THE FUTURE

The world is in a period of rapid change, so much so that, as late as 1985, it would have been difficult if not impossible to predict what the world would look like by 1992. The end of the Cold War and the economic opening of Central and Eastern Europe, the unification of Germany, the rise of Japan and the relative decline of the United States as major international investors have all occurred in the past few years, and are re-defining international relations. While such rapid change makes it difficult to speculate about what the world will look like at the beginning of the twenty-first century, one thing that seems very likely is that international competition will increasingly be based on economic rather than military prowess.

Furthermore, the nature of international competition itself is being re-defined by the globalization of economic activity, such that the activities of TNCs rather than domestic firms operating within the boundaries of individual nations are likely to be key determinants of the dynamics of international competition. International production may well become one of the most, if not the most, important characteristics of the world economy in the coming years.

Not only is international production growing, it is also changing. Transnational corporations may increasingly be viewed as networks, in which intra-firm flows of capital, goods, services, training and technology play an important role, and whose major value-adding function is the integration, organization and management of those international flows. Thus, in the 1990s, the term "transnational", which describes firms whose strategies are determined more by considerations of global efficiency rather than by national borders, may become increasingly applicable to the nature of international production.

The policies that govern the world economy have not moved as quickly as have TNCs in adjusting themselves to international production. The growing role of FDI as a basis for international economic relations poses formidable challenges to policy makers. Addressing the discrepancy between the rise of international production and the policies that govern it is likely to be a key policy issue, both on the domestic and multilateral levels, in the 1990s. The increased role of TNCs in the growth and competitiveness of both home and host countries, and the role played by FDI in integrating national economies into regional and international production structures, present new issues and problems with which most national Governments have had little previous experience. Indeed, the domestic policy frameworks of most countries do not reflect the role of TNCs as integrating agents of capital, trade, technology and training flows; hence one of the first tasks of Governments in the new world economy is to adjust their policy-making structures. However, there is clearly a limit to how far domestic policies can go in addressing the international issues posed by the new world economy. In this regard, there is a risk that effective solutions to the current challenges in the international economy could be hampered by the lack of an adequate multilateral governance mechanism, since the institutions currently in place are not fully able to deal with the issues that arise in a world in which TNCs are the primary private economic actors.

A. New domestic policy issues

The emerging shape of international production poses new challenges to policy makers. First of all, the space in which TNCs act is expanding as more countries give a greater role to the private sector and market forces in their economies. The growing role of the private sector through the liberalization of FDI and trade policies, privatization and fiscal reform is likely to continue into the future. Countries face many issues in this regard, a key one being the model of public-private sector relations they choose to adopt. Very different experiences present themselves in the world economy concerning the relationship between state and market, each carrying its own set of costs and benefits. An important consideration in this respect is that the policies that Governments adopt *vis-à-vis* the private sector will influence their ability to attract investment by TNCs in a highly competitive world FDI market. Going hand-in-hand with the greater role that the private sector is meant to play are expectations that TNCs can make a significant contribution in such major tasks of the 1990s as the need to shift towards a more environmentally sustainable growth path (especially by introducing new technologies); efforts to address migration pressures (by alleviating such pressures through investment in source countries); and the transition of the countries of Central and Eastern Europe to market economies (by engaging themselves strongly in that process through FDI). Such expectations need to be examined carefully, and the limits to the role that TNCs can play in meeting them need to be recognized. Finally, the choices that countries make regarding the management of the private sector will, in an increasingly integrated world economy, become issues of not just domestic but international concern as well (see below).

The priorities of domestic policy regimes are also likely to be affected by the changing nature of international production. Rapidly-developing communications technologies are likely to increase greatly the tradability of services, especially of those that have a high information or know-how content. The nature of FDI will be further changed by that trend, allowing TNCs to create an international division of labour in the production of many services as they are already doing in the production of goods. Such a trend would affect both developed and developing countries alike, and it is likely to affect the nature of economic policy-making. With the services sector having become the largest sector in most countries by the early 1990s, its importance will be fully recognized by the end of the century. By that time, economic management policies will likely focus on the services sector, precisely to reflect the importance of this sector in the world economy and in world-wide FDI flows. Technology policy will also probably be given higher priority on national agendas. Indeed, services sector policies, technology policies and human resources policies may in the future overshadow industrial policies as the prime areas of state and market interaction. Those policies, in turn, in both home and host countries, will have to pay special attention to the role of TNCs. Indeed, countries may need to design integrated policy packages centred on FDI, but addressing simultaneously technology and trade issues in order to derive maximum benefit from the activities of TNCs.

Finally, the globalization of economic activity poses a whole new set of policy issues that needs to be dealt with on both national and international levels. The globalization of firms is creating international production structures that represent a new, more far-reaching level of economic integration than was previously accomplished through international trade. Host countries are faced with the prospect of a growing role for non-national firms in their economies; home countries, too, must deal with the challenges that are posed by outward FDI. Among the new issues facing policy makers in that respect is that many countries, especially small ones, may increasingly become specialized in particular stages of an industry as TNCs organize international production by locating discrete value-adding activities among several different locations according to the latters' comparative advantages in the industry in question. Thus, individual countries may become constrained in their ability to develop independent industries dominated by national firms; indeed, such a strategy may prove detrimental to national competitiveness for some countries in certain industries. National policies regarding industrial and services-sector development, trade and technology will thus increasingly have to take into account the global nature of many industries and the policies of other countries in those industries.

B. New international policy challenges

One of the greatest challenges which the policy community will face in the future is that policy-making with respect to a number of issues relating to the management and regulation of firms may be moving, at least partly, from the national to the international arena.[1] In part, that would be required by the logic of international production which weakens national policies in their ability to regulate national economic activities. In part, that will be required by the fact that the distinction between home and host countries is becoming increasingly blurred; some of the developed countries are also major hosts to FDI and some developing countries have emerged as noteworthy investors in both developed and developing countries. Potential policy areas include, in particular, competition policy and corporate law, investment incentives and technology policy, but also infrastructure-development policies and industrial, services and labour policies. More generally, larger parts of the domestic policy-making domain are likely to become increasingly subject to international policy-making, as the rise of international production could lead to more frequent systems friction, or competition between national approaches to economic management.[2] For example, the behaviour of TNCs is to a certain extent affected by the approach to private-sector management adopted by their home countries; the international activities of Japanese TNCs differ from those of United States TNCs in part because of different home-country policy frameworks. In that regard, problems may arise between countries as the level of FDI between them rises. Japanese TNCs may pursue strategies that are considered normal practice in Japan but anti-competitive in the United States, and vice versa. In another example of how domestic policies can become issues of international concern, conflicting requirements placed on TNCs by different countries can lead to disputes at the international level over basic issues of governance that extend to political, social and environmental concerns.

Such problems multiply significantly in a world in which FDI flows to many countries and integration occurs at the production level. They pose a challenge to the international community, whose task is to resolve issues that arise from different approaches to what are increasingly common problems. Consequently, multilateral mechanisms may be needed to deal with the growing interdependence of national economies at the level of production, especially to create a proper enabling framework for international production and to reconcile potential conflicts of interest between countries.

The importance of a multilateral approach is also underlined by the tendency that, as industries become more globalized simultaneously with a greater role accorded to market forces in national policy-making, a part of economic decision-making power over who gets what, when, where and how is shifting to TNCs. One important issue in that regard concerns the development of and access to new technology, which is, after all, at the heart of economic welfare and growth. Technological advances are promoting increasing globalization by shrinking economic space, as well as affecting profoundly the ways in which corporations organize their global activities. International strategic alliances among TNCs may, in some instances, lead to the formation of web-like organizations that do not clearly belong to any one country. Such networks may play a greater role in developing and disseminating new technologies. Yet, given their diffuse nature, it will be increasingly difficult to construct policies designed to promote their positive benefits for specific national economies; this issue is of concern to both home and host countries, for example, in the context of providing subsidies. The growth of multi-firm, globalized strategic alliances in high-technology industries suggests the possibility of declining bargaining power of individual countries *vis-à-vis* firms whose boundaries extend beyond national borders. It also raises the question of how to maintain competition between networks and alliances. In a separate but related issue, the further development of electronic data networks that span international borders will no doubt raise a host of issues regarding access to information (which is increasingly critical to wealth creation) and, more generally, access to the electronic highways of tomorrow's world economy. Mechanisms may be needed to deal with technology issues arising from globalization and, above all, to safeguard competition in a world of globalized firms and industries.

One way in which countries are dealing with the commonality of issues arising in a world in which FDI plays a major role is through regional economic integration. If the current trends towards a regionalization of the world economy continue, the arena for economic and regulatory activities would be increasingly defined along regional rather than national lines. Policy makers thus face a major challenge in ensuring that their countries benefit from an association in regional groupings; the harmonization of economic policies which regionalization entails is likely to be one of the key policy issues of the 1990s. Even as new institutions are being created to deal with those issues (or pre-existing ones strengthened), there is a gap in the policy framework governing interregional relations, which run the risk of being subject to increased frictions. Specifically, the inherent tension between an increasing globalization of the world economy and its simultaneous regionalization demands multilateral initiatives that ensure that efforts to promote an open, efficient and fair international system are not constrained by regional groupings.

Another international policy issue that arises from regionalization is that this trend appears to be evolving in such a manner as to draw selected developing countries into economic groupings with a Triad member, which serves as the pole of economic activity for those countries. Transnational corporations from the Triad are at the forefront of that development by making the investments that integrate home and host countries which, in turn, encourage economic integration initiatives at the policy level. Many developing countries, however, are isolated from that process, either because of their geographical distance from a Triad member or because they are not able to attract the investment from TNCs that promote deep economic integration. Thus, a key issue raised in the current phase of regional economic integration is whether it will lead to the increasing marginalization of a large number of developing countries, and hence to deepening economic inequality in the world economy. Against this, a question that needs to be addressed is what active role the new regional groupings can play in promoting the economic development of non-member countries through increased flows of FDI, both from developed- as well as developing-country members of the regional grouping. Such issues are likely to require the attention of the international community with a view to promoting development in an equitable fashion, while taking into account the realities of emerging regional groupings.

C. The need for new policy initiatives

As any look into the future, the present effort, too, is entirely speculative. But it seems quite clear that, whatever the specific configurations, a new world economy is in the making. And, unless current trends change significantly, international production will be the principal characteristic of the world economy at the beginning of the next century, with TNCs at its centre.

Such a prospect makes it not only possible, but necessary, to look at the world economy from the perspective of FDI and, more specifically, international production. Equally important, the paradigm of international economic relations will have to change and the mechanisms governing those relations will have to be adjusted. In other words, the international public policy framework has to catch up with the globalization of firms and industries, the rise of international production and the new policy issues that are emerging into the international arena by this deeper form of international integration. In short, there is a growing need to arrive at an international governance framework for international production. The various mechanisms outlined in chapter XI can contribute to it. But, by the beginning of the next century, something more comprehensive may be required.

One possibility would be to elaborate international principles and standards and to consolidate them in a global, comprehensive and balanced instrument with a view to ensuring the stability, predictability and transparency of the international investment environment, which would have to deal with the main aspects of the treatment of TNCs by Governments, on the one hand, and issues related to their behaviour on the other hand. Indeed, the intensified normative activity of recent years in a number of international forums—including the Uruguay Round (chapter III), the United Nations, the World Bank and OECD—suggests that the need for a comprehensive, balanced and universal framework which addresses the various concepts, issues, principles and standards affecting transnational investment and operations is becoming increasingly recognized.

Another possibility would be to establish an international framework focusing on global competition and restrictive business practices. In a sense, the creation of such a framework is imperative if one wants to preserve the operation of the market in a world of globalizing firms and industries. This could be achieved through a web of bilateral arrangements (the agreement between the United States and the European Community mentioned in chapter III may be indicative for such a possibility), or through a multilateral agreement. A multilateral undertaking may appear logical if one looks at the world economy from an FDI perspective; but, given the interrelationships between FDI and trade, it may well be that an international governance mechanism dealing with competition and restrictive business practices could also be reached through future negotiations in the framework of GATT, particularly if that organization should pay more attention to FDI matters in the future. It is interesting to note in this context that elements of a paradigm change are already occurring in GATT in the context of the Uruguay Round. There, in the course of the negotiations on services, the discussions began with efforts to adapt the trade rules of GATT to the services sector. In the end, as described in chapter III, the rules that emerged apply to trade *and* transnational production in the services sector. It may well be that, in the next GATT round, this new paradigm will become the basis of negotiations and will be extended to the goods sector. In that event, FDI matters and competition policies would be one logical focus of negotiations.

While an international governance mechanism for competition and restrictive business practices would be a step in the right direction, the issues outlined earlier in this section point to the need for a more far-reaching multilateral framework to meet the challenges of globalization. Specifically, an institution may be needed that would bring the principal forms of international economic transactions (and their interactions) within its purview. The mandate of such an institution would have to be more comprehensive than that of existing multilateral institutions such as the IMF or GATT.

Such an organization could, indeed, serve as a multilateral focal point for issues stemming from the growth of international production. Its mandate would thus encompass not only FDI issues, but also trade and technology issues, along with other policy issues that arise directly from the spread of international production, including competition and restrictive business practices. Among its functions, such an organization could also serve as a forum to resolve international disputes relating to FDI and related issues, and to monitor the policies and actions of both Governments and TNCs that significantly affect the functioning of the international production system. As a multilateral agency, such an organization could be concerned with the role of *all* countries in the international production system, both home and host, and could also be entrusted with the responsibility of meeting the concerns of countries that receive little FDI and risk marginalization and constrained development options. Such an organization could be the focal point for a rules-based system to promote a smooth and equitable process of economic integration brought about through the rise of international production. The constellation of circumstances is currently such that a window of opportunity may exist for taking bold steps in the direction of a comprehensive framework for foreign direct investment.

Notes

[1]See on this point Sylvia Ostry, "The domestic domain: the new international policy arena", *Transnational Corporations*, vol. 1, No. 1 (February 1992), pp. 7-26.

[2]Ibid.

ANNEX TABLES

Page

Annex table 1. Foreign direct investment inward flows, by region and economy, 1980-1990

(Millions of dollars)

Host region/economy	*1980-1985 (Annual average)*	*1986*	*1987*	*1988*	*1989*	*1990*
Developed regions/countries	37 179	64 083	107 916	128 556	165 385	151 970
Western Europe	15 927	24 734	40 235	57 483	82 578	98 941
European Community	14 690	20 013	36 406	54 278	75 492	88 871
Belgium/Luxembourg	1 189	730	2 355	5 212	7 057	8 606
Denmark	87	163	85	503	1 090	1 212
France	2 343	3 256	5 140	8 490	10 310	12 733
Germany, Federal Republic of	693	1 060	1 920	1 170	6 670	1 430
Greece	500	471	683	907	752	1 005
Ireland	198	-43	89	92	85	99
Italy	968	-145	4 102	6 745	2 538	6 413
Netherlands	1 648	3 522	2 889	4 953	8 660	8 017
Portugal	178	239	466	922	1 737	2 123
Spain	1 724	3 451	4 571	7 021	8 428	13 841
United Kingdom	5 163	7 309	14 106	18 263	28 165	33 392
Other Western Europe	1 237	4 721	3 829	3 205	7 086	10 070
Austria	259	284	486	511	850	1 008
Finland	77	348	265	532	490	979
Iceland	21	9	2	-15	-27	6
Norway	149	1 017	187	279	1 514	821
Sweden	283	941	569	1 493	1 432	2 331
Switzerland	896	2 122	2 320	405	2 827	4 925
North America	18 453	35 297	62 338	63 207	74 841	43 133
Canada	-289	1 217	4 198	3 787	4 281	5 943
United States	18 742	34 080	58 140	59 420	70 560	37 190
Other developed countries	2 800	4 052	5 343	7 866	7 967	9 896
Australia	1 968	3 289	3 701	7 290	7 393	7 086
Israel	77	167	256	214	166	129
Japan	325	230	1 170	-520	-1 060	1 760
New Zealand	277	294	176	412	797	229
South Africa	83	-53	-75	116	8	-5
Turkey	71	125	115	354	663	697

/.....

(Annex table 1, cont'd.)

Host region/economy	*1980-1985 (Annual average)*	*1986*	*1987*	*1988*	*1989*	*1990*
Developing regions/economies	12 634	14 184	25 021	29 718	29 756	31 776
Africa	1 411	1 728	2 186	2 325	4 446	2 196
Oil-exporting countries	1 044	1 541	1 664	1 894	3 670	1 633
Algeria	77	5	4	13	12	12
Angola	66	114	-30	-54	-69	-138
Cameroon	154	19	12	67	32	32
Congo	35	22	43	9	25	25
Egypt	665	1 217	948	1 190	1 615	947
Gabon	59	110	90	133	-31	-50
Libyan Arab Jamahiriya	408	-177	-98	98	125	159
Nigeria	210	167	603	377	1 882	588
Tunisia	212	63	92	61	78	58
Other countries	367	188	522	431	776	563
Benin	1	0	0	0	0	0
Botswana	60	70	114	40	98	148
Burkina Faso	1	3	0	2	2	2
Burundi	4	2	1	1	1	1
Central African Republic	5	8	12	7	7	7
Chad	10	28	8	1	19	10
Comoros	0	0	8	4	3	0
Côte d'Ivoire	44	71	88	56	78	-48
Djibouti	0.1	1	0	0	-0	0
Equatorial Guinea	1	6	2	1	1	1
Ethiopia	1	-1	-3	2	0	12
Gambia	0.4	0	2	1	15	8
Ghana	10	4	5	5	15	15
Guinea	0.3	4	6	7	4	1
Guinea-Bissau	1	1	0	1	1	2
Kenya	26	33	43	0	70	26
Lesotho	4	2	6	21	13	17
Liberia	26	-17	39	10	10	10
Madagascar	2	14	4	3	6	0
Malawi	2	0	0	0	0	0
Mali	4	-8	-6	1	20	-1
Mauritania	12	5	2	2	4	2
Mauritius	3	7	17	24	36	41
Morocco	57	1	60	85	167	165
Mozambique	1	-0	0	0	1	0
Niger	11	0	0	0	0	0
Rwanda	16	18	18	21	16	8

/.....

(Annex table 1, cont'd.)

Host region/economy	*1980-1985 (Annual average)*	*1986*	*1987*	*1988*	*1989*	*1990*
Other countries (cont'd.)						
Senegal	9	-8	-4	2	2	2
Seychelles	10	14	19	23	23	27
Sierra Leone	-5	-140	39	-23	21	0
Somalia	-6	0	0	0	0	0
Sudan	3	0	0	0	4	0
Swaziland	10	31	48	51	74	45
Togo	13	7	7	5	5	5
Uganda	1	0	0	5	-2	0
United Republic of Tanzania	8	-8	-1	4	6	-2
Zaire	3	6	-55	-4	-6	-7
Zambia	26	28	75	93	65	65
Zimbabwe	0.5	8	-31	-18	0	0
Latin America and the Caribbean	6 035	5 353	10 826	11 443	8 363	10 055
Oil-exporting countries	1 674	1 650	3 413	2 816	3 455	3 319
Bolivia	30	10	38	-10	-24	45
Ecuador	55	70	75	80	80	82
Mexico	1 331	1 523	3 246	2 594	3 037	2 632
Trinidad and Tobago	146	-15	33	63	149	109
Venezuela	111	16	21	89	213	451
Other countries/territories	4 361	3 749	7 412	8 627	4 908	6 736
Antigua and Barbuda	15	18	29	60	61	85
Argentina	519	574	-19	1 147	1 028	2 036
Bahamas	0.03	-13	11	37	25	-16
Barbados	5	8	7	12	8	0
Belize	0	5	7	14	19	16
Bermuda	638	1 526	3 466	1 272	-769	819
Brazil	1 975	320	1 225	2 969	1 267	2 118
Cayman Islands	208	356	1 661	2 075	1 884	49
Chile	212	60	105	125	269	595
Colombia	502	674	319	203	576	501
Costa Rica	56	61	80	122	101	111
Dominican Republic	54	50	89	106	110	133
El Salvador	9	24	18	17	14	15
Dominica	1	3	9	7	9	8
Grenada	2	5	13	13	10	11
Guatemala	77	69	150	330	76	203
Guyana	2	-9	4	2	-2	8

/.....

(Annex table 1, cont'd.)

Host region/economy	*1980-1985 (Annual average)*	*1986*	*1987*	*1988*	*1989*	*1990*
Other countries/territories (cont'd.)						
Haiti	8	5	5	10	9	8
Honduras	14	30	39	47	37	0
Jamaica	-3	-5	53	-12	57	0
Netherlands Antilles	-78	1	2	0	0	0
Nicaragua	0	0	0	0	0	0
Panama	17	-62	57	-36	12	-30
Paraguay	19	1	5	8	13	79
Peru	25	22	32	26	59	34
Saint Kitts and Nevis	5	6	9	15	30	13
Saint Lucia	22	19	22	16	18	0
Saint Vincent and the Grenadines	1	4	6	10	6	0
Suriname	9	-34	-73	-96	-168	-43
Uruguay	59	37	50	47	44	44
Virgin Islands	6	-4	38	90	117	18
Western Asia	379	283	255	690	447	1 004
Oil-exporting countries	221	133	154	476	298	797
Bahrain	-14	-32	-36	222	181	201
Iran (Islamic Republic of)	-17	-112	-308	61	-19	-49
Iraq	1	2	13	0	3	0
Kuwait	1	-15	-6	16	4	0
Oman	136	140	35	92	112	144
Qatar	1	-2	-3	-21	-1	16
Saudi Arabia	85	41	411	-83	-20	572
United Arab Emirates	28	110	47	189	39	-87
Other countries	158	150	102	214	149	207
Cyprus	69	46	52	62	70	130
Democratic Yemen	0	0	1	8	5	0
Jordan	62	23	40	24	-1	0
Lebanon	0.2	11	1	-0	2	6
Syrian Arab Republic	6	65	7	121	74	71
Yemen Arab Republic	20	6	1	0	0	0

/.....

(Annex table 1, cont'd.)

Host region/economy	*1980-1985 (Annual average)*	*1986*	*1987*	*1988*	*1989*	*1990*
East, South and South-East Asia	4 644	6 728	11 636	15 017	16 218	18 328
Oil-exporting countries	1 284	741	808	1 296	2 350	3 865
Brunei Darussalam	-1	-6	-0	1	0	-1
Indonesia	227	258	385	576	682	964
Malaysia	1 058	489	423	719	1 668	2 902
Other countries/territories	3 360	5 987	10 828	13 721	13 868	14 463
Afghanistan	2	0	0	0	0	0
Bangladesh	-0.1	2	3	2	0	3
China	718	1 875	2 314	3 194	3 393	3 489
Hong Kong	542	996	3 298	2 675	1 076	783
India	62	118	212	91	252	129
Korea, Republic of	98	435	601	871	758	715
Lao People's Democratic Republic	-0.3	0	0	0	0	0
Macao	1	0	-0	0	-1	0
Maldives	-0.3	-1	0	0	-0	0
Myanmar	0.3	0	-2			4
Nepal	0.2	1	1	1	0	0
Pakistan	75	105	129	186	210	249
Philippines	35	127	307	936	563	530
Singapore	1 330	1 710	2 836	3 647	4 212	4 808
Sri Lanka	42	30	60	46	20	31
Taiwan Province of China	185	326	715	959	1 604	1 330
Thailand	264	263	352	1 105	1 777	2 376
Viet Nam	5	0	0	8	4	16
Oceania	130	98	92	180	222	79
Fiji	31	8	-11	24	13	66
Kiribati	-0.2	0	0	0	0	0
Papua New Guinea	98	91	93	154	204	0
Western Samoa	0	0	1	0	0	0
Solomon Islands	1	-1	8	3	6	13
Tonga	0	0	0	0	0	0
Vanuatu	5	2	13	11	9	13
Other	36	-6	27	63	61	114
Malta	26	22	19	41	52	46
Yugoslavia	10	-28	7	22	9	68

/.....

(Annex table 1, cont'd.)

Host region/economy	*1980-1985 (Annual average)*	*1986*	*1987*	*1988*	*1989*	*1990*
Central and Eastern Europe	17	16	12	15	11	89
Hungary	1	0	0	0	0	0
Poland	17	16	12	15	11	89
Romania	0	0	0	0	0	0
All countries	49 831	78 283	132 949	158 289	195 153	183 835

Source: Estimates of Transnational Corporations and Management Division, based on International Monetary Fund, balance-of-payments tape, retrieved in December 1991; OECD estimates; and Transnational Corporations and Management Division, *World Investment Directory* (New York, United Nations, 1992).

Annex table 2. Average annual inflows of foreign direct investment to the ten largest developing economies recipients of foreign direct investment

(Billions of dollars)

Host economy	*1970-1979*	*Host economy*	*1980-1990*
Brazil	1.3	Singapore	2.3
Mexico	0.6	Mexico	1.9
Malaysia	0.3	Brazil	1.8
Nigeria	0.3	China	1.7
Singapore	0.3	Hong Kong	1.1
Egypt	0.3	Malaysia	1.1
Indonesia	0.2	Egypt	0.9
Hong Kong	0.1	Argentina	0.7
Iran (Islamic Republic of)	0.1	Thailand	0.7
Uruguay	0.1	Taiwan Province of China	0.5
Share of flows to developing countries (Percentage)	66	Share of flows to developing countries (Percentage)	68

Sources: Estimates of the Transnational Corporations and Management Division, based on International Monetary Fund, balance-of-payments tape, retrieved in December 1991; and Transnational Corporations and Management Division, *World Investment Directory* (New York, United Nations, 1992).

Annex table 3. Pattern of foreign direct investment from the Triad to developing and Central and Eastern European countries, 1989 and 1985-1989

(Numbers show the share, in percentage, of foreign direct investment by a Triad member in the total inward foreign direct investment of the country/territory)

Stock and flow data

Group I. Absolute or relative dominance by a Triad Member [a]

United States				*Japan*				*European Community*			
Stocks		*Flows*		*Stocks*		*Flows*		*Stocks*		*Flows*	
1989		*1985-1989*		*1989*		*1985-1989*		*1989*		*1985-1989*	
Panama	81.4	Colombia	89.5	Republic of Korea	52.0 [d]	Republic of Korea	52.7	Paraguay	46.2	Brazil	51.2 [e]
Honduras	80.7	Mexico	60.5	Thailand	36.7	Fiji	47.2 [h]	Brazil	36.2		
Colombia	71.8	Bolivia	55.3	Taiwan Province of China	28.6	Hong Kong	40.7 [j]	Uruguay	34.1 [d]		
Mexico	63.1	Panama	54.3			Thailand	43.7				
Ecuador	54.1 [d]	Chile	50.1			Taiwan Province of China	29.8	Viet Nam	58.4	Viet Nam	50.9 [h]
Venezuela	53.0	Venezuela	44.7 [e]					Bangladesh	56.5 [d]	India	41.8
Chile	49.3 [d]	Guatemala	40.3 [f]					India	54.2	Sri Lanka	31.7
Peru	46.3	Argentina	40.1 [m]					Pakistan	27.3 [e]		
		El Salvador	31.2								
		Paraguay	30.6 [g]					Kenya	78.8 [e]	Ghana	40.8 [n]
Philippines	55.7	Philippines	68.2					Nigeria	41.7	Morocco	40.0 [l]
		Pakistan	51.2					Morocco	39.8		
		Bangladesh	44.7 [h]					USSR	76.4	Yugoslavia	64.1 [e]
		Papua New Guinea	42.7 [l]					Poland	38.3	Poland	63.2 [e]
		Saudi Arabia	34.3 [e]							Czechoslovakia	44.8 [e]
										Hungary	44.8 [e]
										USSR	38.3 [e]

Group II. Competing shares of two Triad members [b]

United States/Japan				*United States/European Community*				*European Community/Japan*			
Stocks		*Flows*		*Stocks*		*Flows*		*Stocks*		*Flows*	
1989		*1985-1989*		*1989*		*1985-1989*		*1989*		*1985-1989*	
Hong Kong	31.3 29.9	Guatemala	22.1 [f] 21.8	Argentina	41.2 36.8	Ecuador	26.5 18.6	Indonesia	16.5 18.4 [d]	Indonesia	21.1 14.6
		Singapore	33.2 28.7								
						Nigeria	36.4 33.3 [l]				

/.....

(Annex table 3, cont'd.)

Group III. Non-triad countries are the largest investors [c]

Newly industrializing economies				*Other countries*			
Stocks		*Flows*		*Stocks*		*Flows*	
1989		*1985-1989*		*1989*		*1985-1989*	
China	58.2 [e]	Nepal	57.4 [e]	Papua New Guinea	74.0	Uruguay	56.8 [i]
Malaysia	35.1 [e]	China	50.6 [e]	Ghana	18.5/ 15.4 [o]	Peru	23.0/ 18.3 [pq]
Sri Lanka	23.5 [e]	Malaysia	37.0 [e]				
		Mauritius	46.6 [l]				

Sources: Transnational Corporations and Management Division, *World Investment Directory* (New York, United Nations, 1992); Transnational Corporations and Management Division and Economic Commission for Europe, *World Investment Directory 1992, Central and Eastern Europe* (New York, United Nations, 1992).

a Group I: A Triad member has absolute dominance in a host country if it accounts for more than 50 per cent of total inward foreign direct investment in that host country. A Triad member has relative dominance in a host country if it is the largest foreign direct investor by a margin of at least 10 per cent more than the next largest investor.

b Group II shows host countries for which two Triad members hold comparable shares of total inward foreign direct investment and for which the Triad as a whole constitutes the dominant foreign direct investor (greater than 50 per cent share of total inward foreign direct investment).

c Group III shows countries for which foreign direct investment by non-Triad countries exceeds that of the Triad. The home country or region and its share are indicated.

d Data available through 1988 only.
e Data available through 1987 only.
f Data available through 1985 only.
g Data available through 1984 only.
h Average for 1988 and 1989 only.
i Average for 1987 and 1988 only.
j Average for 1986 through 1989 only.
k Average for 1986 through 1988 only.
l Average for 1985 through 1988 only.
m Data exclude 1987 and 1989.
n Data exclude 1987.
o United States/United Kingdom from data available.
p Data exclude the Bahamas, Bermuda, the Cayman Islands and Panama.
q United States/EFTA from data available.

Annex table 4. Foreign direct investment and selected economic indicators, 1990, and growth rates for 1980-1984 and 1985-1990

(Billions of dollars and percentages)

Indicator	*Value of flows, 1990 (Current prices in billions of dollars)*	*Average annual growth rates (Percentage)*	
		1980-1984	*1985-1990*
All countries			
FDI outflows	225 [a]	-3	34
Current GDP at factor cost	17 755 [a b]	1	12
Gross domestic investment	4 095 [a b]	-1	14
Exports	3 326	-2	13
Royalty and fees receipts	30 [a]	-3	22
Developed countries			
FDI outflows	217	-3	33
Current GDP at factor cost	14 654 [a b]	2	13
Gross domestic investment	3 270 [a b]	-0.1	15
Exports	2 501	-0.5	14
Royalty and fees receipts	29 [a]	-3	22

Sources: International Monetary Fund, *Direction of Trade Statistics, Yearbook, 1991* and *1988;* International Monetary Fund, balance-of-payments tape, retrieved in December 1991 and January 1992; OECD estimates; Transnational Corporations and Management Division, *World Investment Directory* (New York, United Nations, 1992); World Bank, World Tables database.

a Estimates.

b For 1989; growth rates for 1985-1989.

Annex table 5. Foreign direct investment and selected economic indicators for developing countries, 1990, and growth rates for 1980-1984 and 1985-1990

(Billions of dollars and percentages)

Indicator	*Values of flows, 1990 (Current prices in billions of dollars)*	*Average annual growth rates (Percentage)*	
		1980-1984	*1985-1990*
FDI inflows	32	3	19
Current GDP at market prices	3 370 [a b]	-0.4	6
Gross domestic investment	883 [a b]	-4	9
Royalty and fees payments	2	5	12
Imports	782	-0.9	15
Capital goods imports [c]	155 [b]	-2	11
Technical cooperation grants [c]	13 [b]	1	12

Sources: International Monetary Fund, *Direction of Trade Statistics, Yearbook 1991* and *1988;* International Monetary Fund, balance-of-payments tape, retrieved in December 1991 and January 1992; OECD estimates; Transnational Corporations and Management Division, *World Investment Directory* (New York, United Nations, 1992); World Bank, World Tables database; and UNCTAD computations based on OECD data.

a Estimates.
b For 1989; growth rates for 1985-1989.
c From developed countries.

/.....

Annex table 6. The ratio of foreign-direct-investment inflows to gross domestic capital formation and ratio of gross domestic capital formation to gross domestic product (in brackets), annual averages, 1971-1975, 1976-1980, 1981-1985, 1986-1989

(Percentages)

Region/economy	*1971-1975*	*1976-1980*	*1981-1985*	*1986-1989*
Developed countries				
Australia	4.5	4.6	4.6	9.1
	(24.8)	(24.6)	(24.5)	(25.5)
Austria	1.8	0.9	1.7	1.9
	(29.0)	(27.3)	(23.7)	(32.7)
Belgium/Luxembourg	7.1	5.8	7.6	14.9
	(22.9)	(21.8)	(16.3)	(17.0)
Canada	3.6	1.7	-0.7	3.4
	(24.4)	(24.2)	(20.6)	(21.8)
Denmark	3.0	0.3	0.9	2.4
	(24.1)	(21.4)	(17.1)	(19.3)
Germany, Federal Republic of	2.1	0.8	0.6	1.2
	(23.4)	(22.4)	(20.3)	(20.4)
Finland	0.6	0.4	0.7	1.6
	(31.8)	(25.5)	(24.9)	(26.7)
France	1.8	1.9	2.0	3.8
	(26.1)	(24.1)	(20.6)	(20.5)
Greece	1.0	5.4	6.0	7.8
	(30.0)	(28.0)	(21.8)	(18.7)
Iceland	4.4	1.3	3.0	-0.8
	(33.6)	(33.0)	(28.6)	(31.4)
Ireland	3.8	6.7	4.0	1.0
	(25.7)	(29.0)	(24.7)	(17.6)
Israel	2.9	1.1	1.6	3.0
	(29.0)	(23.2)	(20.3)	(16.9)
Italy	1.8	0.8	1.1	2.1
	(22.6)	(23.2)	(23.1)	(21.1)
Japan	0.1	0.05	0.1	-0.01
	(35.8)	(31.9)	(29.2)	(30.4)
Netherlands	6.1	4.5	6.1	11.9
	(30.2)	(21.5)	(18.7)	(20.1)
New Zealand	4.8	6.1	4.9	5.2
	(29.6)	(27.2)	(26.2)	(22.2)
Norway	3.1	3.2	1.2	3.3
	(32.2)	(30.7)	(25.3)	(27.1)
Portugal	3.1	1.5	3.0	7.9
	(25.7)	(29.6)	(28.4)	(27.7)
Spain	1.9	2.8	5.3	8.2
	(27.8)	(23.8)	(20.1)	(23.1)
Sweden	0.6	0.5	1.6	3.4
	(23.1)	(20.4)	(17.6)	(19.4)
Switzerland	..	..	3.9	4.1
			(24.6)	(27.8)
United Kingdom	7.3	8.4	5.4	12.3
	(19.0)	(20.1)	(19.0)	(20.1)
United States	0.9	2.0	3.0	6.7
	(19.0)	(20.0)	(18.4)	(17.7)

/.....

(Annex table 6, cont'd.)

Region/economy	*1971-1975*	*1976-1980*	*1981-1985*	*1986-1989*
Developing economies				
Asia and the Pacific				
Bangladesh	..	..	-0.01 (13.0)	0.1 (11.0)
Fiji	12.2 (21.6)	6.7 (26.8)	10.7 (24.0)	4.6 (15.5)
Hong Kong	5.9 (24.7)	4.2 (31.9)	6.9 (28.0)	19.1 (26.1)
India	0.3 (19.2)	0.1 (22.2)	0.1 (24.2)	0.2 (23.9)
Indonesia	4.6 (18.3)	2.4 (20.7)	1.0 (27.8)	2.3 (24.5)
Korea, Republic of	1.9 (26.5)	0.4 (31.3)	0.5 (29.2)	1.6 (29.2)
Malaysia	15.2 (24.0)	11.9 (27.2)	10.8 (34.1)	9.6 (26.2)
Nepal	0.3 (9.8)	0.1 (16.7)	0.04 (19.2)	0.2 (20.0)
Pakistan	0.5 (15.3)	0.9 (13.9)	1.3 (17.8)	2.0 (18.2)
Papua New Guinea	..	8.7 (22.7)	15.1 (28.3)	17.8 (24.8)
Philippines	1.0 (25.3)	0.9 (30.1)	0.7 (24.0)	8.5 (15.3)
Singapore	15.0 (41.4)	16.6 (42.0)	17.4 (46.8)	35.2 (38.0)
Sri Lanka	0.1 (14.9)	2.6 (22.1)	2.9 (27.5)	2.9 (23.3)
Taiwan Province of China	1.4 (30.5)	1.2 (31.2)	1.5 (23.5)	3.6 (21.4)
Thailand	3.0 (24.7)	1.5 (27.3)	3.1 (23.5)	4.9 (24.8)
Latin America and the Caribbean				
Argentina	0.1 (21.7)	2.1 (24.4)	5.0 (14.8)	6.5 (11.0)
Barbados	20.4 (21.7)	4.1 (23.5)	2.5 (20.0)	3.7 (16.6)
Bolivia	4.6 (19.7)	2.3 (20.4)	5.8 (12.9)	0.8 (9.3)
Brazil	4.2 (29.3)	3.9 (24.2)	4.3 (18.5)	2.4 (21.1)
Chile	-7.3 (15.2)	4.2 (17.6)	6.3 (15.1)	3.8 (17.5)
Colombia	1.7 (18.8)	2.2 (18.5)	7.7 (19.8)	6.0 (19.9)
Costa Rica	11.3 (23.7)	6.0 (24.9)	7.1 (25.2)	7.5 (25.9)
Dominican Republic	9.4 (22.1)	5.0 (23.8)	2.8 (21.2)	7.2 (22.5)

/.....

(Annex table 6, cont'd.)

Region/economy	*1971-1975*	*1976-1980*	*1981-1985*	*1986-1989*
Latin America and the Caribbean (cont'd.)				
Ecuador	13.6	1.8	1.9	3.3
	(24.3)	(26.1)	(20.3)	(21.7)
El Salvador	4.0	1.7	1.7	2.7
	(19.0)	(19.4)	(12.3)	(13.9)
Guatemala	10.0	7.9	5.7	15.4
	(15.4)	(19.2)	(13.0)	(12.8)
Guyana	-9.1	-4.3	2.1	-0.9
	(26.2)	(29.4)	(26.4)	(27.8)
Honduras	2.5	2.6	3.0	6.5
	(19.8)	(24.5)	(17.3)	(13.6)
Jamaica	12.9	-1.6	-1.4	1.9
	(27.7)	(16.0)	(22.1)	(23.2)
Mexico	3.5	3.6	2.7	8.7
	(21.2)	(24.3)	(22.8)	(19.1)
Panama	4.8	0.03	3.1	-1.9
	(32.1)	(27.5)	(21.8)	(14.2)
Paraguay	6.2	3.9	1.2	0.4
	(19.8)	(27.3)	(24.2)	(24.3)
Peru	3.3	2.0	0.4	0.3
	(21.7)	(22.4)	(26.7)	(25.3)
Suriname	1.5	-2.6	4.9	-64.0
	(25.9)	(30.6)	(18.8)	(9.8)
Trinidad and Tobago	22.3	10.7	7.3	3.0
	(27.0)	(28.9)	(24.8)	(20.0)
Uruguay	..	15.7	1.5	6.5
		(16.5)	(12.5)	(9.3)
Venezuela	-0.9	-0.9	1.0	0.3
	(32.2)	(39.7)	(19.5)	(17.7)
West Asia				
Cyprus	13.8	11.1	9.3	5.5
	(26.4)	(35.3)	(32.1)	(26.6)
Jordan	4.6	2.9	4.5	2.4
	(24.3)	(37.7)	(38.7)	(24.8)
Kuwait	0.02	0.02	0.01	-0.03
	(9.6)	(16.6)	(20.5)	(18.8)
Oman	3.6	8.9	6.4	5.3
	(29.7)	(27.3)	(27.1)	(22.4)
Yemen	..	2.6	1.9	0.6
	(18.7)	(36.9)	(25.9)	(13.7)
Africa				
Algeria	1.9	1.4	-0.01	0.04
	(41.6)	(44.4)	(36.3)	(31.1)
Botswana	-24.3	24.1	16.1	25.7
	(47.6)	(40.1)	(33.9)	(19.1)
Congo	31.6	3.9	4.0	5.2
	(30.6)	(30.9)	(40.3)	(22.7)
Côte d'Ivoire	5.4	2.5	2.3	5.9
	(22.2)	(27.3)	(18.2)	(11.7)

/.....

(Annex table 6, cont'd.)

Region/economy	*1971-1975*	*1976-1980*	*1981-1985*	*1986-1989*
Egypt	..	7.1 (29.9)	6.9 (28.2)	8.1 (20.8)
Gabon	10.8 (44.3)	3.2 (38.8)	5.0 (35.6)	9.3 (35.3)
Ghana	9.7 (11.4)	1.8 (6.8)	2.4 (5.8)	0.9 (10.3)
Kenya	2.9 (22.9)	4.4 (25.9)	1.0 (24.4)	1.4 (23.1)
Liberia	37.3 (26.1)	18.7 (33.6)	13.8 (17.8)	8.6 (11.2)
Madagascar	4.2 (14.0)	-0.6 (19.0)	0.6 (14.5)	2.4 (13.9)
Mauritius	1.1 (27.7)	1.2 (21.6)	1.8 (17.3)	9.3 (9.8)
Morocco	0.4 (18.8)	1.6 (25.6)	1.7 (22.4)	1.4 (19.8)
Nigeria	4.9 (29.6)	0.5 (34.8)	3.6 (13.7)	11.8 (8.6)
Rwanda	4.4 (10.5)	5.9 (16.0)	6.7 (15.8)	5.5 (15.9)
Senegal	5.1 (18.6)	4.4 (16.1)	2.2 (15.1)	-0.7 (15.2)
Seychelles	..	20.3 (38.1)	25.2 (26.1)	39.1 (20.2)
Sierra Leone	8.6 (13.6)	5.0 (15.2)	-1.1 (12.2)	-28.5 (10.6)
Somalia	4.3 (9.8)	2.4 (10.5)	-2.0 (12.2)	..
Sudan	-0.2 (0.6)	..	0.4 (0.7)	0.2 (0.3)
Swaziland	16.1 (21.5)	18.8 (38.4)	4.3 (32.4)	30.3 (25.7)
Togo	-5.3 (21.6)	11.7 (41.3)	3.5 (24.6)	2.2 (23.8)
Tunisia	5.2 (24.6)	6.1 (30.0)	8.4 (30.3)	3.7 (20.8)
Uganda	-0.8 (4.8)	1.0 (7.3)	-0.3 (16.3)	0.9 (10.8)
Zimbabwe	..	0.02 (16.4)	0.02 (20.1)	-1.5 (18.3)

Sources: International Monetary Fund, balance-of-payments tape, retrieved in December 1991; OECD estimates; Transnational Corporations and Management Division, *World Investment Directory* (New York, United Nations, 1992); and United Nations Department of Economic and Social Development data base on major economic indicators showing historical development trends.

Annex table 7. The ratio of foreign-direct-investment inward stock to gross domestic product, by sector, selected years

(Percentage)

Region/economy	*Primary*	*Secondary*	*Tertiary*	*Total*
A. Developed countries				
Australia				
1975	22.4	15.3	5.7	9.2
1980	15.7	13.1	5.3	8.0
1985	25.9	27.1	11.0	15.3
1988	39.0	35.8	13.2	19.2
Austria				
1975	..	8.7	4.0	5.1
1980	..	9.0	2.8	4.4
1985	..	9.2	3.0	4.6
1988	..	11.6	3.4	5.5
Canada				
1970	50.2	99.1	10.9	34.0
1975	23.9	78.5	8.4	24.1
1980	15.6	75.7	7.8	21.8
1985	10.4	68.9	8.3	20.3
1989	13.5	63.2	9.5	20.5
France				
1975	0.8	2.1	1.3	1.5
1980	1.3	3.7	2.2	2.5
1985	1.0	4.9	2.7	3.1
1989	1.6	7.4	4.3	4.9
Italy				
1975	4.8	10.7	2.4	5.0
1980	2.5	5.1	1.0	2.1
1985	1.9	10.8	2.1	3.9
1989	2.8	11.6	3.7	5.3
Japan				
1975	n.a.	0.8	0.1	0.3
1980	n.a.	0.7	0.1	0.3
1985	n.a.	1.2	0.2	0.5
1989	n.a.	1.2	0.3	0.6
Netherlands				
1975	59.3	16.8	4.7	12.0
1980	42.9	19.0	6.6	12.1
1985	44.1	20.6	12.5	16.4
1989	94.9	25.6	14.1	22.2
Norway				
1970	0.4	4.4	0.9	1.6
1975	0.3	3.0	1.1	1.4
1980	0.1	3.5	1.3	1.4
1985	0.8	3.4	1.3	1.5
1988	3.3	5.2	2.2	2.8
Portugal				
1975	2.6	3.3	3.8	3.5
1980	2.2	3.4	2.9	2.4
1985	3.6	5.5	2.7	3.5
1989	6.1	8.3	7.7	7.7

/.....

(Annex table 7, cont'd.)

Region/economy	*Primary*	*Secondary*	*Tertiary*	*Total*
A. Developed countries (cont'd.)				
Spain				
1975	0.4	7.2	0.8	2.4
1980	0.5	8.1	1.0	2.7
1984	1.7	11.0	1.9	4.1
1989	..	..	..	9.6
Sweden				
1986	0.1	4.5	3.5	3.6
1988	0.1	7.9	3.5	4.4
United States				
1970	6.4	2.4	0.6	1.3
1975	6.6	3.2	0.9	1.7
1980	2.1	7.2	1.9	3.1
1985	4.0	10.3	3.2	4.7
1989	5.1	19.2	4.3	7.3
B. Developing economies				
Asia and the Pacific				
Bangladesh				
1977	0.4	3.0	0.1	0.5
1980	0.4	2.3	0.1	0.4
1985	0.4	3.9	0.6	0.7
1988	0.4	3.4	0.7	0.8
Hong Kong				
1975	..	..	..	6.3
1980	..	..	..	6.5
1985	..	23.5	..	10.9
1989	..	25.1	..	22.2
India				
1970	1.3	1.7	0.9	1.0
1975	0.8	2.2	1.1	1.3
1980	0.2	1.9	1.0	1.1
1985	0.1	1.5	0.8	0.9
Indonesia				
1970	2.7	11.2	0.5	2.5
1975	3.9	57.1	2.1	7.5
1980	2.8	33.5	1.5	5.6
1985	4.2	37.6	1.7	7.5
1989	6.3	33.0	2.1	9.3
Korea, Republic of				
1980	0.1	4.4	1.2	2.0
1985	0.1	4.4	1.2	2.0
1988	0.2	4.0	1.4	2.1
Pakistan				
1975	0.6	9.9	2.6	3.0
1980	0.7	8.9	2.0	2.8
1985	1.5	8.5	3.0	3.6
1988	1.4	7.2	2.9	3.3

/.....

(Annex table 7, cont'd.)

Region/economy	*Primary*	*Secondary*	*Tertiary*	*Total*
B. Developing economies				
Asia and the Pacific (cont'd.)				
Philippines				
1975	0.7	4.3	2.4	2.4
1980	2.5	7.3	2.2	3.5
1985	4.3	8.3	1.7	4.0
1989	4.3	7.2	1.6	3.7
Singapore				
1970	6.0	67.5	22.0	30.9
1975	4.4	80.6	28.5	40.1
1980	7.9	97.0	35.4	53.5
1985	15.1	143.3	48.6	70.7
1989	40.8	130.9	75.4	91.7
Sri Lanka				
1980	0.0	17.1	5.1	6.1
1985	3.2	17.4	8.6	8.7
1988	4.1	19.6	8.4	9.2
Thailand				
1975	1.6	5.7	3.9	3.5
1980	1.4	4.8	3.1	3.0
1985	4.9	8.3	4.1	5.1
1989	3.9	13.4	5.5	7.0
Africa				
Morocco				
1970	0.4	4.2	1.4	1.7
1975	0.6	6.0	2.3	2.5
1980	1.2	10.4	3.9	4.4
1985	2.0	11.6	4.8	5.3
1988	2.2	10.6	5.1	5.4
Nigeria				
1970	13.9	40.8	6.4	12.1
1975	9.3	22.2	7.5	9.7
1980	3.3	32.7	6.3	7.2
1985	2.2	36.7	14.1	9.5
1988	4.0	33.9	9.5	7.9
Latin America and the Caribbean				
Brazil				
1971	0.9	17.9	1.6	5.9
1975	1.3	15.6	2.1	5.9
1980	2.5	18.2	2.5	6.9
1985	3.3	29.7	4.2	11.3
1988	3.5	25.1	4.1	10.0
Chile				
1983	28.9	12.3	5.3	10.5
1987	34.8	25.8	7.9	15.5
Colombia				
1975	10.6	14.1	2.7	7.4
1980	6.6	9.6	1.3	4.4
1985	10.3	14.8	1.8	6.4
1987	16.2	16.1	1.8	8.2

/.....

(Annex table 7, cont'd.)

Region/economy	*Primary*	*Secondary*	*Tertiary*	*Total*
Latin America and the Caribbean (cont'd.)				
Peru				
1975	41.7	7.3	1.1	10.4
1980	32.0	12.1	3.0	12.2

Source: Transnational Corporations and Management Division, *World Investment Directory* (New York, United Nations, 1992); and United Nations Department of Economic and Social Development, data base on major economic indicators showing historical development trends.

Annex table 8. The relative importance of foreign direct investment in host countries, various years

(Percentages)

Region/economy	*Ratio of FDI stock to GDP (1988)*	*Ratio of FDI inflows to GDCF (1986-1988)*	*Exports*	*Assets*	*Employment*	*Value-added*	*Sales*	*Profits*
			(Share of foreign affiliates in total)					
Developed countries								
Australia	22.2 [a]	9.1	..	..	..	..	..	22.6 (1983)
Austria	5.5	1.9	..	..	13.5(1985)	..	..	..
Belgium/Luxembourg	..	14.9	..	..	18.0 (1985)	..	39.8 (1985)	..
Canada	20.5 [a]	3.4	..	25.0 (1990)	..	..	25.8 (1990)	26.6 (1990)
Denmark	..	2.4	..	11.6 [b] (1986)	12.4 [b] (1986)	14.2 [b] (1986)	13.3 [b] (1986)	13.2 [b] (1986)
Finland	3.3	1.6	..	..	4.4 (1988)	..	..	..
France	4.9 [a]	3.8	25.9 [b] (1982)	..	20.2 [b] (1982)	..	25.3 [b] (1982)	..
Germany, Federal Republic of	5.6 [a]	1.2	..	..	8.3 (1982)	..	..	..
Greece		7.8	18.5 [b] (1977)	..	21.3 [b] (1977)	..	25.5 [b] (1977)	..
Ireland	..	1.0	..	..	42.8 [b] (1987)	..	65.0 [b] (1987)	..
Israel	1.0 [d]	3.0	..	..	..	..	..	..
Italy	5.3 [a]	2.1	..	..	11.8 (1985)	..	..	..
Japan	0.6 [a]	-0.01	..	0.8 (1986)	0.4 (1986)	1.0 (1986)	..	..
Netherlands	22.2 [a]	11.9	..	..	..	..	..	..
New Zealand	8.5	5.2	..	..	..	..	..	28.9 (1980)
Norway	2.8	3.3	..	..	4.0 (1981)	..	..	..
Portugal	7.7	7.9	..	..	8.2 (1984)	..	..	..
South Africa	12.5	..	..	42.0 (1978)	..	..	..	..
Spain	9.6 [a]	8.2	..	..	46.6 (1977)	..	..	..
Sweden	..	3.4	..	..	..	..	..	11.1 (1988)
Turkey	..	..	..	..	2.0 (1988)	..	..	..
United Kingdom	16.2	12.3	38.0 (1988)	..	..	..	..	10.0 (1988)
United States	7.3 [a]	6.7	..	13.2 [b] (1987)	3.7 (1987)	4.3 (1987)	11.4 [b] (1987)	5.9 [b] (1987)
Asia and the Pacific								
Bangladesh	0.8	0.1	..	..	..	..	..	..
China	2.7	..	..	..	..	..	..	..
Fiji	26.3 [a]	4.6 [c]	35.6 (1985)	..	25.0 (1985)	44.0 (1985)	40.6 (1985)	56.9 (1985)
Hong Kong	22.2 [a]	19.1	..	17.7 (1986)	5.4 [b] (1987)	..	7.1 [b] (1987)	..
India	0.6	0.2	..	..	..	..	..	..
Indonesia	9.3 [a]	2.3	..	..	10.9 [b] (1980)	27.6 [b] (1980)	..	..
Malaysia	27.7 [d]	9.6	45.7 (1988)	19.0 (1988)	32.2 (1988)	..	31.4 (1988)	45.7 (1988)
Nepal	1.6	0.2	..	..	..	..	..	..
Pakistan	3.3	2.0	6.0 (1988)	..	..	..	..	..
Papua New Guinea	38.6 [a]	17.8 [c]	..	..	..	..	..	..
Philippines	3.7 [a]	8.5	34.7 (1987)	18.9 (1987)	2.7 (1987)	..	26.0 (1987)	30.8 (1987)
Republic of Korea	2.1	1.6	29.0 (1986)	..	2.7 (1986)	..	..	..
Singapore	91.7 [a]	35.2	86.1 [b] (1988)	..	59.5 [b] (1988)	71.7 [a] (1988)	53.0 [b] (1988)	..
Sri Lanka	9.2	2.9	26.2 (1987)	..	..	..	..	..
Taiwan Province of China	5.5	3.6	..	..	..	..	..	..
Thailand	7.0 [a]	4.9	..	16.3 (1986)	..	..	39.3 (1986)	..

/.....

(Annex table 8, cont'd.)

Region/economy	*Ratio of FDI stock to GDP (1988)*	*Ratio of FDI inflows to GDCF (1986-1988)*	*Exports*	*Assets*	*Employment*	*Value-added*	*Sales*	*Profits*
			(Share of foreign affiliates in total)					
Latin America								
Argentina	8.9 [o]	6.5	37.3 (1990)	..	26.8 [b] (1984)	26.8 [b] (1984)	51.6 (1988)	..
Barbados	..	3.7	..	..	..	..	..	..
Bolivia	13.4	0.8 [c]	..	..	..	..	..	..
Brazil	10.0	2.4	26.7 [b] (1987)	..	16.2 (1987)	..	17.7 (1987)	43.3 (1987)
Chile	..	3.8	..	..	..	..	..	..
Colombia	8.3 [a]	6.0 [c]	22.8 [b] (1987)	..	12.0 [b] (1987)	24.8 [b] (1987)	..	..
Costa Rica	28.2	7.5	..	..	..	..	..	..
Dominican Republic	12.1	7.2	..	..	..	..	..	..
Ecuador	11.7	3.3	..	..	..	..	..	..
El Salvador	3.3 [a]	2.7 [a]	..	..	..	..	..	..
Guatemala	0.8 [f]	15.4	..	..	..	..	..	..
Guyana	..	-0.9	..	..	..	..	..	..
Honduras	3.6 [g]	6.5 [c]	..	..	..	..	..	..
Jamaica	..	1.9	..	..	..	..	..	..
Mexico	..	8.7	..	..	..	..	..	..
Panama	11.4	-1.9	..	..	..	..	..	..
Paraguay	4.0	0.4	20.1 (1988)	..	..	..	..	..
Peru	3.0	0.3	25.3 [k] (1988)	..	6.5 [a] (1988)	57.2 [l] (1988)	51.1 [l] (1988)	13.5 (1988)
Suriname	..	-64.0	..	..	..	..	..	..
Trinidad and Tobago	..	3.0	..	..	..	..	..	..
Uruguay	..	6.5	..	..	..	..	13.6 [b] (1987)	..
Venezuela	4.2	0.3	..	..	..	..	..	..
West Asia	..	..	..	..	..	..	..	..
Bahrain	17.1 [a]	..	..	..	..	..	..	..
Cyprus	18.2	5.5 [c]	..	..	..	..	..	..
Jordan	7.7 [a]	2.4	..	..	..	..	..	..
Kuwait	1.5 [a]	-0.03 [c]	..	..	..	..	..	..
Oman	45.6 [d]	5.3	..	..	..	..	..	..
Qatar	2.1 [j]	..	..	..	..	..	..	..
Saudia Arabia	29.8 [d]	..	..	..	..	..	..	..
United Arab Emirates	4.8	..	..	..	..	..	..	..
Yemen	..	0.6 [h]	..	..	..	..	..	..
Africa	..	..	..	..	..	..	..	..
Algeria	..	0.04	..	..	..	..	..	..
Botswana	22.9	25.7	..	..	..	..	..	..
Congo	..	5.2	..	..	..	..	..	..
Côte d'Ivoire	..	5.9	..	..	..	..	..	..
Egypt	..	8.1	..	..	..	..	..	..
Gabon	..	9.3	..	..	..	..	..	..
Ghana	..	0.9	..	..	48.4 [b] (1986)	48.4 [b] (1986)	45.7 [b] (1986)	..
Kenya	..	1.4	..	..	..	..	..	..
Liberia	..	8.6	..	..	..	..	..	..
Madagascar	..	2.4	..	..	..	..	..	..
Mauritius	6.2	9.3	..	..	65.4 (1984)	..	..	..
Morocco	5.4	1.4	..	..	..	..	..	..
Nigeria	7.9	11.8	..	..	..	..	..	..
Rwanda	..	5.5	..	..	..	..	..	..
Senegal	7.5 [d]	-0.7	..	..	..	..	..	..

/.....

(Annex table 8, cont'd.)

Region/economy	*Ratio of FDI stock to GDP (1988)*	*Ratio of FDI inflows to GDCF (1986-1988)*	*Exports*	*Assets*	*Employment*	*Value-added*	*Sales*	*Profits*
			(Share of foreign affiliates in total)					
Africa (cont'd.)								
Seychelles	..	39.0	..	..	..	..	..	..
Sierra Leone	..	-28.5 [h]	..	..	..	..	..	..
Sudan	..	0.2 [a]	..	..	..	..	..	..
Swaziland	..	30.3	..	..	..	..	..	..
Togo	..	2.2	..	..	..	..	..	..
Tunisia	..	3.7	..	..	..	..	..	..
Uganda	..	0.9 [i]	..	..	..	..	..	..
Zimbabwe	58.3	-1.5	..	25.3 [b] (1988)	..	..	..	..

Sources: Internationl Monetary Fund, balance-of-payments tape, retrieved in December 1991; OECD estimates; Transnational Corporations and Management Division, *World Investment Directory* (New York, United Nations, 1992); and United Nations, Department of Economic and Social Development, database on major economic indicators showing historical development trends.

a 1989.
b Secondary sector.
c 1986-1989.
d 1987.
e 1986.
f 1985.
g 1984.
h 1986-1987.
i 1988.
j 1990.
k Primary sector.
l Primary and secondary sectors.

Annex table 9. Changes in the relative importance of the activities of transnational corporations in selected industries and host countries, 1970s and 1980s

I. The significance of foreign affiliates in assets (Percentage of foreign affiliates in total assets)

Industry	*Canada*				*United States*		*Malaysia*				
	1970	*1975*	*1980*	*1985*	*1977*	*1987*	*1970*	*1975*	*1980*	*1985*	*1988*
Mining	59	58	49	39	..	..	60	51	15	6	3
Petroleum	61	54	48	41	..	..	87	65	33	22	22
Primary	..	..	..	..	..	..	67	57	31	20	22
Agriculture	..	..	..	..	..	..	66	53	31	19	23
Manufacturing	53	50	48	46	6	13	53	45	42	24	32
Food	30	26	32	39	10	10	..	..	..	..	..
Textiles	24	29	26	25	4	6	..	..	..	..	..
Paper	60	52	55	33	4	9	..	..	..	..	..
Chemicals	66	63	70	68	15	32	..	..	..	..	..
Petrochemicals	..	..	..	..	15	18	..	..	..	..	..
Rubber	69	72	78	85	4	14	..	..	..	..	..
Non-metals	..	..	..	..	7	34	..	..	..	..	..
Metals	11	10	10	12	5	14	..	..	..	..	..
Mechanical equipment	64	59	60	40	6	6	..	..	..	..	..
Electrical equipment	61	63	62	63	11	11	..	..	..	..	..
Motor vehicles	87	88	82	92	3	3	..	..	..	..	..
Other transport	52	48	47	74	..	..	..	..	..	..	..
Other manufacturing	49	48	43	40	3	11	..	..	..	..	..
Transport	16	16	28	35	..	..	..	..	..	..	..
Services	..	..	..	..	..	..	39	40	29	18	16
Construction	..	..	..	..	..	..	28	17	46	42	28
Trade	..	..	..	..	..	..	51	37	30	21	21
Finance	..	..	..	..	..	..	..	45	20	18	16
Other services	19	23	29	30	..	..	31	24	19	12	13
Total	35	34	35	33	..	..	51	44	31	19	19

/.....

(Annex table 9, cont'd.)

II. The significance of foreign affiliates in exports (Percentage of foreign affiliates in total exports)

			Secondary sector				*Tertiary sector*
Region/Economy	*Year*	*Primary sector*	*Electrical and electronic products*	*Chemical products*	*Motor vehicles*	*Total*	*Total*
Africa							
Côte d'Ivoire	1978	..	..	..	..	14.1 [a]	..
	1984	..	..	..	..	15.0 [a]	..
Tunisia	1986	..	..	..	..	37.0	..
Asia and the Pacific							
Fiji	1985	100.0	..	50.1	11.5	21.5	..
Hong Kong	1984	..	..	..	..	16.5 [b]	..
Malaysia	1980	81.0	..	..	..	41.0	32.0
	1984	34.0	..	..	..	64.0	19.0
	1986	32.6	..	..	..	51.2	15.9
Philippines	1980	..	..	..	..	48.1	..
	1983	..	..	..	..	51.5	..
Republic of Korea	1978	..	..	..	..	24.6	..
Sri Lanka	1976	..	..	..	..	17.1	..
	1981	..	..	..	..	26.9 [c]	..
	1987	..	..	..	..	51.3	..
Singapore	1985	..	..	..	..	82.0	..
	1988	..	..	..	..	86.0	..
Taiwan Province of China	1981	..	..	..	..	25.6	..
	1986	18.5	43.6	30.8	..	18.5	3.6
Thailand	1971	..	..	..	..	22.7	..
	1980	..	..	..	..	37.3	..
Latin America							
Argentina	1983	..	..	..	..	26.6	..
Brazil	1980	..	..	..	..	32.3	..
	1987	..	12.3	35.5	79.4	26.7	..
Chile	1979	..	..	..	..	21.7	..
Colombia	1978	..	..	..	..	14.4	..
	1980	..	..	..	..	16.9	..
Costa Rica	1980	..	..	..	..	70.1	..
Mexico	1977	..	..	..	..	42.4	..
	1986	..	28.9	65.6	97.0	58.0	..
Paraguay	1988)	29.8	..	..	..	46.3	..
Peru	1978	..	..	..	..	8.0	..
	1988	25.3	..	..	..	..	..
Uruguay	1978	..	..	..	..	12.6	..
	1986	..	..	..	..	12.0	..
	1988	..	..	..	..	10.0	..

/.....

III. The significance of foreign affiliates in sales (Percentage of total sales)

Host country	Year			
	1982	1985	1987	1988
United States				
Manufacturing	7	..	11	..
Food, beverages and tobacco	5	..	7	..
Textiles, leather and clothing	5	..	5	..
Paper	8	..	6	..
Chemicals	31	..	32	..
Coal and petroleum	..	..	19	..
Rubber products	4	..	10	..
Non-metallic mineral products	11	..	25	..
Metals	6	..	12	..
Mechanical equipment	7	..	7	..
Electrical equipment	9	..	13	..
Motor vehicles	5	..	3	..
Other manufacturing	..	..	7	..
Singapore				
Manufacturing	..	70	..	75

Source: Transnational Corporations and Management Division, *World Investment Directory* (New York, United Nations, 1992).

a Including only majority-owned French companies that account for the largest part of foreign investment in Côte d'Ivoire.
b As a percentage of profits.
c Textile exports, which amounted to 81 per cent of total manufactured exports in 1981.

Annex table 10. Regional distribution of bilateral investment treaties signed by OECD countries

(Number of treaties)

Country	*Asia and the Pacific*	*Africa*	*Latin America*	*Caribbean*	*Middle East*	*Central and Eastern Europe*	*OECD countries*	*Total*
Germany, Federal Republic of	13	36	7	5	7	6	3	77
Switzerland	8	25	9	1	2	5	1	51
United Kingdom	11	14	6	8	2	5	1	47
France	11	16	5	1	5	7	-	45
Netherlands	9	12	1	1	2	6	1	32
Belgium/Luxembourg	9	10	2	-	1	6	1	29
Italy	5	8	2	-	1	5	1	22
Sweden	4	6	1	-	1	4	-	16
United States	1	7	1	2	-	1	1	13
Denmark	4	3	-	-	-	5	1	13
Austria	2	-	-	-	-	7	1	10
Norway	4	1	-	-	-	4	-	9
Finland	3	1	-	-	-	5	-	9
Turkey	2	-	-	-	1	3	6	12
Spain	-	1	1	-	-	3	-	5
Japan	2	1	-	-	-	1	-	4
Canada	-	-	-	-	-	3	-	3
Greece	-	1	-	-	-	1	1	3
Portugal	-	2	-	-	-	-	1	3
New Zealand	1	-	-	-	-	-	-	1
Australia	1	-	-	-	-	-	-	1
Ireland	-	-	-	-	-	-	-	-
Iceland	-	-	-	-	-	-	-	-
Total	90	144	35	18	22	77	20	406

Source: UNCTC and ICC, *Bilateral Investment Treaties* 1959-1991 (United Nations publication, Sales No. E.92.II.A.16), p. 5.

/.....

Annex table 11. Changes in main national legislation relating to foreign direct investment in 1991 [a]

Country	*Law/regulation*	*Content*
Asia		
China	Income Tax Law of the People's Republic of China for Enterprises with Foreign Investment and Foreign Enterprises of 9 April 1991 effective 1 July 1991 and Detailed Rules and Regulations effective 1 July 1991.	Establishes a single flat tax rate for all foreign investment; abolishes withholding tax on profits remitted; and grants tax holidays and 40 per cent tax refund for profits reinvested.
India	Statement on Industrial Policy of 24 July 1991.	Creates a more favourable investment climate to stimulate FDI flows, but restrictions still exist in such industries as energy and minerals. Foreign investment procedures have been simplified with the formation of the Foreign Investment Promotion Board.
Mongolia	Ministry of Finance Public Notices Nos. 91-3 and 91-4 of 27 February 1991; effective on 1 March 1991.	Tax incentives have been changed by allowing 100 per cent tax exemption for first three years of the investment project, and 50 per cent reduction during the next two years.
	Privatization Law ratified by President on 31 May 1991.	Specifies the State-owned enterprises that are subject to privatization and the methods of privatization. It also regulates the privatization of agricultural cooperatives.
	Banking Law effective 1 May 1991.	Regulates the activities of foreign banks and banking transactions of foreigners.
	Petroleum Law ratified by the President on 13 February 1991.	Declares petroleum the exclusive property of the State and governs the operations of Mongolian or foreign companies engaged in the exploration of petroleum.
Philippines	An Act to Promote Foreign Investments, Prescribe the Procedures for Registering Enterprises Business in the Philippines, and for other purposes (Republic Act No. 7042).	Allows 100 per cent foreign equity in main areas of the economy.
	Transitory Foreign Investment Negative List issued by the Philippine National Economic and Development Authority on 28 October 1991.	Lists areas in which foreign direct investment is prohibited or restricted to a maximum of 25-40 per cent.
Republic of Korea	The Foreign Capital Inducement Law (No. 4316) and Enforcement Decree (Presidential No. 13317) and Enforcement Regulations Ministry of Finance (Ordinance No. 1843) of 1 March 1991.	Liberalizes FDI by dispensing prior Government approval for foreign investments except in certain designated sectors.

/.....

(Annex table 11, cont'd.)

Country	*Law/regulation*	*Content*
Asia (cont'd.)		
Taiwan Province of China	Statute for Upgrading Industries effective 1 January 1991 until 30 June 1998 (replaced Statute for the Encouragement of Investment).	Incentives offered apply to both domestic and foreign investment organized as stock companies. The most significant incentive is the investment tax credit.
Viet Nam	Decree No. 28/HDBT of 6 February 1991 of the Council of Ministers (repealed Decree No. 139/HDBT of 5 September 1988).	Implements liberalization provisions contained in the Law on Foreign Investments as amended in 1990.
Africa		
Egypt	Regulation of June 1991 of the General Authority for Investment (GAFI) of the Ministry of Economy and Foreign Trade.	Expanded areas for foreign investments to include air and sea transport and consultancy services for electricity, water and waste-water projects. Also lists activities where foreign investors are barred and manufacturing activities subject to local-content requirements.
Uganda	The Investment Code, of 25 January 1991.	Establishes the Uganda Investment Authority whose functions are to promote and supervise investments. Foreign investors cannot operate a business without an investment license. Transfer of foreign exchange requires approval also. Incentives include exemption from import duties and sales tax on machinery and construction items not available in Uganda, plus three-year tax holidays from corporate and dividend taxes.
Zambia	Investment Act of 1991.	Establishes an "Investment Centre" as a "one stop" facility for the promotion, coordination, regulation and monitoring of investments. Enumerates incentives granted to licensed investors in specific industries; guarantees include protection of property from expropriation except upon payment of compensation equivalent to the market value of the property; transfer of profits, interests, royalties and dispute settlement by arbitration.

/.....

(Annex table 11, cont'd.)

Country	*Law/regulation*	*Content*
West Asia		
Bahrain	Decree No. 13 of 1991 (amends Article 278 of the Commercial Companies Law).	Allows the establishment of non-Bahrainis wholly-owned companies for the purpose of forming an industrial enterprise; or using Bahrain as a main centre for investment of funds in activities involving distribution of goods which it produces or services which it provides; or if the majority capital of said companies will be invested in industrial development projects.
Saudi Arabia	Ministry Circulars issued in 1991.	Ministries involved in FDI have issues circulars relaxing rules relating to foreign businesses. Thus, the Ministry of Commerce has made registration easier. Likewise, applications for investment licenses are processed faster.
Syrian Arab Republic	Investment Promotion Law No. 10 of 4 May 1991 and Implementing Instructions of 10 June 1991.	Provides incentives such as tax holidays; repatriation of capital and profits; exemption from customs duties and foreign exchange regulations on importations of certain fixed assets worth at least 10 million Syrian pounds.
Yemen	Presidential Decree Law 22 for the Year 1991 Concerning Investment effective 11 July 1991.	Provides for guarantees, privileges, customs and tax exemptions for licensed projects such as right o transfer profits; freedom from nationalization; and tax-exempt importation for immovable properties for use of the project.
Latin America		
Bolivia	Mining Code 1243 (as amended on 11 April 1991 by Decree Nos. 21060, 21216, 22175, 22407, 22408.	Allows joint ventures with foreign companies within 50 kilometers from the border and with COMIBOL, the state mining company.
Colombia	Law 45 of January 1991 (new foreign investment law).	Foreign and local investors are accorded equal treatment; dispenses with Government approval on most investment projects; raises ceiling on profits that can be remitted; and liberalizes reinvestments.

/.....

(Annex table 11, cont'd.)

Country	*Law/regulation*	*Content*
Latin America (cont'd.)		
Ecuador	Decree 2501 of June 1991.	Foreign and local investors are treated equally; provides for registration of foreign investments with the proper Government office instead of approval of the Ministry of Commerce and Industry, and allows foreign investments in all sectors except defense, national security, media and areas governed by special laws.
	Mining Code as amended on 31 May 1991.	Grants new incentives to foreign investors in the mining sector.
Nicaragua	Law No. 127 on Foreign Investment of June 1991.	Allows 100 per cent foreign ownership; guarantees repatriation of capital after three years, and remittances of profits; grants prompt, adequate and effective compensation upon expropriation; requires prior approval from the Committee on Private Investment.
Peru	Decree 662 of September 1991.	Eliminates restrictions and grants several guarantees to foreign investors. Among its main features are automatic approval of foreign investments; and repatriation of capital, remittance of profits and dividends.
Regional norms:		
Andean Pact (Bolivia, Colombia, Ecuador, Peru, Venezuela)	Decision of 291 of the Commission of the Cartagena Agreement enacted on 21 March 1991 (repealed Decision 220 of 1987).	Among the restrictions lifted are "fade out" requirements, that is, "foreign" companies (those with less than 51 per cent national control) transform themselves into "mixed" companies (with at least 51 per cent national control) or "local" companies (with at least 80 per cent national control). Also, permits investments by way of contributions of intangible assets (before foreign investments could be made only in the form of money and tangible goods).
Caribbean		
Jamaica	Exchange Control Order dated 25 September 1991.	Liberalized exchange controls by allowing persons who receive or earn foreign currency to retain the same in Jamaica or elsewhere; allowing dealings in securities by residents and non-residents; and allowing all forms of importations.

/.....

(Annex table 11, cont'd.)

Country	*Law/regulation*	*Content*
Central and Eastern Europe		
Albania	Decree No. 7512 of 10 August 1991, "On Sanctioning and Protection of Private Property, Free Initiative of Independent Private Activities and Privatization".	Provides for protection of FDI; opens all reas to foreign investments, including presently state-owned enterprises which are subject to privatization; guarantees repatriation of capital and profits. Expropriation and nationalization are allowed only for public use and upon payment of full compensation.
Belarus	The Law "On Foreign Investments on the Territory Republic of Belarus" of 14 November 1991.	Allows 100 per cent foreign investment except in banks, insurance companies, mixed companies and other financial and credit institutions which shall not exceed 50 per cent of the authorized stock capital; guarantees the free transfer of income in foreign currency and compensation in case the foreign investment is requisition due to natural calamities, accidents, epidemics, epizootics and other emergencies.
Bulgaria	Foreign Investment Law No. 193 effective 14 June 1991.	Features include: FDI may be allowed in any economic activity unless prohibited; license to invest is not required except in cases provided by law; foreign investors are allowed to transfer profits, interest, dividends and earnings; investments effected through the formation or expansion of a wholly-owned enterprise or the acquisition of an interest in a new or existing enterprise; or a long-term (five year) investment credit extended to an enterprise by someone other than a bank.
Czechoslovakia	Company Law of 5 November 1991 effective on 1 January 1992 (repealed Act 173 of 1988 as amended, the Law on Enterprise with Foreign Property Participation).	A foreign person is allowed to establish a legal entity either as a sole proprietor or as founder of a stock company, under this law, foreigners have the same rights and obligations as nationals have.
Estonia	Foreign Investment Law effective 17 September 1991.	Foreign and local investors are afforded equal treatment unless otherwise provided by Estonian law or international agreement; determines which sectors of economy are open or closed to foreign investments; contains guarantees against nationalization and confiscation.

/.....

(Annex table 11, cont'd.)

Country	*Law/regulation*	*Content*
Central and Eastern Europe (cont'd.)		
Hungary	Foreign Investment Law as amended on 1 January 1991.	Features include: 100 per cent foreign-owned company is allowed and after-tax profits may be transferred in convertible currency without any limitation.
	Banking Law effective 1 January 1991.	Allows foreign banks to acquire up to 100 per cent equity of small banks provided that the total foreign equity participation in the banking system shall not exceed 40 per cent.
Kazakh Republic [b]	Law on Foreign Investment effective 17 January 1991.	Authorizes foreign investment in all areas of the economy except the manufacture of products for military purposes; grants tax concessions to legal entities with foreign participation in the form of exemption from the payment of a tax on profits for five years, and the payment of only 50 per cent of tax on profits for the next five years provided that the share of the foreign investor in the legal entity is in excess of 30 per cent and the legal entity is engaged in the production of certain goods and services enumerated in the law.
Latvia	Law on Foreign Investment of 5 November 1991.	Notable features include: foreign investors may form limited liability companies or joint stock companies even without a local partner; foreign investors cannot have a controlling share in enterprises which are involved in the following sectors: defense, manufacture and sale of narcotics, weapons and explosives, printing (or minting) of stocks, bank notes, coins and stamps, mass media, grants a foreign investor the same rights and obligations as local legal entities and private persons in making investments unless otherwise provided by Latvian law or an international agreement.

/.....

(Annex table 11, cont'd.)

Country	Law/regulation	Content
Central and Eastern Europe (cont'd.)		
Poland	Law on Companies with Foreign Participation of 14 June 1991.	Simplifies registration procedures; liberalizes profits' repatriation procedures; guarantees compensation for expropriation; and provides for cancellation of the automatic "tax holiday" benefit by making the grant discretionary on the Minister of Finance.
	Corporate Income Tax Law effective 1 January 1992.	Dividends, royalties, and interests due to foreign investors are subject to a flat rate of 20 per cent to be withheld by the foreign company unless otherwise provided by tax treaties.
Romania	Foreign Investment Law of 3 April 1991.	Provides liberal conditions to attract FDI such as 100 per cent foreign ownership; free transfer of profits, royalties, and proceeds from the sale of stocks, shares, bonds and other securities in freely convertible currencies; guarantees against nationalization and expropriation in the public interest and upon payment of compensation; grants a tax holiday in the form of exemption of certain investments from the payment of the profit tax subject to certain conditions; also allows foreign investments in all sectors of the economy (including the exploration and production of natural resources) provided that said investments do not violate environmental regulations, or affect national security or cause harm to public order, health and good morals.
Russian Republic [c]	Law on Foreign Investments of 4 July 1991.	Allows foreign investments in areas not prohibited by law; foreign investments shall not be accorded a treatment less favourable than the treatment of property, property rights, and investment activity of legal local entities and citizens of the Russian Republic except as provided by law; it may not be nationalized and confiscated except in cases provided by legislative enactment in the public interest and upon payment of adequate compensation; and foreign investors may transfer abroad their share of profits, dividends, interest, licensing and other fees after payment of appropriate taxes.

/.....

(Annex table 11, cont'd.)

Country	*Law/regulation*	*Content*
Central and Eastern Europe (cont'd.)		
Ukraine [d]	Law on Protection of Foreign Investments in Ukraine of 10 September 1991.	Guarantees the right to transfer profits and reinvest profits in Ukraine; State cannot requisition foreign investments except in certain cases and upon payment of adequate compensation. Areas open to FDI shall be determined by the Cabinet of Ministers.
Uzbekistan [e]	Law on Foreign Investments of 14 June 1991.	Foreign investments shall not be treated in a manner less favourable than that accorded to enterprises and citizens of the republic except as provided by law. Areas of the economy where foreign investments are allowed are determined by law. Foreign investment guarantees include protection against subsequent changes in law; compensation in case of requisition; and free repatriation of profits.
Developed countries [f]		
Japan	Amendment to the Foreign Exchange and Foreign Trade Control Law Concerning Inward Investment and Importation of Technology, passed by the Diet on 19 April 1991 and took effect on 1 January 1992.	Allows practically all inward FDI to be executed without prior notification. Sufficient to submit *ex post facto* reports to the Investment Authority after the execution of investment. Prior notification is required only by investments in the four sectors mentioned in Articles 2 and 3 of the OECD Code of Liberalisation of Capital Movements and in investments in industries related to national security or related interests. Inward FDI may not be restricted except where no liberalization obligation under the OECD Code exists and when the investment is deemed to threaten national security or related interests or might adversely and seriously affect the performance of the Japanese economy. Previous prior notification procedures for the importation of technology were also changed in favour *ex post facto* report procedures.
Sweden	Foreign Takeover Law No. 991/92.71 of December 1991; effective 1 January 1992.	Liberalizes foreign takeovers of local companies in Sweden.

/.....

(Annex table 11, cont'd.)

Country	*Law/regulation*	*Content*
Switzerland	Revised Company Law effective 1992.	Main features include: ownership structure of companies must be disclosed; consolidated accounts required; banks can refuse to register transaction on securities when shares of stocks exceed a certain percentage as provided by company statutes, when federal law has been violated and when false declarations have been made; voting instructions from shareholders must be secured before annual meetings by custodians of stocks; and shareholders have power to demand special audits or put an item in the agenda.
United States	Public Law 102-99 of 17 August 1991. (Defense Production Act Extension and Amendments of 1990).	Declared the Exon-Florio Amendment to the Defense Production Act permanent and exempt from the termination of the Act. The Exon-Florio Amendment empowers the President of the United States to ban foreign investments which endanger national security.

Sources: Transnational Corporations and Management Division, based on various sources.

a This table contains complete information—according to available sources—primarily on laws and regulations directly addressing foreign direct investment. In addition, it includes some legal statutes that are not directly addressed to foreign investors but contain important provisions affecting their operations.

b Also in 1991, the former Kazakh SSR adopted the Law on Free Economic Zones (17 January 1991); the Law Governing Ownership (8 January 1991); the Law on Freedom Of Economic Activities and Development of Business Undertakings (15 January 1991); and the Law on Basic Principles of Kazakh SSR Foreign Economic Activities (17 January 1991).

c Also in 1991, the Russian Republic adopted, among others, the Law on Privatization of State and Municipal Enterprises (3 July 1991); the Law on Employment of Populace (19 April 1991); the Land Code (25 April 1991); the Law on Competition and Limitation of Monopolistic Activities in Goods Markets (22 March 1991); the Decree of the Presidium of the RSFSR Supreme Soviet on the Introduction on the Territory of the RSFSR of a Temporary Procedure for the Levying of Taxes on Enterprises, Associations, Organizations and Citizens (9 May 1991); the Presidential Decree on Liberalization of Foreign Economic Activity on the Territory of the RSFSR (15 November 1991).

d In 1991, Ukraine adopted also, among others, the Law on Economic Partnership (19 September 1991); the Law on Investment Activity (18 September 1991); the Law on Legal Succession of Ukraine (12 September 1991); the Law on Enterprises, Institutions and Organizations Under Union Subordination Located Within the Territory of Ukraine (10 September 1991); the Law on Taxation of Income of Citizens of the Ukrainian SSR, Foreign Citizens, Stateless Persons (5 July 1991); the Law on the Taxation System (25 July 1991); the Law on the Protection of Natural Environment (25 June 1991); the Law on Foreign Economic Activities (April 1991), the Law on Property (7 February 1991); and Temporary Regulations on the Procedure for the Registration of Joint Enterprises Established Within the Ukrainian SSR with the Participation of Soviet and Foreign Organizations, Firms, and Management Agencies (17 January 1991).

e Also in 1991, Uzbekistan adopted, among others, the Law on Business Undertakings (15 February 1991), and the Law on Enterprises (15 February 1991).

f Increasingly there is a tendency in most Western countries to avoid the existence of different legal regimes for foreign and local investors. Accordingly, most provisions affecting foreign investment are found in laws addressing specific issues (that is, antitrust, mergers and acquisitions, taxation of income and capital) which normally apply to both local and foreign investors.

Annex table 12. Share of pollution-intensive industries [a] in inward investment stock

(Percentage and millions)

Economy and year	Total FDI	Total FDI in manufac-turing	Chemicals	Pulp and paper	Petroleum and coal products	Metals	Total (1) [b]	Share of (1) in total FDI	Share of (1) in total FDI in manu-facturing
Developing economies									
Africa									
Nigeria									
(naira)									
1970	1 003	225	18	13	18	13	62	6	28
1980	3 620	1 504	140	62	4	128	334	9	22
1987	9 994	3 122	356	128	-4	256	736	7	24
Asia									
Hong Kong									
(Hong Kong dollars)									
1975	..	1 695	97	62	..	50	209	12	12
1984	..	11 448	804	677	..	630	2 112	18	18
1989	..	91 224	1 806	2 181	..	1 479	5 466	6	6
Korea, Republic of									
(won)									
1971	51 435	39 637	14 751	125	6 180	3 722	24 778	48	63
1980	752 300	502 228	197 673	2 453	- 5 445	42 593	237 274	32	47
1988	2 706 549	1 665 408	455 749	20 137	- 27 115	77 027	525 798	19	32
Malaysia									
(ringgit)									
1984	..	3 615	421	138	174	..	733	..	20
1987	..	4 961	392	73	517	..	982	..	20
Philippines									
(Philippine pesos)									
1980	9 312	4 716	1 385	118	205	225	1 933	21	41
1989	35 195	17 207	4 688	262	817	1 428	7 195	20	42
Singapore	1 744	778	18	22	400	26	466	27	60
(Singapore dollars)									
1970	1 744	778	18	22	400	26	466	27	60
1980	12 986	7 090	275	95	3 089	372	3 831	30	54
1989	50 732	21 490	3 023	428	5 376	1 256	10 083	20	47

/.....

(Annex table 12, cont'd.)

Economy and year	Total FDI	Total FDI in manufacturing	Chemicals	Pulp and paper	Petroleum and coal products	Metals	Total (1) [b]	Share of (1) in total FDI	Share of (1) in total FDI in manufacturing
Asia (cont'd.)									
Taiwan Province of China (United States dollars)									
1960	36	31	18	1	..	..	19	53	61
1970	559	434	81	4	..	17	102	18	24
1980	2 772	2 084	311	16	..	176	503	18	24
1990	13 252	9 398	2 217	96	..	948	3 261	25	35
Thailand (baht)									
1970	891	447	79	..	100	..	179	20	40
1980	20 231	6 406	861	..	218	295	1 374	7	21
1989	142 224	60 875	8 091	..	1 907	6 355	16 353	11	27
Latin America									
Argentina (United States dollars)									
1976	3 505	2 502	389	27	294	230	940	27	38
1980	5 186	3 358	519	34	294	259	1 106	21	33
1986	6 480	4 045	788	33	294	286	1 401	22	35
Brazil (United States dollars)									
1971	2 912	2 384	541	68	197	214	1 020	35	43
1980	17 480	13 005	2 765	374	393	1 389	4 921	28	38
1990	37 143	25 729	5 198	859	993	3 028	10 078	27	39
Colombia (United States dollars)									
1970	457	317	149	39	..	6	194	42	61
1980	1 061	750	289	83	..	14	386	36	51
1990	3 500	1 485	590	176	..	19	785	22	53
Venezuela (United States dollars)									
1975	1 270	687	185	37	..	27	249	20	36
1980	1 604	989	245	46	..	39	329	21	33
1990	3 581	2 731	704	142	..	274	1 120	31	41

/.....

(Annex table 12, cont'd.)

Economy and year	*Total FDI*	*Total FDI in manufac-turing*	*Chemicals*	*Pulp and paper*	*Petroleum and coal products*	*Metals*	*Total (1)* [b]	*Share of (1) in total FDI*	*Share of (1) in total FDI in manu-facturing*
Developed economies									
France (French francs)									
1975	21 868	8 177	1 812	..	..	2 941	4 735	22	58
1980	69 803	24 969	7 185	..	..	8 800	15 985	23	64
1989	295 888	94 481	19 418	7 255	..	18 096	44 769	15	47
Germany, Federal Republic of (Deutsche marks)									
1976	63 531	41 997	5 992	594	7 164	5 477	19 227	30	46
1980	71 758	42 537	6 933	669	8 514	5 320	21 436	30	50
1989	124 954	49 095	10 052	1 134	4 977	3 221	19 384	26	40
Japan (United States dollars)									
1977	1 920	1 539	498	..	257	114	869	45	57
1980	2 979	2 316	714	..	451	152	1 317	44	57
1989	15 654	10 202	2 722	..	692	497	3 911	25	38
United Kingdom (Pounds sterling)									
1981	16 962	12 188	2 402	663	..	655	3 720	22	31
1987	54 631	19 779	4 232	1 320	..	1 107	6 659	12	34
United States (United States dollars)									
1973	20 556	8 231	2 892	..	..	960	3 852	19	47
1980	83 046	42 320	10 439	2 262	9 309	3 576	25 586	31	61
1990	403 735	189 042	41 678	13 026	29 044	17 596	101 344	25	54

Source: Transnational Corporations and Management Division, *World Investment Directory* (New York, United Nations, 1992).

a The coverage of data for different industries may vary from country to country.

b Total FDI in the industries shown only.

Select list of publications of the Transnational Corporations and Management Division

A. Individual studies

World Investment Report, 1992: Transnational Corporations as Engines of Growth. 354 p. Sales No. E.92.II.A.19.

Transnational Corporations and Industrial Hazards Disclosure. 98 p. Sales No. E.92.II.A.18.

World Investment Directory 1992, Volume I, Asia and the Pacific. 356 p. Sales No. E.92.II.A.11.

Climate Change and Transnational Corporations: Analysis and Trends. 110 p. Sales No. E.92.II.A.7. $16.50.

Foreign Direct Investment and Transfer of Technology in India. 150 p. Sales No. E.92.II.A.3.

The Determinants of Foreign Direct Investment: A Survey of the Evidence. 84 p. Sales No. E.92.II.A.2.

The Impact of Trade-related Investment Measures on Trade and Development: Theory, Evidence and Policy Implications. 108 p. Sales No. E.91.II.A.19. $17.50. (Joint publication with UNCTAD.)

Transnational Business Information: A Manual of Needs and Sources. 216 p. Sales No. E.91.II.A.13. $45.

World Investment Report, 1991: The Triad in Foreign Direct Investment. 108 p. Sales No.E.91.II.A.12. $25.

Transnational Corporations: A Selective Bibliography, 1988-1990. 618 p. Sales No.E.91.II.A.10. $65. (English/French.)

Transnational Corporations in South Africa: A List of Companies with Investments and Disinvestments. 282 p. Sales No. E.91.II.A.9. $50.00.

*University Curriculum on Transnational Corporations:**

Vol. I	*Economic Development.*	188 p.	Sales No. E.91.II.A.5. $20.00.
Vol. II	*International Business.*	156 p.	Sales No. E.91.II.A.6. $20.00.
Vol. III	*International Law.*	180 p.	Sales No. E.91.II.A.7. $20.00.
* The Set:			Sales No. E.91.II.A.8. $50.00.

Directory of the World's Largest Service Companies: Series I. 834 p. ISSN 1014-8507. (Joint publication, UNCTC/Moody's Investors Service.)

The Challenge of Free Economic Zones in Central and Eastern Europe. 444 p. Sales No. E.90.II.A.27. $75.

Accountancy Development in Africa: Challenge of the 1990s. 206 p. Sales No. E.91.II.A.2. $25. (Also available in French.)

Transnational Banks and the International Debt Crisis. 157 p. Sales No. E.90.II.A.19. $22.50.

Transborder Data Flows and Mexico: A Technical Paper. 194 p. Sales No. E.90.II.A.17. $27.50.

Debt Equity Conversions: A Guide For Decision-Makers. 150 p. Sales No. E.90.II.A.22. $27.50.

Transnational Corporations and Manufacturing Exports from Developing Countries. 124 p. Sales No. E.90.II.A.21. $25.

Transnational Corporations in the Transfer of New and Emerging Technologies to Developing Countries. 141 p. Sales No. E.90.II.A.20. $27.50.

Transnational Corporations, Services, and the Uruguay Round. 252 p. Sales No. E.90.II.A.11. $28.50.

The Uruguay Round: Services in the World Economy, 220 p., ISBN 0-8213-1374-6. (Joint publication, UNCTC/World Bank.)

Transnational Corporations in the Plastics Industry. 167 p. Sales No. E.90.II.A.1. $20.

Objectives and Concepts Underlying Financial Statements. 32 p. Sales No. E.89.II.A.18. $8.

Services and Development: The Role of Foreign Direct Investment and Trade. 187 p. Sales No. E.89.II.A.17. $20.

Transnational Corporations in South Africa and Namibia: A Selective Bibliography. 98 p. Sales No. E.89.II.A.13. $12.

Transnational Corporations in the Construction and Design Engineering Industry. 60 p. Sales No. E.89.II.A.6. $9.

Foreign Direct Investment and Transnational Corporations in Services. 229 p. Sales No. E.89.II.A.1. $26.

Data Goods and Data Services in the Socialist Countries of Eastern Europe. 103 p. Sales No. E.88.II.A.20. $13.50.

Conclusions on Accounting and Reporting by Transnational Corporations: The Intergovernmental Working Group of Experts on International Standards of Accounting and Reporting. 58 p. Sales No. E.88.II.A.18. $7.50. (Also available in Arabic, Chinese, French, Russian, Spanish.)

Transnational Corporations in World Development: Trends and Prospects. 628 p. Sales No. E.88.II.A.7. $56. (Also available in Arabic, Chinese, French, Russian, Spanish.)

Executive Summary. Transnational Corporations in World Development: Trends and Prospects. 66 p. Sales No. E.88.II.A.15. $3.

Transnational Corporations: A Selective Bibliography, 1983-1987.

Vol. I	441 p.	Sales No. E.88.II.A.9. $45.
Vol. II	463 p.	Sales No. E.88.II.A.10. $49.

Joint Ventures as a Form of International Economic Co-operation: Background Documents of the High-Level Seminar Organized by the United Nations Centre on Transnational Corporations in Co-operation with the USSR State Foreign Economic Commission and the USSR State Committee on Science and Technology, 10 March 1988, Moscow. 210 p. Sales No. E.88.II.A.12. $21.

International Income Taxation and Developing Countries. 108 p. Sales No. E.88.II.A.6. $13.50.

Transnational Corporations in Biotechnology. 136 p. Sales No. E.88.II.A.4. $17.

Foreign Direct Investment in the People's Republic of China: Report of the Round-Table Organized by the United Nations Centre on Transnational Corporations in Co-operation with the Ministry of Foreign Economic Relations and Trade, People's Republic of China, Beijing, 25 and 26 May 1987. 115 p. Sales No. E.88.II.A.3. $15.50.

Bilateral Investment Treaties. 194 p. Sales No. E.88.II.A.1. $20.

UNCTC Bibliography, 1974-1987. 83 p. Sales No. 87.II.A.23. $12.

Licence Agreements in Developing Countries. 108 p. Sales No. E.87.II.A.21. $13.50.

Consolidated List of Products Whose Consumption and/or Sale Have Been Banned, Withdrawn, Severely Restricted or Not Approved by Governments, Second Issue (UNCTC in collaboration with FAO, WHO, ILO and other relevant intergovernmental organizations). 655 p. Sales No. E.87.IV.1. $60.

Transnational Corporations and Non-fuel Primary Commodities in Developing Countries. 89 p. Sales No. E.87.II.A.17. $10.

Transnational Corporations in the Man-made Fibre, Textile and Clothing Industries. 154 p. Sales No. E.87.II.A.11. $19.

Transnational Corporations and Technology Transfer: Effects and Policy Issues. 77 p. Sales No. E.87.II.A.4. $11.

Analysis of Engineering and Technical Consultancy Contracts. 517 p. Sales No. E.86.II.A.4. $45.

Transnational Corporations in the International Semiconductor Industry. 471 p. Sales No. E.86.II.A.1. $41.

Trends and Issues in Foreign Direct Investment and Related Flows. 96 p. Sales No. E.85.II.A.15. $11.

Environmental Aspects of the Activities of Transnational Corporations: A Survey. 114 p. Sales No. E.85.II.A.11. $12.50.

Transnational Corporations and International Trade: Selected Issues. 93 p. Sales No. E.85.II.A.4. $11.

B. Serial publications

UNCTC Current Studies, Series A

No. 1 Patrick Robinson, *The Question of a Reference to International Law in the United Nations Code of Conduct on Transnational Corporations.* 22 p. Sales No. E.86.II.A.5. $4.

No. 2 Detlev Vagts, *The Question of a Reference to International Obligations in the United Nations Code of Conduct on Transnational Corporations: A Different View.* 17 p. Sales No. E.86.II.A.11. $4.

No. 3 *Foreign Direct Investment in Latin America: Recent Trends, Prospects and Policy Issues.* 28 p. Sales No. E.86.II.A.14. $5.

No. 4 *The United Nations Code of Conduct on Transnational Corporations.* 80 p. Sales No. E.86.II.A.15. $9.50.
(Also published by Graham & Trotman, London/Dordrecht/Boston. $31.50)

No. 5 *Transnational Corporations and the Electronics Industries of ASEAN Economies*. 55 p. Sales No. E.87.II.A.13. $7.50.

No. 6 *Technology Acquisition under Alternative Arrangements with Transnational Corporations: Selected Industrial Case Studies in Thailand*. 55 p. Sales No. E.87.II.A.14. $7.50.

No. 7 *Foreign Direct Investment, the Service Sector and International Banking*. 71 p. Sales No. E.87.II.A.15. $9. (Also published by Graham & Trotman, London/Dordrecht/Boston. $25).

No. 8 *The Process of Transnationalization and Transnational Mergers*. 91 p. Sales No. E.89.II.A.4. $12.

No. 9 *Transnational Corporations and the Growth of Services: Some Conceptual and Theoretical Issues*. 96 p. Sales No. E.89.II.A.5. $12.

No. 10 *Transnational Service Corporations and Developing Countries: Impact and Policy Issues*. 50 p. Sales No. E.89.II.A.14. $7.50.

No. 11 *Transnational Corporations and International Economic Relations: Recent Developments and Selected Issues*. 50 p. Sales No. E.89.II.A.15. $7.50

No. 12 *New Approaches to Best-practice Manufacturing: The Role of Transnational Corporations and Implications for Developing Countries*. 76 p. Sales No. E.90.II.A.13. $12.50.

No. 13 *Key Concepts in International Investment Arrangements and Their Relevance to Negotiations on International Transactions in Services*. 66 p. Sales No. E.90.II.A.3. $9.

No. 14 *The Role of Free Economic Zones in the USSR and Eastern Europe*. 84 p. Sales No. E.90.II.A.5. $10.

No. 15 *Economic Integration and Transnational Corporations in the 1990s: Europe 1992, North America and Developing Countries*. 52 p. Sales No. E.90.II.A.14. $12.50.

No. 16 *The New Code Environment*. 54 p. Sales No. E.90.II.A.7. $7.50.

No. 17 *Government Policies and Foreign Direct Investment*. 68 p. Sales No. E.91.II.A.20.

No. 18 *Foreign Direct Investment and Industrial Restructuring in Mexico*. 114 p. Sales No. E.92.II.A.9. $12.

No. 19 *New Issues in the Uruguay Round of Multilateral Trade Negotiations*. 52 p. Sales No. E.90.II.A.15. $12.50.

No. 20 *Foreign Direct Investment, Debt and Home Country Policies*. 50 p. Sales No. E.90.II.A.16. $12.

No. 22 *Transnational Banks and the External Indebtedness of Developing Countries: Impact of Regulatory Changes* 48 p. Sales No. E.92.II.A.10. $12.

UNCTC Advisory Studies, Series B

No. 1 *Natural Gas Clauses in Petroleum Arrangements*. 54 p. Sales No. E.87.II.A.3. $8.

No. 2 *Arrangements Between Joint Venture Partners in Developing Countries*. 43 p. Sales No. E.87.II.A.5. $6.

No. 3 *Financial and Fiscal Aspects of Petroleum Exploitation.* 43 p. Sales No. E.87.II.A.10. $6.

No. 4 *International Debt Rescheduling: Substantive Issues and Techniques.* 91 p. Sales No. E.89.II.A.10. $10.

No. 5 *Negotiating International Hotel Chain Management Agreements*, 60 p. Sales No. E.90.II.A.8. $9.

No. 6 *Curricula for Accounting Education for East-West Joint Ventures in Centrally Planned Economies.* 86 p. Sales No. E.90.II.A.2. $10.

No. 7 *Joint Venture Accounting in the USSR: Direction for Change.* 46 p. Sales No. E.90.II.A.26. $12.

International Accounting and Reporting Issues:

1984 Review.	122 p.	Sales No. E.85.II.A.2. $13.50.
1985 Review.	141 p.	Sales No. E.85.II.A.13. $15.
1986 Review.	158 p.	Sales No. E.86.II.A.16. $15.
1987 Review.	140 p.	Sales No. E.88.II.A.8. $17. (Also published by Graham & Trotman, London/Dordrecht/Boston. $65).
1988 Review.	95 p.	Sales No. E.88.II.A.3. $12.
1989 Review.	152 p.	Sales No.E.90.II.A.4. $12.
1990 Review.	254 p.	Sales No. E.91.II.A.3. $25.
1991 Review.	244 p.	Sales No. E.92.II.A.8.

National Legislation and Regulations Relating to Transnational Corporations:

Vol. I (Part One)	302 p.	Sales No. E.78.II.A.3. $16.
Vol. I (Part Two - Supplement)	114 p.	Sales No. E.80.II.A.5. $9.
Vol. II	338 p.	Sales No. E.83.II.A.7. $33.
Vol. III	345 p.	Sales No. E.83.II.A.15. $33.
Vol. IV	241 p.	Sales No. E.85.II.A.14. $23.
Vol. V	246 p.	Sales No. E.86.II.A.3. $23.
Vol. VI	322 p.	Sales No. E.87.II.A.6. $45.
Vol. VII	320 p.	Sales No. E.89.II.A.9. $36.

Transnational Corporations in South Africa and Namibia: United Nations Public Hearings:

Vol. I	*Reports of the Panel of Eminent Persons and of the Secretary-General.*	242 p.	Sales No. E.86.II.A.6. $65.
Vol. II *	*Verbatim Records.*	300 p.	Sales No. E.86.II.A.7.
Vol. III	*Statements and Submissions.*	518 p.	Sales No. E.86.II.A.8. $54.
Vol. IV *	*Policy Instruments and Statements.*	444 p.	Sales No. E.86.II.A.9.

Four-volume set — $200.

* May not be purchased separately.

Transnational Corporations in South Africa: Second United Nations Public Hearings, 1989

Vol. I	*Report of the Panel of Eminent Persons, Background Documentation.*	162 p.	Sales No. E.90.II.A.6. $19.
Vol. II	*Statements and Submission.*	209 p.	Sales No. E.90.II.A.20. $21.

Transnational Corporations (formerly ***The CTC Reporter***). Published three times a year. Individual issues $15. Annual subscription, which includes three issues and the report of the annual meetings of the Commission on Transnational Corporations — $35.

Transnationals, a quarterly newsletter, is available free of charge.

United Nations publications may be obtained from bookstores and distributors throughout the world. Please consult your bookstore or write to:

United Nations Publications

Sales Section
Room DC2-0853
United Nations Secretariat
New York, N.Y. 10017
U.S.A.

Tel: (212) 963-8302
Fax: (212) 963-4116
Telex: 422311 UN UI

OR

Sales Section
United Nations Office at Geneva
Palais des Nations
CH-1211 Geneva 10
Switzerland

Tel: (41)(22) 734-6011
Fax: (41)(22) 733-9879
Telex: 23711 ONU CH

All prices are quoted in United States dollars.

For further information on the work of the Division, please address inquiries to:

Transnational Corporations and Management Division
Department of Economic and Social Development
Room DC2-1322
United Nations
New York, N.Y. 10017, U.S.A.

Telephone: (212) 963-3176
Telefax: (212) 963-3062
Telex: UNCTNC 661062

QUESTIONNAIRE

World Investment Report 1992:

Transnational Corporations as Engines of Growth

(ST/CTC/130)

In order to improve the quality and relevance of the work of the Transnational Corporations and Management Division (TCMD), it would be useful to receive the views of readers on this and other similar publications. It would therefore be greatly appreciated if you could complete the following questionnaire and return it to:

Readership Survey
Transnational Corporations and Management Division
United Nations, Room DC2-1322
New York, N.Y. 10017, USA

1. Name and address of respondent (optional):

____

____

____

2. Which of the following best describes your area of work?

Government	☐	Public enterprise	☐
Private enterprise	☐	Academic or research institution	☐
International organization	☐	Media	☐
Non-profit organization	☐	Other (specify) ______________	

3. In which country do you work? ___________________________

4. What is your assessment of the contents of this publication?

Excellent	☐	Adequate	☐
Good	☐	Poor	☐

5. How useful is this publication to your work?

Very useful ☐ Of some use ☐ Irrelevant ☐

6. Please indicate the three things you liked best about this publication:

____

____

____

7. Please indicate the three things you liked least about this publication:

____

____

____

8. If you have read more than the present TCMD publication, what is your overall assessment of them?

Consistently good ☐ Usually good, but with some exceptions ☐

Generally mediocre ☐ Poor ☐

9. On the average, how useful are these publications to you in your work?

Very useful ☐ Of some use ☐ Irrelevant ☐

10. Are you a regular recipient of ***Transnational Corporations*** (formerly ***The CTC Reporter***), the Division's tri-annual publication which reports on the Division's and related work?

Yes ☐ No ☐

If not, please check here if you would like to receive a sample copy sent to the name and address you have given above ☐

World Investment Report 1992:

Transnational Corporations as Engines of Growth

Foreign-direct-investment flows have maintained their upward trend since the mid-1980s, reaching $225 billion in 1990. With sales of foreign affiliates amounting to an estimated $4.4 trillion in 1989—exceeding the volume of world exports—transnational corporations have become the driving force of international economic transactions.

It is against this background that the present report addresses the theme of *Transnational Corporations as Engines of Growth.* It focuses on the role of transnational corporations in the economic growth of developing countries through in-depth analyses of the impact of those corporations on capital formation, technology, human resource development, trade and sustainable development. Furthermore, as the activities of transnational corporations are growing in importance in a rapidly changing international economic environment, policy implications are explored in an attempt to view the world economy from the perspective of foreign direct investment, transnational corporations and international production.

The *World Investment Report 1992* is the second in a series of annual reports, which provide state-of-the-art data and analysis on trends in global foreign direct investment, along with in-depth examinations of selected themes related to transnational corporations.

How to obtain United Nations Publications

For more information on how to obtain United Nations Publications, or to receive a copy of our most recent catalogue, please write to:

United Nations Publications
United Nations
Room DC2-0853, Dept. 600
New York, New York 10017
Fax no. (212) 963-4116, or:

United Nations Publications
Sales Section
Palais des Nations
1211 Geneva 10
Switzerland

Litho in United Nations, New York
21889—June 1992—3,925
Reprinted in United Nations
80889—October 1992—775
ISBN 92-1-104396-4

United Nations publication
Sales No. E.92.II.A.19
ST/CTC/130